List of Chapters

Chapter 1	**Getting answers, 1**	
	How do I use this book and other QuickBooks information sources?	
Chapter 2	**Business basics, 7**	
	I'm new to starting a business. What do I need to know?	

Your company data

Chapter 3	**Setting up your company in QuickBooks, 23**	
	How do I set up and find my way around QuickBooks?	
Chapter 4	**Organizing data effectively, 39**	
	How much detail do I need to track—and where?	
Chapter 5	**Protecting your data, 61**	
	How can I keep my data safe?	
Chapter 6	**Sharing QuickBooks Pro on a network, 69**	
	How can we use the same company file at the same time?	
Chapter 7	**Creating a professional image, 77**	
	How do I create a professional image for my business?	

Banking

Chapter 8	**Banking, credit cards, and financing, 95**	
	How do I meet my banking and financing needs?	

Sales and customers

Chapter 9	**Items—your services, products, and more, 113**	
	What are items, and why are they so important?	
Chapter 10	**Customers and jobs, 141**	
	Who are my customers, and do I need to track information about them?	
Chapter 11	**Tracking income, 169**	
	How should I track the money my business brings in?	

Purchases and vendors

Chapter 12	**Working with vendors, 211**	
	Why should I enter vendors in QuickBooks?	
Chapter 13	**Inventory, 223**	
	Should I use QuickBooks to track my inventory?	
Chapter 14	**Tracking and paying expenses, 247**	
	How should I track the money I spend?	

Taxes

Chapter 15 — **Tracking and paying sales tax, 275**
How can I collect and pay the right amount of sales tax?

Chapter 16 — **Gathering income tax information for the IRS, 297**
How can QuickBooks save me time in filing my tax forms?

Time and payroll

Chapter 17 — **Time tracking, 309**
How can I base payroll or invoices on time worked?

Chapter 18 — **Payroll, 341**
Should I use QuickBooks to track my payroll?

Analyzing your business

Chapter 19 — **Tracking your progress with reports and graphs, 397**
How can I use reports in my business?

Chapter 20 — **Keeping on target with budgets, 413**
Why should I budget?

Chapter 21 — **Periodic tasks, 419**
What should I be doing weekly, monthly, quarterly, and annually?

Resources

Chapter 22 — **Updating QuickBooks, 431**
How can I keep my software up to date?

Chapter 23 — **Staying in touch with important contacts, 437**
Can QuickBooks help me keep in touch with key contacts?

Chapter 24 — **Working with an accountant or advisor, 447**
How can I get help with my bookkeeping or computers?

Chapter 25 — **Importing and exporting data, 455**
How can I transfer information between QuickBooks and other software?

Appendix A — **Troubleshooting, 459**
How do I solve a QuickBooks problem?

Appendix B — **Intuit services, supplies, and technical support, 467**
Want more help running your business?

Index, 473

QuickBooks keyboard shortcuts, last page

Contents

Chapter 1 **Getting answers, 1**

How do I use this book and other QuickBooks information sources?

Where to start, 2
    If you're new to QuickBooks, 2
    If you want to use QuickBooks Pro multi-user capabilities on a network, 2
Using this manual, 3
    Finding the step-by-step instructions, 3
Getting answers while using QuickBooks, 4
    Finding the step-by-step instructions, 4
    Finding information about fields in a window, 5
    Exploring QuickBooks with a sample company, 5
    Finding industry-specific information, 5
    Using the Information & Support window, 6

Chapter 2 **Business basics, 7**

I'm new to starting a business. What do I need to know?

Key business strategies, 8
Business tax issues, 10
    Tax year definition, 11
    Accounting methods, 11
Handling your accounting, 13
    Your company's chart of accounts, 13
    Powerful accounting reports, 17
Organizing your paper documents, 20
Additional tasks, 21

Chapter 3   Setting up your company in QuickBooks, 23

How do I set up and find my way around QuickBooks?

Setting up your QuickBooks company, 24
    Setup tasks, 24
    Things to think about after setup, 36
Creating reports to check your setup, 36
Finding your way around QuickBooks, 37
    Begin with the Welcome to QuickBooks window, 37
Your company at a glance, 38

Chapter 4   Organizing data effectively, 39

How much detail do I need to track—and where?

Where the detail is, 40
    Tracking detail while keeping a simple chart of accounts, 40
    What are the advantages of using subaccounts?, 43
    What's the best way to track my type of detail?, 45
    Tracking income and expenses with classes, 47
    Should I use classes, jobs, or types?, 49
    You get out only what you put in, 50
    What you shouldn't try to track in QuickBooks, 50
Tracking the detail you need, 51
    Fine-tuning your chart of accounts, 51
    Setting up accounts to track equity details, 53
    Entering detail on transactions, 56
    Customizing estimates, sales forms, and purchase orders, 58
    When you no longer need the detail, 59

Chapter 5   Protecting your data, 61

How can I keep my data safe?

Using passwords, 62
    Do you need to use passwords?, 62
    Setting up users, 63
    Using permissions to close an accounting period, 64

Recording who changed what, 65
Backing up your company data, 66
    Recommended backup routine, 67

Chapter 6 Sharing QuickBooks Pro on a network, 69

How can we use the same company file at the same time?

How multi-user ready QuickBooks Pro works, 70
    Network options, 71
Setting up the multi-user environment, 73
    If you add other computers to your network, 74
Using multi-user QuickBooks Pro, 74
    Switching between modes, 74
    Refresh after entering data, 75
    Improving performance, 75

Chapter 7 Creating a professional image, 77

How do I create a professional image for my business?

How can QuickBooks help?, 78
    Establishing a Web site, 78
    Timely reminders and notes, 79
    Checks that reflect your business, 80
    Choosing the right business forms, 80
Customizing your checks, 83
Creating custom business forms, 84
    Customizing and designing your QuickBooks business forms, 86
    Customizing a form's content, 87
Printing your forms and checks, 91
    Paper options for business forms, 92
    Printer setup, 92
    Printing issues, 93
    Can I fax a form?, 94

Chapter 8   Banking, credit cards, and financing, 95

How do I meet my banking and financing needs?

Choosing the right bank (or other financial institution), 96
- Shopping around for the financial institution, 96
- Benefits of online banking, 97
- Choosing credit cards, 98
- Startup and growth financing, 99

Setting up banking information, 99
- Setting up online banking (account access and payment), 99

Handling banking transactions, 101
- Day-to-day activities, 101
- Once-a-month activities, 107
- As-needed activities, 110

Chapter 9   Items—your services, products, and more, 113

What are items, and why are they so important?

Why you probably need to set up items, 114
- Items for what you sell, 114
- Items for what you purchase, 116
- Deciding how items should affect accounts, 116
- How many different items do you need?, 117

Setting up items, 118
- Where to find information about your items, 118
- Types of QuickBooks items, 119
- Adding items to your Item list, 123
- Items for reimbursable costs in QuickBooks Pro, 125

Working with items, 128
- Using items, saving time, 128
- Using items to subtotal on sales forms, 130
- Entering a group of items, 130
- Applying a discount to one or more items, 131
- Showing partial payments received at the time of sale, 132
- Adding sales tax to a sale, 134
- Changing prices or rates, 135
- Editing item information, 135

Reports and graphs about items, 137
    What's a quick way to get a list of transactions for an item?, 137
    How can I create a list of my items and their prices?, 138
    Which items sell the most?, 139
    Other reports about items, 139

Chapter 10   Customers and jobs, 141

Who are my customers, and do I need to track information about them?

Should I track customers and jobs?, 142
    What does QuickBooks mean by a customer?, 142
    What does QuickBooks mean by a job?, 143
    If you set up customers and jobs in QuickBooks, 144
    If you charge your customers sales tax, 144
    Classifying customers and jobs, 144
    Defining custom fields for customers, 146
Setting up customers and jobs, 147
    Setting up customers, 147
    Setting up jobs, 150
Working with customers and jobs, 153
    Using the Customer and Customer Detail centers, 153
    Viewing and changing customer and job information, 155
    Viewing the customer register, 158
    Contacting customers by mail, 158
    Changing the opening balance for a customer or job, 159
    Changing customer types, 160
    Changing job types, 160
    Changing job status, 161
Reports about customers and jobs, 162
    How can I create a list of customer contact information?, 162
    How can I get a list of customer transactions quickly?, 163
    Exactly how much do my customers owe me?, 164
    Can I see a breakdown of all income and expenses for a job?, 165
    Which billable costs have I not yet charged for?, 166
    Which items are still on order for a customer or job?, 166
    Other reports by customer and job, 167

Chapter 11   Tracking income, 169

How should I track the money my business brings in?

How QuickBooks can track your income, 171
    If your customers pay in full at time of service or sale, 171
    If your customers owe you money or pay in advance, 172
    Should I record estimates?, 177
Setting up for tracking sales, 178
    Setting up to track reimbursed expenses as income, 180
Tracking sales and customer payments, 182
    How to track sales and payments, 182
    Charging for actual time and costs, 193
    Making changes while tracking sales, 198
    Repeating similar transactions, 200
    Managing what customers owe you, 201
Getting information about sales and what people owe you, 205
    Which items or customers bring in the most income?, 205
    How do my actual costs and income so far compare to the estimate for the total job?, 207
    Are my customers paying me on time?, 208
    Other reports about sales and accounts receivable, 210

Chapter 12   Working with vendors, 211

Why should I enter vendors in QuickBooks?

Tracking vendor information, 212
    How can the Vendor Detail Center help manage my business?, 212
    How much information should I add for each vendor?, 212
Setting up vendors, 215
Using vendor names and managing your Vendor list, 217
    Using vendors in QuickBooks, 217
    Managing your Vendor list, 217
    Adding notes, 219
    Contacting your vendors by mail, 219
Reports about vendors, 220
    Am I in danger of paying late charges for any of my bills this month?, 220
    How can I see a list of unpaid bills for each vendor?, 221
    Didn't I pay my wholesaler last month?, 221
    What's my vendor's phone number?, 221

Chapter 13   Inventory, 223

Should I use QuickBooks to track my inventory?

Is QuickBooks inventory right for my business?, 224
- Which types of inventory can I track in QuickBooks?, 224
- What QuickBooks inventory can do for you, 226

Setting up for tracking inventory, 228
- List for setting up for inventory tracking in QuickBooks, 228
- Accounts for tracking inventory, 230
- Setting up inventory items, 230
- Tips for setting up inventory items, 231

Working with QuickBooks inventory, 233
- Ordering inventory items, 233
- Receiving inventory items, 234
- Buying inventory items over the counter, 236
- Selling inventory items, 238
- Managing your inventory, 239
- Inventory and your QuickBooks accounts, 242

Getting information about your inventory, 244
- How can I print a price list of my items?, 244
- How do I find out about items I've ordered for a customer?, 244
- Which items do I need to reorder?, 244
- What is the current value of my inventory by item?, 245
- What is my profit on the items I sell?, 245
- Which purchases and sales affected my quantity on hand?, 245
- Other reports about inventory items, 246

Chapter 14   Tracking and paying expenses, 247

How should I track the money I spend?

Ways to track and pay expenses in QuickBooks, 248
- Tracking expenses, 248
- Paying for expenses, 251
- Paying for expenses on the spot, 252
- Paying bills at a later time, 253

Setting up to track and pay expenses, 255
- Setting up online payment, 256

Using A/P to track and pay expenses, 256
- Paying bills, 257
- Applying a vendor's discount, 259

Handling bills you receive regularly, 261
Editing bills and payments, 261
Sending an online payment inquiry, 261
Deleting bills and payments, 262
Viewing an A/P transaction history, 262
Entering and applying credits from vendors, 263
Receiving items with a bill, 263
Accounts payable reports, 263
Paying bills immediately (non-A/P), 264
Using checks, 265
Using credit cards, 267
Using cash to pay for expenses, 269
Tracking a vendor's discount, 270
Mixing business and personal funds, 271
For owners or partners, 271
For employees, 272

Chapter 15 Tracking and paying sales tax, 275

How can I collect and pay the right amount of sales tax?

How QuickBooks tracks sales tax, 276
Your sales tax rates and tax districts, 277
Do I need to group individual sales taxes in QuickBooks?, 279
Setting up sales tax, 280
If your business collects only one tax for one agency, 282
If your business collects sales taxes based on location, 282
If your business collects a combination rate, 283
If your business reports nontaxable sales to out-of-state customers, 283
If your business reports nontaxable sales to resellers, 284
Which customers are subject to sales tax?, 284
Which items are subject to sales tax?, 285
How do I specify when my sales tax is payable?, 286
Tracking and paying sales tax, 286
Applying sales tax to an invoice or cash sale, 287
Special tax situations, 289
Keeping track of how much sales tax you owe, 291
Paying sales tax, 292

Changing information about your sales tax, 293
Getting reports about sales tax, 294
What is the breakdown of my sales tax, taxable sales, and nontaxable sales by sales tax district?, 294

Chapter 16 Gathering income tax information for the IRS, 297

How can QuickBooks save me time in filing my tax forms?

Figuring it all out, 298
- Consulting tax experts, 298
- Keeping current with tax information, 298
- What QuickBooks can do for you, 299
- Other taxes you may need to pay, 300

Setting up income tax tracking, 300
- Why are tax line assignments important?, 301

Reporting income tax information, 302
- Getting the numbers you need to file your income taxes, 302
- Transferring income tax information to TurboTax, 304

Handling assets, 304
- Buying assets, 304
- Handling depreciation of assets, 305
- Selling assets at a gain or loss, 305
- Theft or loss of a fixed asset, 306

Handling 1099-MISC forms, 307
- Setting up to track 1099-MISC information, 307
- Verifying amounts and printing 1099-MISC forms, 308
- Why doesn't my 1099 report have anything on it?, 308

Chapter 17 Time tracking, 309

How can I base payroll or invoices on time worked?

Should I track time?, 310
- Should I make time billable?, 310
- Should I track time for subcontractors?, 311
- How much detail should I track for time activities?, 311
- Choosing a method to track time, 313

Setting up QuickBooks for tracking time, 314
    List for preparing QuickBooks to track time, 314
    Setting up to use time tracking with payroll, 315
Setting up and using the Timer, 315
    How the Timer works with QuickBooks, 315
    Setting up the Timer, 316
    Using the Timer, 318
    Importing Timer data into QuickBooks, 322
Using the Stopwatch or entering time manually, 323
    Using the Stopwatch to time an activity, 323
    Entering time manually into QuickBooks, 324
Tasks you can do with time data, 325
    Viewing, editing, and printing time data, 325
    Using time data with payroll, 326
    Paying nonemployees for time, 326
    Charging customers for time, 328
    Costs of work and invoicing for work, 329
Reports about time, 330
    How many hours did each person work?, 330
    How much time did we spend on each job?, 332
    How much time did we spend on each type of work?, 333
    Is there a detailed list of each time activity?, 333
Installing the Timer, 335
    Installing the Timer from the CD-ROM, 335
    Creating install disks for the Timer, 336
    Installing the Timer from 3.5-inch disks, 336
Quick Reference Sheet for the QuickBooks Pro Timer, 338

Chapter 18   Payroll, 341

Should I use QuickBooks to track my payroll?

An overview of QuickBooks payroll, 342
    If you don't use the payroll feature in QuickBooks, 342
    What the payroll feature in QuickBooks can do for you, 343
    QuickBooks Payroll Services, 346
How QuickBooks payroll works, 348
    The importance of payroll items, 348
    Payroll expense and liability accounts, 349
    How QuickBooks tracks company-paid taxes and benefits, 353

Setting up payroll, 354
  Setting up your payroll items, 358
  Setting up employees, 361
  Summarizing amounts for this year to-date, 364
  Checking your payroll data, 369
Managing payroll and employee information, 371
  Changing payroll item information, 371
  Changing employee information, 374
  Contacting your employees by mail, 377
  Setting up employees for direct deposit of paychecks, 378
Running payroll and paying taxes, 379
  Paying your employees, 379
  Paying payroll taxes and liabilities, 386
  Filing your payroll tax forms, 388
  Adjusting the liability balance for a payroll item, 392
Getting information about your payroll, 393
  How much do I owe for payroll tax liabilities?, 393
  How much money do I spend on my payroll?, 394
  How can I tell if I'm withholding the correct tax amounts?, 395
  How can I get information for state payroll tax forms?, 395
  Other reports about employees and payroll, 396

Chapter 19 Tracking your progress with reports and graphs, 397

How can I use reports in my business?

Setting up for reporting and graphing, 398
Generating reports and graphs, 399
  Keeping your reported data accurate, 399
  Making preset reports work for you, 399
  Creating a report from scratch, 405
  Saving report settings, 405
  QuickReports: reports at your fingertips, 406
  Portraying your data with graphs, 407
  Investigating transactions or values on reports and graphs, 408
  Printing reports and graphs, 410
  Exporting the report to a Microsoft Excel spreadsheet, 410

Chapter 20 Keeping on target with budgets, 413

Why should I budget?

How can QuickBooks help me budget?, 414
Reporting tools, 415
    Reports, 415
    Budget vs. actual graphs, 416
Planning and setting up your budgets, 417
Checking your progress against your budgets, 418

Chapter 21 Periodic tasks, 419

What should I be doing weekly, monthly, quarterly, and annually?

Weekly tasks, 420
Monthly tasks, 421
Quarterly tasks, 422
Year-end tasks, 422
    What QuickBooks does at year end, 422
    Making year-end accounting entries, 423
    Safeguarding last year's data, 423
    Yearly tax forms, 424
As-needed tasks, 425
    Synchronizing QuickBooks Pro with your contact manager, 425
    Changing company information, 425
    Condensing data, 426
    How condensing data affects your reports, 428
    How to condense a data file when you use one of the QuickBooks Payroll Services, 429

Chapter 22 Updating QuickBooks, 431

How can I keep my software up to date?

Updating your copy of QuickBooks, 432
    Getting updates from the Internet, 432
    Choosing an updating method, 433
    Using both updating methods concurrently, 434
    Installing a maintenance release and other updates, 435
    Sharing updates among multiple users, 436

Chapter 23	**Staying in touch with important contacts, 437**
	Can QuickBooks help me keep in touch with key contacts?
	Sharing QuickBooks Pro information with your contact manager, 438
	Setting up and synchronizing QuickBooks with Symantec ACT! or Microsoft Outlook, 439
	Creating reports about contacts, 441
	Writing letters, 441
	Printing labels and Rolodex cards, 442
	Making To Do notes, 444
	Remind me!, 445
Chapter 24	**Working with an accountant or advisor, 447**
	How can I get help with my bookkeeping or computers?
	Working with an accountant who doesn't use QuickBooks, 449
	Making adjustments, 449
	Working with an accountant who uses QuickBooks, 450
	Option 1: Use the Accountant's Review feature, 450
	Option 2: Have your accountant work onsite, 453
	Option 3: Give your accountant a backup copy, 453
Chapter 25	**Importing and exporting data, 455**
	How can I transfer information between QuickBooks and other software?
	Importing and exporting to other software programs, 456
	If you use Microsoft Word, Microsoft Excel, Microsoft Outlook, or Symantec ACT!, 456
	Importing customer names from a list, 457
	Transferring QuickBooks lists between company files, 457

Appendix A Troubleshooting, 459

How do I solve a QuickBooks problem?

Finding the information you need, 460
    Using QuickBooks onscreen Help features, 460
    Frequently asked questions, 461
Exploring problems on your own, 462
    Guidelines for solving typical problems, 462
    If the program "hangs" or locks up on you, 463
Getting Technical Support, 464
    Talking to a technical support representative: Be prepared when you call, 464
    In case you need to restore a file, 465

Appendix B Intuit services, supplies, and technical support, 467

Want more help running your business?

Intuit services and supplies, 468
    Intuit supplies, 468
    QuickBooks Support Network (QBSN), 468
    QuickBooks Payroll Services, 469
    QuickBooks Online Banking and Bill Payment, 470
    QuickBooks.com Web site, 471
    QuickBooks Learning Guide, 471
    QuickBooks Certified Professional Advisors Program, 471
    QuickBooks Training Seminars, 472
    New services, 472

Index, 473

QuickBooks keyboard shortcuts, last page

CHAPTER 1

Getting answers

Where to start	2
Using this manual	3
Getting answers while using QuickBooks	4

How do I use this book and other QuickBooks information sources?

This user's guide is designed to show you the best ways to set up and use QuickBooks for your type of business. Other QuickBooks information sources are designed to give you the detail you need while you use the program.

(Please note that this manual and the program's onscreen Help system don't contain the same information.)

Where to start

If you're new to QuickBooks

1. Look at the List of Chapters to get a sense of the scope of QuickBooks capabilities and to assess which features you want to use.

    For example, do you want to use one of the QuickBooks Payroll Services? If not, you can skip that chapter.

2. Read Chapter 2, *Business basics,* beginning on page 7, to learn a few business and accounting basics and to see the two most important reports for any business.

3. Read Chapter 3, *Setting up your company in QuickBooks,* beginning on page 23, to ensure that you set up QuickBooks properly.

4. Read Chapter 4, *Organizing data effectively,* beginning on page 39, to learn how to fine tune your accounts, items, and other data so that you can track the detail you need.

5. Read other chapters applicable to you.

If you want to use QuickBooks Pro multi-user capabilities on a network

- Read Chapter 6, *Sharing QuickBooks Pro on a network,* beginning on page 69, to learn about the networking feature and how to set it up.

Using this manual

This book provides information on how you can use QuickBooks for your particular business. Here you'll find answers to "big picture" questions such as:

- Which QuickBooks features should I use for my type of business?
- How much detail do I need to enter to get useful reports?
- How do I set up a specific feature?
- What are the weekly, monthly, quarterly, and annual tasks that I need to do?

Because this manual serves as a guide for both QuickBooks and QuickBooks Pro, all references to "QuickBooks" will mean both programs.

Finding the step-by-step instructions

As you use this book, you'll notice that the chapters don't include many step-by-step instructions. Instead, we direct you to specific onscreen Help topics that will give you more information and guide you through a given task while you're using QuickBooks.

For example, the following type of table is designed to direct you to the appropriate Help topic.

To learn about...	Search the Help index for...
Writing checks	checks, writing for expenses and items

To search the QuickBooks Help index:

1 From the Help menu, choose Help Index.
2 Type the word(s) you are searching for.
3 Double-click the term you are interested in.

Getting answers while using QuickBooks

While you're using QuickBooks to perform daily and weekly tasks, you have a variety of ways to obtain useful information and answers to your questions. To contact Intuit for assistance, choose Phone Directory from the Help menu and then click General Product Support.

Finding the step-by-step instructions

How Do I menus

Throughout QuickBooks you'll find windows with a **How Do I** drop-down menu. These menus provide quick access to information and instructions for this window.

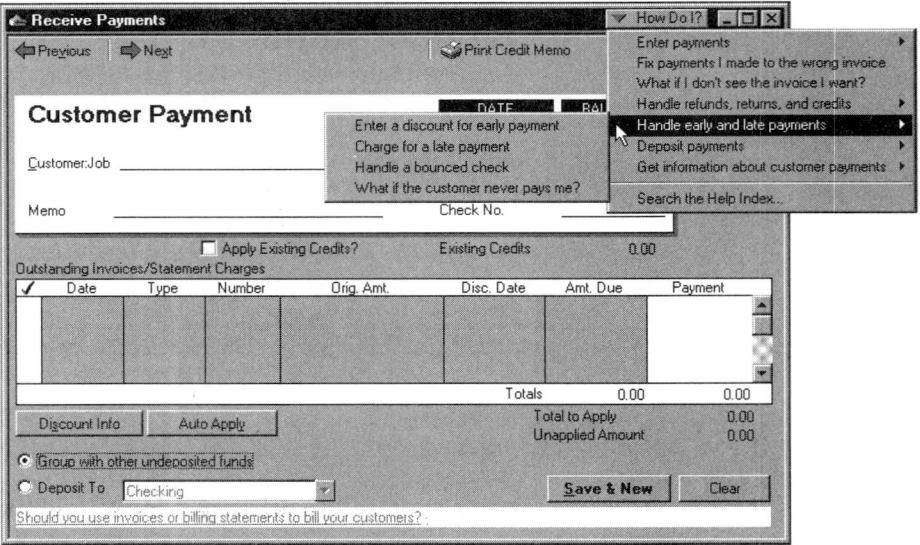

Using the Help Index

The tables in the manual and the **How Do I** menus on the windows are not exhaustive, so we encourage you to search the extensive QuickBooks Help system. (Go to the QuickBooks Help menu and choose Help Index; then enter your subject. You can get back to the index from any Help topic.)

Finding information about fields in a window

If you're unsure of a field or control (such as a button) in a particular window, you can press F1 to get help on the key parts of the window. These "What's important about..." topics provide answers to questions such as:

- What does this button do?
- What kind of information is displayed in this column?
- What happens when I select this option?

Exploring QuickBooks with a sample company

You can use one of the sample companies that we provide to explore QuickBooks to enter data, run reports, and try all the features.

To view a sample company:

1. From the File menu, choose Open Company.
2. In the Open a Company window, choose a sample company file.

Finding industry-specific information

A collection of information, customized for various industries, provides specific information about how to set up and best use QuickBooks for the industries listed.

To view the industry-specific information:

1. From the Help menu, choose "Optimizing QuickBooks for Your Industry."
2. Click "List of industries" and then select an industry name in the window that displays.

   A list of the industry's topics appears (see the following Consulting businesses example).
3. Click the topic that interests you. You can also print a topic using the Options menu in the Help window.

Topics exist for the following industries:

- Accounting and CPA firms
- Advertising and public relations
- Architecture
- Construction and contracting
- Consulting
- Farming and ranching
- Franchises
- Graphic design and printing
- Insurance
- Law firms
- Manufacturer's or sales representatives
- Medical practices
- Non-profit organizations
- Periodic billing businesses (member organizations)
- Real estate brokerages
- Restaurants
- Retail
- Service businesses
- User groups
- Wholesalers/Distributors
- Writers, photographers, and other artists

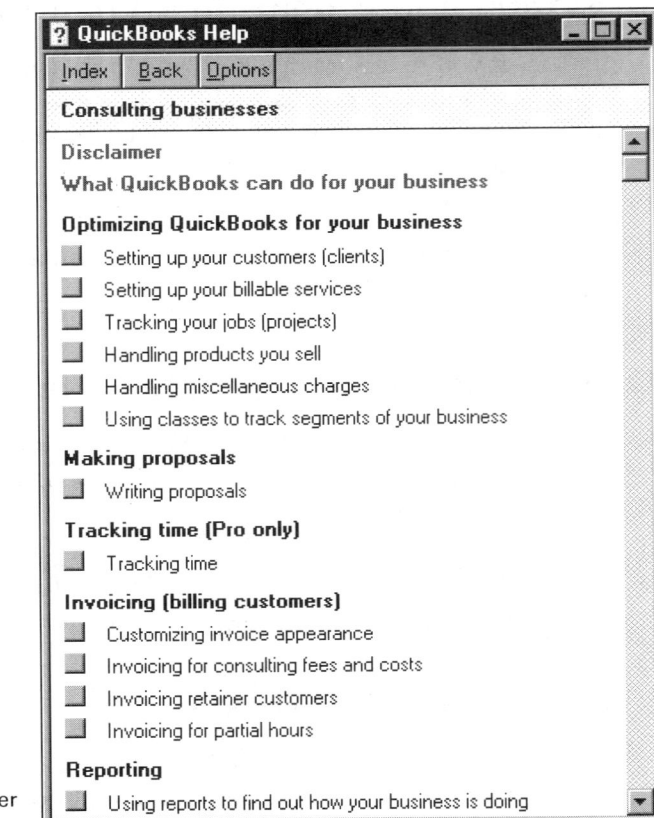

Using the Information & Support window

The Information & Support window consolidates the many ways of getting QuickBooks help and support information into a single, convenient location. The information available from this window draws upon advice, help, and tips provided within QuickBooks, as well as from various sources on the World Wide Web.

To display the Information & Support window, choose Information & Support from the Help menu.

CHAPTER 2
Business basics

Key business strategies	8
Business tax issues	10
Handling your accounting	13
Organizing your paper documents	20
Additional tasks	21

> I'm new to starting a business. What do I need to know?

Congratulations! You're doing what millions of people only dream about doing; taking a skill, a set of knowledge, or a product and building your own business with it. Like any venture—remodeling your house, going back to school, or starting a new business—the more you know about the rules, the goals, and the cost, the better your chance for success.

Key business strategies

Whatever the business, the following strategies will assist you in reaching the goals you have set for your business.

- **Start with a business plan.** A business plan is a written document defining your business, its goals, and its direction. Even if you've been in business a few years, creating a simple business plan will force you to think about your competition, take a hard look at your finances, and help set your business focus.

- **Develop short- and long-term goals.** Business goals keep you focused on what's important and help provide a means of measuring success. Make goals realistic, specific, and measurable. Review and adjust them from time to time.

Sample goal worksheet

Goals for 1/00-6/00	Ideas
Establish three new, long-term clients.	■ Send out introduction letters to key companies in the area. ■ Create a Web site! See "Establishing a Web site" on pag e78.
Grow business sufficiently to enable hiring a part-time office assistant to handle bookkeeping, mail, and scheduling.	Covered by the efforts above. ■ Visit http://qbpaweb.intuit.com to search for an accountant with QuickBooks expertise.
Reduce overhead costs by 15% over the next six months.	Reduce the cost of ■ Office space ■ Phone services ■ Bank charges

- **Develop key relationships.** Every small business, at one time or another, will benefit from outside advice and services.
    - **Attorneys.** Contact an attorney to help you decide the legal structure of your business (sole proprietorship, partnership, or corporation), and to help you deal with licenses, permits, zoning laws, and other regulations. Ask your accountant for a reference to a good attorney who works with small businesses.

- **Accountants.** Accountants can act as tax preparers, financial advisors, and consultants. Initially, your accountant can help you determine the structure and level of detail of your accounts. (For more information about accounts, see "Your company's chart of accounts" on page 13.)

    To find an accountant with an in-depth knowledge of QuickBooks, visit http://qbpaweb.intuit.com, where you can search for a certified QuickBooks professional advisor in your area. Or solicit recommendations from other small business owners in your area.

- **Find the right financial institution.** The bank you use for your personal accounts may not be the best fit for your business. Many banks offer special services for small businesses including different types of checking accounts, retirement plans (SEPs and KEOGHs), a variety of business loans, lines of credit, and credit cards. In addition to these, ask about online banking availability through QuickBooks, courier service for deposits, and tax deposits.

- **Utilize government resources.** The Small Business Administration (SBA) at www.sba.gov provides loans, business development workshops, counseling, literature, videotapes, and up-to-the-minute news on laws and regulations affecting small businesses.

    The IRS wants to make it easy for small businesses to understand their obligations. Key forms of assistance include:

    - **Your Business Tax Kit**—This collection of IRS forms and publications for small business owners and self-employed individuals includes publication 334, *Tax Guide for Small Businesses*.

    - **Small Business Tax Education Program STEP)**—This program is a partnership between the IRS and local organizations who provide workshops on taxes, starting a business, recordkeeping, and more.

- **Tax Tips Calendar for Small Businesses**— "contains helpful hints, general tax information, a listing of the most common tax filings dates, and more, all in one comprehensive publication."
- IRS Web site

To find out more information, contact your local IRS office, phone 1-800-829-1040, or visit their Web site at **www.irs.gov**.

Stay "connected" through professional associations. Whatever your business, joining a society or association can help you keep abreast of trends, network with others in your industry, receive discounts on services, and so forth. Check the Internet, the phone book, or with other professionals in your industry to find an association that's right for you.

Business tax issues

With any new business, you have to figure out all the tax requirements: federal (includes income and employment), state, local, and sales. You can find details about these taxes from a variety of sources.

Accountants, tax professionals, small business consultants, and other small business owners can help you understand your tax requirements and wade through the many forms and schedules.

Tax	Resource
Federal taxes include, but are not limited to: income, federal income tax withholding, social security, Medicare, FUTA, and excise. You may also need to file information returns like 1099s.	Request the IRS publication 334, Tax Guide for Small Businesses (For Individuals Who Use Schedules C or C-EZ), Circular E, Employer's Tax Guide; and 533-Self-Employment Tax. Also, request the Small Businesses and Taxes kit, which includes a video about an entrepreneur starting a new business. Contact: **www.irs.gov** or 1-800-829-1040.
State taxes could include, but are not limited to, tax on income, sales, and capital gains.	Contact your state tax board. For example, the California Franchise Tax Board.
Local	Contact your county officials.
Sales	Contact state officials. For example, the California Board of Equalization or the New York Department of Taxation and Finance.

Tax year definition

You figure your taxable income and file your returns based on an annual accounting period called a tax year. Your tax year can follow the **calendar year** (12 consecutive months beginning January 1 and ending December 31) or follow a **fiscal year** (12 consecutive months ending on the last day of any month except December).

Accounting methods

An accounting method is a set of rules that determines when and how you report your income and expenses for tax purposes.

Tip: The IRS publishes guidelines for your business entity (sole proprietor, partnerships, corporations, and so forth). Check IRS Publication 538, *Accounting Periods and Methods*.

Cash basis

Many small businesses track income at the time they receive the money and expenses when they pay the bills. This method is known as bookkeeping on a cash basis. If you've been recording deposits of your customers' payments but have not been including the money customers owe you as part of your income, you've been using cash basis. Similarly, if you've been tracking expenses at the time you pay them, rather than at the time you first receive the bills, you've been using cash basis.

Accrual basis

In bookkeeping on an accrual basis, you record income at the time of the sale, not at the time you receive the payment. Similarly, you enter expenses when you receive the bill, not when you pay it. Accountants usually recommend accrual basis because it gives you a better picture of how your business is doing.

The choice is yours

QuickBooks allows you to enter your transactions the same way no matter which method you use for taxes. And, at any time, you can create reports that follow either method. (See page 398.) However, note that the IRS requires that you file your taxes using the "same method from year to year." Changing your tax accounting method requires IRS consent.

QuickBooks comes set up to do your reports on an accrual basis. That is, it shows income on a profit and loss statement for invoices as soon as you record them, even if you haven't yet received payment. It shows expenses as soon as you record bills, even if they are unpaid.

Handling your accounting

Using QuickBooks requires very little accounting knowledge. You need to understand a chart of accounts and the different types of accounts on it. You don't have to know about debits and credits, journal entries, or closing periods.

Your company's chart of accounts

When you keep books for a business or organization, you want to track where your income comes from, where you put it, what your expenses are for, and what you use to pay them. You track this flow of money through a list of accounts called the **chart of accounts**. Your QuickBooks chart of accounts can have:

- Balance sheet accounts
- Income accounts
- Expense accounts
- Cost of goods sold accounts
- Non-posting accounts (includes purchase orders and estimates, which do not appear on your balance sheet)

Some of these accounts are created for you automatically. For example, the first time you create an invoice or statement charge, QuickBooks automatically creates an accounts receivable (A/R) account. You'll add other accounts, such as your checking account, during setup using the EasyStep Interview. You can create and modify your accounts as needed at any time.

Types of accounts

Balance sheet accounts

Your chart of accounts includes **balance sheet accounts**. These accounts track the following:

- What you have (assets)
- What people owe you (accounts receivable)
- What your company owes to other people (accounts payable and other liabilities)

- The net worth of your company (equity)

The following table describes the various types of QuickBooks balance sheet accounts.

Balance sheet account type	QuickBooks account type	Use to track
Asset		**What you have and what people owe you**
	Bank	Transactions in checking, savings, and money market accounts. You can also use this type of account for petty cash.
	Accounts Receivable (A/R)	Transactions between you and your customers, including invoices, statement charges, payments from customers, deposits of customer payments, refunds, and credit memos. QuickBooks automatically creates an A/R account when you first create an invoice or statement charge.
	Other Current Asset	Assets that are likely to be converted to cash or used up within one year, such as the value of your inventory on hand, notes receivable due within a year, prepaid expenses, and security deposits.
	Fixed Asset	Depreciable assets your business owns that aren't liquid (not likely to be converted into cash within a year), such as equipment, furniture, or a building.
	Other Asset	Any asset that is neither a current asset nor a fixed asset, such as long-term notes receivable.
Liability		**What your company owes to other people**
	Accounts Payable (A/P)	Outstanding bills. When you first enter a bill, QuickBooks automatically creates an A/P account.
	Credit Card	Credit card transactions for your business expenses. One account per credit card.
	Other Current Liability	Liabilities that are scheduled to be paid within one year, such as sales tax, payroll taxes, accrued or deferred salaries, and short-term loans. Some businesses include the current portion of long-term liabilities in this kind of account.

Balance sheet account type	QuickBooks account type	Use to track
	Long-Term Liability	Liabilities such as loans or mortgages scheduled to be paid over periods longer than one year.
Equity		**Net worth of your company**
	Equity	A company builds equity from three sources: ■ Investment of capital in the business by the owners ■ Net profit from operating the business during the current accounting period ■ Retained earnings, or net profits from earlier periods that are carried forward into the current fiscal year and that have not been distributed to the owners

Balances for balance sheet accounts

The Chart of Accounts window shows a balance for each balance sheet account (except for the special equity account, Retained Earnings).

The IRS recommends opening a business checking account as one of the first things you do when starting a new business.

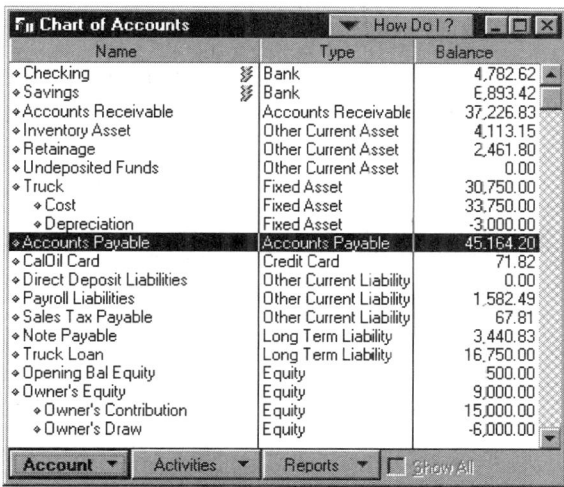

Handling your accounting | 15

In QuickBooks, each balance sheet account has its own register, just like your check register. The register shows every transaction for that account, as well as the account balance.

For example, the A/P register shows every bill from vendors, every payment to vendors, and the total amount you owe vendors.

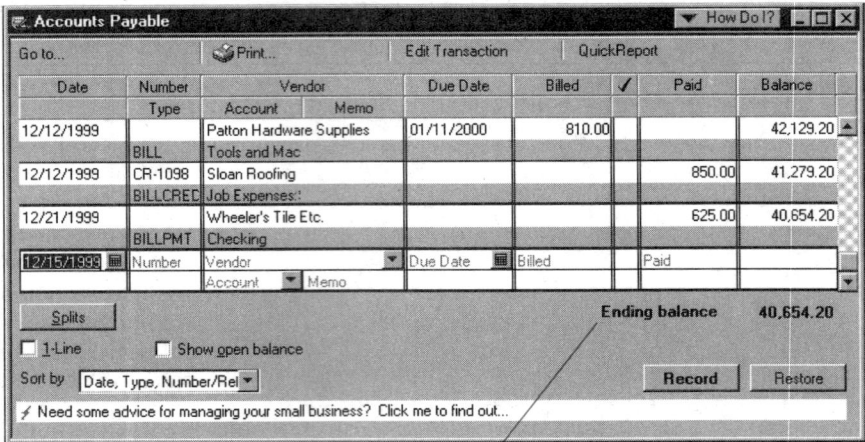

Balances are always referred to as the ending balance in the register.

Income and expense accounts

Income and expense accounts (which are the same as Quicken categories) track the sources of your income and the purpose of each expense. When you record transactions in a balance sheet account, you usually assign the amount of the transaction to one or more income or expense accounts. For example, you not only record that you took money out of your checking account, but you keep track of what you spent the money on, such as utilities, advertising, or office supplies.

There are no registers for income and expense accounts, but you can create reports to show totals for these accounts over a period of time.

You may also want to track reimbursed expenses as income. See "Setting up to track reimbursed expenses as income" on page 180 for details.

Cost of goods sold (COGS) account

Many businesses that track inventory have one cost of goods sold account, which is similar to an expense account. A COGS account contains the cost of inventory you have sold.

Powerful accounting reports

The value and performance of your company can be summarized by two reports: the balance sheet and the profit and loss statement. How you set up your accounts will greatly influence the level of detail you can get on these reports. You may also want to create the statement of cash flows report, which details the net change in your cash during a period.

- See Chapter 4, *Organizing data effectively,* beginning on page 39, for more information about how to get the level of detail you need.
- See Chapter 19, *Tracking your progress with reports and graphs,* beginning on page 397, for information about generating and customizing these reports.

Your company's balance sheet

A balance sheet is a financial snapshot of your company on one date. This report is useful when applying for a business loan or at year-end to get an accounting of your company's equity, assets, and liabilities.

Assets include what you have and what people owe you. Examples include:
- cash on hand
- money in your checking account
- money you are owed
- furniture
- vehicles

total assets = total liabilities + equity

Liabilities include what your company owes to other people or your company debts. Examples include:
- unpaid bills
- money you owe on credit cards
- loans
- sales tax you owe

Equity is the net worth of your company:

equity = assets - liabilities

```
              Rock Castle Construction
                    Balance Sheet
                  As of March 31, 1998

ASSETS
  Current Assets
    Checking/Savings                       29,454.55
    Accounts Receivable                    94,246.05
    Other Current Assets                       93.19
  Total Current Assets                    123,793.79

  Fixed Assets                             43,900.00
TOTAL ASSETS                              167,693.79

LIABILITIES & EQUITY
  Liabilities
    Current Liabilities
      Accounts Payable                     44,118.16
      Credit Cards                          1,129.36
      Other Current Liabilities             2,655.72
    Total Current Liabilities              47,903.24

    Long Term Liabilities                   8,470.96
  Total Liabilities                        56,374.20

  Equity                                  111,319.59
TOTAL LIABILITIES & EQUITY                167,693.79
```

Your company's profit and loss statement

Profit and loss statements (also known as "income statements") show your income and expenses over a period of time.

Profit and Loss Statement

Oct - Dec '97

Ordinary Income/Expense		
Income		
Construction		
Labor	▶ 29,965.75 ◀	
Materials	35,540.21	
Miscellaneous	3,002.20	
Subcontractors	47,946.63	
Total Construction		116,454.79
Total Income		116,454.79
Cost of Goods Sold		
Cost of Goods Sold		5,651.38
Total COGS		5,651.38
Gross Profit		110,803.41
Expense		
Automobile		
Fuel	140.35	
Repairs and Maintence	114.75	
Total Automobile		255.10
Bad debt		33.99
Bank Service Charges		10.00
Freight & Delivery		70.00
Insurance		
Disability Insurance	150.00	
Liability Insurance	1,050.00	
Work Comp	825.00	
Total Insurance		2,025.00

Your cost of goods sold account always appears after income accounts and before any other expense accounts, so you can see what your net income is before subtracting your business's indirect expenses, such as utilities and office supplies.

Net income = income - expenses

Page 2

Oct - Dec '97

Interest Expense		
Finance Charge	-5.65	
Interest Expense - Other	539.80	
Total Interest Expense		534.15
Job Expenses		
Equipment Rental	850.00	
Job Materials	18,395.36	
Permits and Licenses	700.00	
Subcontractors	40,099.00	
Total Job Expenses		60,044.36
Payroll Expenses		19,780.38
Professional Fees		
Accounting	250.00	
Total Professional Fees		250.00
Rent		2,400.00
Repairs		
Computer Repairs	0.00	
Total Repairs		0.00
Tools and Machinery		1,135.00
Utilities		
Gas and Electric	154.40	
Telephone	100.71	
Water	61.85	
Total Utilities		316.96
Total Expense		86,854.94
Net Ordinary Income		23,948.47
Other Income/Expense		
Other Income		
Interest Income	93.42	
Other Income	12.50	
Total Other Income	105.92	
Net Other Income		105.92
Net Income		**24,054.39**

Statement of cash flows report

The statement of cash flows summarizes your business's sources (inflows) and uses (outflows) of cash. From the report, you can see how your cash position changed over a period of time.

Rock Castle Construction
Statement of Cash Flows
October 1 through December 15, 1999

12/15/99

	Oct 1 - Dec 15, '99
OPERATING ACTIVITIES	
Net Income	19,919.42
Adjustments to reconcile Net Income to net cash provided by operations:	
Accounts Receivable	-37,251.83
Inventory Asset	-4,113.15
Retainage	-2,461.80
Accounts Payable	40,779.20
CalOil Card	5.14
Payroll Liabilities	-838.39
Sales Tax Payable	-792.50
Net cash provided by Operating Activities	15,246.09
FINANCING ACTIVITIES	
Note Payable	-17,059.17
Opening Bal Equity	-8,863.39
Owner's Equity:Owner's Draw	-6,000.00
Retained Earnings	8,863.39
Net cash provided by Financing Activities	-23,059.17
Net cash increase for period	-7,813.08
Cash at beginning of period	35,071.57
Cash at end of period	27,258.49

The report shows how much cash was provided by profit-making activities.

The report shows how much cash was provided by long-term liabilities and equity.

QuickBooks also has the capability to display investing activities, which show you how much was invested in assets such as equipment and furniture.

Organizing your paper documents

A well thought-out and executed filing system means that your important paper documents are readily available to support a tax return, provide information for a bank loan, or return a faulty product with the original receipt and warranty information.

Save the following documents.

Form	Keep for...	Examples
Legal documents	permanent collection	■ Incorporation papers ■ Partnership agreement ■ Fictitious business name filings ■ Board of directors' meeting minutes ■ Leasing agreements
Insurance records	permanent collection	■ Policy contracts ■ Amendment letters ■ Claim information ■ Riders ■ Correspondence
Banking records	10 years	■ Canceled checks ■ Bank statements ■ Loan agreements and payment receipts
Filed tax returns (federal and state)	permanent collection	■ Income tax returns ■ Excise tax returns ■ Forms and correspondence sent to the Social Security Administration
Employment records	permanent collection IRS - "at least 4 years after the date the tax becomes due or is paid (whichever is later)"	■ W-2 and W-3 wage statements ■ 940 (annual) and 941 (quarterly) payroll tax returns ■ Any state payroll tax returns ■ Any related correspondence
Annual financial statements	permanent collection	■ Year-end balance sheet ■ Year-end profit and loss statement
Vendor bills for supplies and services	7 years	■ Receipts from the vendor ■ Credit or collection correspondence

Form	Keep for...	Examples
Vendor bills for fixed assets	7 years after you sell or dispose of the asset	■ Receipts from the vendor ■ Credit or collection correspondence
Customer invoices	7 years	■ Customer invoices, statements, and credit memos ■ Credit or collection correspondence

Additional tasks

We've put together a list of additional tasks appropriate for new businesses.

Note: This list is not exhaustive and some items may not be applicable for your type of business.

✔ File a fictitious business name. (You can find information on the Internet on who needs to file and how to file.)

✔ Find out which licenses and permits are required by your local and state governments.

Contact city, county, and state authorities.

✔ Decide your tax year, accounting method, and tax and reporting responsibilities.

See the IRS information described on page 9.

✔ Apply for an EIN (Employee Identification Number) from the IRS.

✔ Secure financing and a line of credit.

Sources of funding include your local bank and the Small Business Administration (see page 9).

✔ Lease or purchase necessary equipment and space. For your space considerations, make sure you understand the local zoning laws. For example, some locales may restrict home-based businesses.

Contact your city planning board.

✔ Line up suppliers.

✔ Decide on your phone line needs (phone, fax, ISDN, cell phone, pager, 800, call waiting, and so forth) and contact a phone company for the appropriate numbers and services.

- ✔ Plan for your staffing needs. Consider the pros and cons of hiring independent contractors, employees, or family members.
- ✔ Get business cards, letterhead, and so forth.
- ✔ Start marketing/advertising campaign.
- ✔ Set up your QuickBooks company.

    See "Handling your accounting" on page 13 and "Setting up your QuickBooks company" on page 24.

CHAPTER 3

Setting up your company in QuickBooks

Setting up your QuickBooks company	24
Creating reports to check your setup	36
Finding your way around QuickBooks	37
Your company at a glance	38

How do I set up and find my way around QuickBooks?

We recommend that you use the QuickBooks EasyStep Interview to set up your company data file if you do not have existing QuickBooks or Quicken data for your company. If you have existing data, refer to the *Installation and Conversion Guide*.

The EasyStep Interview helps you enter information about your company so you can begin working with QuickBooks as soon as possible. The Interview also provides industry-specific tips for your type of business.

If you skip the Interview, you will miss critical information needed to make the right choices about setting up your company in QuickBooks. As a result, your reports may not give you the information needed to make decisions about your business. You can save time by avoiding later changes (and calls to technical support) if you use the Interview to set up your company file.

QuickBooks is designed to track most functions that small businesses need. You may not need to use all of the features in QuickBooks (such as inventory or payroll), but this setup chapter covers all the areas available to you. If an area does not apply to your company, you can skip it.

Tip: By this point, you should know which IRS tax forms you need to file, when your tax year starts, and if you'll be reporting income and expenses on an accrual or cash basis.

Setting up your QuickBooks company

The time required for setting up QuickBooks varies, depending on how many vendors, customers, inventory items, and so on, you have. Generally, you'll want to set aside time each day for the setup process until completed.

Setup tasks

Follow the order of tasks on this list. Detailed information about each task is given in the following pages.

1. Choose your QuickBooks start date.
2. Gather the necessary business information and documents.
3. Set up your company using the EasyStep Interview.
4. Fine-tune your chart of accounts.
5. Enter any historical transactions.
6. Complete customer and vendor information.
7. Complete the Item list.
8. Enter any optional adjustments.

1 Choose your QuickBooks start date

If you are setting up your company at the same time you are setting up QuickBooks, your start date is today. Continue reading on page 37.

Your QuickBooks start date is the date for which you give QuickBooks a financial snapshot of your company. After you complete the Interview, you'll enter all transactions that occurred from your start date through today to make your records and reports up to date.

The date you choose determines what information you will enter in the Interview. To choose a start date that's best for your company, consider the following questions:

- When does your company's fiscal year start?
- How close is today to the end of your fiscal year?
- Do you have an accurate balance sheet for your current fiscal year?
- Do you have an accurate profit and loss statement for your current fiscal year?
- How far back in time are you willing to enter historical transactions?

Many people want to have accurate books without spending days or weeks entering historical transactions. If your business generates many invoices, bills, or checks, you probably don't want to enter more than three months of historical transactions. On the other hand, if your business has few invoices, bills, or checks, you may be willing to enter more than three months of historical transactions so that QuickBooks will have full detail for the entire fiscal year.

If it's almost the end of the fiscal year, consider finishing the fiscal year using your old system of bookkeeping. Then set up your company in QuickBooks with a start date of your fiscal year end so you can use QuickBooks for the new fiscal year. You'll have the detail for each fiscal year, and you won't have to do a lot of work setting up.

---

start date

The date QuickBooks will begin to track complete information about your company finances. The start date can be in the past if you enter historical records; it can be the current date; or it can be some day in the future if you prefer to enter information gradually.

If your fiscal year began some time ago, decide which is more important to you:

- Do you want to have full detail in QuickBooks for the current fiscal year?

  OR

- Do you want to enter fewer than three months of historical transactions (covering the period between your start date and today)?

Note: **Although you can change your start date at a later time, your start date determines much of your setup.** It's easier to decide on the best start date now than to change it later.

2 Gather information you'll need to set up your business in QuickBooks

The following table lists the information you need and where to find it. You will enter some of this information in the EasyStep Interview and some of it after you've finished the Interview and are completing your company setup.

Information you need	Where to find it
Company legal name and address	Owner, your accountant, or tax forms
Federal identification number You can use your social security number as your identification number, unless you: ■ Pay wages to one or more employees OR ■ File pension and excise tax returns If your business fits either of these situations, you must have an employer identification number (EIN).	The EIN is a nine-digit number that the IRS issues. If you do not have an EIN, you can obtain one by submitting Form SS-4. Call **1-800-TAX-FORM** to get this form.
Fiscal year dates	Your records or accountant

Information you need	Where to find it
Income tax form you file The tax forms you file depend on your type of business ownership. Check with your accountant to make sure you are filing the correct forms for your business. **Tip:** In the EasyStep Interview, be sure to select your company income tax form. QuickBooks uses this information to associate accounts with tax form lines and create tax reports.	Your accountant, the IRS, or tax forms
Chart of accounts for your business **Tip:** If you do not have an existing chart of accounts, don't worry. The EasyStep Interview helps you choose an appropriate chart of accounts for your industry.	Your accountant or previous bookkeeping method
Names of QuickBooks users in your company and which areas of your books and financial records you want them to have access to.	See "Using passwords" on page 62.
Sales tax rates, how much you owe, and the agency you pay sales tax to	Your accountant or the State Board of Equalization or a corresponding sales tax agency
List of types of items you sell (products and services), including: ■ Item number or name ■ Current sales price (or hourly rates) ■ Whether the item is taxable ■ Income account for tracking sales of the item For inventory only: ■ Purchasing cost ■ Quantity on hand ■ Total value of inventory for the item	Your company records
List of customers, including: ■ Addresses ■ Contact names ■ Phone numbers ■ Outstanding invoices	Your company records. QuickBooks Pro can integrate information from Symantec® ACT! and Microsoft® Outlook if you use these applications for customer information.

Information you need	Where to find it
List of vendors, including: ■ Addresses ■ Contact names ■ Phone numbers ■ Outstanding bills	Your company records. QuickBooks Pro can integrate information from Symantec® ACT! and Microsoft® Outlook if you use these applications for vendor information.
Balances for these accounts: ■ Credit card ■ Line-of-credit ■ Loan ■ Bank	■ Statements dated from your start date to today for all bank accounts, including checking, savings, certificates of deposit, and money market funds ■ All uncleared checks, deposits, or other items (credit card receipts, for example) ■ Balance sheet prepared by your accountant
Value of your assets For fixed assets, you also need the original cost and accumulated depreciation.	Balance sheet prepared by your accountant
Equity information All the money you have put into the company, plus the sum of the retained earnings (the net profit or loss) for each year your company has been operating.	Your accountant

3 Set up your company with the EasyStep Interview

If you haven't yet set up a data file, QuickBooks displays a window with several options at startup. One is to create a new company. Choosing this option starts the EasyStep Interview.

To open the EasyStep Interview at other times:

- Choose New Company from the File menu.

  OR

- With your company file open, choose EasyStep Interview from the File menu.

  If you need to open your company file first, choose Open Company from the File menu, select the filename, and click Open to open the file.

The tabs across the top are for topics within the same section.

A checkmark indicates you have completed the topic.

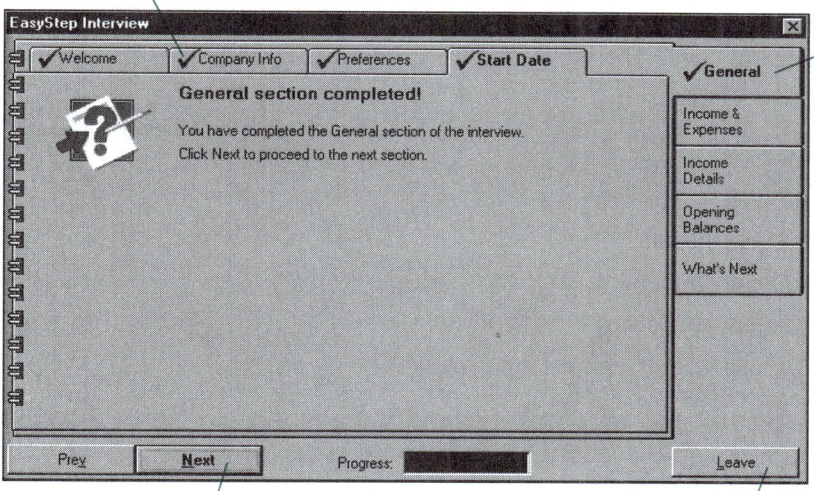

The tabs down the side are for major sections of the Interview.

A checkmark indicates you have completed all the topics in that section.

Click Next (or press Enter), and the Interview guides you through your company setup. To return to the previous screen, click Prev.

To leave the Interview, click Leave. The best stopping points are at the end of topics.

Complete the General section of the Interview before going on to other areas.

QuickBooks won't know enough about your company to ask the rest of the Interview questions unless you fill in your basic company information and start date first. See "Setup tasks" on page 24.

Setting up your QuickBooks company | 29

After you complete the EasyStep Interview, your QuickBooks company file contains basic information about your business.

If you want to change any of the information you entered, change it directly in QuickBooks.

You cannot return to the EasyStep Interview and change answers to questions.

4 Fine-tune your accounts

QuickBooks set up a chart of accounts during the Interview. Before you begin entering transactions, make sure your chart of accounts is complete and that it accurately represents your business. Change account names and edit, delete, or add accounts to make your chart of accounts reflect your company's financial activity. (You can edit your chart of accounts at any time as needed.) For suggestions and examples, see Chapter 4, *Organizing data effectively,* beginning on page 39.

You can also add a numbering scheme to your accounts. For example,

- 100-199 - Assets
- 200-299 - Liabilities
- 300-399 - Equity
- 400-499 - Income
- 500-599 - Expenses
- 600-699 - Other income and expenses

Adding numbers can help you identify the type of accounts, thereby speeding up your account selection on various forms.

Tip: Develop and follow consistent account naming and numbering conventions.

To learn about...	Search the Help index for...
Changing your chart of accounts	▪ accounts, adding to your chart of accounts
	▪ accounts, editing information about
	▪ accounts, deleting

CHAPTER 3 Setting up your company in QuickBooks

5 Enter any historical transactions

If you've decided on a start date that is before today's date, you'll need to enter past transactions to have complete financial records from your start date forward. Then your QuickBooks records will be as complete as if you had started using the program on your start date.

Enter historical transactions in this order:

1   Invoices you've sent out since your start date
2   Purchase orders you've issued since your start date that have not been received in full
3   Cash or checks you've received since your start date
4   Bills you've received since your start date
5   Bills you've paid since your start date
6   Deposits you've made to any of your accounts since your start date
7   Any other checks you've written (for things other than bills) since your start date

The order in which you enter historical transactions is important.

Enter historical transactions in sequential order. For example, QuickBooks won't know how to credit a customer payment unless you've previously recorded the invoice to that customer.

Enter transactions in your bank account last, because your accounts payable and accounts receivable affect your bank account. By the time you enter all of your historical transactions, your check register will be mostly up to date.

Entering current and historical transactions simultaneously

If you don't have time to enter all your historical transactions right away, don't worry. You don't have to enter all your past transactions before you start using QuickBooks for your current transactions. Start entering current transactions as they occur, so you don't get behind. Then catch up with historical transactions when you can.

Setting up your QuickBooks company | 31

Note: If current and historical transactions are related, enter the earlier one first. For example, if you receive a payment today for an invoice you have not yet entered, enter the invoice first and then use QuickBooks to record the payment. That way, QuickBooks correctly links your transactions to each other.

Remember, though, that your account balances will be off until you've entered all the past transactions.

To learn about...	Search the Help index for...
Entering historical information	historical transactions

Entering bank account information

If you entered all your historical transactions, your checking account or savings account register already contains entries reflecting bills you've paid, checks you've written for other purposes, and deposits you've received. But there are other transactions that you must now enter to make your account registers complete:

- Checks or other charges that happened before your start date but didn't appear on statements before your start date.

    For example, if you wrote a check a few months ago that wasn't cashed until recently, it would show up on your current bank statement.

- Other checks you wrote after your start date that were not for bills or accounts payable (credit card payments, for example).

- Deposits made after your start date that were not customer payments.

- Deposits made before your start date, but which didn't appear on statements before your start date.

- Bank charges and fees.

- Interest paid on your account.

To learn about...	Search the Help index for...
Entering information in account registers	registers, entering transactions in

6 Complete your customer and vendor information

During the Interview, you only entered information about customer and vendor open balances. Now you need to enter more information, such as addresses, phone numbers, and credit limits—though it's not necessary to enter this additional information for all customers and vendors at once.

Note: If you use Symantec ACT! or Microsoft Outlook, information about customers and vendors in your contact manager, such as addresses and phone numbers, can be synchronized with QuickBooks Pro so that you don't have to re-enter this information. See "Sharing QuickBooks Pro information with your contact manager" on page 438.

For information about customers and vendors, see Chapter 10, *Customers and jobs*, beginning on page 141 and Chapter 12, *Working with vendors*, beginning on page 211.

7 Complete your Item list

Items are goods, services, or other things you buy or sell. QuickBooks starts a list of items when you go through the Interview, but you'll want to add to this list. See Chapter 9, *Items—your services, products, and more*, beginning on page 113 for more information.

8 Enter any optional adjustments

After you have created a company in the EasyStep Interview, you may need to make a few adjustments as of your start date.

Enter sales tax liability

If you collect sales tax, record the sales tax owed as of your start date in the Sales Tax Payable account register. Make sure that each sales tax agency is a vendor on your Vendor list.

Note: **Do not enter the amounts in the register if you have entered historical invoices.** Your sales tax will already be included on them. However, you will want to check to see if you owe more sales tax than is represented on the invoices. In that case you will need to enter an adjustment in the Sales Tax Payable account register for the remaining tax liability.

To learn about...	Search the Help index for...
Recording the sales tax you owed as of your start date	sales tax, historical data
Setting up sales tax agencies as vendors	sales tax, agencies

Adjust the Uncategorized Income account and the Uncategorized Expenses account (for accrual basis only)

When you enter unpaid balances for customers, QuickBooks assigns the income to an account called Uncategorized Income. Similarly, when you enter unpaid balances for vendors, QuickBooks assigns the expenses to the Uncategorized Expenses account.

Read the following to see which situation applies to your business:

- **If you keep your books on a cash basis** (you recognize income when you receive payment), QuickBooks does not show these two accounts on your profit and loss statement until payment occurs, which is the expected behavior. You do not need to make any adjustments.

- **If you keep your books on an accrual basis** (you recognize income when you make the sale or incur an expense), QuickBooks

cash basis

A method of bookkeeping in which you regard income or expenses as occurring at the time you actually receive a payment or pay a bill.

shows these two accounts on a profit and loss statement as of your start date. You may want to make an adjustment so that the income from all invoices and the expenses from all bills before the start date is also tracked on an accrual basis, regardless of whether payment has occurred.

To learn about...	Search the Help index for...
Adjusting for Uncategorized Income and Uncategorized Expenses	■ Uncategorized Expense account ■ Uncategorized Income account

accrual basis

A method of bookkeeping in which you regard income or expenses as occurring at the time you ship a product, render a service, or receive a purchase rather than at the time you pay or receive cash. With this method, the first time you enter the transaction into your records and the moment when you pay or receive cash may be two separate events.

Adjust for current income and expenses if your start date is not at the beginning of your fiscal year

If you are setting up with a midyear start date and you know what your income and expenses are for the period from the beginning of the fiscal year through the start date, you can enter an adjustment for them. Then, your QuickBooks profit and loss statement will be accurate for the period starting with the beginning of the fiscal year and ending on any date after your start date.

To get this information, have your accountant create a year-to-date profit and loss statement for the current fiscal year through your start date.

To learn about...	Search the Help index for...
Adjusting income and expenses for midyear setup	adjustments, income and expenses

Distribute earnings and equity from before your start date

After you have entered all opening balances and made other adjustments, you may want to move the amount in your Opening Bal Equity account to your other equity accounts if you want to identify retained earnings or the equity of several owners. For more information about equity accounts, see "Setting up accounts to track equity details" on page 53.

Setting up your QuickBooks company | 35

To learn about...	Search the Help index for...
Distributing earnings and equity from before your start date	Opening Bal Equity account
Equity carried over from previous fiscal periods	equity, retained earnings from
Moving the amount in the Opening Bal Equity account to other equity accounts	equity, transferring from Opening Bal Equity

Things to think about after setup

If you have more than one company file

If you set up QuickBooks with more than one company file, you should keep those company files in the same directory. If you update QuickBooks to an interim release, receive alerts, and so forth, you will download multiple copies of the new information—if the company files are not in the same directory. (See *Updating QuickBooks,* beginning on page 431, for information about updating QuickBooks.)

Your previous accounting system

If your business is an existing business, make sure your previous accounting system is complete and backed up. You are required by the IRS to keep this information for 10 years. You should also keep any software and hardware that it runs on—or have printouts of all the information and accounting reports.

Creating reports to check your setup

After you've finished setting up your company and making any adjustments, create a profit and loss statement and a balance sheet to check that QuickBooks has the right numbers. For each report, the date range should match the fiscal year-to-date that ends with your start date. For example, if your fiscal year began on July 1 and your QuickBooks start date was September 1, create a report with a date range of July 1 to September 1.

For information about the profit and loss statement and balance sheet report, see Chapter 2, *Business basics,* beginning on page 7. For information on creating and customizing reports, see Chapter 19, "Tracking your progress with reports and graphs" on page 397.

Finding your way around QuickBooks

Begin with the Welcome to QuickBooks window

When you open QuickBooks, Welcome to QuickBooks appears in the center of the main QuickBooks window and the navigation bar displays on the left. If you're new to QuickBooks, Welcome to QuickBooks guides you through the next steps after you've set up your company file. If you've used QuickBooks before, it highlights the new features in QuickBooks 2000. In either case, it shows you how to find your way around QuickBooks.

The navigation bar lets you perform tasks quickly—simply click the name of the window to move to that window. You can choose Hide Navigation Bar from the Window menu if you don't want to display it.

To redisplay the Welcome window once you've closed it, choose Welcome to QuickBooks from the Help menu.

Click the heading for a group to use its navigator. The navigator flowchart guides you in performing tasks in the correct order.

Click QuickAdd to add the current window to the navigation bar. Or, Customize to add and remove windows, change back to the default settings, and so forth.

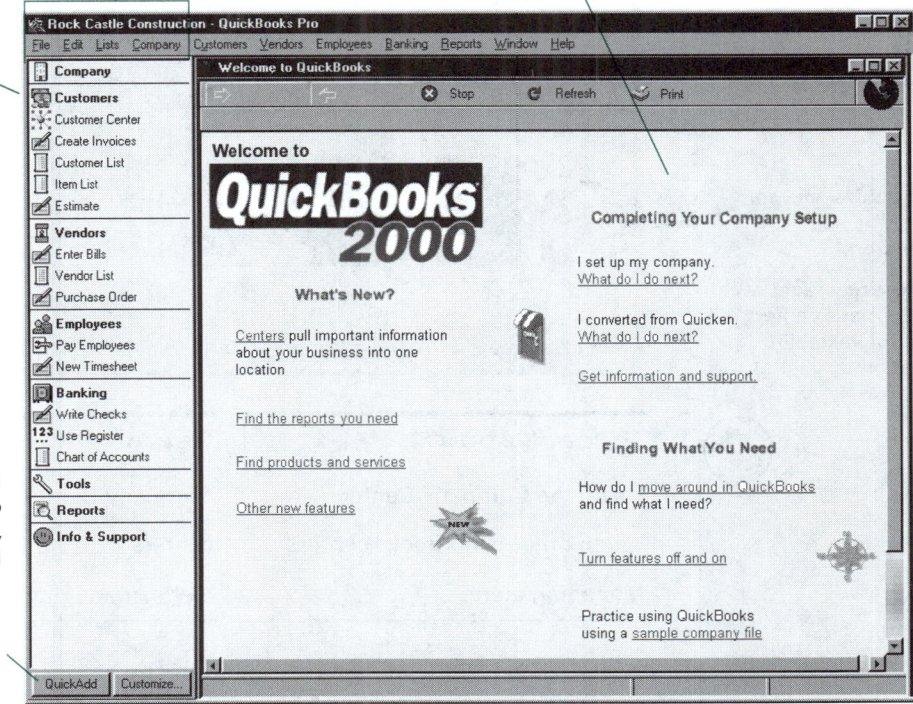

To learn about...	Search the Help index for...
Using, customizing, or hiding the navigation bar	navigation bar
Displaying and using the QuickBooks navigator	navigator

Your company at a glance

The Company Center gathers information from your QuickBooks data and displays it in one location—to help you manage your business.

QuickBooks alerts keep you informed regarding important business information—tax deadlines, updates to QuickBooks, and new services as they become available.

See account balances and amounts due.

Get summary information, such as total unpaid invoices.

Get a graphical view of your income and expense trend.

Click these messages at the bottom of a center or form for valuable information.

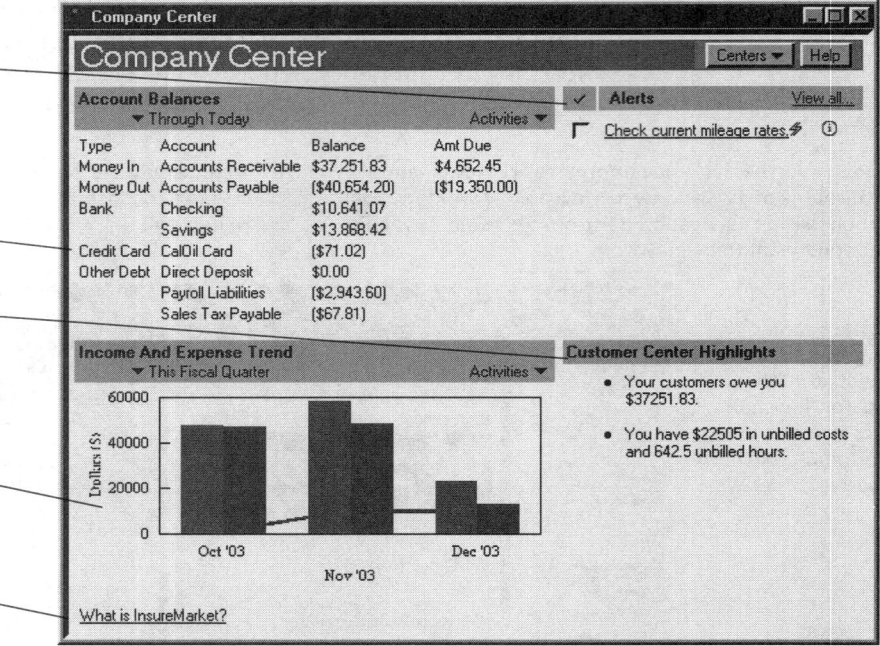

To learn about...	Search the Help index for...
Using the Company Center	Company Center
Using other QuickBooks centers	centers
Managing alerts	alerts, managing

38 | CHAPTER 3 Setting up your company in QuickBooks

CHAPTER 4

Organizing data effectively

Where the detail is — 40

Tracking the detail you need — 51

How much detail do I need to track—and where?

If you set up and use QuickBooks wisely, you can track enough detail to understand how your business is doing. Yet you can have a streamlined chart of accounts.

You may be used to having a separate account (or subaccount) on your chart of accounts for every detail about your business. With QuickBooks, you can get detailed reports about what you sell, what you buy, your payroll, and so on, without having this detail on your chart of accounts.

The fundamental guidelines for tracking detail in QuickBooks are:

- Track at least as much detail on your chart of accounts as you need for income tax reporting. Any further detail is up to you.
- QuickBooks usually has a particular way of tracking each type of detail that saves you time and gives you meaningful reports. This chapter describes these ways of tracking detail. Unless you also need the detail for income tax reporting, you don't need to duplicate it on your chart of accounts.

Where the detail is

This section contains the following topics:

Tracking detail while keeping a simple chart of accounts	**40**
What are the advantages of using subaccounts?	**43**
What's the best way to track my type of detail?	**45**
Tracking income and expenses with classes	**47**
Should I use classes, jobs, or types?	**49**
You get out only what you put in	**50**
What you shouldn't try to track in QuickBooks	**50**

Tracking detail while keeping a simple chart of accounts

A main advantage to using QuickBooks is that as you write invoices, write checks, write purchases orders, and pay employees, QuickBooks is helping you do your bookkeeping.

To make it easy to perform regular tasks, QuickBooks saves information on various lists so you don't have to retype it each time you need it. For example, on the Customer:Job list, you can save addresses, phone numbers, payment terms, and the correct sales tax to charge the customer.

Three of these lists can provide detail for reports while keeping your chart of accounts simplified: the Item list, Payroll Item list, and Class list.

Getting information about your services and products

Will you use QuickBooks to write invoices or statements or track what you sell? If so, you'll use the *Item list,* where you store descriptions of what you sell (or the services you perform).

For example, Stan is a consultant who helps small businesses purchase and set up computers and software. His Item list has separate items for pre-sales consulting, computer systems, installation, accounting software (QuickBooks, of course), word processing software, spreadsheets, and ongoing consulting.

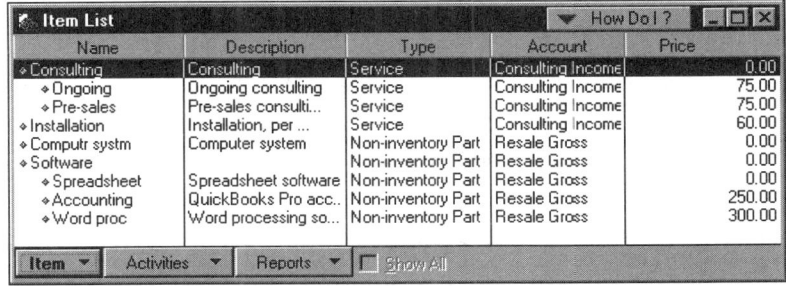

Stan's Item list for his services and products has many different items that he can track on sales reports. For more about using items, see Chapter 9, *Items—your services, products, and more,* beginning on page 113.

You may be accustomed to tracking all your detail by assigning different accounts on your chart of accounts. Stan, on the other hand, can use QuickBooks sales reports to see detailed information about income, hours of consulting, software units, and so on. His chart of accounts has just two income accounts: Consulting Income and Resale Gross. He doesn't need to duplicate the breakdown that is already on his Item list.

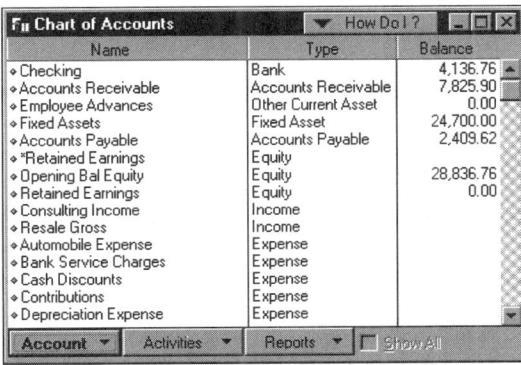

Tracking depreciation

You can set up accounts in QuickBooks to track depreciation. However, it is important to consult your tax advisor or the IRS about taking tax deductions for depreciation of assets. For more information, see "Handling depreciation of assets" on page 305.

If you simply want to track depreciation so that your financial statements are more accurate, choose Decision Tools from the Company menu.

Getting information about your payroll

Rosemary uses QuickBooks for payroll for her three employees. She keeps track of all payroll taxes and insurance deductions.

QuickBooks uses payroll items on its *Payroll Item list* to track all this detail, which Rosemary can see when she runs payroll reports. (For an illustration of a Payroll Item list, see page 371. For examples of payroll reports, see "Getting information about your payroll" on page 393.)

Her chart of accounts has a single expense account for payroll because she doesn't need to duplicate the breakdown that is already on her Payroll Item list.

Getting information for fund accounting

Richard keeps the books for his church. In addition to the general operating fund, the church has a separate building fund and a pastor's discretionary fund. Each fund has its own income and expenses. Instead of trying to subdivide each income and expense account into subaccounts for each fund, Richard has set up a QuickBooks class on the *Class list* for each fund.

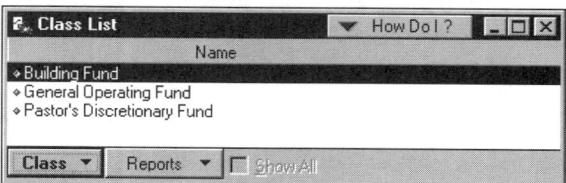

Whenever he records an income or expense transaction, he assigns a fund from his Class list. (See "Entering detail on transactions" on page 56.) He can then create a profit & loss by class report. Because this report has a column for each class, he can tell the board how the income and expenses are broken down by fund.

Because each fund is set up as a class, the profit & loss by class report shows income and expenses broken down by fund.

(Richard can rename his report "Inc and Exp by Fund" so his board can interpret it more easily.)

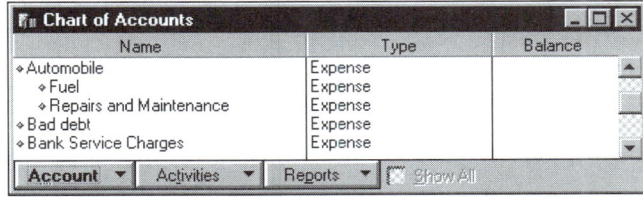

For more about QuickBooks classes, see "Tracking income and expenses with classes" on page 47.

What are the advantages of using subaccounts?

When you use subaccounts of a "parent" account, reports such as the profit and loss statement and the balance sheet show amounts for each subaccount plus a total for the parent account.

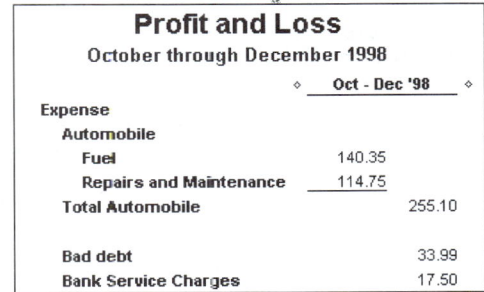

On this chart of accounts, the Automobile expense account has two subaccounts:

- Fuel
- Repairs and Maintenance

The expense part of the resulting profit and loss statement shows amounts for each subaccount and a total for the Automobile "parent" account.

You may want to use subaccounts for two reasons:

- You want a further breakdown of amounts for an existing account. To accomplish this, set up subaccounts for the existing account. From now on, use the subaccounts instead of the parent account.

Where the detail is | 43

(You may want to edit earlier transactions so the breakdown shows up on reports covering a period before today.)

For example, suppose you have an Automobile expense account for all automobile expenses. You add subaccounts for Fuel and for Repairs and Maintenance, as in the previous example.

- You already have related accounts that you want to subtotal on reports. (Or you may want to find them more easily.) You set up a new parent account and then make the related accounts subaccounts of the new parent.

For example, suppose you have separate accounts for Health Insurance, Fire Insurance, and Liability Insurance. You set up a new account called Insurance, and make the three separate accounts subaccounts of it.

What does "Other" refer to on reports?

If you use subaccounts, subitems, or jobs, then sooner or later you will see the word "Other" on a report:

The $18.45 expense for Automobile-Other is for the Automobile main account and not for either of the subaccounts.

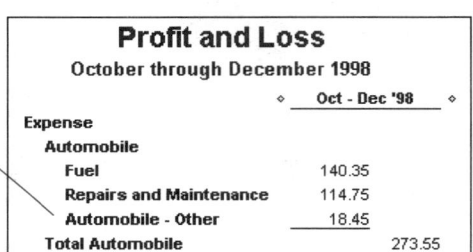

The word "Other" appears when the report has subaccounts (or subitems or jobs) but there is at least one transaction that is for the main account (or item or customer).

To avoid seeing a line or column for "Other," be sure to use subaccounts (and subitems and jobs) consistently.

Tip: **To remove the "Other" line or column on a report, double-click its dollar amount to learn why it occurs.** When QuickBooks displays a report listing one or more transactions, double-click each transaction in turn. On the transaction itself, replace the problem name with the correct subaccount, subitem, or job.

What's the best way to track my type of detail?

The following table describes situations that require a business to track a particular type of detail. The table suggests the best way to track this detail in QuickBooks.

Situation	How to record in QuickBooks	Comments	See...
You need to track details of services you are providing or products you are selling.	■ Set up items on the Item list for your services and products. ■ Record the sale, using the appropriate items. On sales forms you can edit the item descriptions to add detail you want the customer or client to see.	You can get reports about the items for services and products that you have sold, including quantities and dollar amounts by item.	Chapter 9, *Items—your services, products, and more,* beginning on page 113
You need to track multiple jobs for the same customer.	■ Set up jobs for the customer on your Customer:Job list. ■ When entering any sales for a job, enter both the job and customer name in the Customer:Job field.	Reports by customer or by job give subtotals by job and then a total of jobs for the customer.	Chapter 10, *Customers and jobs,* beginning on page 141
You need to track expenses by customer or job.	■ If you don't have QuickBooks Pro, turn on the preference for tracking expenses by job. ■ When entering any expenses for a customer or job, enter the customer name or the job and customer name in the Customer:Job field.	You can track expenses by customer alone if you don't use jobs. The profit & loss by job report lists both income and expenses with a separate column for each customer and job.	■ "Setting up customers and jobs" on page 147 ■ "Entering detail on transactions" on page 56
You need to track income and expenses by fund, location, department, or business segment. **Examples:** Religious and arts organizations, retail stores with multiple locations	■ Turn on class tracking, and set up a class on your Class list for each fund. ■ On every transaction, enter a class as well as an account (where appropriate).	The profit & loss by class statement has a column for each fund (class), so you can see income and expenses by fund.	"Tracking income and expenses with classes" on page 47

Where the detail is   45

Situation	How to record in QuickBooks	Comments	See...
You have employees and need to see detail about payroll taxes and other payroll expenses. **Example:** Any company with employees	Use the QuickBooks payroll feature to track your payroll.	The payroll reports show all your payroll information.	Chapter 18, *Payroll*, beginning on page 341
You need to track certain details about your customers and vendors. **Example:** Payment terms, customer's sales tax, customer's "ship to" address, vendor's tax ID for 1099 forms, your account number with a vendor	Find and fill in the appropriate field in the New or Edit Customer window or the New or Edit Vendor window. The field you want may be on the Additional Info tab.	If you set up customers and vendors by using the QuickAdd option, go back later, to add missing information.	▪ "Setting up customers" on page 147 ▪ "Using the Customer and Customer Detail centers" on page 153 ▪ "Setting up vendors" on page 215 ▪ "Editing vendors" on page 218
You want to see reports for a particular group of customers, jobs, or vendors. **Examples:** Residential vs. commercial customers; remodeling jobs vs. new construction; vendors that sell materials vs. subcontractors	When setting up a customer, job, or vendor, assign a type. (Job types are available only in QuickBooks Pro.)	You can filter a relevant report to limit the transactions to those for customers, job, or vendors of the type (or types) you specify. You can filter a report of your Customer:Job list or Vendor list to limit the names to those for the type (or types) you specify.	▪ "Customer types" on page 145 ▪ "Job types" on page 145 ▪ "Setting up vendors" on page 215 ▪ "Customizing the look of the report" on page 400
On your Item list, you want to group similar items together. **Example:** A school store wants to group clothing items and also group book items	▪ Set up a main, or parent, item (for example, clothing). Then set up subitems of the parent item (for example, T-shirt, cap). ▪ Use the appropriate subitem when entering a sale or purchase of items.	On reports that summarize amounts by item, QuickBooks provides an amount for each subitem, and then a subtotal for all subitems of the same item.	"Using items to subtotal on sales forms" on page 130

Situation	How to record in QuickBooks	Comments	See...
You want to track information that QuickBooks doesn't already track for customers, vendors, employees, or the items you sell. **Examples:** Patient's insurance company, item size or color	■ Set up a custom field for tracking the particular kind of information. ■ Fill in the custom field, where relevant, for new and existing customers, vendors, employees, or items. ■ To display and print the custom field on sales forms or purchase orders, customize the form to add the new field.	You can use the same custom field for customers, vendors, and employees if you choose. Custom fields for items are only for items you sell or purchase (services, parts, and other charges). You can filter a relevant report to limit the transactions to forms that have specific text in a custom field.	■ Search the Help index for: **custom fields, about** ■ Read "Customizing estimates, sales forms, and purchase orders" on page 58
On your profit and loss statement, you want to see subtotals for accounts that have something in common. **Example:** A construction company wants a subtotal for construction income for labor, materials, and subcontractors	■ Set up a main, or parent, account for the subtotal (for example, construction income). Then set up subaccounts of the parent account (for example, labor, materials, subcontractors). ■ Use the appropriate subaccount when QuickBooks requires you to specify an account.	On reports that summarize amounts by account, QuickBooks provides an amount for each subaccount and then a subtotal for all subaccounts of the same account.	"What are the advantages of using subaccounts?" on page 43

Tracking income and expenses with classes

Do you need to track income and expenses for separate parts of your business or organization? The following table has examples of what you can track by using classes in QuickBooks. (The word *class* has nothing to do with teaching or learning—instead, it is a way of classifying income or expenses *in addition to* assigning an income or expense account.)

Where the detail is

Use classes to track the following	Industry examples
Account executives (particularly useful if you plan on using an employee incentive program linked to the employee's business goals and profitability)	■ Advertising ■ PR ■ Consulting
Construction industry standard categories (General, Site Work, Concrete, Masonry, and so on)	■ Construction contractors
Departments	■ Businesses that budget by department ■ Retailers
Funds (General, Building, Outreach, and so on) You could start with two main classes for restricted and unrestricted funds, and then make each fund a subclass of a main class.	■ Nonprofit organizations ■ Religious groups
Locations (if the business has more than one)	■ Restaurants ■ Retailers ■ Service businesses
Manufacturers	■ Distributors ■ Manufacturing reps
Partners	■ Law firms ■ Consulting ■ Any other partnerships
Product lines	■ Distributors ■ Manufacturing reps ■ Sales agents

After you set up classes, you can enter them on any income or expense transaction including payroll transactions. For examples of entering a class on a deposit or a check, see "Entering detail on transactions" on page 56.

You cannot assign classes to transactions that involve only balance sheet accounts (for example, transfers from checking to savings, setup of inventory, setup of fixed assets).

You can set up subclasses of existing classes if you need to subtotal information about classes on reports.

	To learn about...	Search the Help index for...
	Turning on the preference for using classes	classes, turning on in QuickBooks
	Adding classes and subclasses	classes, adding

Should I use classes, jobs, or types?

Ask yourself: Am I trying to track income or expense activity associated with a particular customer or group of customers or group of jobs?

If your answer is Yes, then you use jobs, customer types, or job types or track expenses by job. The following table shows what you can do with each of these.

To do the following...	Do this in QuickBooks...	Examples of reports to use
Keep track of sales for separate jobs or projects for one customer.	Set up and use jobs for the customer on the Customer:Job list.	Sales by customer summary (which shows each job separately)
See income or expenses for one type of customer, as distinguished from another type. **Example:** A PR writer wants to compare a restaurant with retail clients.	When entering or editing a customer, assign a customer type.	■ Sales by customer summary, filtered for one customer type ■ Profit & loss by job, filtered for one customer type
(QuickBooks Pro only) See income or expenses for one type of job, as distinguished from another type. (Jobs of the same type can be for different customers.) **Example:** A construction contractor wants to compare kitchen remodels with office remodels.	When entering or editing a job, assign a job type.	■ Sales by customer summary, filtered for one job type ■ Profit & loss by job, filtered for one job type
Assign expenses to a customer (or to a particular job for a customer).	On every expense transaction for that customer or job, enter the customer name (or the customer and job name) in the Customer:Job field.	The following reports always break down amounts by customer. If you have jobs, they also break down amounts by job. ■ Profit & loss by job ■ Job profitability (QuickBooks Pro only) ■ Profit & loss budget vs. actual

If you are tracking a segment of your business that is independent of your customers and jobs, set up a class for the particular business segment. Then enter the class name in the Class field of every income or expense transaction for that segment.

You get out only what you put in

If you want to see detail on reports, be sure to track the detail somewhere in QuickBooks.

For example, if Susan needs to know how her yearly travel expenses break down by airfare, lodging, and meals, first she needs to subdivide her expense account for travel expenses into three subaccounts. Then she needs to break down her expenses each time she enters them in QuickBooks.

Similarly, if Richard needs to know what the income and expenses are for each of his church funds, then he must assign at least one fund to every transaction.

What you shouldn't try to track in QuickBooks

Some things should not be tracked in QuickBooks:

- Personal finances

    For tax purposes, it's usually best to keep your business income and expenses completely separate from your personal income and expenses. (If you still want to track personal finances in QuickBooks, set up a separate company file for them.)

- Investments in stock and mutual funds

    If the business owns these investments, you can track the cost basis as an asset. However, QuickBooks doesn't have the investment tracking found in Quicken.

- Details that are not specifically related to your business accounting (even though they may be very important)

    For example, Rachel needs to track when subscriptions expire so she can send reminder notices. Jon sells antiques on consignment and needs to track details about each unique item. Other software, such as a database, spreadsheet, or membership software, can help you track these details.

QuickBooks has a To Do List, where you can record notes you want to see on the Reminder list on a specific date. You can list personal as well as business notes. See "Making To Do notes" on page 444. To schedule events at specific times, you'll need other software.

Tracking the detail you need

This section covers the following topics:

Fine-tuning your chart of accounts	51
Setting up accounts to track equity details	53
Entering detail on transactions	56
Customizing estimates, sales forms, and purchase orders	58
When you no longer need the detail	59

Fine-tuning your chart of accounts

You can fine-tune your chart of accounts at any time by doing the following:

- Add new accounts or subaccounts.

    You can add subaccounts to balance sheet accounts (for example, fixed asset accounts) as well as to income and expense accounts.

- Turn on and use account numbers.

    QuickBooks has an option for specifying account numbers in addition to names. If the account is one that QuickBooks added for you, it already has a number but you can change it.

- Change the name or number of an existing account.

- Enter or edit an opening balance for a balance sheet account if the original opening balance is incorrect.

- Arrange accounts of the same type in alphabetical order (or numerical order if account numbers are turned on).

- Rearrange the order of accounts within the same account type.

- Make one existing account the subaccount of another (or, conversely, move a subaccount to a higher level).

You can drag accounts to a new position on the chart of accounts. When your accounts are not in alphabetical or numerical order, and you add a new account, QuickBooks places the new account above the other accounts of the same type.

Place the mouse pointer over the diamond at the left of the account you want to move.

When the pointer becomes a 4-headed arrow, click and drag the account up or down the list.

To make the account a subaccount of the account above, drag it to the right.

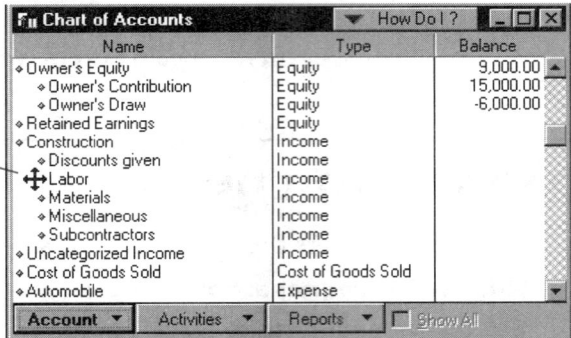

If you want to remove accounts from your chart of accounts, see "When you no longer need the detail" on page 59.

To learn about...	Search the Help index for...
Adding new accounts or subaccounts	accounts, adding to your chart of accounts
Turning on account numbers	accounts, numbering
Changing account names or numbers	accounts, editing information about
Changing or entering an opening balance for a balance sheet account	<ul><li>opening balances, changing for existing accounts</li><li>opening balances, entering for existing accounts</li></ul>
Arranging accounts (and other lists) in alphabetical or numerical order	lists, sorting entries
Reorganizing accounts within the same account type; also, reorganizing other lists that allow subentries (for example, Customer:Job list)	lists, reorganizing entries

52 | CHAPTER 4 Organizing data effectively

Setting up accounts to track equity details

equity

The net worth of a company, equal to the total assets minus the total liabilities. All the equity belongs to the owners.

Your company's equity comes from two sources:

- Money invested in your company (capital investments)
- Profits of your company

Of course, the owner can also take money out of the company. Such withdrawals, called owner's draws, reduce the company equity.

QuickBooks sets up two equity accounts automatically:

- Opening Bal Equity

  For every balance sheet account you set up with an opening balance, QuickBooks records the amount of the opening balance in the Opening Bal Equity account. (Asset account opening balances increase the equity; liability account opening balances decrease the equity.)

- Retained Earnings

  If you have data for more than one fiscal year, the QuickBooks balance sheet has a balance for the Retained Earnings account equal to the net profit from prior fiscal years. The balance for the Retained Earnings account does not display on the chart of accounts.

Some people like to track owner investments, owner's draws, and retained earnings prior to the QuickBooks start date by putting them in separate equity accounts. If you decide to add additional equity accounts, QuickBooks still adds the Retained Earnings and Net Income lines on your balance sheet.

Equity accounts for sole proprietorships

sole proprietorship

An unincorporated company owned by one person.

Because all equity of a sole proprietorship company belongs to one person, tracking equity can be very simple.

As of your QuickBooks start date, all equity is in the Opening Bal Equity account. You have several options:

- Keep the equity in this account and perhaps rename the account to something such as "Owner's Equity."

- Transfer all the equity out of Opening Bal Equity into Retained Earnings.

    This action is appropriate for companies that have built up assets as a result of earnings prior to the QuickBooks start date. From now on, you can take owner's draws out of the Retained Earnings account.

- Set up additional accounts (or subaccounts) to track owner's investments, owner's draws, and earnings before your QuickBooks start date.

In this example, a sole proprietor has changed the name of Opening Bal Equity to Owner's Equity and set up three subaccounts with opening balances.

The balance for Owner's Equity equals the total for the three subaccounts.

Name	Type	Balance
Owner's Equity	Equity	17,363.39
Owner's Contribution	Equity	15,000.00
Owner's Draw	Equity	-6,000.00
Company Earnings	Equity	8,363.39
Retained Earnings	Equity	

Tip: When setting up a new account for owner's draws, enter a negative opening balance to show the total draws prior to the QuickBooks start date. The negative opening balance indicates that the draws have reduced the company's equity. (Or, enter a zero opening balance and simply record draws from now on.)

Partnerships

partnership

An unincorporated company owned by two or more persons.

In a partnership, each partner owns a share of all assets and liabilities. Each partner may have invested in the partnership, and each receives a specified share of profits. Because partners are not employees, they don't receive salaries or wages, but they may withdraw money against their share of profits.

As of your QuickBooks start date, all the equity is in the Opening Bal Equity account.

- Set up separate equity accounts for each partner.

    If you don't want to see further detail, the opening balance for each partner's equity account should equal the partner's equity as of your QuickBooks start date. Because the company's equity belongs to the partners, setting up the new accounts should reduce the balance of the Opening Bal Equity account to zero.

From now on, record each partner's capital investment, draws, and share of profits in the partner's single equity account.

If you want to see further detail by adding subaccounts, the opening balance for each partner's "parent" equity account should equal zero.

- (Optional) Add subaccounts to provide the level of detail you'd like to see on the chart of accounts and on the balance sheet. For example, add subaccounts for each partner's investments, share of profits, and draws.

In this partnership, the balance for Marilyn's Equity equals the total of her subaccounts. Similarly, the balance for Peggy's Equity equals the total of her subaccounts.

The balance for Opening Bal Equity is zero after the partners' equity accounts have been set up.

Name	Type	Balance
Marilyn's Equity	Equity	10,579.76
Marilyn's Draw	Equity	-6,000.00
Marilyn's Investment	Equity	10,000.00
Marilyn's Profits	Equity	6,579.76
Opening Bal Equity	Equity	0.00
Peggy's Equity	Equity	7,783.63
Peggy's Draw	Equity	-6,000.00
Peggy's Investment	Equity	9,000.00
Peggy's Profits	Equity	4,783.63
Retained Earnings	Equity	

Corporations

corporation

A business organization that has been incorporated. A corporation is owned by its stockholders.

In a corporation, you'll usually want to separate stockholders investment of capital from the stockholders share of earnings.

To track paid-in capital or investments of stockholders, add an equity account with a name such as "Capital Stock." Although you do need to have records of the names and investments of each stockholder, you probably won't want to show this detail on your chart of accounts. For the opening balance, enter the total paid-in capital as of your QuickBooks start date.

After you have set up all your accounts, the amount remaining in Opening Bal Equity represents retained earnings prior to the start date. You can rename this account with a name such as "Prior Earnings" or "Pre-1995 Earnings."

QuickBooks automatically tracks the corporation's retained earnings for completed fiscal years in the Retained Earnings equity account.

After the end of the year, you may distribute some or all of the Corporations retained earnings to stockholders as dividends.

To learn about...	Search the Help index for...
Renaming Opening Bal Equity	accounts, editing information about
Adding equity accounts or subaccounts	accounts, adding to your chart of accounts
Transferring equity out of Opening Bal Equity	equity, transferring from Opening Bal Equity

Entering detail on transactions

Once you have set up to track a particular kind of detail, you should track the detail where appropriate on transactions you record.

- For information about recording checks, bills, and credit cards, see Chapter 14, *Tracking and paying expenses,* beginning on page 247.

- For information about recording deposits, see "Receiving payments and making deposits" on page 105.

For example, Stefan has subaccounts for his expense accounts, so he chooses the correct subaccount when recording a check or bill.

When Stefan chooses the subaccount Equipment Rental from the drop-down list in the **Account** field, QuickBooks enters the account name (Job Expenses) followed by a colon (:) and the subaccount name.

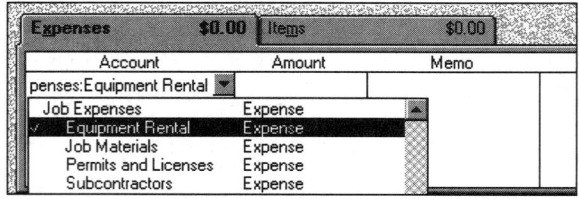

Tip: **To get reports to show the breakdown you want, use subaccounts or subitems consistently.** That is, if you record expenses for a subaccount of a main account, do not sometimes record expenses directly for the main account. Similarly, if you record sales of a subitem of a main item, do not sometimes record sales directly for the main item. To choose a subaccount or subitem in a field, display the drop-down list for that field.

Deborah needs to track the costs as well as the income for each customer's job. Whenever she records an expense or purchases an item for the job, she assigns the job to the expense or item. She can even indicate that the expense or item is billable to the job so she can invoice the customer for it later. (See "Charging for actual time and costs" on page 193.)

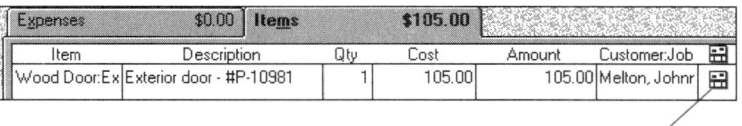

In the **Customer:Job** field of checks, bills, or credit card charges, Deborah enters the name of the customer (and job) for the expense or purchase.

If you track customers but not jobs, you can enter the customer name alone.

The invoice symbol indicates the expense or purchase is billable to the customer or job.

Tip: You can assign customers and jobs to purchases of items as well as expenses only in QuickBooks Pro. If you don't have QuickBooks Pro, you can assign customers and jobs to expenses but not purchases of items.

Richard is using classes to keep track of each fund his church has set up. When Richard records income for a fund, he assigns both an income account and the class for that fund.

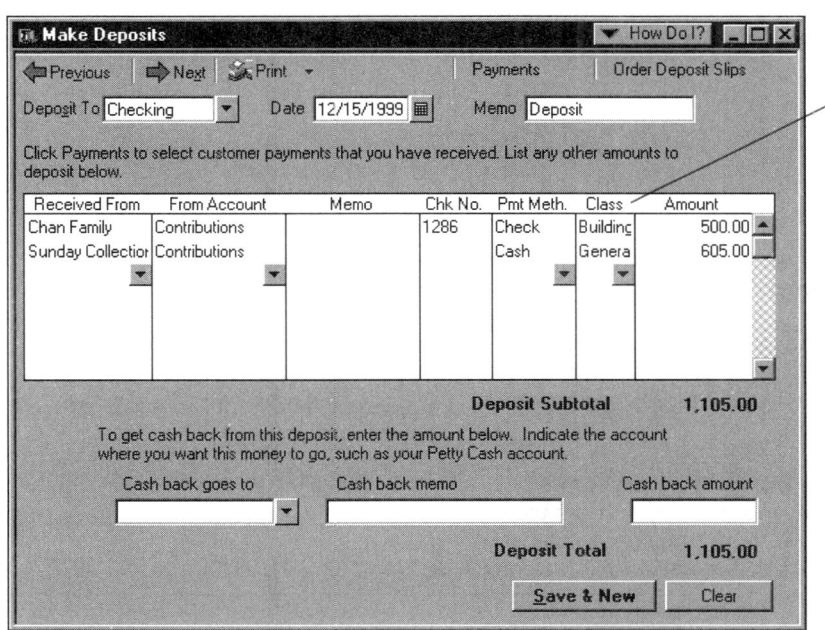

In the **Class** field for the deposit, Richard indicates the fund each contribution is for.

Tracking the detail you need | 57

Similarly, when he writes a check, he assigns both an expense account and a class for the appropriate fund.

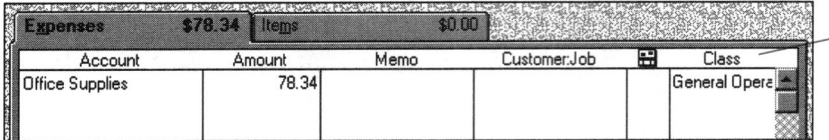

In the **Class** field for the check detail, Richard indicates the fund each expense is for.

Customizing estimates, sales forms, and purchase orders

You can customize your estimates (available only in QuickBooks Pro), sales forms, and purchase orders to show standard fields (such as service date, and customer:job) or custom fields you have set up.

For example, Justine has a custom field for the color of her items. She can add a column for color to all of her forms by customizing the template for each form.

Ralph wants his invoices to display the customer's contract number. He sets up a custom field for contract number for customers. Then he adds this field to the top of his invoices by customizing his invoice template.

Note: **You cannot add custom fields to statements.** However, you can customize statements by adding or deleting some standard fields (such as quantity and rate). You can add custom fields to all other sales forms.

For more information, see Chapter 7, *Creating a professional image*, beginning on page 77.

To learn about...	Search the Help index for...
Setting up custom fields to track additional information about customers, vendors, employees, or items	■ custom fields, for customers, vendors, or employees ■ custom fields, for the items you purchase or sell
Customizing estimates, sales forms, and purchase orders to add standard and custom fields for customers, vendors, or items	■ customizing forms, fields ■ customers, special orders for

When you no longer need the detail

In some situations, you may want to remove detail from lists or reports:

- The detail is for something you needed at one time but no longer need.

- You realize you don't need all the detail you set up and would like to consolidate some of it.

If the detail is on a particular list (for example, old, completed jobs on the Customer:Job list), the easiest solution is to simply hide the unwanted name on the list. You do this by making the name "inactive." It remains on the old transactions, but you won't see it on drop-down lists.

If you never used the name at all and don't plan to, you can delete it altogether. However, if you did use it, QuickBooks doesn't allow you to delete it.

If you want to consolidate all transactions for one name with those of another name, QuickBooks allows you to merge the names. This is a good solution if you inadvertently set up and used two different names for the same thing.

Finally, if your data file grows large and you want to remove old transactions as well as old names that are not in current transactions, you can use the Condense feature. You can specify from which lists you want to remove old names. See "Condensing data" on page 426.

To learn about...	Search the Help index for...
Hiding unwanted names on lists	hiding, list entries
Deleting unused names from lists	deleting, entries from lists
Merging transactions for one name with transactions for a second name	merging, list entries
Removing old transactions along with old names	condensing data

CHAPTER 5

Protecting your data

How can I keep my data safe?

Using passwords	62
Recording who changed what	65
Backing up your company data	66

Keeping your data safe can include limiting access to the data through passwords, making regular backup copies of your data, and maintaining an audit trail to track changes to transactions.

Tip: To prevent other people from accessing your QuickBooks company file, always close it when you are finished using it or if you plan to be away from your workstation for an extended period of time.

If you suspect that your QuickBooks company file has become damaged, refer to Appendix A, "Troubleshooting" on page 459 for information.

Using passwords

Intuit recommends that you use both Windows system and QuickBooks passwords, which are designed to limit access to your desktop and to certain areas of your QuickBooks company file—and thereby help to safeguard sensitive company information.

Each QuickBooks user in your company can be set up with a unique password and given designated areas of the program that he or she can work in. Areas include sales and accounts receivable, purchases and accounts payable, checking and credit cards, inventory, time tracking, payroll, sensitive accounting activities, and sensitive financial reports.

Until you set up users (and passwords) in your QuickBooks company file, any person who accesses the file through QuickBooks, will have full access.

The QuickBooks password feature provides a basic degree of protection for your data, but it is not a complete security system.

For example, it will not prevent someone from using Windows Explorer to delete a company file. If you need stronger protection, keep your computer and backup disks in a secure area and ensure any network connections to your computer.

Do you need to use passwords?

Situation	Action	Comments
If you are the only person in your office who uses QuickBooks	Set up system and QuickBooks passwords for yourself to help prevent others from accessing your QuickBooks data. Or, you can choose not to use one. However, Intuit recommends that you use passwords as safety precautions in helping protect your data.	If you used passwords in your previous version of QuickBooks, QuickBooks remembers the owner password you used in that version. When you first open your company file in QuickBooks 2000, you'll be prompted to enter this password. Later, you can change the password or choose not to use passwords any longer.
If you allow others to access your QuickBooks data	Set up users with passwords and specific access areas.	For example, you can allow your business partner to write payroll checks but limit a data-entry person to entering invoices.

Situation	Action	Comments
If you want to have two or more people working in the QuickBooks file at the same time	Set up users with passwords and specific access areas.	You must have two or more copies of QuickBooks Pro 2000.

Setting up users

When you create a new QuickBooks company file, QuickBooks creates a user called "Admin." This is the QuickBooks Administrator for that company file.

Tip: **When you choose a password for the Administrator, make sure you write it down and store it in a safe place.** If you forget this password and need assistance, choose Phone Directory from the Help menu and click General Product Support.

The Administrator has unlimited access to all data in the company file and is the only person who can add additional users and access privileges. For each user being set up, the Administrator designates:

- A password which the user can change later. (The password can contain up to 16 alphanumeric characters and is not case sensitive.)
- Full access, selective access, or no access for each QuickBooks area.

After setup, a summary screen displays the access selections for that user.

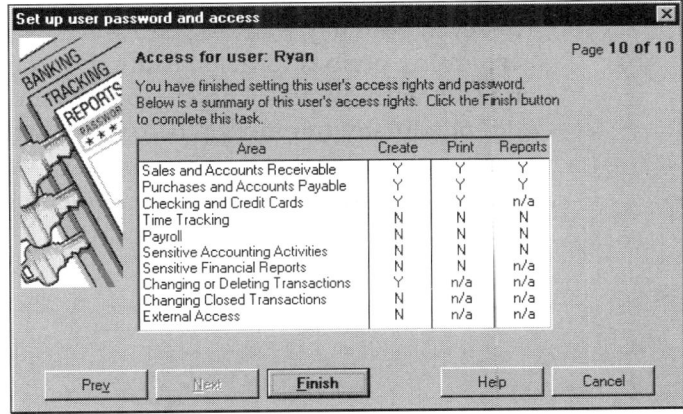

Using passwords 63

Once you have set up more than one user, QuickBooks prompts you for a login when you open the company file.

Only the QuickBooks Administrator can set up new users and their levels of access.

Once set up, each individual user can change or delete his or her own password. However, the QuickBooks Administrator will still be the only user able to make changes to a user's access.

To learn about...	Search the Help index for...
The different access areas of QuickBooks	passwords, access areas
The role of the QuickBooks Administrator	admin
Setting up users with passwords and access	users, adding
Changing passwords	passwords, changing
Deleting passwords	passwords, deleting

Using permissions to close an accounting period

Unlike most other accounting systems, QuickBooks does not require you to "close the books" at the end of a period. Closing books is often a complicated process that involves transferring information from one ledger to another and summarizing it. You can ask QuickBooks for reports at any time, not just at the end of a period.

However, you may want to restrict access to the transactions of prior accounting periods to help ensure that the transactions are not changed without your knowledge. By requiring permission to delete, add, or edit any transaction before a chosen date, you can discourage accidental or casual changes made in or with QuickBooks to closed periods, but still make corrections when necessary.

You can grant or deny this access in QuickBooks when setting up a user.

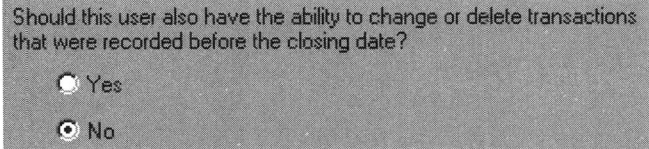

To learn about...	Search the Help index for...
Using permissions to "close" your books	closing, an accounting period

Recording who changed what

You can have QuickBooks keep a record of all changes made to transactions, including the name of the user who made the changes, and then review the changes in the audit trail report.

This transaction has been edited. The "Current Transaction" shows what the transaction is like now; the "Previous Transaction" shows what the transaction was like before the change.

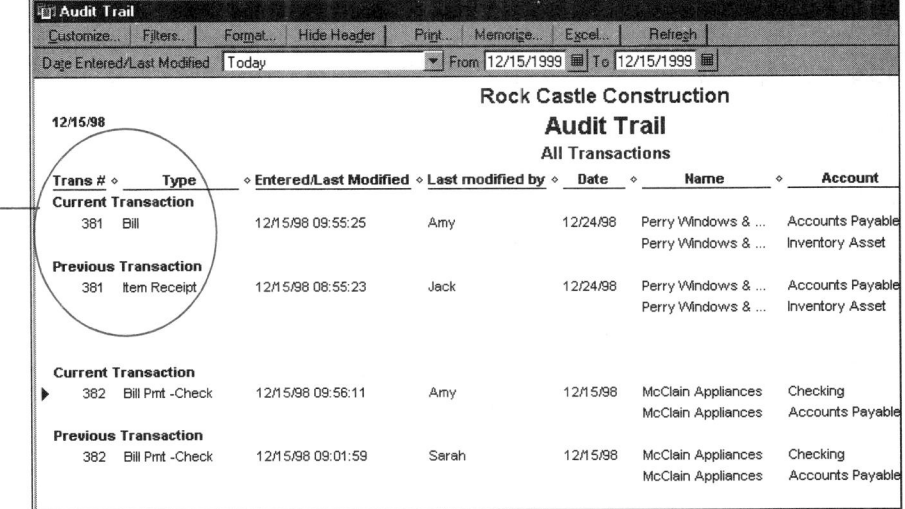

Any transactions labeled "Previous Transaction" have been modified. You can compare the previous transaction to the current transaction to see which part or parts of the transaction have changed. The report shows the user who entered modifications and the date and time of the modification.

To keep a record of changed transactions, you must have the audit trail preference turned on.

If the preference is turned off, QuickBooks will no longer keep a record of the changes to transactions. If the audit trail was turned off during part of the period covered by the report, QuickBooks may not show the modification date of some transactions, but it will retain old audit trail information.

If you turn the audit trail preference on, you may find that QuickBooks works more slowly, and your data takes up more disk space and may require more memory. These drawbacks occur because QuickBooks records not only the changed transaction, but also its previous versions. In contrast, QuickBooks overwrites the previous version of a transaction when the audit-trail preference is turned off.

To learn about...	Search the Help index for...
Using the audit trail feature and creating the report	audit trail

Backing up your company data

Your data is valuable! No technique can recover all possible file damage or protect against theft or natural disasters.

Tip: **Help protect your computer from electrical surges by using surge protectors.** Surge protectors are inexpensive and can be purchased in most hardware stores. In addition, you may want to unplug your computer during electrical storms. If you suffer from regular brownouts or blackouts, you might consider an Uninterruptible Power Supply (UPS).

You might lose data if you delete the data file by mistake, if your hard disk fails, or if your computer is stolen or damaged. To prevent or minimize data loss, you should make regular backup copies of your QuickBooks company data. In the event of a data loss you can restore your data from a backup copy. To initiate the process of making a backup copy, choose Back Up from the File menu.

Note: The QuickBooks Back Up command does not simply copy the data file for your QuickBooks company. Instead, it compresses the data into a compact backup file. You can name the backup file whatever you want.

Recommended backup routine

- Prepare your backup disks by completing a full format.
- Label the outside of your disks accordingly, such as "QuickBooks Backup Monday," "QuickBooks Backup Tuesday," and so on. (If you're backing up onto multiple 3.5-inch disks, QuickBooks provides a convenient on-disk labeling feature that makes it easier for you to keep track of basic labeling information such as year, month, date, filename, and disk number.)
- Each day, back up onto 3.5-inch disks to keep in the office.

   If you are using QuickBooks Pro with multiple users, you must switch QuickBooks to **single-user mode** before you can create a backup. (For more information on single-user mode, see Chapter 6, *Sharing QuickBooks Pro on a network,* beginning on page 69.)

- At least once a month, make a backup to keep off your premises.

   For your monthly backup to keep off premises, you may want to alternate between two sets of disks. If a disaster strikes your office, you'll want to have a reliable record of your data to fall back on.

- Periodically, replace the backup disks with new disks formatted on your machine.

   Disks are susceptible to damage and should be replaced periodically.

- At the end of the fiscal year, make an archive copy of your data to store off site.

To learn about...	Search the Help index for...
Backing up your company data	backups

CHAPTER 6

Sharing QuickBooks Pro on a network

How multi-user ready QuickBooks Pro works	70
Setting up the multi-user environment	73
Using multi-user QuickBooks Pro	74

> How can we use the same company file at the same time?

As your business grows larger, more people in your office may need access to the company file. If you have QuickBooks Pro running on a network, you can have up to five people working in your QuickBooks Pro company file at the same time. For example, your business partner can be using QuickBooks Pro to write payroll checks while a data-entry person enters invoices.

Note: The ability for two or more people to work in the same QuickBooks Pro file at the same time over a network is available only in QuickBooks Pro.

How multi-user ready QuickBooks Pro works

Using QuickBooks Pro on a network is basically the same as using QuickBooks Pro on a single computer, with a few exceptions. For most of the tasks you perform everyday, up to five users can access the company file at the same time. When users are allowed to work simultaneously in the company file, the file is in *multi-user mode*.

multi-user mode

The status of a QuickBooks Pro company file that allows more than one person to access the file at the same time.

However, there are some activities in QuickBooks Pro that allow only one person at a time to be in the company file. These activities require the file to be in *single-user mode*. In this mode, other users must close the company file on their computer. Then the person who wants to perform the activity must switch the file to single-user mode. After finishing the activity, the person switches back to multi-user mode, and then the others may open the file and continue working as before.

single-user mode

The status of a QuickBooks Pro company file that allows only one person to access the file.

Single-mode activities include:

- Setting up a new company file
- File operations such as backing up, condensing, or exporting data
- Some types of changes to lists
- Activities involving an Accountant's Review copy

> **QuickBooks Pro 2000 will not work with QuickBooks Pro 6.0 or QuickBooks Pro 99 in a multi-user environment. Also, QuickBooks Pro 6.0 will not work with QuickBooks Pro 99 in a multi-user environment.**
>
> QuickBooks Pro 99 users: If you don't want to upgrade all users to QuickBooks Pro 2000, you can still purchase copies of QuickBooks Pro 99 from Intuit by calling 1-888-2-INTUIT. QuickBooks Pro 6.0 users: You can still increase the number of multi-users by purchasing copies of QuickBooks Pro 2000 for all users in your multi-user environment (call 1-888-2-INTUIT).

Network options

The company file should be located on a shared resource, like a server or a hard disk, that others have read/write access to.

Peer-to-peer network

In a peer-to-peer network, Jack, Sarah, and Amy all have a copy of QuickBooks Pro installed on their networked computers. Because Sarah does the most work on QuickBooks Pro, the company file resides on her computer in a folder or directory that both Jack and Amy have read/write access to.

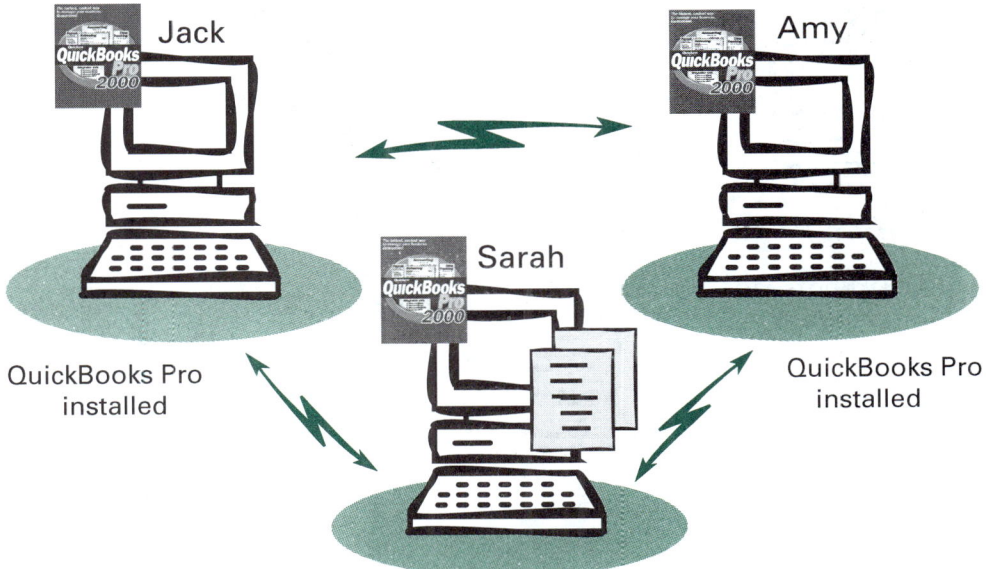

Client-server network

In a client-server network environment, Jack, Sarah, and Amy all have a copy of QuickBooks Pro installed on their networked computers. They all also have access to a file server. The company file is stored on the file server in a place that they all have access to.

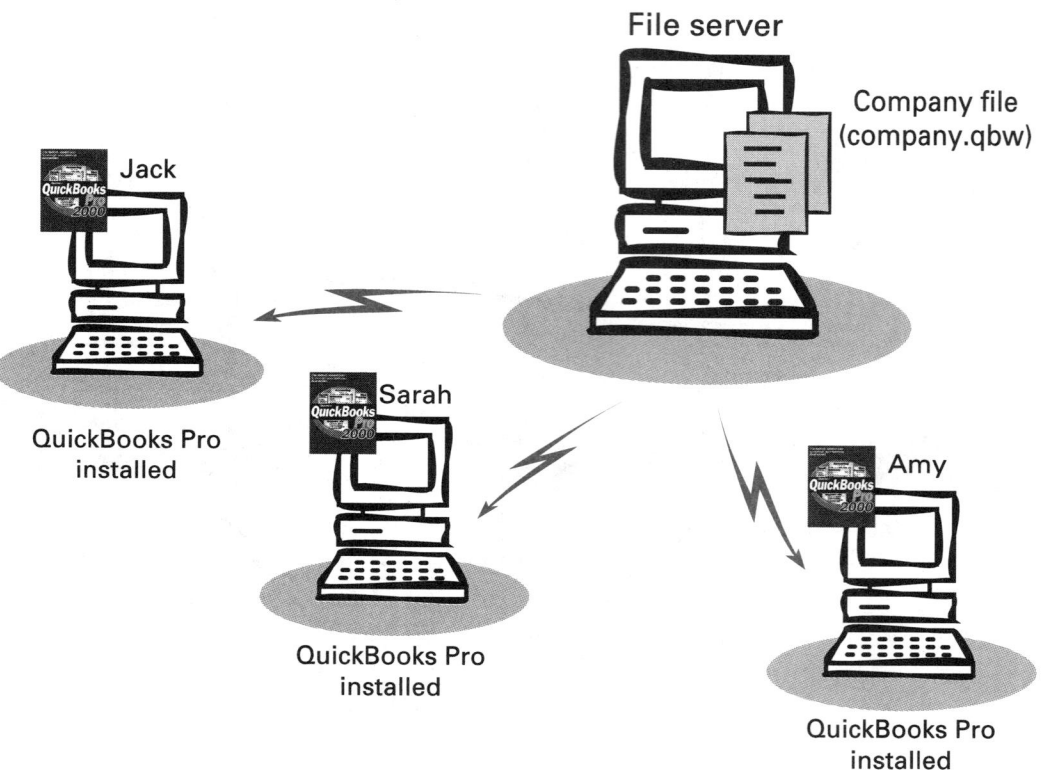

Setting up the multi-user environment

Follow these steps to set up a multi-user environment for QuickBooks Pro.

1 Make sure you have your computers properly networked.

Please refer to your networking software documentation for instructions.

2 Install a copy of QuickBooks Pro 2000 on each of the computers you are working with.

Your installation routine will vary slightly depending on if you are installing a 5-User Value Pack, or multiple individual copies of QuickBooks Pro. For complete installation instructions, be sure to read *System requirements and installation,* beginning on page 1 of the "Installation and Conversion Guide."

3 Have your QuickBooks Administrator add your users.

For more information about the Administrator and setting up users and passwords, see "Using passwords" on page 62.

Note: Up to five users may have access to the company file simultaneously. However, you can set up as many users as you wish. For example, if you have five full-time employees and three part-time employees who need access to the data file, you can set up all eight employees as users of the company file. All eight are considered valid users of the company file, but only five can access the company file at the same time.

4 Register your copies of QuickBooks Pro after you have begun sharing the company file.

This allows us to properly register the different copies of QuickBooks Pro you are using. For more information about how to register, see "Registering QuickBooks" on page 8 of the *Installation and Conversion Guide.*

5 (Optional) Have users customize their QuickBooks Pro working environment.

For example, each user can decide which menus will appear in his or her copy of QuickBooks Pro, the kinds and frequency of various reminders, and so forth.

To learn about...	Search the Help index for...
Adding users	users, adding
Setting up user preferences	preferences, general

If you add other computers to your network

As your business grows, you may want to add additional computers to your office and, therefore, additional copies of QuickBooks Pro.

Note: Your networked computers must all use the same multi-user version and release of QuickBooks Pro.

After you add the computer to your network

1   Install QuickBooks Pro on the new machine.

2   Have a user open the company file.

3   Once a user has accessed the company file, register this copy of QuickBooks Pro.

To learn about...	Search the Help index for...
Adding new users	users, adding
Finding out what version of QuickBooks Pro you're using	version

Using multi-user QuickBooks Pro

After you have set up the multi-user environment, up to five users can now log in to your QuickBooks Pro company file. They will only be able to access the features set up for them by the Administrator.

Switching between modes

To switch from multi-user mode to single-user mode:

1   Inform others working in QuickBooks Pro so they may close the shared company file and their copy of QuickBooks Pro.

2   From the File menu, choose **Switch to single-user mode**.

To switch from single-user mode to multi-user mode:

- From the File menu, choose **Switch to multi-user mode**.

Refresh after entering data

Anytime you are working with others in the company file, you can use the Refresh button to make sure you have the most current information on your reports or lists. The Refresh button will update your screen with the information that others have entered into QuickBooks Pro since you selected the report or list.

To learn about...	Search the Help index for...
Your refresh options	Refresh button

Improving performance

If you have multiple people using QuickBooks Pro at the same time, you may notice that QuickBooks Pro runs a little slower than before. There are a few ways to improve the performance of QuickBooks Pro and increase its speed:

- Store the company file on the fastest or most powerful computer.

- Keep your company file size under 20 megabytes. See "Condensing data" on page 426.

- Try to run reports during off hours. Day-to-day activities such as entering invoices, receiving payments, or entering purchase orders and bills have no effect on performance. However, running reports can slow QuickBooks Pro.

- Wait to refresh reports until you are ready to use or print the report.

- Avoid keeping unnecessary windows open.

To learn about...	Search the Help index for...
More tips for improving performance	performance

CHAPTER 7

Creating a professional image

How can QuickBooks help?	78
Customizing your checks	83
Creating custom business forms	84
Printing your forms and checks	91

How do I create a professional image for my business?

Creating a professional image for your business involves several aspects. For a home-based business, one aspect includes investing in a business phone line and voice mail. Other aspects include establishing a presence on the World Wide Web, creating a consistent graphic look for business materials (such as invoices, checks, and business cards), and client courtesy, which includes timely responses to phone messages and prompt arrival for meetings.

How can QuickBooks help?

QuickBooks and Intuit provide features, tools, and supplies to help you create and maintain a professional business image.

Establishing a Web site

Having your own Web site with your own Internet address is like having a display ad in a phone book with millions of readers. With your own Web site, you can:

- Establish an Internet presence that looks as professional as your other forms of communication.
- Publish information about your services and policies.
- List your hours, address, phone numbers, and directions on how to get to your business.
- Receive e-mail from vendors, customers, and potential customers through your own Internet address.

By simply answering a few questions, you can create a unique, professional Web site with QuickBooks.

Creating your Web site

You can create a Web site when you register QuickBooks. Later you can change your Web site to further personalize it or to update it if information such as your phone number changes. When you create a Web site through QuickBooks, you get:

- A unique Internet address (or domain name), like www.weplant.com for We Plant, Inc. QuickBooks searches the Internet for unique names and registers the one you choose.
- A Web site filled with information about your industry and your company.
- E-mail forwarding so that e-mail sent to your new Internet address is forwarded to the e-mail account you normally use.

To create your Web site:

- Register QuickBooks. Completing online registration creates your Web site.

- From the Company menu, choose My Company Web Site. If you did not create your Web site during registration, you will be able to create it when you choose to view or manage it.

To view or manage your Web site, choose My Company Web Site from the Company menu.

To learn about...	Search the Help index for...
Creating and personalizing your Web site	Web site, creating for your company

Timely reminders and notes

QuickBooks Reminder and To Do lists help you manage your important tasks, meetings, and commitments.

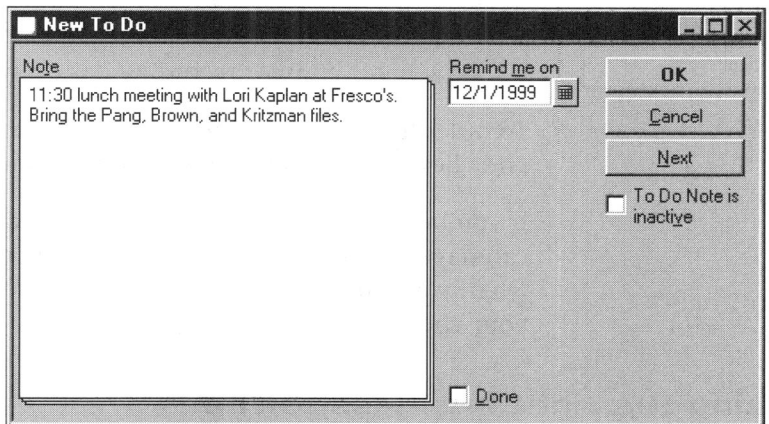

You can use the To Do list to look at your notes at any time, or use the Reminders list to see which notes are currently due when you start up QuickBooks.

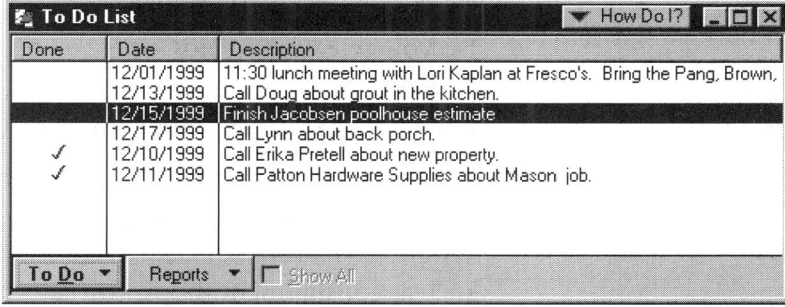

You can create the To Do notes list report that shows the status, date, and description for each To Do note.

For more information, see "Making To Do notes" on page 444.

Checks that reflect your business

While your vendors won't be picky about the checks you use for payment, you'll want checks that reflect your business.

If you want to have checks preprinted with your company logo, Intuit offers multiple check formats in a variety of colors and designs that are guaranteed to work with the latest version of QuickBooks.

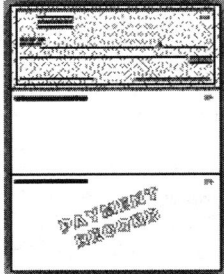

Intuit check formats include:

- Voucher checks have a detachable stub you can use for payroll or accounts payable information. These checks are standard business size.
- Standard checks are business size with no voucher area.
- Wallet checks are the size of personal checks and include a detachable stub for recording date, payee, amount, and memo.

To order Intuit checks, choose Phone Directory from the Help menu and click QuickBooks Supplies, or visit **www.intuitmarket.com**.

If you buy checks printed without your company information, you can have QuickBooks print your logo and company name and address when you print your checks. For more information, see "Customizing your checks" on page 83.

Choosing the right business forms

To help you decide which forms you'll want to use in QuickBooks, review the following questions:

- Do you give quotes, bids, or estimates to prospective clients? (QuickBooks Pro only)

    If yes, you can create your own custom estimate forms.

- Do you receive full payment at the time of sale?

    For high-volume businesses, you'll want to use your point-of-sale system for cash sales receipts, but for lower-volume businesses, such as consignment shops, you can create your own sales receipts in QuickBooks using custom cash sales forms.

- Do you buy inventory that is later resold?

    If yes, QuickBooks has a purchase order form that can be customized to meet your needs.

- Do you need to bill customers or patients?

    If yes, you can use either the Professional, Service, or Product invoices or the standard statement or create a custom invoice or statement.

    Unsure if you should use invoices or statements? Read the discussion found in "If your customers owe you money or pay in advance" on page 172.

Standard Intuit forms

Standard forms have layouts that match preprinted Intuit forms. You can also print these invoices (and statements) on your own letterhead, plain paper, or multi-purpose forms. (To order Intuit preprinted forms, choose Phone Directory from the Help menu and click QuickBooks Supplies.)

Form	Characteristics
Intuit Professional Invoice Used by businesses such as law firms and consultants.	■ Prints only two columns: description and amount. ■ Has the widest column for descriptions, so is the best choice for long, detailed descriptions.
Intuit Service Invoice Used by businesses that bill by the hour or item, such as design firms or caterers.	Prints columns for quantity, description, rate, and amount.
Intuit Product Invoice Used by businesses that have product sales, such as retailers.	■ Prints fields designed for shipping products, such as Ship To and FOB. ■ Prints a column for the item name or code, in addition to columns on the Intuit Service Invoice. (It has a Price Each column instead of a Rate column.)
Intuit Standard Statement	■ Prints columns for the date, transaction, amount, and balance. ■ Aging information is tracked along the bottom.

Other business forms

Many other business forms are available in QuickBooks and can be created and customized as needed. See "Creating custom business forms" on page 84 for details.

With the exception of deposit slips, you can print these forms on letterhead, plain paper, or multi-purpose forms from Intuit.

Form	Preset characteristics
Invoice	■ Prints columns for description, quantity, rate, and amount. ■ Fields include purchase order number, terms, and project.
Finance Charge	Prints description and amount.
Progress Invoice (QuickBooks Pro only) Used by construction and architecture firms.	Prints columns for item, description, estimate amount, prior amount, prior %, quantity, rate, current %, total %, and amount.
Custom Credit Memo	Prints fields for credit number, purchase order, and project.
Custom Cash Sale	■ Title is Sales Receipt. ■ Prints fields for sale number, check number, payment method, and project.
Custom Purchase Order	■ Prints fields for FOB and expected date. ■ Prints columns for description, quantity, rate, and amount.
Statement	■ Prints columns for the date, description, amount, and balance. ■ Aging information is tracked along the bottom.
Custom Estimate (QuickBooks Pro only) Can be used by any business that creates estimates, bids, or quotes.	■ Prints columns for description, quantity, rate, and total. ■ Includes a signature line and a standard disclaimer, "This estimate is good for 30 days."

Form	Preset characteristics
Printable Deposit Slips	- These slips are personalized with your company name, address, and financial institution information. - You can print customer payments made by cash or check and other income made by cash or check on these slips. For more information or to order Printable Deposit Slips, visit **www.intuitmarket.com**

Customizing your checks

Using QuickBooks, you can customize your checks to print the following:

- Your company name and address
- Your logo

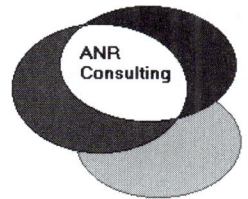

- Your check information in the font of your choice

To learn about...	Search the Help index for...
Adding a logo and changing fonts	checks, customizing

Creating custom business forms

Creating a custom invoice or other business form is made up of two basic concepts: **customizing** and **designing**. You customize the forms by specifying the fields and columns you want on the form in the Customize window. Design the layout of forms with the Layout Designer window in which you can move and resize objects using the mouse.

Here are just a few examples of how you can customize and design your business forms with QuickBooks:

- Create different versions of a form for use in specific situations. For example, if you ship goods with a packing slip, you can create an invoice form with the title "Packing Slip" instead of "Invoice."
- Change fonts.
- Add new columns and fields and delete ones you don't need. For example, if you've created custom fields for your inventory, you can have the fields appear on the form.
- Decide which fields you want to see for your own use onscreen, and which fields you want your customer to see on the printed form.
- Change the names of fields to make them appropriate for your business.
- Move a field to give it greater visibility.
- Add your company logo.
- Add a field containing up to 1,000 characters to print on forms. For example, you can print a tax ID number for customers, product warranty information, or legal text.

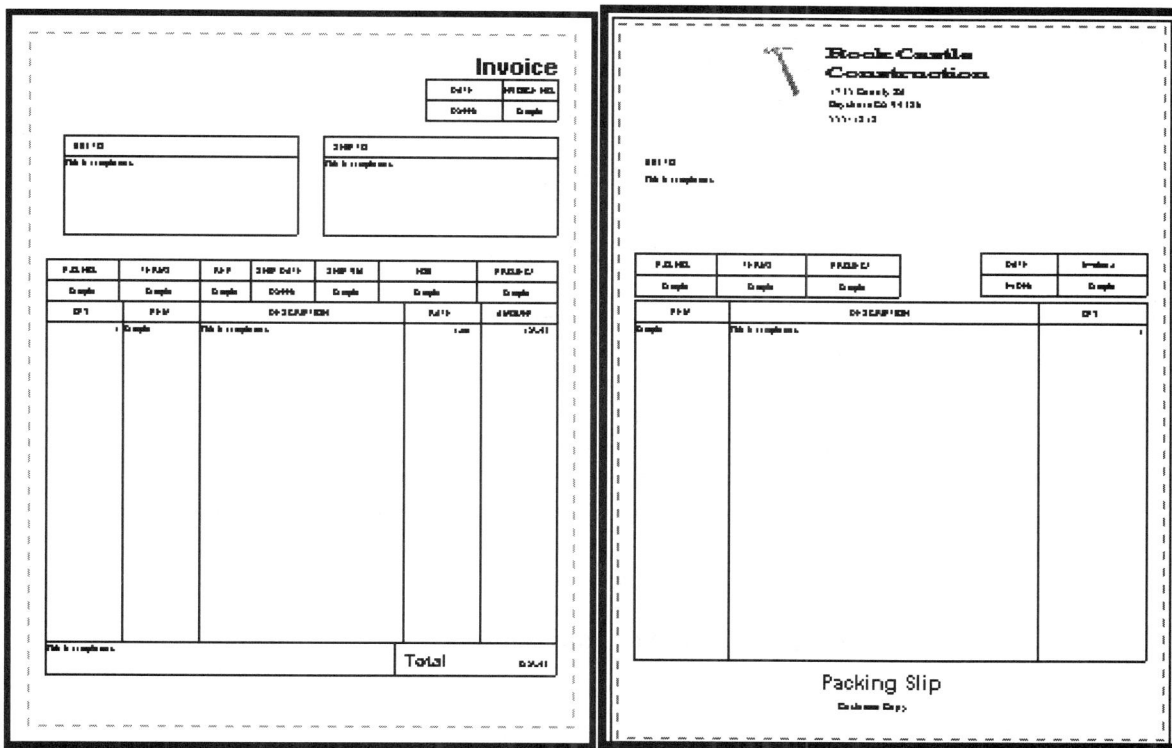

Standard Intuit Product Invoice form

A sample custom form created with the Customize window and the Layout Designer window

Customizing and designing your QuickBooks business forms

This section has the following information:

Using the Templates list	**86**
Customizing a form's content	**87**
Designing the layout of a form	**89**
Paper options for business forms	**92**

Using the Templates list

When you first set up your QuickBooks company, the Templates list will display only the Standard Intuit forms (see page 81). As you use certain features, additional templates will be added to the list automatically. For example, as you enter your first cash sale, QuickBooks puts "Custom Cash Sale" on your Templates list. You can choose to customize this form or leave it "as is." At any time, you can create customized templates of QuickBooks business forms (invoices, credit memos, cash sales receipts, purchase orders, statements, and estimates) to suit your business needs.

To view the Templates list:
- From the Lists menu, choose Templates.

Use the Templates menu button to do the following:
- Create a new template.
- Edit an existing template.
- Delete a template.
- Make a copy (duplicate) of a template to edit.
- Make a template inactive.
- Use a template for a form.

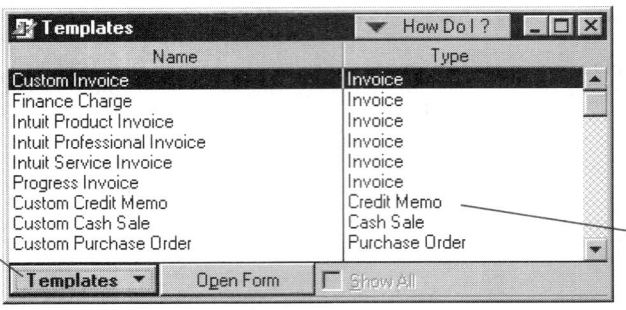

Note that some of these templates will appear on the list only after you have used the feature. For example, after you create a credit memo, the Custom Credit Memo template appears on the list.

The Templates list shows all the templates and the type of form each template is used for.

To preview what the templates look like:

1 From the Lists menu, choose Templates.

2 From the Templates list, select a template and click Open Form.

The onscreen version of the form displays.

3   To see what the printed version of the template will look like, click the down arrow next to Print and then choose Preview. In some cases, you'll only need to click Preview.

Customizing a form's content

You can customize any template form and create any number of versions.

Tip: **If you plan on printing your invoices or statements on preprinted forms from Intuit, you should make only minor adjustments to the Intuit templates.** For example, adding a logo, adding your company name and address, or changing fonts still allows you to use preprinted forms and double-window envelopes you purchase from Intuit. You cannot, however, add, change, delete, or move columns.

For each form you customize, you decide which fields (including custom fields) and columns to include, what they are labeled, and where to place them.

Enter a unique name for the template in the **Template Name** field.

You can specify if a field or column should appear on the screen version and/or on the printed version you send to your customers.

The last four fields are custom fields that you may want to add to your forms.

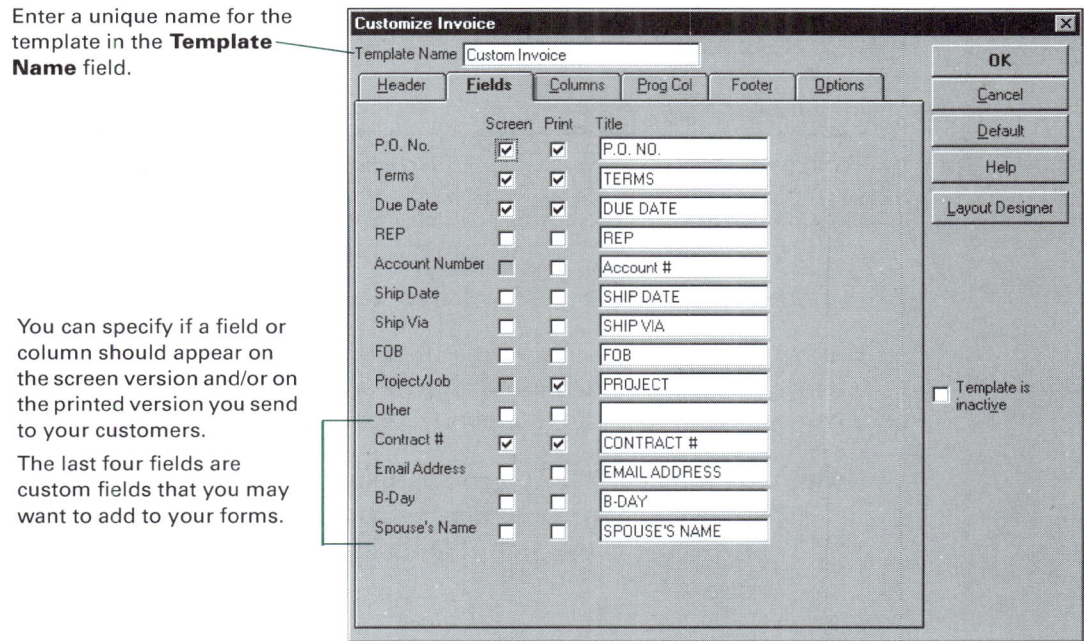

Once you've created your forms, you can save them to use whenever you wish and modify them whenever you want.

Creating custom business forms   87

The following diagram shows the areas of the form that you can change using various tabs of the Customize window.

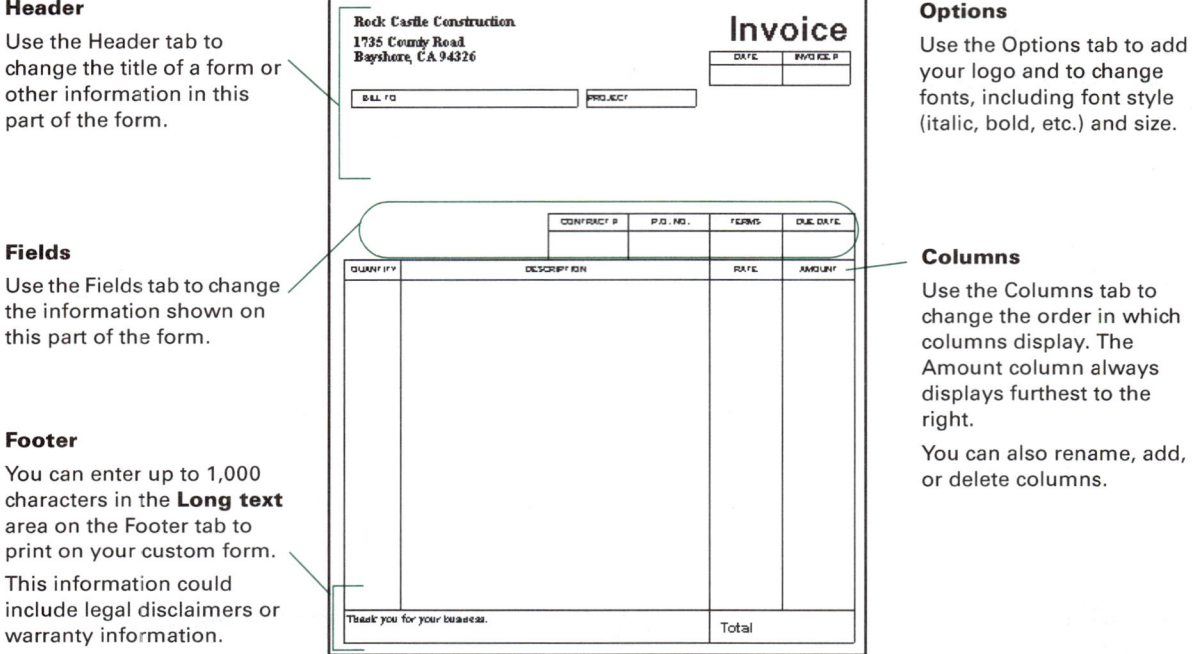

Header
Use the Header tab to change the title of a form or other information in this part of the form.

Fields
Use the Fields tab to change the information shown on this part of the form.

Footer
You can enter up to 1,000 characters in the **Long text** area on the Footer tab to print on your custom form.

This information could include legal disclaimers or warranty information.

Options
Use the Options tab to add your logo and to change fonts, including font style (italic, bold, etc.) and size.

Columns
Use the Columns tab to change the order in which columns display. The Amount column always displays furthest to the right.

You can also rename, add, or delete columns.

To learn about...	Search the Help index for...
Creating custom business forms	customizing forms, about

Adding your company logo to forms

You can specify a logo from a file which QuickBooks then prints to the left of your company name and address on forms. If you like, you can move your logo to a different part of the form.

Note: **The logo must be a bitmap (.BMP) file.** For best results, use a bitmap file with the same height and width. You can reduce or expand the size of the logo by using the mouse to select and resize it.

To learn about...	Search the Help index for...
Adding a logo to a business form	logos, adding to sales and purchase forms

What happens if I remove a field or column that I've previously used?

If you remove a field or column from a form after you have used it in a transaction, QuickBooks retains all the data that you entered. You can still create reports based on the data.

For example, suppose you have been using a custom field labeled "Color" on your sales forms, and you decide to remove the Color field. When you display invoices that you created before you removed the Color field, the field no longer appears, but you can still create reports based on the color of items you sold. If you decide to restore the Color field at a later time, the field reappears on all the invoices where it originally appeared.

If you delete or add columns, QuickBooks automatically resizes the remaining columns, but you can adjust the widths with the Layout Designer window.

Designing the layout of a form

Another aspect of creating customized business forms can include changing the form's layout. Once you've specified in the Customize window which fields, columns, header and footer elements you want to print, and how you want them labeled, you can use the Layout Designer tool to move and resize these objects.

Objects are the elements that make up the layout of a business form, including:

- A field
- A column
- The title of a field or column
- The title of the form
- Your company name and address
- Your company logo

Form setup issues

Before you begin moving and resizing objects on your form:

1 Check your printer setup orientation and paper size.

For example, if you need to lay out a form to fit legal-size paper, you'll need to check that your printer setup is set for legal-size paper.

2 Within the Layout Designer, specify your margins.

When you know the size and margins of your form, it is easier to adjust the fields and columns on the form to get the appearance you want.

How you can create a custom layout

- You can give your company name, address, and logo special treatment on the form. For example, you can center the logo at the top, and put your company name and address in a special font immediately below the logo.

- You can enlarge a custom field so that it can hold more information. For example, if you're using a custom field to enter e-mail addresses, you can lengthen the field so that it can hold a long e-mail address.

- You can position the customer's billing address so that it coincides with the address window in the envelopes you use. (You can also remove the box around the address so that just the address shows through.)

Note: *Only sample text appears in the fields and columns when you are in the Layout Designer window.* To see what the finished form will look like, you need to print the form, or access a form window and click Print Preview.

To learn about...	Search the Help index for...
Using the Layout Designer	Layout Designer, how to use

What if I use double-window envelopes?

You can adjust the fields in the header area of your form so that when you fold the form and place it in one of Intuit's specially designed double-window envelopes, the appropriate fields show through.

QuickBooks displays shadowed areas to show you which part of the form will show through the envelope windows. You can then adjust your fields accordingly.

Aligning your fields to match the shadowed areas will allow you to use a double-window envelope with a mailing name and address and your return name and address.

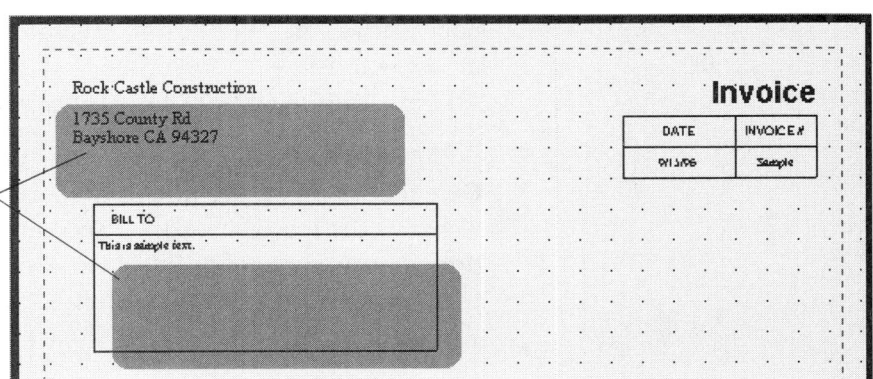

To learn about...	Search the Help index for...
Adjusting forms to fit window envelopes	windowed envelopes

Printing your forms and checks

QuickBooks can print any of your business forms and checks, but before printing your forms and checks, make sure you've specified any customization.

Paper options for business forms

When you print your business forms you have three paper options:

- **Preprinted forms**

    These may include your logo, company name, and address. (You can purchase preprinted forms through Intuit. Choose Phone Directory from the Help menu and click QuickBooks Supplies.)

    QuickBooks does not print the title of the form on preprinted paper, however, it will print your company name and address unless you deselect "Print Company Name" and "Print Company Address" on the Options tab of the Customize window.

- **Blank paper**

    QuickBooks prints the title of the form (shown onscreen) in large letters at the top of the paper. You can specify whether to print lines around each field. Select this option when printing forms that you have customized with the Layout Designer window.

- **Letterhead**

    QuickBooks does not print in the upper 1.9 inches of your letterhead. You can specify whether to print lines around each field.

You may want to consult your Intuit Checks, Forms and Supplies Catalog for examples of available forms.

Note: **You cannot print customized invoices on Intuit forms if your customization includes changes to columns or fields.** However, you can use Intuit's multi-purpose forms preprinted with your company name and address.

Printer setup

Checks

From the Printer setup window for checks, you'll choose your printer from a list of your installed printers and the check type you'll be printing on (voucher, standard, or wallet). You can also print partial pages of checks when necessary.

Tip: **Before you print checks, you may want to set different preferences for how they print.** For example, you can replace the preset date with the date that you print the checks, or control whether certain information prints on the voucher portion of the checks.

To learn about...	Search the Help index for...
Setting up your printer to print checks	printer setup, general

Forms

You can set up your printer to print any QuickBooks form, including invoices, cash sales receipts, credit memos, estimates, statements, and purchase orders. From the Printer setup window for invoices (and other forms), you'll choose your printer from a list of installed printers and the paper type you'll be printing on (see "Paper options for business forms" on page 92 for details).

To learn about...	Search the Help index for...
Setting up your printer to print your business forms	printer setup, general

Printing issues

You can print any business form or check directly from the window where you created it, or use the Print Forms command (found on the File menu) to print, in a single operation, a group of forms or checks.

Alignment

You can print samples of your QuickBooks forms and checks to see if the forms line up correctly, and you can make alignment adjustments. If you have trouble getting forms to print correctly at first, print sample forms on blank paper. After printing a sample, place it on top of the real form and hold them both up to the light to see if the text printed correctly.

When you change a form's alignment, QuickBooks shifts all text by the same amount. You cannot change the alignment of individual columns.

If you're printing on preprinted forms with a continuous-feed printer, you usually need to make coarse alignment adjustments first, and then make fine alignment adjustments. If you are using a page-oriented printer, you need to make only fine alignment adjustments.

To learn about...	Search the Help index for...
Printing your business forms	printing, sales forms
Printing and reprinting checks	printing checks
Alignment	aligning forms in printer
Printing batches of forms	printing, batches of forms

If the data won't fit on one form

If an invoice or receipt is too long to fit on one page, QuickBooks automatically adds additional pages as needed. Each page of a multiple-page form is numbered. The transaction total appears only on the last page.

Can I fax a form?

Any form that you can print from QuickBooks, you can also fax from QuickBooks!

To learn about...	Search the Help index for...
Faxing documents from QuickBooks	faxing forms

CHAPTER 8

Banking, credit cards, and financing

Choosing the right bank (or other financial institution)	96
Setting up banking information	99
Handling banking transactions	101

How do I meet my banking and financing needs?

Whether your business is brand new or has been around for years, you probably have certain business needs that must be met by banks and other financial institutions, including startup and growth financing, checking account(s) for bill and payroll payment, credit cards for everyday expenses and small equipment purchases, and online account access and payments.

Choosing the right bank (or other financial institution)

This section contains the following information:

Shopping around for the financial institution	96
Benefits of online banking	97
Choosing credit cards	98
Startup and growth financing	99

Shopping around for the financial institution

The bank you use for your personal accounts may not be the best fit for your business. Many banks offer special services for small businesses, including different types of checking accounts, retirement plans (SEPs and KEOGHs), a variety of business loans, lines of credit, and credit cards.

Some questions to ask prospective banks:

- What types of business checking accounts do you offer? Is there a monthly service charge? If so, can it be waived if you keep a large balance in the account? (Non-profit organizations and sole proprietors may be eligible for an interest-earning checking account.)
- How quickly are deposits available for use?
- Do you have ATM surcharges?

    There can be surcharges and fees for non-account holders using a bank-owned ATM for transactions by account holders who use an ATM through networks, and for cards, card replacement, and so on.

- What are your requirements to issue a line of credit?
- Do you specialize in loans to certain types of businesses?
- Do you offer online banking for QuickBooks users?

Some banks have other services that might be of interest to you:

- Merchant accounts for credit card payments (QuickBooks lets you apply for a merchant account online—see "Applying for and handling merchant accounts for credit card payments" on page 104.)
- Courier service for deposits
- Tax deposit

Do not mix personal and business finances!

You may be tempted when you first start your business to use your personal checking account and credit cards for business expenses. *We recommend that you open business accounts as soon as possible.* Some of the benefits include the following:

- Simpler bookkeeping procedures, including expense tracking for tax purposes
- Enhanced professional image

Benefits of online banking

Online banking offers you the following advantages:

- Flexible **online account access** to help you manage your cash flow better.
    - You can get answers to your questions, night or day. (Did the check clear? What's my account balance?)
    - You can transfer funds between online accounts at your bank to maximize the interest you earn and replenish your checking account.
    - You can download your account balances and cleared transactions right into QuickBooks to make sure that bank-initiated transactions, such as fees and interest, are recorded.
    - You can access your checking, savings, credit card, and line of credit accounts.
    - You can match your bank and credit card transactions with those cleared at the financial institution for speedier account reconciliation.
- Flexible **online payment** to help you save time and improve control when paying bills.
    - You can record and pay bills to anyone.
    - You can designate who is authorized to make payments and use password protection to add control.
    - You can send remittance information with your payment so that your payee knows how it should be applied.
    - You can schedule payments up to a year in advance.

- You can make online payments from any U.S. bank account with check-writing privileges or through Intuit Online Payment service. See the illustration, "How Your Bills Get Paid" on page 254.

To use online account access or payment you must choose a participating financial institution. Visit our Web site at www.intuit.com/ofs for more information or call the number listed in the phone directory. Choose Phone Directory from the Help menu and choose "Online account access or online payment support".

To safeguard the data you send online, Intuit uses state-of-the-art encryption and authentication tools.

Some differences between Quicken and QuickBooks online banking features

Quicken	QuickBooks
You can create repeating payments.	You cannot create repeating payments, but you can set up scheduled payments up to a year in advance.
N/A	You can send remittance information on an online payment check voucher.

Choosing credit cards

The bank you choose for checking and savings may offer credit cards as well; however, you may want to shop around depending on how you plan to use your business credit cards.

Situation	Consider...
You plan to pay off the balance every month.	A credit card with a higher interest rate, but no annual fee.
You plan to pay only some of the balance every month.	A credit card with a lower interest rate, even if it has an annual fee.
You want to download your credit card account transactions into QuickBooks.	A credit card from a bank that supports online account access for QuickBooks users.

Startup and growth financing

All businesses experience the need for extra cash for equipment, inventory, or a new facility. If your capital needs extend beyond what is currently invested in your business, you'll need to do some research.

- Talk to the representatives at your local bank about their small business loan programs. Or, you may want to visit the Web sites of your local banks.
- Check out the loan programs of the U.S. Small Business Administration (SBA) at **www.sbaonline.sba.gov**.

Setting up banking information

Note: You may have already added your various bank accounts in the EasyStep Interview. These accounts include checking, savings, and credit card accounts.

What to set up	Comments	Search the Help Index for...
Bank accounts that haven't been added to QuickBooks yet	Enter an opening balance for these accounts or create the opening balance by adding all the necessary historical transactions.	■ accounts, adding to your chart of accounts ■ accounts, opening balances ■ historical transactions
Credit card accounts that haven't been added to QuickBooks yet	None	■ accounts, adding to your chart of accounts ■ accounts, opening balances
Reconcile each bank account (and credit card account) with your bank statements, from the first statement after your start date to your last statement.	Then you'll know that QuickBooks and your bank are in agreement. See "Reconciling bank and credit card accounts" on page 108.	reconciling, bank statements

Setting up online banking (account access and payment)

QuickBooks online banking encompasses both account access and payment features. The Online Banking Setup Interview will answer your questions and walk you through the account setup process.

To access the Online Banking Setup Interview:

- From the Banking menu, choose Set Up Online Financial Services, and then Apply for Online Banking.

The following table gives you a brief overview of the online banking setup process. These steps are completed over a period of days or weeks, depending on how quickly your application for online banking is processed at the financial institution.

Also, if you are planning on using online payment, you'll need to set up your payees. See "Setting up online payees" on page 256.

What to set up	Comments	Search the Help Index for...
Internet access through an ISP if you haven't already set this up for another QuickBooks feature	Choose Internet Connection Setup from the Help menu.	Internet connection setup
If you don't already have an account (checking, savings, money market, credit card) at a financial institution that provides online banking through QuickBooks, you'll need to open one.	**Note:** You can use the Intuit Online Payment service with any U.S. account with check-writing privileges.	online banking, financial institutions
Submit an application for online banking to your financial institution.	You can access application information over the Internet or contact your institution directly. There will be a period of days or weeks until you receive confirmation.	online banking, setting up
When you receive your confirmation and a PIN/password from your financial institution, complete the "Enable Accounts" section of the Online Banking Setup interview.	Verify that the information sent to you by the financial institution is correct.	confirmation information for online services

Going online for the first time

You should use online banking within the first month of enrolling for online services. The first time you go online, we recommend that you download the most recent transactions that have cleared at your financial institution.

From the Banking menu, choose Online Banking Center.

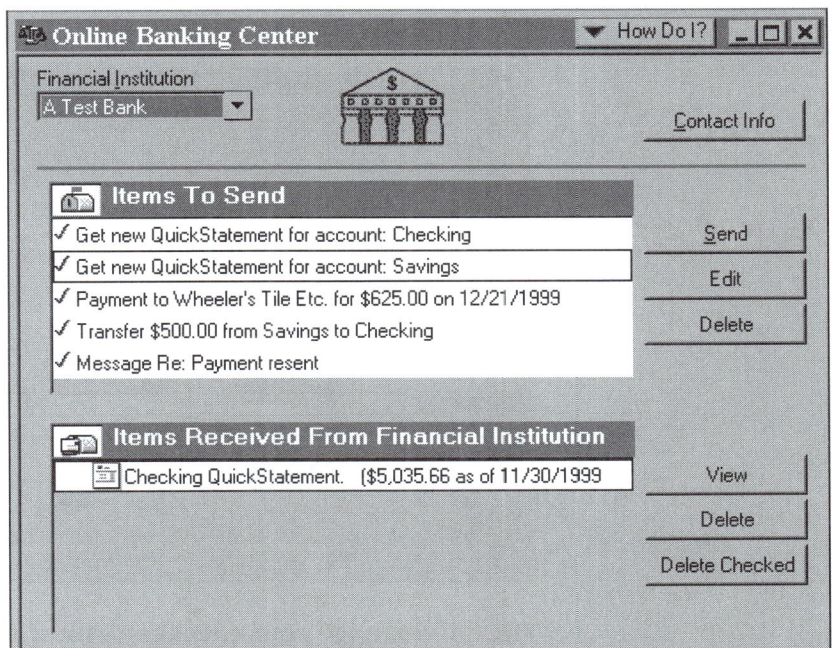

To learn about...

Going online for banking

Search the Help index for...

online banking, sending

Handling banking transactions

Day-to-day activities

Managing your checkbook

Whether you handwrite checks, print them from QuickBooks, or use online payment, you'll need to enter all the information into QuickBooks to keep your checking account accurate and up to date.

Information is entered into your check register from various QuickBooks sources: the Write Checks window; windows where you pay bills, sales tax and payroll liabilities; windows that record deposits; the monthly reconciliation process (fees, interest, and adjustments);

and online banking downloads. You can add and modify transactions directly in the register.

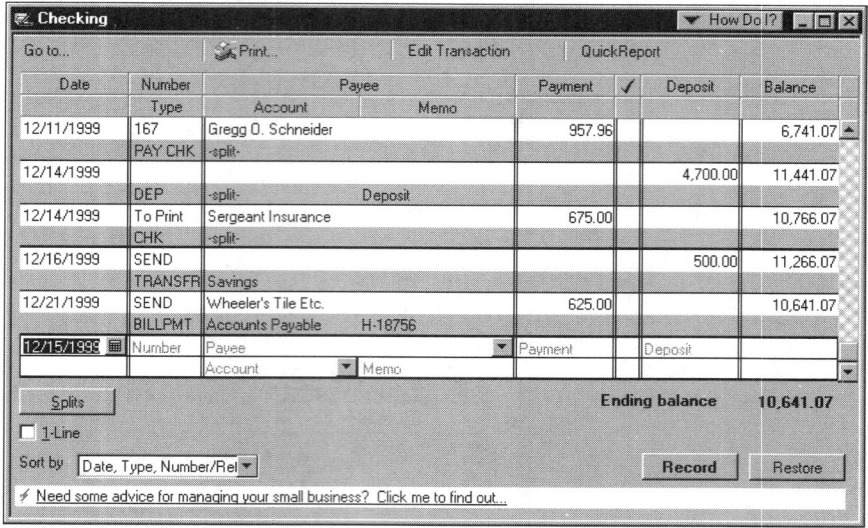

Tip: To manage your checkbook most effectively, enter your transactions on a regular basis, and reconcile the account when you receive your bank statement.

Some daily checking-related tasks may include the following:

Task	Comments	Search the Help index for...
Writing a check for expenses	Review the Accounts Payable information before you start writing checks. See "Ways to track and pay expenses in QuickBooks" on page 248. See also "Using checks" on page 265 and "Using online payment" on page 253.	▪ checks, writing for expenses and items ▪ online payments, writing checks for
Printing checks	You can print checks singly or in batches. You may need to experiment with alignment features the first time you print checks. You can also change the look of your printed checks by changing the fonts or adding a logo.	▪ printing checks ▪ logos, adding to checks and paychecks

Task	Comments	Search the Help index for...
Sorting your check register	The preset sort is by Date, Type, and Document #.	registers, sort by different criteria
Finding a particular check	Use the Find feature on the Edit menu.	finding transactions
Voiding or deleting a check	Choose to void (rather than delete) a check if you want to keep its history in QuickBooks. See also "Voiding or deleting checks" on page 266.	checks, voiding or deleting
Canceling an online payment	You can only cancel payments that the payment processor has scheduled but not yet sent or mailed.	online payments, canceling a payment
Editing information on a check	You can edit check information in the Write Checks window or in the checking account register.	checks, editing
Making a deposit	See page 105.	deposits, bank or checking account
Making an ATM withdrawal	Watch out for ATM surcharges. They can add up!	ATM withdrawals
Reconciling your accounts	See "Reconciling bank and credit card accounts" on page 108. See "Reconciling online accounts" on page 109.	■ reconciling, bank statements ■ reconciling, clearing an online transaction

Handling business credit card accounts

Your business may use a credit card for various purchases.

Task	Comments	Search the Help index for...
Making purchases with a credit card	Enter the charge with all appropriate information. For example, was this item purchased for a customer?	"Using credit cards" on page 267
Handling credit card fees	Enter the fee in the credit card register as "Annual Fee" or "Interest Owed," as appropriate. You can also enter these fees when you reconcile the account with the statement.	"Handling fees and interest earned on accounts" on page 107

Handling banking transactions

Task	Comments	Search the Help index for...
Reconciling your credit card accounts	At the end of the reconcile process, you are prompted to write the check to pay for the credit card bill or enter a bill.	"Reconciling bank and credit card accounts" on page 108

Applying for and handling merchant accounts for credit card payments

Many businesses use merchant accounts, allowing you to accept credit cards as a form of payment, to increase sales and enhance customer convenience. You can easily apply for a merchant account online, right from QuickBooks.

Task	Comments	Search the Help index for...
Opening a merchant account	■ Open a merchant account online. To apply, choose Accept Credit Card Payments from the Customers menu. ■ Set up your QuickBooks accounts for handling transactions and processing fees for a merchant account.	merchant account service
Recording customer payments from credit cards	■ Choose Accept Credit Card Payments from the Customers menu, and then choose Process Credit Card Payments to authorize a credit card payment online. ■ If you are not authorizing credit card payments online, use the Receive Payments window or the Enter Cash Sales window. You can deposit the payment to your checking account or to Undeposited Funds. ■ Choose Make Deposits and select all the credit card payments that have been processed.	receiving payments, credit cards

To learn about...	Search the Help index for...
Handling merchant account processing fees	merchant account service

104 | CHAPTER 8 Banking, credit cards, and financing

Receiving payments and making deposits

Depending on your type of business or organization, your deposits may include payments from customers, gifts from donors, loans from family members, investment money from partners, down payments, tax refunds, or other income. Before you enter any income in QuickBooks, review a recent bank statement.

For ease of reconciliation, you'll want to *imitate* your bank statement in terms of how you receive payments and make deposits in QuickBooks. For example, if your bank statement shows a lump sum for a deposit, you should enter your payments (in the Receive Payments or Enter Cash Sales windows) and choose to "Group with other undeposited funds" for later deposit; if the statement shows each individual check and merchant charge deposited, you should choose to deposit directly to the account.

Additionally, if your bank separates credit card and check deposits on your bank statement, you should too.

Note: **Always list all merchant credit card payments that have been processed in one deposit transaction and your checks and cash in another.** See page 106.

To learn about...	Search the Help index for...
Receiving payments	receiving payments, about
Separating deposits by payment method	deposits, separating by payment method
Making deposits	deposits, bank or checking account
Finding a particular deposit	deposits, viewing a list of
Editing or deleting a deposited payment	deposits, editing
Reminders to make deposits	deposits, reminding yourself to make

Dealing with nonpayment income

For income you receive that is not a customer payment, you can enter the deposit in the Make Deposits window.

In this example, a nonprofit organization is depositing a day's donations.

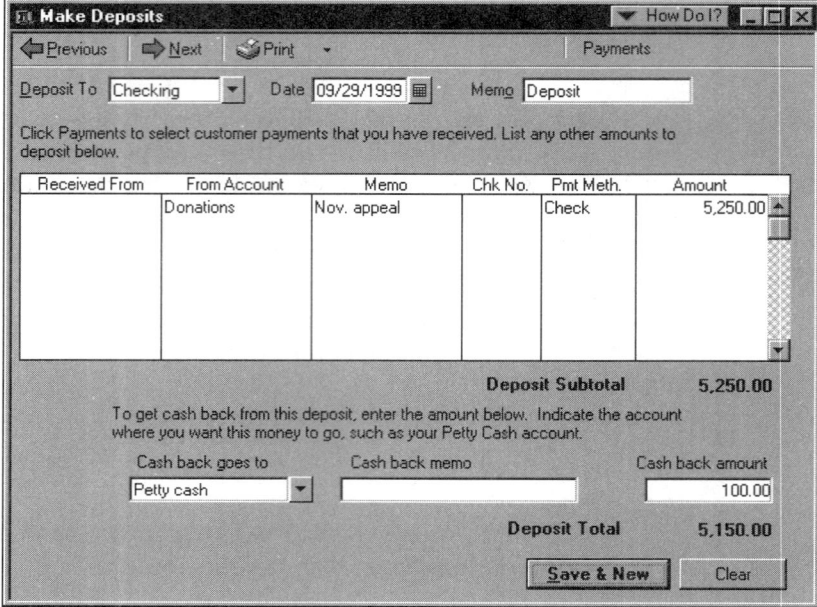

Cash back from your deposit

If you need cash back from your deposit, you can specify the necessary account and amount using the Make Deposits window.

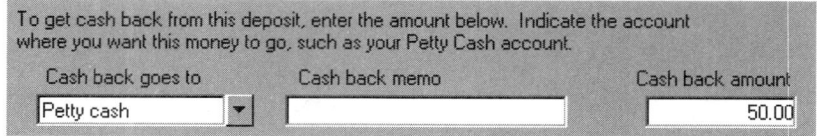

To learn about...	Search the Help index for...
Getting cash back from a deposit	deposits, cash back

Printing deposit slips and summaries

Before you take your deposit to the bank, you can print a deposit slip and/or deposit summary that lists customer payments made by cash or check, other income received by cash or check, and any cash back that you will receive.

Note: Do not create deposit slips for merchant credit card payments.

Printable deposit slips, along with a complete selection of printable checks, are available through Intuit. To order printable deposit slips, choose Phone Directory from the Help menu and click Intuit Supplies.

To learn about...	Search the Help index for...
Printing deposit slips and summaries	deposit slips

Once-a-month activities

Handling fees and interest earned on accounts

Generally, you'll enter these fees, surcharges, and interest earned on an account when you receive the account's monthly bank statement or when you reconcile the account.

- Bank accounts (checking, savings, money market)

    Enter **bank service charges** and **interest earned** when you reconcile your bank accounts (using the Reconcile window), or you can enter them directly into the account's register.

    Be sure to add any **ATM surcharges** you incur during the course of the month to your checking account register.

- Credit card accounts

    You must enter any **finance charges** if you carry a balance forward. The charge can be added to the account's register or in the **Finance Charges** field when you reconcile the account.

    If the card has an **annual fee**, enter this fee directly in the account register.

To learn about...	Search the Help index for...
Entering a fee or interest in a register	registers, entering transactions in

Handling banking transactions | 107

Reconciling bank and credit card accounts

You should plan to reconcile your bank (checking, savings, and money market accounts) and credit card statements on a regular basis to make sure your records and the bank's agree.

Situation	What to do in QuickBooks
You haven't reconciled these accounts for a month or more.	Reconcile each month you skipped. Balance each month separately, starting with your earliest statement since you've been using QuickBooks, through your most recent statement.
You added earlier transactions in QuickBooks.	After you add earlier transactions, and you want to reconcile past months, you should reconcile month by month only if you've never used the QuickBooks reconcile feature.
	However, if you've already reconciled one or more months, you should reconcile forward only, that is, reconcile months after your start date. Use the previous months' data for reporting only. You need to mark all older transactions as cleared to reconcile future months.
You are reconciling for the first time.	Enter all uncleared transactions in your account.
	Update the Opening Balance transaction to reflect the amount actually in your account when you began using QuickBooks.
You cancel in the middle of reconciling.	QuickBooks keeps track of the items you've marked as cleared with an asterisk (*) in the cleared column of the account's register. This indicates that the items are still pending and reconciliation wasn't complete.
	When you start reconciling again, you'll need to re-enter your ending balance and your service charges and interest earned. You'll also need to check off additional payments and deposits.

When you reconcile, be sure to add any bank service charges, interest earned, and finance charges.

To learn about...	Search the Help index for...
Reconciling a bank account	reconciling, bank statements

To learn about...	Search the Help index for...
Reconciling a credit card account	reconciling, credit card statements
Adjusting for differences	reconciling, adjusting for differences

Reconciling online accounts

Reconciling your online accounts is a three-phase process.

1 Download your transactions from your financial institution.

2 Match transactions.

View a QuickStatement for the account. The QuickStatement includes all transactions that have cleared your financial institution since the last time you downloaded, including deposits, checks, transfers, and ATM withdrawals, as well as any transactions that were downloaded previously but not been matched.

Click Match to have QuickBooks match your QuickStatement transactions to the transactions in your register. You can add unmatched transactions to your register to keep your register up to date with your bank.

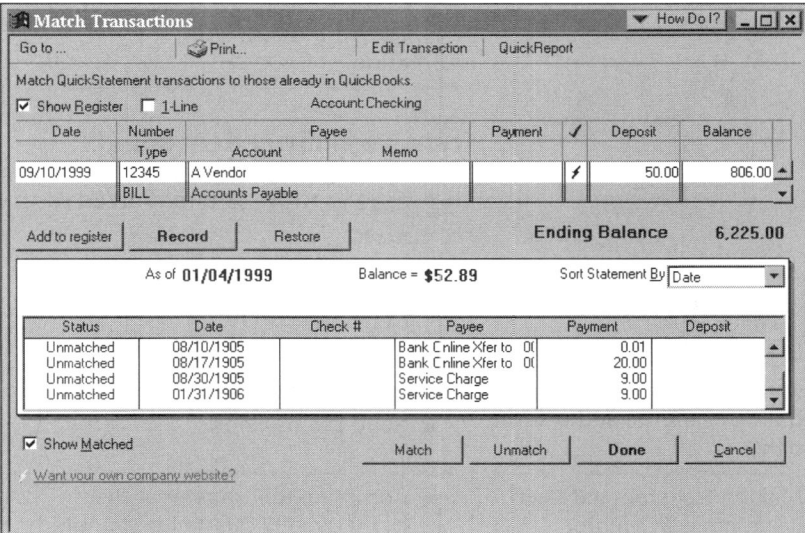

3 When you receive your bank statement for the account, use the Reconcile window.

Note: With QuickBooks, you can reconcile only to the paper statement you receive from your financial institution. With Quicken, you can reconcile to either the online or paper statement.

To learn about...	Search the Help index for...
Downloading and matching online transactions	transactions, online
Account reconciliation	■ reconciling, bank statements ■ reconciling, credit card statements

As-needed activities

Obtaining up-to-date account information

Through online account access, you can obtain up-to-date account balance or activity information. You can find out which checks have cleared and verify that deposits have been posted.

To learn about...	Search the Help index for...
Getting up-to-date account information	online banking, balances

Transferring funds

From time to time, you may need to transfer money from one account to another.

Task	Comments	Search the Help index for...
Making transfers between online accounts at the same bank	■ Enter the transfer in QuickBooks. ■ Send the transfer.	transferring funds, between online accounts
Making transfers between accounts (not online)	■ Complete the transfer at the bank; usually this can be handled with a phone call. ■ Enter the transfer in QuickBooks.	transferring funds, between balance sheet accounts

Tracking loans

You can track both the loans you receive from lending institutions and the loans you make to customers.

- For loans your business receives, use a liability account.

  Note: If you take out a loan to pay for a new asset, such as a new vehicle for your business, the asset account (for the vehicle) and the liability account (for the loan) are not connected in QuickBooks in any way.

- For loans you make to customers, use an other asset account.

To learn about...	Search the Help index for...
Adding a loan account	loans, setting up
Tracking a loan for an asset	loans, paying for assets
Tracking loan payments (reporting on the principal and interest paid)	loans, recording a payment on
Depositing loan money	loans, depositing money
Loans to customers	loans, customer

Handling a customer's bounced check and bad debt

When a customer's check bounces, you need a way to record both the adjustment to your bank account (including any bank charges) and that the customer owes you the amount of the check (plus any penalties or fees you want to impose).

If the amount becomes uncollectable, you'll need to write it off as bad debt.

To learn about...	Search the Help index for...
Handling a customer's bounced check	bounced checks
Writing off bad debt	bad debts

Depositing employment taxes

You can deposit your employment taxes with your coupon (Form 8109) to an authorized financial institution or Federal Reserve Bank. These coupons can also be mailed.

Contact the IRS for more information. Their Web site has downloadable publications, forms, and small business information (**www.irs.gov**).

Sending and viewing online messages

With QuickBooks, you can send messages to any financial institution at which you have accounts enabled for online banking. For example, you might want to send a message to:

- Inquire about account activity
- Inquire about a payment
- Obtain interest rate or fee information
- Request a loan application

To learn about...	Search the Help index for...
Sending and viewing online messages	online payments, inquiring about

Modifying online account information

Your QuickBooks account information must be identical to the information on record with your financial institution.

You may need to change the account information in one or both places:

- In the **Enable Accounts** portion of the Online Banking Setup Interview
- In the account's Edit window (in the chart of accounts, select the account, click the Account button, and choose Edit)

To learn about...	Search the Help index for...
Modifying an online account	online banking, editing online account information

CHAPTER 9

Items—your services, products, and more

Why you probably need to set up items	114
Setting up items	118
Working with items	128
Reports and graphs about items	137

What are items, and why are they so important?

QuickBooks uses *items* to keep track of the services and products that are your source of income. It also has special items to make it easy to do calculations on your sales forms (for example, discounts or sales tax). When you use items, you save time typing, allow QuickBooks to do the calculations, and keep track of your business income.

Why you probably need to set up items

This section contains the following topics:

Items for what you sell	**114**
Items for what you purchase	**116**
Deciding how items should affect accounts	**116**
How many different items do you need?	**117**

Items for what you sell

If your business provides a service—writing, haircutting, consulting, legal advice, house painting, or any other service—you may charge by the hour and list the number of hours and your rate on your sales forms. Or, you may simply charge a flat rate for the service.

If your business sells products or parts, you probably list them on sales forms that you give your customers.

In QuickBooks, both kinds of businesses—service and product—can benefit by setting up items to track the services they provide or the products they sell to customers.

Note: **In QuickBooks, "sales" is a broad term.** It refers to any business action that generates income in exchange for services or products, even if you don't think of what you do as selling. For example, a psychologist with patients, a graphic designer with clients, and a roofing contractor with customers all would set up items in QuickBooks for what they sell.

Benefits of setting up items

Here are some specific benefits of setting up items:

- You can use sales forms in QuickBooks to track the details of how your business earns its income. Estimates and all sales forms—invoices, cash sales receipts, credit memos—require items. So do QuickBooks statement charges, which print on statements.

  (If you're a professional, you may not think of your statements as sales forms, but they are.)

- You can fill out sales forms or enter statement charges quickly. QuickBooks automatically enters the description and rate or price you entered in the item's setup window. When you enter a quantity, QuickBooks calculates the amount.

- When you record a sale (remember, it can be for a service), QuickBooks automatically tracks the income in the appropriate income account. You can fill out a sales form (or enter a statement charge), keep track of your sales, and keep track of income—all in one step.

- You can create reports that show total units of each service or product sold as well as dollar amount totals.

If you're still not sure you need items

Here are some examples of businesses or organizations that use items:

- Rebecca is the bookkeeper for a country club whose members sign for meals, drinks, and fees and receive a statement at the end of the month. Rebecca uses items in QuickBooks for each of these. She uses the items to enter statement charges for each member and create monthly statements.

- Mario is a dentist. He has items set up for the various services he provides to his patients: cleaning, x-rays, filling cavities, and so on.

In contrast, some businesses or organizations probably don't need items. Here are some examples:

- John is keeping the books for his church. The church has members who pledge and contribute money, but the church doesn't sell anything or charge for specific services, so John doesn't need to create any sales forms.

- Marina does facials in her home evenings and weekends. Her clients pay at the time of their visit. Marina simply wants to track the income received. She doesn't care to track in QuickBooks how many facials she gives or to whom.

- Rick is a commissioned sales representative. He takes orders for a manufacturer that then invoices the customers directly. Rick tracks the orders in a spreadsheet, not QuickBooks, because the sales are income for the manufacturer, not Rick. When Rick receives a commission check, he enters it in QuickBooks as a deposit.

Items for what you purchase

Once you've decided to set up items for the services or products you sell, you may want to use items for the services and products you purchase.

If you purchase products or parts for resale, keep them in inventory, and then sell them, be sure to read Chapter 13, *Inventory,* beginning on page 223. It will help you decide whether to track inventory in QuickBooks.

If you purchase services or products for a specific customer or job, QuickBooks Pro allows you to set up items that you can use for both purchases and sales. See "Items for reimbursable costs in QuickBooks Pro" on page 125.

On the other hand, if you don't have QuickBooks Pro and you don't track inventory, you should not use the same items for both purchases and sales. Instead, use items for entering sales only.

Deciding how items should affect accounts

When you set up most items, you must specify which account it should affect when you use the item on a sale or purchase. Then, when you record the sale or purchase, each item on it affects the appropriate account.

In other words, while you are recording the items on a sale or purchase, QuickBooks is adjusting all the right accounts behind the scenes.

Which are the right accounts? If you sell an item, you normally associate an income account with it. If you purchase the same item, QuickBooks Pro provides a way to associate a second account, usually an expense account, to be used on purchases. See "Items for reimbursable costs in QuickBooks Pro" on page 125. (Inventory items each have three different accounts, as explained in "Accounts for tracking inventory" on page 230.)

Before you set up your items, you have to decide how much detail from your sales and purchases needs to show up in reports about your accounts. (The profit and loss statement, for example, is a report on your income and expense accounts.)

You can see details of your sales (such as number of units and dollar amount of each item sold) on the QuickBooks sales reports. You don't need to have the same level of detail on your profit and loss statement. For example:

- Cynthia has a single income account for all sales income. She doesn't want to see any further breakdown on her profit and loss statement, and she doesn't need it for her tax returns.

- Derek, on the other hand, wants to split up income from services and income from materials he buys for a job and then puts on the customer's invoice. Thus, he uses one income account for all his service items and a second income account for all his non-inventory part items (for his materials). Like Cynthia, he has far more items than income accounts.

How many different items do you need?

Every business is different, but knowing how QuickBooks works can help you decide how specific your items should be.

First, once you use an item in a transaction, you can never delete the item unless you delete the transaction or condense your file to remove old transactions and old items. Thus, if you sell unique items or a rapidly changing assortment of items, you probably want to use more general items. If the prices vary, you can enter prices on the sales form.

For example, Tomas has a men's clothing store. Because his inventory of styles changes so much, he doesn't use QuickBooks to track inventory. To track his sales, he has more general items such as Suit, Sports Jacket, Dress Shirt.

On the other hand, if you have two standard services or products that are similar except for their rate or price, you can save time recording sales by having a separate item for each. Then QuickBooks can fill in the correct rate or price on the sales form.

For example, Mali employs three stylists in her beauty salon. When she cuts a client's hair, she charges more than the rate for a haircut by one of the employees. So she has two separate items for haircuts.

You can change the rate or price of any item at any time. You don't have to create a new item in order to raise your prices.

Finally, if there are things you purchase but never sell (supplies for your office, for example), you probably shouldn't bother to put them on your Item list. They will lengthen your list, and you'll find it harder to pick out the items that you do sell. However, if you plan on using QuickBooks purchase orders, you'll need to set up the items you purchase, even though they are only for your office use.

Setting up items

This section contains the following topics:

Where to find information about your items	**118**
Types of QuickBooks items	**119**
Adding items to your Item list	**123**
Items for reimbursable costs in QuickBooks Pro	**125**

The EasyStep Interview helps you set up a few items, so you may already have some items.

This section is about adding items to QuickBooks. You can add items at any time—as part of setting up QuickBooks or whenever you think of an item you need to use.

Remember, items are for the services or items you buy and sell. You also may need special calculating items that calculate subtotals and discounts, and that apply specific sales tax rates.

Where to find information about your items

When you set up an item, you enter information you can use over and over again, without retyping, such as the following:

- Name or code
- Description
- Price per unit or rate per hour, if applicable
- For items you sell, the income account to assign income from the sale; for items you purchase, the expense account for purchases of the item

QuickBooks stores information about your items on the Item list.

On the Item list, items are in order of item type.

Within the same item type, they are usually in alphabetical (or numerical) order, but you can change this order.

Subitems are indented under the parent item.

Use the menu buttons to add, edit, sort, or perform other activities on items.

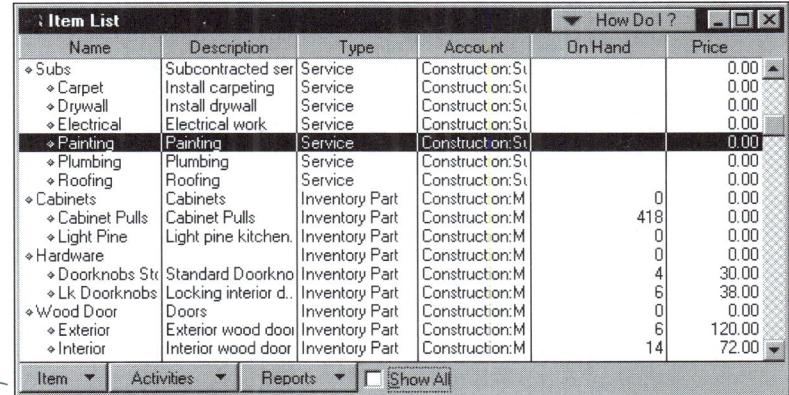

To learn about...	Search the Help index for...
Displaying the Item list	items, list of
Sorting the Item list (and other lists)	sorting, list entries
Moving items (and other list entries)	lists, reorganizing entries

Types of QuickBooks items

In addition to items for services or products, QuickBooks has several other types of items. This section explains what each type of QuickBooks item is designed to do.

Tip: Use one of the Part item types for any product, not just a part of another product. If you decide to use QuickBooks inventory to track your products, set up inventory parts for them. Otherwise, set up non-inventory parts for your products.

Item type	Use for...	Usual effect on accounts	Comments
Service	Services you charge for or services you purchase **Examples:** professional fees, labor	■ On sale: Increases income. ■ On purchase: Increases expenses.	In QuickBooks Pro you can set up a service item so that it can affect either income or expenses, depending on where you use it.

Setting up items   119

Item type	Use for...	Usual effect on accounts	Comments
Inventory Part	Products you purchase, track as inventory, and then resell **Examples:** Electrical outlets, T-shirts	■ On sale: Increases income, increases cost of goods sold, and decreases inventory assets. ■ On purchase: Increases inventory assets.	Available only if the inventory feature is turned on. Read "Is QuickBooks inventory right for my business?" on page 224 before deciding whether to track inventory in QuickBooks.
Non-inventory Part	Products you sell but do not purchase; items you purchase and resell but do not track as inventory; items you enter on purchase orders **Examples:** Custom-made slipcovers	■ On sale: Increases income. ■ On purchase: Increases expenses.	In QuickBooks Pro you can set up a non-inventory part item so that it can affect either income or expenses, depending on where you use it.
Other Charge	Other charges on a sale or a purchase **Examples:** Shipping charge, delivery charge, finance charge	■ On sale: Increases income. ■ On purchase: Increases expenses.	In QuickBooks Pro you can set up an other charge item so that it can affect either income or expenses, depending on where you use it. Can be either a percentage or a flat amount.
Subtotal	Calculating and printing a subtotal on sales forms	Subtotal items have no effect on accounts.	On sales forms, if you want to apply a discount or add a percentage charge to several items at once, subtotal first.
Group	Fast entry of a group of individual items already on the list **Example:** A group of services and food items provided by a caterer.	Each item in the group affects the same account it affects when used by itself.	Available for either sales or purchases.
Discount	Calculating an amount to be subtracted from a total or subtotal **Example:** A 10% discount given to nonprofit organizations.	Either decreases income or increases expenses (depending on item setup).	Available for sales forms only; not available for statement charges or purchase forms.

Item type	Use for...	Usual effect on accounts	Comments
Payment	■ On invoices: Payment received at the time of invoicing, so that amount owed on invoice is reduced ■ On cash sales summaries: To show totals for each type of payment (cash, checks, credit card charges)	Increases the balance of either a specific checking account or the account for undeposited funds (depending on item setup).	Available for sales forms only; not available for statement charges or purchase forms.
Sales Tax Item	Calculating a single tax Available only if the sales tax feature is turned on (see "Setting up sales tax" on page 280)	Increases the balance in the Sales Tax Liability account.	Available for sales forms only; not available for statement charges or purchase forms.
Sales Tax Group	Calculating two or more sales taxes grouped together and applied to the same sale Available only if the sales tax feature is turned on (see "Setting up sales tax" on page 280)	Increases the balance in the Sales Tax Liability account.	Available for sales forms only; not available for statement charges or purchase forms.

Items that calculate

The table of items includes some items used to perform a calculation on one or more lines above it on a sales form.

For example, if you need to subtotal on sales forms, then you need a subtotal item. A subtotal item adds the amounts of the items above it on the sales form and enters the subtotal on the form.

If you have to add sales tax to your sales forms, then you need at least one sales tax item. (You need one for each separate district you collect tax for.)

Finally, there are some items that can be set up either as percentages or with flat amounts, depending on what you need. For example, Carol adds a 10% service charge to her invoices. She has set up an other charge item with a rate of 10%. She uses a subtotal item before the service charge, so that the 10% will be based on the subtotal amount.

Steve gives a 15% discount to certain customers. He has set up a discount item with a rate of 15%. He also uses a subtotal item, so that the discount will be based on the subtotal amount.

For examples of how to use items that calculate, see page 130 for subtotals, page 131 for discounts, and page 287 for sales tax.

Subitems vs. group items

Just as you can set up an account with related subaccounts under it on your chart of accounts, you can have an item with related subitems. For example, Cherril keeps the books for her symphony association's gift shop, which sells T-shirts and other items. She has an item called T-shirts and subitems called Adult and Child, each with its own price.

Subitems allow you to put similar items together on your Item list, so you can locate them easily on the drop-down list in any **Item** field. Each subitem can have its own rate or price and its own description. Each subitem can even have its own account, although you would probably assign the same account to all subitems of the same parent item.

In this example, Hardware is a parent item with two subitems under it.

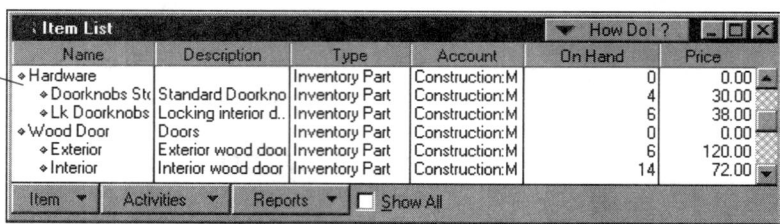

On sales forms, you use subitems the same way you use other items. On reports based on items, QuickBooks subtotals each group of subitems. For example, see the sales by item summary report on page 206.

Group items have a completely different purpose from subitems. Group items allow you to enter a group of items—that is, several different items— at once on a sale or purchase. For example, Margo makes up gift baskets that contain three jars of her homemade jam. She has a group item for the gift basket that includes one wicker basket and one jar each of the three varieties in the gift basket. For an example of entering a group of items, see page 130.

Adding items to your Item list

As the table starting on page 119 shows, QuickBooks has 10 different item types. Here is some general information about what to enter for most types of items when adding a new item to your Item list.

Information to enter	How QuickBooks uses this information
Type of item	After you choose the item type, QuickBooks requests only the information it requires for that particular item type. After you set up an item, depending on the type, you may not be able to change it to a different type.
Item name or code	Displays this name or number on reports of items and in the drop-down list in the **Item** field (for example, on sales forms).
Item description (optional)	Prefills the entire description in the **Description** field of sales or purchase forms. Displays the beginning of the description in the drop-down list in the **Item** field. You can set up some types of items to have separate descriptions for sales and for purchases.
Rate or price (optional)	Prefills the rate or price in the **Rate** or **Price** fields of sales or purchase forms. Some types of items can have a rate that is a percentage. You can set up some types of items to have separate rates or prices for sales and for purchases.
Account or accounts	Profit and loss statements report on the income or expense account associated with items used in transactions. You can set up some types of items to have separate accounts for sales and for purchases. Some types of items (for example, payment items) require a balance sheet account instead of an income or expense account. Inventory items require three separate accounts.

Information to enter	How QuickBooks uses this information
Taxability (required only if you collect sales tax)	If a taxable item is on a sales form and the customer is taxable, QuickBooks includes the item when calculating the sales tax.
Subitem status	You can make an item a subitem of an existing item. QuickBooks displays subitems of the same item together.
Custom fields (optional)	You can set up custom fields that fill your company's needs (for example, size or unit of measure). You can also customize sales and purchase forms to display a column for a custom field. Then QuickBooks prefills the column with the custom field information for the item.

To learn about...	Search the Help index for...
Adding a new item for one of the following: ■ A service ■ A product or part that is not held in inventory ■ A miscellaneous charge	■ items, services ■ items, non-inventory parts ■ items, miscellaneous charges
Adding a new item for a product or part held in inventory	items, inventory
Adding a new item that puts a group of several items on a sales or purchase form	items, grouped together
Adding a new item that calculates a subtotal	items, subtotal types
Adding a new item that calculates a discount on a sales form	items, discount types
Adding a new item that records a customer payment or deposit received at the time of sale	items, payment types
Adding a new item that calculates a sales tax for a single sales tax rate and single sales tax district	items, sales tax

To learn about…	Search the Help index for…
Adding a new item that calculates the total sales tax for a combination of sales tax rates	items, sales tax
Creating subitems of another item	items, subitems
Creating custom fields for items	items, custom fields on
Turning sales tax on	sales tax, setting up

Items for reimbursable costs in QuickBooks Pro

Perhaps your business purchases services or products for specific customers or jobs and then invoices the customer for the items (with or without markup). For example, Frank is a general contractor who uses subcontractors and invoices for their costs at a higher rate than what they charge him. Tina is an interior designer who buys furniture at wholesale and sells it to the client at retail.

In QuickBooks Pro only, service items, non-inventory parts, and other charge items each have a checkbox that allows you to pass through their costs at a markup and track costs and revenues in separate accounts. Then you can track both the expenses and the income for these items for a particular job. (For example, the checkbox for a non-inventory part is "This item is purchased for and sold to a specific customer:job.")

Note: **If you don't have QuickBooks Pro, use expense accounts, not items, for reimbursable costs.** See "Reimbursable expenses in QuickBooks" on page 194.)

There are several advantages to using items for reimbursable costs in QuickBooks Pro:

- It is easy to associate the cost of an item with an expense account and the income with a separate income account when you set up the item.
- You can track the number of units or hours purchased or sold.
- You can use items on estimates and purchase orders.
- If you write a purchase order for an item, you can create a bill from the purchase order and assign a job. Then you can invoice the customer for the item.

- When you enter a bill, check, or credit card charge, QuickBooks Pro fills in the description of the item and the unit cost after you choose the item from the drop-down list on the Items tab.

- When you invoice the customer for the cost of the item, QuickBooks Pro fills in the sales description of the item and the sales price.

- You can create reports that compare costs to revenues for each item.

For more information on invoicing for reimbursable time and costs, see "Reimbursable time and costs in QuickBooks Pro" on page 195.

Services performed by subcontractors or owners

If you charge for services performed by outside subcontractors or you pay owners (or partners) for time worked, set up a service item for each type of service. Be sure to select the checkbox "This service is performed by a subcontractor, owner, or partner." Then you can designate separate income and expense (or equity) accounts, and separate descriptions for sales and purchases.

You can enter different hourly rates for your cost and the sales price to your customer. If you write checks based on time tracked or enter the item on a purchase order, purchase, or estimate, QuickBooks fills in the rate from the **Cost** field. If you enter the item on a sales form, QuickBooks fills in the rate from the **Sales Price** field. However, if the subcontracted service is usually billed as a flat fee, and the fee varies, leave the **Cost** and **Sales Price** fields 0.00 when you set up the item.

If you pay owners (or partners) and vendors for the same service, you need separate service items because the accounts for the costs must be different. See "Service items for the time data" on page 327.

Products and materials purchased for a job

If you invoice for actual costs of products and materials purchased for a specific customer or job, set up a non-inventory part item for each type of product or service. Be sure to select the checkbox for "This item is purchased for and sold to a specific customer:job." Then you can designate separate income and expense accounts, and separate descriptions for sales and purchases.

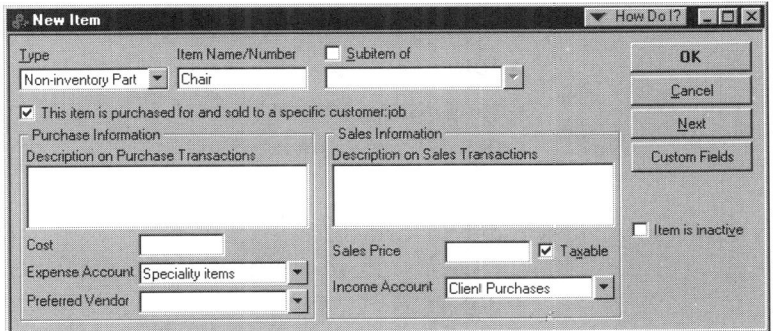

You can enter different rates for your cost and the sales price to your customer. However, if the cost of the product or material varies, leave the **Cost** and **Sales Price** fields 0.00 when you set up the non-inventory part item.

Tip: **To further aid in tracking the item, you can also specify the customer and job on the purchase order.** When you receive the item, this information will prefill on the item receipt or bill. You can use the open purchase orders by job report to find out which items are still on order for your customers.

Miscellaneous charges you pass on

If you invoice for miscellaneous charges incurred on a job, you can set up an other charge item for each type of miscellaneous charge. For example, Frank has an other charge item called Equipment Rental. Be sure to select the checkbox for "This is a reimbursable charge." Then you can designate separate income and expense accounts, and separate descriptions for sales and purchases.

As with products and materials, you can enter different cost and sales prices or leave the fields 0.00 when you set up the other charge item.

Working with items

This section contains the following topics:

Using items, saving time	**128**
Using items to subtotal on sales forms	**130**
Entering a group of items	**130**
Applying a discount to one or more items	**131**
Showing partial payments received at the time of sale	**132**
Adding sales tax to a sale	**134**
Changing prices or rates	**135**
Editing item information	**135**

After you have set up items, you use them to enter estimates, sales, purchase orders, and actual purchases. Remember, QuickBooks uses the term *sales* broadly; it can mean the performance of services or the assessment of fees as well as the sale of products.

You can enter all ten item types listed in the table on page 119 on any sales form. You can enter all but payment items on estimates. However, you cannot enter the following item types on purchase orders or purchases (on the Items tab of bills, checks, and credit card charges):

- Other charge items set up as a percentage
- Discount items
- Payment items
- Sales tax items
- Sales tax groups

(To learn how to record discounts from vendors, enter payments to vendors, and enter sales tax for purchases, see Chapter 14, *Tracking and paying expenses,* beginning on page 247.)

Using items, saving time

When you fill out a sales form, you list each service or product you're selling on its own line of the invoice or cash sale, along with the amount the customer owes for that item. Similarly, when you write a purchase order or receive a bill, each service or product is listed on its own line.

Because information about individual items is listed on separate lines, the items are called "line items." In QuickBooks, you enter line items by choosing from the drop-down list in the **Item** field of a sales or purchase form. You can also type in the **Item** field and let QuickBooks fill in the rest of the item's name.

Enter an item in the **Item** field by typing or by choosing from the drop-down list.

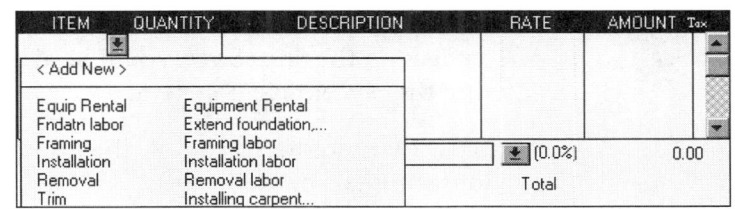

Each item on the Item list can contain all the information you need to fill in one line. You can always change any information, such as the description and rate, as you're filling in a form.

When you enter a quantity, QuickBooks calculates the amount for you.

When you enter items, QuickBooks keeps track of how much of each item you sell and to whom.

You can edit an item rate or description at any time.

Each item that you sell is associated with an income account. This association allows QuickBooks to provide useful sales and income reports.

The **Item** field shows the item name you entered when you created the item.

QuickBooks multiplies the **Quantity** by the **Rate** to calculate the **Amount**.

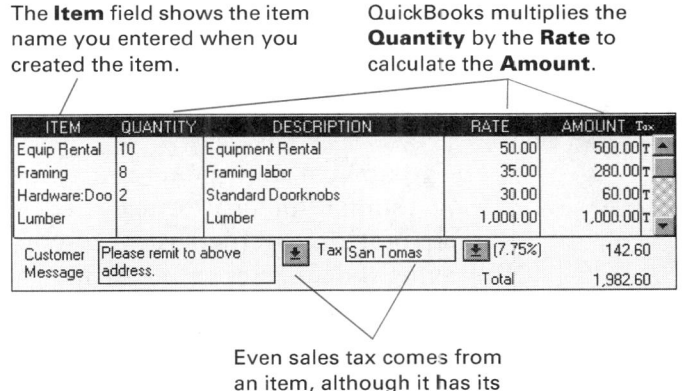

Even sales tax comes from an item, although it has its own field on the sales form.

You'll have separate items not only for each service rendered and each product sold, but also for discounts, markups, sales taxes, and subtotals. If the customer makes a partial payment at the time of the sale, you can add an item for the payment.

Working with items | 129

Using items to subtotal on sales forms

The subtotal item adds up the amounts of the items above it, up to the last subtotal.

You'll need a subtotal item if you ever want to apply a percentage discount or surcharge to several items. Because QuickBooks calculates percentages on the line above, you'll need to subtotal the items before entering the percentage line item.

If you use two subtotals in a row, the last subtotal will add up all the previous subtotals on the form.

The first subtotal line shows a total for all materials.

The second subtotal shows a total for all labor.

This second subtotal also makes the third subtotal include all amounts on the invoice, so a percentage markup can apply to the total sale.

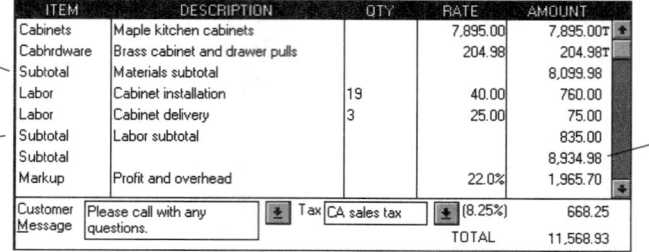

The third subtotal line adds up the two previous subtotals, so that a markup can be applied to the entire sale.

Entering a group of items

The group item allows you to enter several items all at once on a sales form, estimate, purchase order, check, or bill. If you often sell the same group of items together, using a group item saves you the trouble of entering the same set of line items again and again.

When you use a group item, you can enter a quantity for the group that affects the quantity and amount of each item in the group. You can also edit the individual quantity of each item in the group, and edit descriptions and rates.

Using a group item to hide details on a sales form

The more detailed you are in tracking items, the more information you can get from reports. The QuickBooks group item allows you to be very detailed in tracking the items you sell without showing all that detail to your customers. When you set up a group item, you specify whether to print each item or just the group item. (Of course, if you use a group item on a purchase order, you must show the detail to the vendor so the vendor will know what you want.)

For example, Frank has a construction company that sends invoices for full jobs, such as complete remodels. If he used one general service item called "Remodel," a sales report would show his income from remodels.

If you use very general items, like this one, your reports won't be as useful as if you used detailed items grouped together.

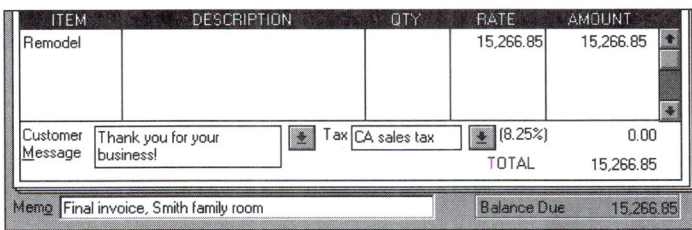

However, Frank uses more detailed items, so he can learn more from his sales reports. Frank breaks down the remodel cost and uses items such as "Lumber," "Hardware," "Markup," "Carpentry Hours," and "Laborer Hours."

He groups these items under one item called "Remodel." Even though he chooses not to print the items in the group on the invoice for his customers to see, he still has those details on his sales reports.

QuickBooks shows you the items in the group onscreen, whether you choose to print them or not.

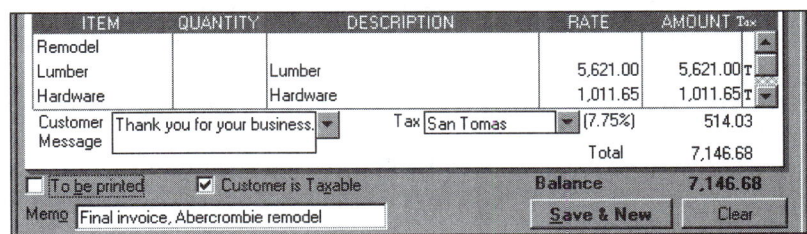

Applying a discount to one or more items

To apply a discount, you have to enter a discount item. If the discount item's rate is a percentage, the item reduces the amount due by a percentage of the line above it.

To take a percentage off several items at once, you must first subtotal the items. On the other hand, if you want to discount one particular

Working with items | 131

item you've sold and not the entire sale, add a discount item directly beneath the one discounted item.

The first discount line follows a subtotal line, so that the discount percentage is calculated for all labor.

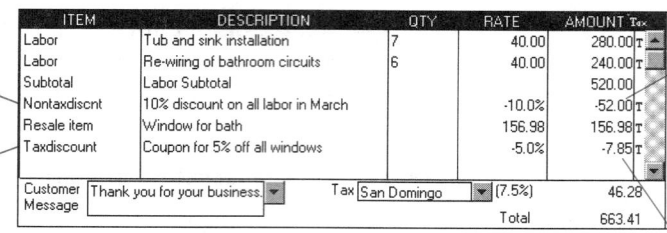

The first discount has no effect on the sales tax calculation for this sale.

The second discount line applies only to one item, so a subtotal is not needed.

The second discount (with a T in the Tax column) reduces the amount of taxable sales, so it lowers the tax amount on the sale.

If you give discounts of different percentages, you can either set up a separate discount item for each percentage or edit the amount right on the sales form.

Don't use a discount item for discounts that you give for early payment.

Enter discounts for early payment through the Receive Payments window. See "Receiving and depositing payments" on page 189.

Showing partial payments received at the time of sale

If you receive a partial payment toward the amount of an invoice at the time you create the invoice, you'll need to enter a payment item.

The payment item tells QuickBooks to subtract the amount of the payment from the total invoice amount. To record the payment on the invoice, enter a payment item for the amount you've received after you've entered all the items sold.

Use a payment item when you receive a partial payment at or before the time you create the invoice.

ITEM	DESCRIPTION	QTY	RATE	AMOUNT
Cleaning			65.00	65.00
Payment	Co-payment at time of service Patient to present invoice to insurance company. Full payment due in 30 days.		-5.00	-5.00
Customer Message	Happy Holidays!	Tax CA sales tax	(8.25%)	0.00
			TOTAL	60.00

QuickBooks subtracts a payment item amount from the invoice total.

You can set up a payment item so that it automatically deposits the payment directly to a checking or other account. Alternatively, you can set it up so that QuickBooks automatically puts the payment amount into your Undeposited Funds account so you can deposit it with other funds. (See "Receiving and depositing payments" on page 189.)

If you need to track the payment method (check, cash, credit card charge), you can have different payment items for different methods of payment.

Using a payment item is not the only way to record a payment. For some types of payment, you should use a different method:

Type of payment	How to record in QuickBooks
Partial payment received at time of sale	Enter payment item on invoice.
Full payment received at time of sale.	Use cash sales receipt, not invoice. No payment item is necessary, as QuickBooks assumes sale is fully paid.
Summary of payments, by method, for daily sales summary	Use cash sales receipt to summarize the daily sales. Enter a different payment item for the summary of each payment method.
Payment from customer to pay outstanding invoice or statement	Enter payment in Receive Payments window. Indicate which invoices or statement charges have been paid by the payment.
Advance payment from customer before work is done or sale is made.	Use one of the following options: ■ Enter payment in Receive Payments window. ■ Enter payment item on a credit memo. ■ Record a retainer. See the QuickBooks and Your Industry help for law firms, or search the Help index for **retainers**.

Avoid entering double payments.

If you receive payment before the sale and record a deposit before you record the invoice, do not also enter a payment item on the invoice or you will record a double payment.

Adding sales tax to a sale

Sales tax varies greatly from region to region. Read Chapter 15, *Tracking and paying sales tax,* beginning on page 275, for a complete picture of how QuickBooks handles sales tax.

To have QuickBooks calculate the sales tax on your sales forms, you have to do the following:

- Create the sales tax items or sales tax groups you need.
- Specify the sales tax item or group for each customer or job subject to sales tax.
- Identify whether each saleable item (service, non-inventory part, inventory part, other charge) or discount item is taxable.

Even though you use a sales tax item or sales tax group to specify a sales tax, you don't need to enter sales tax as a line item. Instead, sales tax has its own field at the bottom of the sales form.

On invoices, cash sales receipts, and credit memos, QuickBooks automatically displays the sales tax you have set up for the customer or job named on the sales form. QuickBooks calculates the correct tax and prints it on the sales form after all the other line items.

To learn about...	Search the Help index for...
Assigning a sales tax rate to a customer or job	sales tax, tax assignments
Identifying an item as taxable	sales tax, identifying which items are taxable
Applying a different tax from the one displayed on the sales form	invoices, sales tax on

Changing prices or rates

You can change the prices or rates of many items at one time through the Change Item Prices window. In this window you can tell QuickBooks to raise (or lower) prices or rates by a specified amount or percentage. You can change prices or rates for items individually, or have QuickBooks calculate new prices or rates on several or all items of the same type at once.

To learn about...	Search the Help index for...
Changing prices or rates of items	items, prices

Editing item information

After you've created an item, you can edit information about it at any time, subject to certain restrictions.

Changing item type

In both QuickBooks and QuickBooks Pro, you can change a non-inventory part or other charge item to a service, non-inventory part, inventory part, or other charge item.

However, you cannot change the item type of any other type of item.

Hiding and redisplaying items on lists

You can hide an item on the Item list without deleting it by making the item *inactive*. For example, you may have an inventory item on your Item list that you have not stocked in the last six months, but which you may want to stock in the future.

When you make an item inactive, QuickBooks keeps the information associated with that item, but hides the item on the Item list and removes it from any drop-down lists that use items. You do not need to change or delete any transaction that uses the item. If you start to use the item again, you can make it active at any time.

You can display all your items, including the inactive ones, on the Item list by selecting Show All. (Inactive items still appear on reports, but never display on drop-down lists.)

Deleting items

You can delete an item only if it is not used in any transaction or group item. To locate all transactions that use a given item, create a QuickReport for the item for all dates. See "What's a quick way to get a list of transactions for an item?" on page 137.

If you condense your QuickBooks data through a specified date (to reduce the file size and remove detail), you can also remove items that are not used after that date. See "As-needed tasks" on page 425.

To learn about...	Search the Help index for...
Changing item type	items, changing type of
Changing information about an item	items, editing information
Hiding and showing items on the Item list and drop-down lists in **Item** fields	items, hiding and showing
Making hidden items visible on the Item list as well as on drop-down lists	lists, hiding and showing entries
Deleting items	items, deleting

Reports and graphs about items

This section contains the following topics:

What's a quick way to get a list of transactions for an item? 137
How can I create a list of my items and their prices?   138
Which items sell the most?   139
Other reports about items   139

What's a quick way to get a list of transactions for an item?

A QuickReport for an item shows all transactions involving that item for the fiscal year to date.

12/15/98

Item QuickReport
October 1 through December 15, 1998

Type	Date	Num	Name	Memo	Qty	Amount
Service						
Framing						
Invoice	10/05/98	1	Abercrombie, Kristy:Rem...	Framing labor	0	0.00
Invoice	10/15/98	4	Cook, Brian:Kitchen	Framing labor	-8	-440.00
Invoice	10/25/98	6	Abercrombie, Kristy:Rem...	Framing labor	-16	-1,144.00
Invoice	10/26/98	7	Pretell Real Estate:155 W...	Framing labor	-32	-1,760.00
Invoice	10/28/98	8	Natiello, Ernesto:Kitchen	Framing labor	0	0.00
Paycheck	10/29/98	170	Pretell Real Estate:155 W...		24	478.85
Paycheck	10/29/98	170	Cook, Brian:Kitchen		24	478.85
Paycheck	10/29/98	172	Abercrombie, Kristy		1.5	38.81
Paycheck	10/29/98	172	Abercrombie, Kristy:Rem...		8	138.00
Paycheck	10/29/98	172	Pretell Real Estate:155 W...		8	138.00
Invoice	10/30/98	10	Cook, Brian:Kitchen	Framing labor	-24	-1,320.00
Paycheck	11/12/98	173	Natiello, Ernesto:Kitchen		16	319.23
Paycheck	11/12/98	173	Melton, Johnny:Dental off...		20.5	409.01
Paycheck	11/12/98	173	Pretell Real Estate:155 W...		11.5	229.45
Invoice	11/15/98	12	Pretell Real Estate:155 W...	Framing labor	-19.5	-1,072.50
Invoice	11/16/98	14	Natiello, Ernesto:Kitchen	Framing labor	-32	-2,112.00

For a service, part, other charge, discount, payment, or sales tax item, the QuickReport lists each invoice, cash sales receipt, credit memo, bill, credit, check, or credit card receipt that has this item on it.

For an inventory part item, the QuickReport also lists inventory adjustment transactions that affect the quantity or value on hand and open purchase orders that affect the quantity on order.

Note: You cannot create a QuickReport for a subtotal item or for a group item.

To learn about...	Search the Help index for...
Creating a QuickReport for a selected item	items, reports about

How can I create a list of my items and their prices?

The item price list shows the name, description, sales rate or price, and preferred vendor for each item.

```
                    Item Price List
                    December 15, 1998

    Item                 Description              Price    Preferred Vendor
►   Framing              Framing labor            55.00
    Installation         Installation labor       35.00
    Removal              Removal labor            35.00
    Repairs              Repair work              35.00
    Subs                 Subcontracted services    0.00
    Subs:Carpet          Install carpeting         0.00    Larson Flooring
    Subs:Drywall         Install drywall           0.00    Middlefield Drywall
    Subs:Electrical      Electrical work           0.00    C.U. Electric
    Subs:Insulating      Install insulation        0.00    Keswick Insulation
    Subs:Metal Wrk       Metal Work                0.00    Hamlin Metal
    Subs:Painting        Painting                  0.00    Washuta & Son Painting
    Subs:Plumbing        Plumbing                  0.00    Lew Plumbing
    Subs:Roofing         Roofing                   0.00    Sloan Roofing
    Subs:Tile &Counter   Install tile or counter   0.00    Wheeler's Tile Etc.
    Cabinets             Cabinets                  0.00    Thomas Kitchen & Bath
    Cabinets:Cabinet Pulls  Cabinet Pulls          2.00    Patton Hardware Sup...
```

The item listing report has additional information, such as whether the item is taxable and, for inventory part items, the quantities on hand and on order. You can customize either report to add or delete columns.

To learn about...	Search the Help index for...
Creating a list of information about your items	lists, reports about
Finding the report you need with the Report Finder	reports, finding

Which items sell the most?

The sales graphs include a pie chart showing the percentage of sales income from each item for the fiscal year. The sales reports by item show your unit and dollar sales and returns, subtotaled by item type and item.

For illustrations of the sales graphs and the summary sales by item report, see "Which items or customers bring in the most income?" on page 205.

To learn about...	Search the Help index for...
Creating reports and graphs about your sales by item	■ report types, sales ■ graphs, sales

Other reports about items

QuickBooks has many reports that show sales by item, purchases by item, job and project information by item, and information about inventory items. (For descriptions of the inventory reports, see "Getting information about your inventory" on page 244.)

You can customize and filter reports to meet your needs, and then memorize the changed report for later use. See "Customizing the look of the report" on page 400 for more information.

Are some items not included on item reports?

The reports of sales, purchases, and job and project information by item include only the following types of items:

- Service
- Non-inventory parts
- Inventory parts
- Other charges
- Discounts

They do not include payment items, group items (although they include the members of the group), reimbursed expenses, sales tax items, or sales tax groups.

To learn about...	Search the Help index for...
Finding the report you need with the QuickBooks Report Finder	reports, finding
Creating one of the preset reports by item	■ jobs, reports about (QuickBooks Pro only) ■ purchases, reports about ■ reports, creating ■ report types, sales
Changing what is in a report	■ reports, changing the scope of ■ report customization

CHAPTER 10

Customers and jobs

Should I track customers and jobs?	142
Setting up customers and jobs	147
Working with customers and jobs	153
Reports about customers and jobs	162

> Who are my customers, and do I need to track information about them?

QuickBooks uses the word *customer* to mean any person, business, or group that buys or pays for the services or products that your business or organization sells or provides. By entering information about customers, you save time entering customer transactions later—and you can get reports about them. In addition, entering customer information provides valuable business management information through the Customer Center and the Customer Detail Center.

Should I track customers and jobs?

This section contains the following topics:

What does QuickBooks mean by a customer?	142
What does QuickBooks mean by a job?	143
If you set up customers and jobs in QuickBooks	144
If you charge your customers sales tax	144
Classifying customers and jobs	144
Defining custom fields for customers	146

What does QuickBooks mean by a customer?

customer

Any person, business, or group that buys or pays for the services or products that your business or organization sells or provides.

In QuickBooks, a customer can be any of the following:

- A person or company that buys products from your retail business
- A company that buys products from your wholesale business
- A client of your consultant business or law firm
- A patient of your medical or dental practice
- A homeowner who buys your home repair or remodeling services
- A condominium owner who pays fees to your condo association
- A renter who pays rent to your real-estate management firm

Some businesses do not need to keep track of the names of customers. An example is a retail store or service business that always receives payment with the sale or service.

However, here are some situations in which you would want to keep track of customer names:

- Customers receive your goods or services and then pay you later.
- Customers are supposed to pay a regular monthly fee, and you want to track who has paid and who hasn't.
- You want to track income (and perhaps expenses as well) by customer.

If you are using QuickBooks for an organization that receives money but doesn't really sell anything, you probably don't need to set up customers. For example, a nonprofit or religious organization with members making contributions or paying dues can simply track the deposits without making the members customers. Specialized membership software can keep track of membership details such as pledges, contribution history, and names of family members.

What does QuickBooks mean by a job?

job

A project done for a particular customer.

In QuickBooks, a job is a project done for a particular customer. You must always associate a job with a customer. Use jobs if you do (or expect to do) more than one job for the same customer. For example, Jan does freelance writing for a large company that supplies a separate purchase order for each job. Hank's plumbing business has to keep track of the separate jobs it does for a general contractor.

On the other hand, if your company never does more than one job per customer, or you do not want to track individual jobs, you don't have to enter job names. For example, Doug's printing company refers to each customer order as a "job." However, even though Doug gets repeat business from customers, all he cares about is whether the customer has paid, so he doesn't need to set up jobs for his customers.

Besides using projects for jobs, you can be creative. For example:

- If you manage several apartment buildings, set up the building addresses as customers and the individual apartments as jobs.
- If you invoice against purchase orders, set up each purchase order number as a job.
- If you have a practice or organization that sends one statement to a family to cover individual members of the family, set up the family members as jobs.
- If you have multiple estimates per customer, see the tip in "Estimates and proposals" on page 184.

Tip: **QuickBooks reports about jobs apply to customers as well.** You don't have to set up jobs in order to use these reports. For example, the profit and loss by job report actually applies to both customers and jobs. If you have customers but not jobs, you will still see information about your customers.

If you set up customers and jobs in QuickBooks

When you set up a customer or job in QuickBooks, you enter information you can use over and over again, without retyping, for the following tasks:

- Fast entry of name, address, payment terms, and tax status on invoices and other sales forms
- Tracking payments received and amounts owed
- Contacting customers with overdue balances, including merging names, addresses, and balance information with Microsoft Word letters
- Reporting of sales or income by customer, profit and loss by job, and profit and loss budget vs. actual by job
- Tracking reimbursable expenses by customer and job
- Printing mailing labels

Note: **If you use Symantec ACT! or Microsoft Outlook contact management software to store customer data, you can transfer basic customer information (such as name, address, phone, and so on) from your contact manager to QuickBooks Pro and vice versa.** See Chapter 23, "Sharing QuickBooks Pro information with your contact manager" on page 438.

If you charge your customers sales tax

QuickBooks allows you to assign the appropriate sales tax (such as for a particular county) to each customer. When you enter the customer name on a QuickBooks sales form, the correct sales tax shows up on the form.

Classifying customers and jobs

Both customer types and job types are completely optional. They allow you to get additional information on reports.

Customer types

If your business wants to be able to report on types of customers, you have the option of assigning a customer type to your customers. Then you can filter (restrict) reports to customers of a particular type or group of types, create mailing labels for customers of one type or of certain types, or choose to print statements for all customers of one type. For example:

- Laura wants to know whether her interior design business is earning more money from its residential clients or its corporate clients. She assigns her customers to one of these types: Residential or Corporate. Then she can filter her profit and loss report for one customer type at a time and compare the profits for the two customer types.

- Hugh is a portrait photographer. Every October he mails a brochure to previous customers who have come in for family portraits to remind them to get updated portraits for holiday greeting cards or gifts.

Job types

Job types (available only in QuickBooks Pro) are useful as an additional way of filtering information on reports. Use job types to classify your jobs differently from customer types. For example:

- Tony, a construction contractor, uses customer types such as Residential and Commercial. In addition, he wants to compare profits for job types such as:
    - Kitchen Remodels
    - Bath Remodels
    - Decks
    - New Houses
    - New Commercial Buildings
    - Restaurant Remodels

- Connie, a freelance writer, classifies customers with customer types such as Corporate, Startup, Retail, or Nonprofit. In addition, she wants to compare income from job types such as:
  - Writing Business Plans
  - Writing Brochures

Tip: **Do you want to learn more about using customer and job types in your business?** Choose Optimizing QuickBooks for Your Industry from the Help menu. Then select the industry type closest to your own.

Defining custom fields for customers

To track additional information about your customers, you can define up to seven custom fields. For example, you might want to define fields for:

- Web site address
- Spouse's name
- Birthday

After you add custom fields, you can customize your sales forms to include these fields. You can also display and filter for customized field data in your reports. See *Customizing a form's content,* beginning on page 87.

Setting up customers and jobs

You may have already used the EasyStep Interview to set up customers and jobs that had open balances as of your QuickBooks start date. You should also set up any customers who owed you money between your QuickBooks start date and today. As your business gains new customers, you should add them as well.

If you want to transfer customer information from Symantec ACT! or Microsoft Outlook contact management software to get you started, see "Sharing QuickBooks Pro information with your contact manager" on page 438.

Setting up customers

You'll use the New Customer window when you set up a customer. Enter as much or as little information as you need to get started. If you don't have all the information now, you can add it later.

Custom fields provide a way to gather more customer detail. Press the Define Fields button to set these up.

This user has set up customer types to further categorize her customer base.

If your customers are taxable, set up sales tax items before setting up your customers.

What to set up	Comments	See...
Sales tax (if you collect it from customers)	Before you can assign a sales tax to a customer, you must first set up your sales tax rates.	■ "Setting up sales tax" on page 280 for information about setting up sales tax ■ In the Help Index: sales tax, setting up
Customer types (optional)	Customer types provide you with another way of categorizing your customer base.	In the Help Index: customers, types
Customers	Refer to the following table "Customer information and how it's used in QuickBooks" to help you decide what information to add.	In the Help Index: customers, adding new
Custom fields for customers	Use these fields to record additional information about the customer, like a spouse's name. Once you've set up the custom fields for one customer, the fields will appear for all customers.	In the Help Index: custom fields, for customers, vendors, employees
Preference to track expenses by customer and job (QuickBooks Pro only)	In QuickBooks, when you first install the program, you are set up to track expenses by customer and job. However, there is a preference that allows you to turn this feature on and off. If your Write Checks and Enter Bills windows do not have a Customer:Job column, the feature is off. QuickBooks Pro is automatically set up to track expenses by customer and job.	In the Help Index: preferences, accounting

Customer information and how it's used in QuickBooks

Information needed	How QuickBooks uses this information
Customer name (short) or number	- Displays on Customer:Job list; sorted alphabetically (or numerically) - Displays on all drop-down lists where you choose the customer (for example, on sales forms) - Displays on all reports that are by customer or that show the customer name on a transaction
Company name, title, first and last name (optional)	- Exports to mail merge file for use with word processor - Prefills the name in the "Bill To" field
"Bill To" name and address (optional)	Displays and prints on sales forms and checks
"Ship To" name and address (optional)	Displays and prints on sales forms that have this field
Contact information (name, phone, FAX—optional)	Name and phone display and print on the A/R collections report
Account number (optional)	Required only if you make online payments to this customer; otherwise, QuickBooks does not use this number.
Customer type (optional)	Available as a filter for reports
Payment terms if payment has a due date (optional)	Determines due date on invoices and on statements that include statement charges
Rep associated with sales to this customer (optional)	Determines sales by rep on sales by rep reports
Credit limit (optional)	Warns you if you try to record an invoice that would put the customer balance above this limit
Sales tax information (recommended if you collect sales tax)	Calculates correct sales tax for taxable items on sales forms

Information needed	How QuickBooks uses this information
Custom field information (optional)	After you set up any custom fields relevant to your business, you can customize sales forms to display and print this information. Also, you can filter reports for customers that share the same information
Job information (QuickBooks Pro only, optional)	Use only if you do NOT plan to set up separate jobs for the customer. Job status displays on Customer:Job list. You can display and filter by job information on any customer list report.

Setting up jobs

You can add your current jobs all at once or as you need them on transactions. As you start new jobs, you can add them as well.

What to set up	Comments	See...
Job types (optional)	You can filter for job types on reports.	In the Help Index: job types
Job status	Five preset descriptions include: ■ Pending ■ Awarded ■ In progress ■ Closed ■ Not awarded	"Setting descriptions for job status" for information on where job status information displays and how to change the preset descriptions.
Jobs	You can add as much or as little information as you need. Refer to the following table "Job information and how it's used in QuickBooks" on page 152 to help you decide what information to add.	In the Help Index: jobs, adding new

Setting descriptions for job status

In QuickBooks Pro (but not in QuickBooks) you can note the status of a job when you set up or edit the job. QuickBooks Pro uses the descriptions for the choices in the following places:

- Drop-down list in the **Job Status** field on the Job Info tab of the New Job, Edit Job, New Customer, and Edit Customer windows
- Job Status column of the Customer:Job List window (page 155)
- Job progress invoices vs. estimates report (and when a job status column is added to the customer phone list report or customer contact list report)
- The job status filter on the customer phone list report, customer contact list report, and job progress invoices vs. estimates report

Five preset descriptions include:

- Pending
- Awarded
- In progress
- Closed
- Not awarded

You can change any or all of the descriptions that are meaningful to your company. The only one that QuickBooks Pro treats in a special way is the Closed description. If you use the Condense feature to reduce the size of your file, QuickBooks deletes estimates only for jobs with the job status of Closed. If you change this description, be sure it still applies to a job that has been completed.

To learn about...	Search the Help index for...
Changing the descriptions for job status	job status

Setting up customers and jobs | 151

Job information and how it's used in QuickBooks

In QuickBooks, a job is associated with a particular customer. You can also have a subjob of another job.

To set up a job for a customer, you need to enter the following information.

Information needed	How QuickBooks uses this information
Job name or number	- Displays on Customer:Job list; sorted alphabetically (or numerically), indented under the customer name - Displays on all drop-down lists where you choose the customer and job (for example, on sales forms) - Displays on all reports that are by customer or job or that show the customer:job name on a transaction - Prints in the Project field of sales forms that have this field
Name, address, and contact information	QuickBooks copies what you already entered for the customer, but you can change it if necessary.
Account number, customer type, credit limit, custom fields (optional)	QuickBooks copies what you already entered for the customer, but you can change it if necessary.
Job status (optional, available in QuickBooks Pro only)	- Displays on Customer:Job list - Displays on the job progress invoices vs. estimates report and is available as a filter for that report - Available as a possible column and as a filter for any customer list report
Start, projected end, and end dates (optional, available in QuickBooks Pro only)	Available as a possible column and as a filter for any customer list report
Job description (optional, available in QuickBooks Pro only)	Available as a possible column and as a filter for any customer list report
Job type (optional)	Available as a possible column and as a filter for any customer list report

Working with customers and jobs

This section contains the following topics:

Using the Customer and Customer Detail centers	153
Viewing and changing customer and job information	155
Viewing the customer register	158
Contacting customers by mail	158
Changing the opening balance for a customer or job	159
Changing customer types	160
Changing job types	160
Changing job status	161

Using the Customer and Customer Detail centers

Customer Center

QuickBooks conveniently displays integral information about your customers in one place—the Customer Center.

Alerts keep you apprised of important business information such as tax deadlines. Click an alert to act on it.

Easily see which customers have open balances and how much they owe.

View useful comparative information such as the most/least profitable customers.

QuickBooks displays links to tips and useful information.

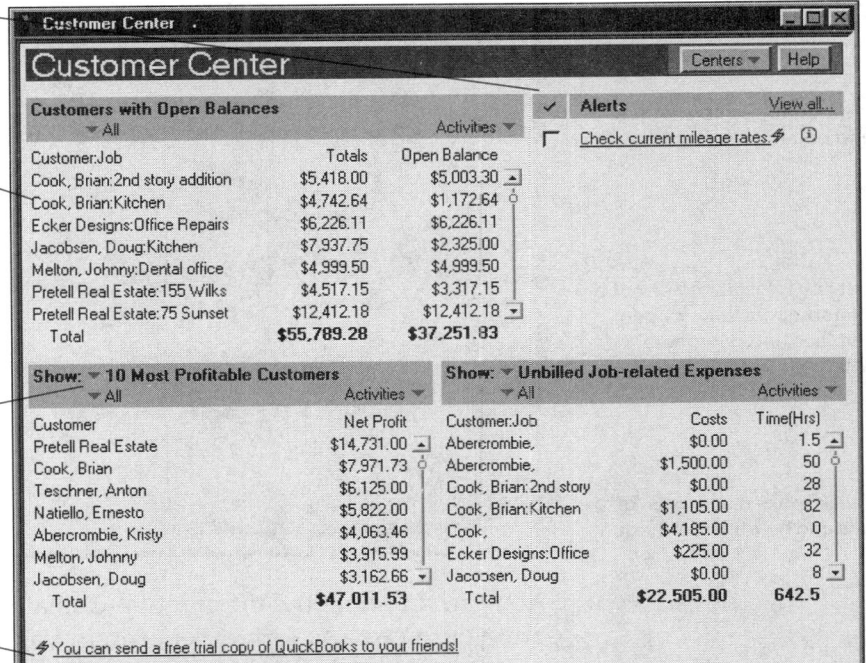

QuickBooks gives you the flexibility to display information that's more meaningful to you. For example, you might want to compare customer profitability for two different time periods. To do so, you can display the same type of information in two separate tables—with each table set to show data for a different time period, such as the current fiscal quarter and last fiscal quarter.

To learn about...	Search the Help index for...
Using centers in QuickBooks	centers
Managing alerts	alerts, managing

Customer Detail Center

The Customer Detail Center serves as a central point for viewing detailed information about a specific customer.

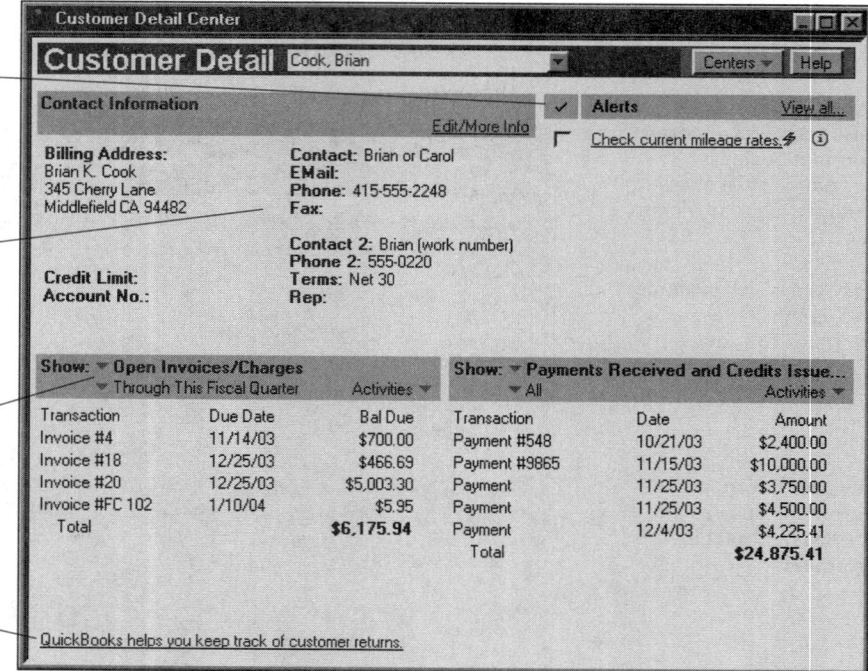

QuickBooks alerts keep you current with information important to your business—including updates to QuickBooks. Click an alert to act on it.

View contact information and edit it if necessary.

Get key information about a customer, including open invoices and payments received.

QuickBooks displays links to tips and helpful information.

You can fine-tune the information displayed in some sections to best suit your needs. As with other centers, you can quickly access the forms from which you can take action on displayed data. For example,

154 | CHAPTER 10 Customers and jobs

you can bring up the Receive Payments form if you're viewing a list of open invoices/charges.

To learn about...	Search the Help index for...
Using centers in QuickBooks	centers
Managing alerts	alerts, managing

Viewing and changing customer and job information

The Customer:Job list displays helpful information at a glance:

- Name of each customer and job
- Current balance owed by each customer (and for each job)
- Whether there is an existing note for the customer or job
- Job status of each customer or job (QuickBooks Pro only)
- Amount of any existing estimate for the customer or job (QuickBooks Pro only)

The Balance column shows the current balance owed by each customer (and for each job).

Double-click in the Notes column to add or view notes about a customer or job.

Use the menu buttons to add, edit, or perform other tasks for your customers.

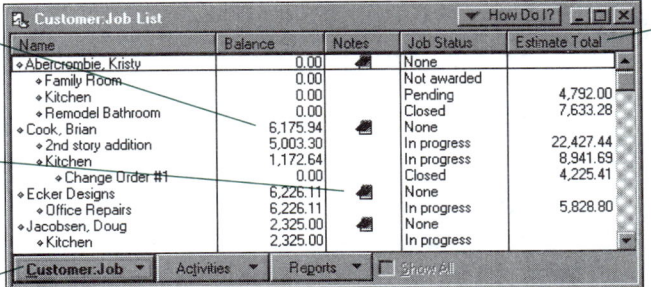

Only QuickBooks Pro has the Job Status and Estimate Total columns.

The Job Status column shows the job status entered in the Add Job or Edit Job window.

The Estimate Total column shows the amount of the estimate if the job (or customer) has an estimate.

Working with customers and jobs | 155

To see further details about a customer or job, you can view the Edit Customer or Edit Job window or you can create a report. You can also change information about a customer or job.

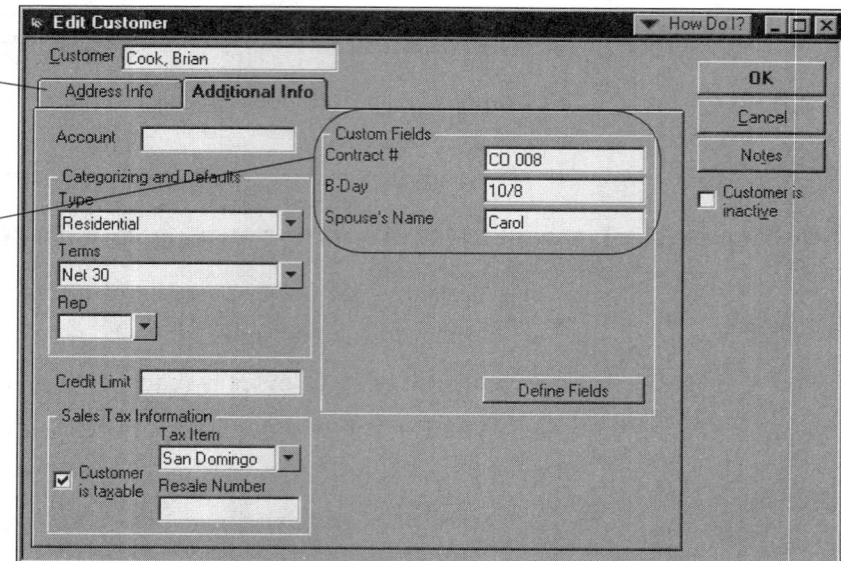

The Address Info tab of this window (not shown) has name, address, and phone information.

You can set up and fill in any custom fields that fit your needs.

QuickBooks does not allow you to delete a customer or job if there are any transactions associated with the customer or job. To delete a customer or job you have used, you must remove the name from every associated transaction.

On the other hand, you can hide a customer or job on the Customer:Job list without deleting the name by making the customer or job *inactive*. For example, you may have customers who have not done business with you in a long time and who owe you no money. You don't want their names to keep appearing on the list.

When you make a customer or job inactive, QuickBooks keeps the information associated with that customer or job, but hides the customer or job name on the Customer:Job list. The names are removed from any drop-down lists that use customers or jobs. You do not need to change or delete any transaction that uses the customer or job. You can make a customer or job active again at any time.

Tip: **To see which names are currently inactive, select the Show All checkbox on the Customer:Job list.** Inactive names display with a hand symbol to their left.

QuickBooks provides a notepad for recording notes about a customer or job. These notes can help you keep track of important dates and information for a customer or job. You can have a different set of notes about each job for one customer.

You can reach the notepad directly from the Customer:Job list. (You can also write on the notepad when viewing a customer's record or when entering a transaction.)

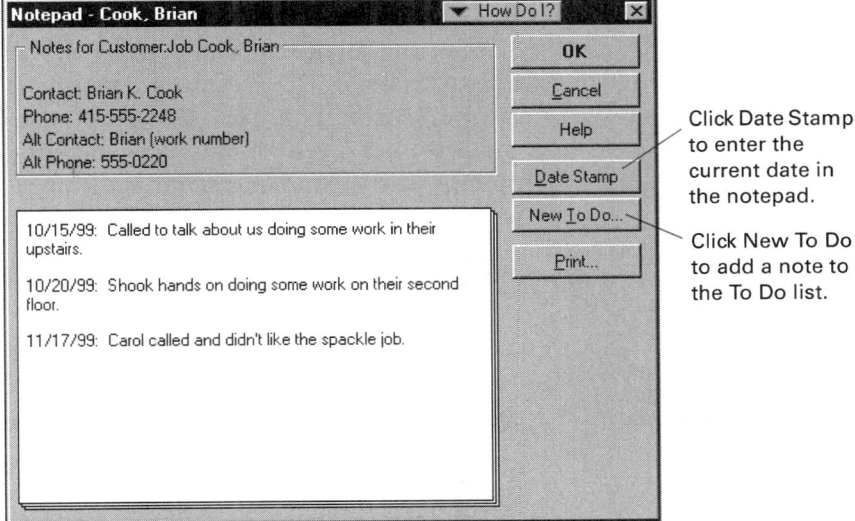

Click Date Stamp to enter the current date in the notepad.

Click New To Do to add a note to the To Do list.

Each customer's notepad can hold roughly 10 windows' worth of text.

Once you fill up this window, use the Up and Down Arrow keys or PgUp and PgDn to see more text.

To learn about...	Search the Help index for...
Displaying the Customer:Job list	customers, list of
Viewing or editing information about an existing customer or job	customers, editing information for
Hiding an inactive customer or job	customers, hiding and showing
Deleting an unused customer or job	customers, deleting
Creating a note for a customer or job	customers, notes about
Viewing or adding to an existing note for a customer or job	customers, notes about

To learn about...	Search the Help index for...
Displaying all hidden (inactive) customers and jobs	customers, hiding and showing
Making an inactive customer or job active again	customers, hiding and showing

Viewing the customer register

The customer register is something like a checkbook register for just one customer or job. A customer register is available for each customer on your Customer:Job list. It lists all transactions that affect how much the customer owes you: invoices, statement charges, payments, credit memos, and customer discounts. (It does not list any transactions in which the customer pays in full at the time of sale.)

The customer's name appears both at the top of the register and in the **Customer:Job** field.

If you choose a customer name, the register shows transactions for all jobs for that customer.

If you choose a job name, the register shows transactions for that job alone.

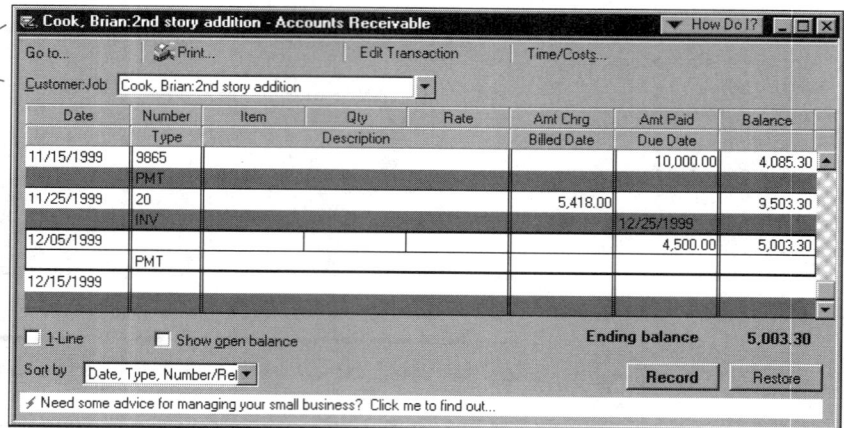

Tip: To locate a particular invoice or payment for a customer, scroll through the customer's register. Sort the register by date, amount, document number, order entered, or paid status.

To learn about...	Search the Help index for...
Viewing a customer register	customers, registers for

Contacting customers by mail

You can use your QuickBooks customer data in conjunction with Microsoft Word letters to send various messages to your customers, including collection notices, thank you letters, and change of address notices.

To learn about...	Search the Help index for...
Getting your QuickBooks data into Microsoft Word letters	letters using QuickBooks data in Microsoft Word
Printing labels	mailing labels, printing

Changing the opening balance for a customer or job

When you first set up a customer or job, you have a chance to enter the opening (unpaid) balance for the customer or job as of a specific date. The date should be your QuickBooks start date (that is, the date when you enter opening balances for all accounts, customers, and vendors).

When you enter the customer's opening balance (in the EasyStep Interview or New Customer window), QuickBooks creates an invoice for the amount and date you specify. This invoice is probably the first transaction in the customer register. (There should not be any opening balance transaction if the customer had no unpaid balance as of the start date.)

You can change the customer's opening balance invoice by finding it in the customer's register and then editing it.

If you failed to enter an opening balance but want to create one now, enter an invoice dated on or before your start date. To summarize the amount owed as of your start date, enter on the invoice an item set up as a nontaxable other charge, and assign the account Uncategorized Income.

To learn about...	Search the Help index for...
Displaying a customer's register	customers, registers for
Editing a transaction displayed in a register	registers, editing entries
Entering an invoice	invoices, creating
Setting up an other charge type of item	other charge items

Changing customer types

If you create customer types to classify your customers, you can rename, reorganize, hide, or delete them.

To learn about...	Comments	Search the Help index for...
Changing an existing customer type	The changes affect all customers already assigned to the type.	customers, types
Hiding a customer type	The hidden (inactive) name is not visible on the drop-down list in the **Customer Type** field.	customers, types
Making a hidden customer type active	Active customer types are visible on the drop-down list in the **Customer Type** field.	customers, types
Deleting an unused customer type	You cannot delete a customer type currently used for any customer or job.	customers, types

Changing job types

If you create job types to classify your jobs, you can rename, reorganize, hide, or delete them. Job types are available only in QuickBooks Pro.

To learn about...	Comments	Search the Help index for...
Changing an existing job type	The changes affect all jobs already assigned to the type.	job types
Hiding a job type	The hidden (inactive) name is not visible on the drop-down list in the **Job Type** field.	job types
Making a hidden job type active	Active job types are visible on the drop-down list in the **Job Type** field.	job types
Deleting an unused job type	You cannot delete a job type currently used for any customer or job.	job types

Changing job status

QuickBooks Pro does not automatically change the job status of any job on the basis of transactions you enter. You must edit the customer or job to change the status (for example, from In Progress to Closed).

You can change the descriptions of the five choices for job status, but you cannot delete or hide any of them. Job status is available only in QuickBooks Pro.

To learn about...	Search the Help index for...
Changing the job status of a customer or job	job status
Changing the description of a job status shown on the **Job Status** drop-down list	job status

Reports about customers and jobs

This section contains the following topics:

How can I create a list of customer contact information?	162
How can I get a list of customer transactions quickly?	163
Exactly how much do my customers owe me?	164
Can I see a breakdown of all income and expenses for a job?	165
Which billable costs have I not yet charged for?	166
Which items are still on order for a customer or job?	166
Other reports by customer and job	167

QuickBooks has reports that give you information about sales to (and payments from) customers, work on specific jobs or projects, and basic information about your customers.

How can I create a list of customer contact information?

You can create two preset reports that show information you are likely to want from your Customer:Job list.

Report	Description
Customer phone list	Shows name and phone number for each customer and job (active names only)
Customer contact list	Shows name, balance, phone and fax numbers, contact name, and billing address for each customer and job (active names only)

You can customize either report to display additional information such as Ship To address, sales tax information, customer type, or job status. You can also filter to restrict the report (such as, to customers in a particular zip code).

To learn about...	Search the Help index for...
Creating a list of information about your customers and jobs	customers, contact management

How can I get a list of customer transactions quickly?

QuickReport

A report that shows a list of transactions you are likely to want to see for the name you have selected. The particular report depends not only on the name you select but also where you select it.

You can create a QuickReport about a customer from the Customer:Job list as well as from a register or any transaction for the customer. (You can also create a QuickReport about a specific job for a customer.)

The QuickReport shows different information depending on how you create it.

When you create a QuickReport while displaying the Customer:Job list, a customer register, sales form, or payment, it shows the estimates, sales forms, statement charges, and payments related to the selected customer for the current month to date.

12/15/98			Customer QuickReport				
			December 1 - 15, 1998				
Type	Date	Num	Memo	Account	Clr	Split	Amount
Pretell Real Estate							
155 Wilks Blvd.							
▶ Payment	12/03/98	87521		Undeposited Funds	✓	Accounts Re...	10,000.00 ◀
Invoice	12/10/98	25		Accounts Receiva...		-SPLIT-	1,715.00
Payment	12/11/98	8602		Undeposited Funds	✓	Accounts Re...	1,200.00

Transactions are grouped by job for the selected customer. You can change the date range of the report by choosing a different date range from the Dates drop-down list.

When you create a QuickReport while displaying the accounts receivable (or A/R) register, it shows all transactions that affect what the selected customer owes you for the selected job. The QuickReport indicates which transactions are paid. For unpaid sales transactions and unapplied payments and credits, the report shows both the open balance and the original amount. The total open balance is what the customer owes for the job. (The report does not include estimates or cash sales because they do not affect what the customer owes you.)

A QuickReport for a customer in the A/R register displays all invoices (or statement charges), credit memos, and payments for the customer.

You can make columns wider to see more detail. Just drag the diamond symbol to the right.

	12/15/03			Register QuickReport All Transactions				
	Type	Date	Num	Memo	Account	Paid	Open Balance	Amount
	Pretell Real Estate							
	155 Wilks Blvd.							
▶	Invoice	10/10/2003	3		Accounts Receiva...	Unpaid	2,239.00	3,439.00 ◀
	Invoice	10/26/2003	7		Accounts Receiva...	Paid		2,320.00
	Invoice	10/30/2003	9		Accounts Receiva...	Paid		4,750.00
	Payment	10/30/2003	5874		Accounts Receiva...	Paid		-2,320.00
	Payment	11/05/2003			Accounts Receiva...	Paid		-4,750.00
	Invoice	11/15/2003	12		Accounts Receiva...	Unpaid	1,072.50	1,072.50
	Invoice	11/20/2003	15		Accounts Receiva...	Paid		15,435.00
	Invoice	11/25/2003	FC 100	Finance Cha...	Accounts Receiva...	Unpaid	5.65	5.65
	Payment	11/25/2003	87521		Accounts Receiva...	Paid		-10,000.00
	Payment	11/25/2003	15785		Accounts Receiva...	Paid		-7,150.00
	Invoice	12/10/2003	25		Accounts Receiva...	Paid		1,715.00
	Payment	12/11/2003	8602		Accounts Receiva...	Paid		-1,200.00
	Total 155 Wilks Blvd.						3,317.15	3,317.15
	Total Pretell Real Estate						3,317.15	3,317.15
	TOTAL						**3,317.15**	**3,317.15**

To learn about...	Search the Help index for...
Creating a QuickReport for a customer or job	customers, reports about

Exactly how much do my customers owe me?

The customer open balance report shows all open invoices, statement charges, and unapplied credits related to a particular customer. The open balance report also shows the due date, the open balance, and the original amount of the invoice or statement charge. The total equals the customer's balance.

12/15/98				Customer Open Balance All Transactions			
Type	Date	Num	Memo	Due Date	Open Balance	Amount	
Pretell Real Estate							
155 Wilks Blvd.							
▶ Invoice	10/10/98	3		11/09/98	2,239.00	3,439.00 ◀	
Invoice	11/15/98	12		12/15/98	1,072.50	1,072.50	
Invoice	11/20/98	15		12/20/98	7,150.00	15,435.00	
Invoice	11/25/98	FC 100	Finance Cha...	11/25/98	5.65	5.65	
Total 155 Wilks Blvd.					10,467.15	19,952.15	
Total Pretell Real Estate					10,467.15	19,952.15	
TOTAL					**10,467.15**	**19,952.15**	

To learn about...	Search the Help index for...
Creating a customer open balance report	customers, reports about

Can I see a breakdown of all income and expenses for a job?

The profit & loss by job report shows income and expenses by customer and job, summarized by income and expense account.

This report is like the standard profit and loss statement (page 18) except that it has a separate column for each job and for all jobs for each customer. You can restrict the report to a single job by filtering for that job.

If you do payroll, the profit & loss by job report always includes expenses for salary and hourly wages by job. It includes expenses for employer-paid taxes, benefits, commissions, and additions prorated by job only if the following conditions were true when the paychecks were recorded:

- The payroll preference for reporting by job was on.
- (For a benefit, commission, or addition) The payroll item was set up with the **Track Expenses by Job** option selected.

Tip: If you get reimbursed for job expenses, do you want to see reimbursement income in a separate income account? See "Setting up to track reimbursed expenses as income" on page 180.

In QuickBooks Pro only, two reports compare costs and revenues for jobs.

- The job profitability summary report shows the total cost, total revenue, and difference, subtotaled by customer and job.
- The job profitability detail report shows the costs, revenues, and difference for one customer or job, subtotaled by item type and item. The report is most useful if you invoice for subcontracted services and for items purchased for a specific job. However, the report includes costs and revenues not associated with any item.

To learn about...	Search the Help index for...
Creating one of the following reports: ■ Profit & loss by job ■ Job profitability summary ■ Job profitability detail	jobs, reports about

Which billable costs have I not yet charged for?

If you make expenses or items billable to a customer or job on bills, credit card charges, or checks, the unbilled costs by job report shows which costs are still unbilled.

12/15/98		Unbilled Costs by Job All Transactions				
Type	Date	Source Name	Memo	Account	Billing Status	Amount
Abercrombie, Kristy						
Remodel Bathroom						
Bill	09/30/98	Sloan Roofing	Opening Balan...	Uncategorized Exp...	Unbilled	500.00
Total Remodel Bathroom						500.00
Total Abercrombie, Kristy						500.00
Cook, Brian						
Kitchen						
Change Order #1						
Bill	10/01/98	McClain Appliances	Microwave an...	Job Materials	Unbilled	385.00
Bill	10/01/98	McClain Appliances	Trash compac...	Job Materials	Unbilled	195.00
Bill	10/01/98	McClain Appliances	Gargage dispo...	Job Materials	Unbilled	95.00
Bill	10/08/98	Middlefield Drywall	Install drywall	Subcontractors	Unbilled	850.00
Bill	10/15/98	Wheeler's Tile Etc.	Install tile or co...	Subcontractors	Unbilled	1,200.00
Bill	10/27/98	Washuta & Son Pain...	Painting	Subcontractors	Unbilled	360.00
Bill	11/03/98	Lew Plumbing	Plumbing	Subcontractors	Unbilled	800.00
Bill	11/05/98	Washuta & Son Pain...	Painting	Subcontractors	Unbilled	300.00
Total Change Order #1						4,185.00

To learn about...	Search the Help index for...
Creating an unbilled costs by job report	unbilled costs report

Which items are still on order for a customer or job?

If you specify customers and jobs on purchase orders, you can use the open purchase orders by job report to find out which items are still on order for your customer and jobs. This report includes the vendor name and delivery date for the items.

To learn about...	Search the Help index for...
Creating an open purchase orders by job report	purchase orders, reports about

Other reports by customer and job

Many other reports are broken down by customer and job. You can use these reports to get specific information about your customers.

For illustrations of graphs and reports about customers whose account balances are past due, see "Are my customers paying me on time?" on page 208.

Remember, you can filter a report to restrict it to a specific kind of information.

For example, Terry wants to see a list of all payments from one customer. She starts with a customer balance detail report (an A/R report). Then she filters the report for the name of the customer and for the payment transaction type. The filtered report shows all payments from this customer, subtotaled by job. (For more information about report filters, see "Changing the scope of the information in the report" on page 402.

If she wants to know how a particular payment was applied, she can double-click the payment on the report to QuickZoom to the Receive Payments window.

To learn about...	Search the Help index for...
Creating a report by customer and job	customers, reports about
Answers to questions about job reports (QuickBooks Pro only)	jobs, reports about
Changing the scope of a report	filtering reports

CHAPTER 11

Tracking income

How QuickBooks can track your income	171
Setting up for tracking sales	178
Tracking sales and customer payments	182
Getting information about sales and what people owe you	205

> # How should I track the money my business brings in?

It depends on your business and when your customers pay you.

If you provide services or sell products, you should be tracking this income using one of QuickBooks many ways to track sales.

Note: In QuickBooks, "sales" is a broad term. It refers to any business action that generates income in exchange for services or products, even if you don't think of what you do as selling. For example, a psychologist with patients, a graphic designer with clients, and a roofing contractor with customers all would track sales in QuickBooks.

On the other hand, if your income is from commissions you receive from a third party or voluntary contributions from the public, you probably don't need to use any of the sales features in QuickBooks. You can simply record the money you receive as a deposit into your bank account and assign an appropriate income account to track the income. See "Receiving payments and making deposits" on page 105.

Scan the first section of this chapter. If the steps and concepts aren't relevant to you, skip the rest of the chapter.

How do I track the money my business earns?

- Your nonprofit receives contributions.
- Or, you receive commissions from a third party.
- Or, you always receive payment in full at time of service or sale, and you do not want to track sales.

Record as a deposit.
See "Receiving payments and making deposits" on page 105.

- You want to track what was sold or provided.
- Or, you receive payment for statements or invoices sent previously.
- Or, you receive advance payments toward future services or sales.

Use the QuickBooks sales feature.

How QuickBooks can track your income

item

A service you provide or a product you sell, which you set up on your Item list. In addition, you can have items for miscellaneous charges and for various calculations on your sales forms.

customer

Any person or business that pays you for your services or products. You may commonly use a different term, such as *client* or *job*.

This section guides you through various QuickBooks options for tracking business income. Use the ones that are right for your business.

If your customers pay in full at time of service or sale	171
If your customers owe you money or pay in advance	172
Should I record estimates?	177

For any particular transaction, record it only once in QuickBooks, or you will duplicate the income. You can use different methods for different situations.

All the options (except depositing directly into your checking account) require that you enter items from your Item list. It is through the items that you keep track of which income account or accounts each sale affects. For a discussion of items, please read Chapter 9, *Items—your services, products, and more*, beginning on page 113.

If your customers pay in full at time of service or sale

If your customers pay in full at the time they receive your service or product, then you don't have to track how much people owe you. Your main decisions are:

- Should you keep track of each sale (what was sold, the quantity—if applicable—and the rate or price)?

    If you want QuickBooks to track each sale, calculate its sales tax, or print a receipt for the sale, then use cash sales receipts in QuickBooks (see page 182).

- Should you track a daily summary of sales in QuickBooks?

    If you need a summary to keep track of sales income and sales tax owed, but you have another means of calculating sales tax on single sales, then summarize daily sales on a cash sales receipt in QuickBooks (see page 182). You would summarize *instead of* entering individual cash sales receipts.

- Should you not track sales in QuickBooks at all but simply record a deposit of the money received?

    When you record the deposit, you can assign an income account for this type of income. See "Receiving payments and making deposits" on page 105.

If customers pay in advance, either in part or in full, you should not use the cash sales receipt. A cash sale requires full payment at the time you record the sale.

If your customers owe you money or pay in advance

accounts receivable

The record of money owed to a business, that is, outstanding invoices or statement charges for which the business has not received payment. Accounts receivable is called A/R for short. (Even though the word *accounts* is plural,

QuickBooks uses a single account on the chart of accounts to track all the money that different people owe you.)

If your customers owe you money at the time you perform your service or provide your product, you need to track how much they owe you—your *accounts receivable,* also called A/R.

If you receive payments in advance, you need to track how much your customers still owe at the time of the sale.

QuickBooks offers two different ways to record a sale for which you receive any payments at another time:

- Invoices
- Statement charges

In both cases, you will be able to track what you sold and what the customer owes you.

For a given business, it's usually easier to use invoices exclusively or statement charges exclusively, rather than both. Read the following to determine which method is right for your business.

When to use invoices

In QuickBooks, an *invoice* is a form on which you record details about a sale to a customer who owes you money. You may use the term *bill* or *statement*; however, in QuickBooks these terms mean other things. (If you have received full payment at the time of sale, you should record a cash sale instead of an invoice. See "Cash sales" on page 182.)

Most businesses use invoices. An invoice lists the services you are providing or the products you are selling. It also shows the quantity and price or rate of each item (unless you choose an invoice design that does not show them).

You should use invoices if you do any of the following:

- Collect sales tax, apply discounts, or use any other item that is calculated as a percentage of charges.
- Write detailed, multiple-line descriptions of services or products.

- Bill at the time of a sale or the completion of a job, rather than at a regular interval.
- Group and total certain types of billings together, for example, all services or all reimbursable expenses. (If you track billable time and want to summarize work done on different days, you will need to be able to group.)
- Create estimates (or proposals) that, when accepted, you want to turn into an invoice (or a series of invoices) based on the estimate.
- Invoice in installments against a purchase order with a preset total.

Examples of businesses likely to use invoices include general contractors, consultants, and mail-order firms.

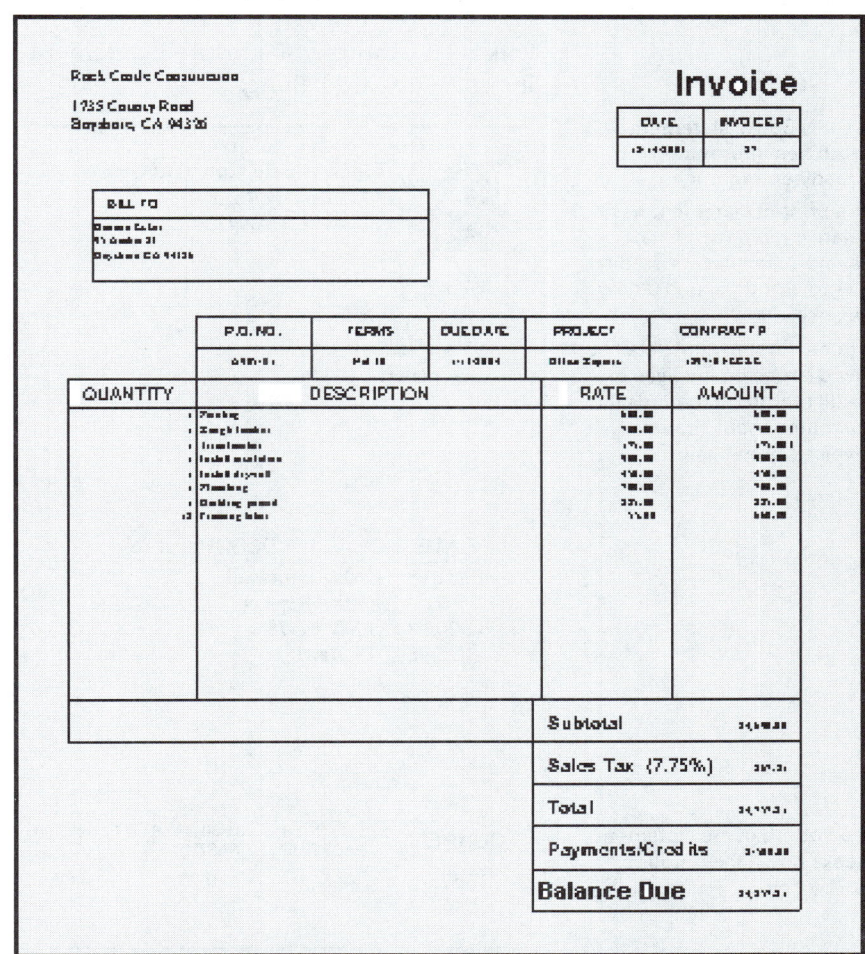

This printed invoice lists each item with its quantity, its rate, and its amount.

You can customize an invoice to print what you want, such as adding fields for Payments/Credits and Balance Due. See Chapter 7, *Creating a professional image,* beginning on page 77.

To learn about creating invoices, see "Invoices" on page 185.

If you send invoices and your customers need to know how much they owe in total, you can send *reminder statements*. These statements show the previous balance, list new invoice amounts, and show payments received (including advance payments) and the new balance. The details about the sales are only on the invoices, not on the statements, so you would have to send invoices as well as statements.

Tip: **If you prefer to mail a collection letter and you have Microsoft Word 97 (or higher), QuickBooks Pro provides a variety of customizable letters.** You can show overdue amounts without having to retype your QuickBooks data. For more information, see "Writing letters" on page 441.

This is an example of a printed statement sent to remind a customer about an unpaid balance.

A QuickBooks statement combines information already entered.

The printed statement has a balance forward, a list of payment, invoice, or credit memo amounts, and a new balance.

It does not show the detail of any charges on invoices or credit memos. It reminds the customer about charges invoiced previously.

Rock Castle Construction
1735 County Road
Bayshore, CA 94326

Statement

DATE: 11/30/98

BILL TO
Deanna Ecker
95 Amber St
Bayshore CA 94326

AMOUNT DUE	AMOUNT ENC.
$5,226.11	

DATE	DESCRIPTION	AMOUNT	BALANCE
10/31/98	Balance forward		1,468.30
	Office Repairs-		
11/20/98	PMT #9478	-1,000.00	468.30
11/25/98	INV #27	4,757.81	5,226.11

The bottom of the statement breaks down the amount due by date.

CURRENT	1-30 DAYS PAST DUE	31-60 DAYS PAST DUE	61-90 DAYS PAST DUE	OVER 90 DAYS PAST	AMOUNT DUE
4,757.81	468.30	0.00	0.00	0.00	$5,226.11

To learn about printing statements, see "Statements" on page 188.

When to use statement charges and billing statements

QuickBooks has an alternative to invoices, called *statement charges*. You enter statement charges one by one, as you perform the services for the customer.

If your charges do not require invoices (see "When to use invoices" on page 172), then statement charges are simpler to record. Statement charges are ideal if you want to accumulate charges before requesting payment, or if you assess a regular monthly charge.

Later, you print a *billing statement* that shows the previous balance, details of all new charges, payments received, and the new balance. The charges become due on or after the statement date, according to the customer's terms.

Here is what a printed billing statement might look like:

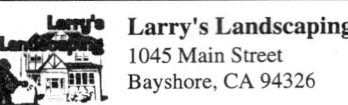

Larry's Landscaping
1045 Main Street
Bayshore, CA 94326

Statement

DATE
11/30/98

BILL TO
Middlefield Elementary School
100 Middlefield Blvd
Middlefield CA 94352

AMOUNT DUE	AMOUNT ENC.
$725.00	

DATE	DESCRIPTION	QTY	RATE	AMOUNT	BALANCE
10/31/98	Balance forward				330.00
11/05/98	Weekly gardening service	1	110.00	110.00	440.00
11/12/98	Weekly gardening service	1	110.00	110.00	550.00
11/12/98	Flats of annuals	6	35.00	210.00	760.00
11/12/98	Pest control service	1	75.00	75.00	835.00
11/19/98	Weekly gardening service	1	110.00	110.00	945.00
11/21/98	PMT			-330.00	615.00
11/27/98	Weekly gardening service	1	110.00	110.00	725.00

CURRENT	1-30 DAYS PAST DUE	31-60 DAYS PAST DUE	61-90 DAYS PAST DUE	OVER 90 DAYS PAST	AMOUNT DUE
725.00	0.00	0.00	0.00	0.00	$725.00

If you have entered statement charges dated within the period of the statement, the statement lists the date, description, and amount of each charge.

You can customize your statements to add a field for due date and columns for quantity and rate, if appropriate.

The bottom of the statement breaks down the amount due by date.

Billing statements (that is, statements that show information about new charges) are appropriate if you want to send monthly statements that show the detail of new charges as well as the previous balance and payments received.

(A QuickBooks statement becomes a billing statement when there are new statement charges for the customer. It becomes a reminder statement when there are only invoices—or only old statement charges—for the customer.)

To learn about creating statement charges, see "Statement charges" on page 187. To learn about printing billing statements, see "Statements" on page 188.

Tip: **QuickBooks can enter regular monthly fees automatically.** You can set up statement charges for automatic monthly entry (or for you to be reminded to enter them yourself). See "Repeating similar transactions" on page 200.

Examples of businesses that could use statement charges and billing statements include medical and dental practices, property management companies, and organizations assess monthly fees.

Should I record estimates?

QuickBooks Pro allows you to record estimates. You can prepare an estimate, using items from the same Item list you use to record sales.

Bids and proposals

The most obvious use for QuickBooks estimates is to prepare a proposal of work you can do and products or materials you can provide.

progress invoice

One of a series of invoices all based on the same estimate for the same job. Use progress invoices when you want to invoice for the job in phases—that is, by milestone or by percentage complete.

QuickBooks keeps track of the amount you have already invoiced and the amount not yet invoiced.

Later, if the proposal is accepted, you can turn the estimate into a single invoice or a series of *progress invoices* (if you invoice in phases).

Invoicing in phases

Progress invoicing (also called *progress billing* or *partial billing*) is invoicing in phases for the same job, based on the same estimate. When you create a progress invoice from an existing estimate, you can choose from among the following:

- Invoice for the entire estimate (100%).
- Invoice for a percentage of the entire estimate.
- Invoice for selected items or for different percentages of each item.

Tip: **Use estimates and progress invoices if you invoice in phases against a purchase order with a preset amount.** For example, if you receive a purchase order (P.O.) for a large amount of work and then invoice in phases, enter an estimate for the P.O. (even if you don't have to submit an estimate). Then create progress invoices for your work against the P.O.

On the other hand, if you send a series of invoices all based on actual time and costs, you should not use progress invoices. Instead, you should transfer the time and costs directly to each new invoice.

To learn how to prepare estimates and turn estimates into invoices, see "Estimates and proposals" on page 184 and "Invoices" on page 185. To learn about invoicing for actual time and costs, see "Charging for actual time and costs" on page 193.

Setting up for tracking sales

To record sales, you must set up items on your Item list. Remember, you can have items for services as well as for products or materials.

If you collect sales tax, you set up your sales tax by having one or more sales tax items on your Item list.

You don't need to set up customers on your Customer:Job list if all your sales are cash sales—that is, if people never owe you money. But if customers do owe you money, you'll need to set them up.

QuickBooks provides preset designs for sales forms that you can print on plain paper, letterhead, or preprinted forms purchased from Intuit. But you can customize both the contents and the layout to get the form you want.

If you assess a finance charge for overdue payments, you can set it up with your usual rate.

Finally, there are preferences you can set for such choices as whether to use estimates, do progress invoicing, or automatically apply payments to the oldest invoices first.

Refer to the following for tracking sales of services or products in QuickBooks.

What to set up	Comments	Search the Help index for...
Items for services, products, other charges, or sales tax that are relevant to your business	See Chapter 9, *Items—your services, products, and more,* beginning on page 113.	- items, services - items, non-inventory parts - items, inventory - items, miscellaneous charges - items, sales tax
Names and information about customers that do not pay at the time they receive the service or product	See Chapter 10, *Customers and jobs,* beginning on page 141.	customers, adding new
Names and information about the individual jobs for customers (optional)	See Chapter 10, *Customers and jobs,* beginning on page 141.	jobs, adding new
Customized columns, fields, or layout for forms you print: estimates, invoices, cash sales receipts, credit memos, statements (optional)	You can have alternative versions of the same type of form. See Chapter 7, *Creating a professional image,* beginning on page 77.	entries under: customizing forms
Company-wide preferences for sales (for example, how to apply payments, whether to track reimbursed expenses as income) (optional)	Only the QuickBooks Administrator can change company-wide preferences.	sales, preferences
Company-wide preferences for estimates (for example, whether to use estimates, whether to use progress invoicing) (optional, available only in QuickBooks Pro)	Only the QuickBooks Administrator can change company-wide preferences.	estimates, preferences for
Finance charges for overdue invoices or statements (optional)	Finance charges appear on printed statements.	finance charges, setting up for

Setting up to track reimbursed expenses as income

reimbursed expenses

Expenses you have incurred on behalf of a customer, and for which you request reimbursement.

If you request reimbursement from your customers for expenses you incur on their behalf, and you want this income from reimbursed expenses to show up on profit and loss statements, you need to follow the steps in the next section to track reimbursable expenses as income. Unless you do the following setup, the reimbursed expense will cancel the original expense and won't show up on profit and loss statements at all.

You may want to do this if reimbursable expenses are a significant portion of your business, such as a construction or remodeling business, so that your profit and loss statement accurately reflects the portion of total sales that these reimbursable expenses comprise.

For example, Mary purchases an antique sink for $100 for a customer's home that she is remodeling. She charges the customer an additional $25 for the sink. Her profit and loss statement shows the following, depending on whether or not she tracks reimbursable expenses as income.

Track reimbursable expenses as income	Do not track reimbursable expenses as income
Income $125	Income..........$25
Expense $100	------------------
------------------	Net Profit......$25
Net Profit.....$ 25	

In both QuickBooks and QuickBooks Pro

In both products, you can make direct expenses billable—that is, you record an expense account and dollar amount for a purchase, assign a customer (and job), and mark the expense as billable. Then you can transfer the expense to an invoice. (See "Charging for actual time and costs" on page 193.)

If you want to have separate accounts for the expense and for the income for the reimbursed expense, do the following:

1 Turn on the "Track reimbursed expenses as income" preference in the Sales & Customer preferences.

2 After turning on the preference, edit the expense accounts you plan to use for reimbursable expenses. In the Edit Account window, you can now select an income account to use for the reimbursement.

Note that you must take *both* actions to track an expense and your customer's reimbursement for the expense in separate accounts.

In QuickBooks Pro only

In addition, in QuickBooks Pro only, you can use items for any expenses associated with a particular customer or job. For example, you can have an item for a subcontracted service, an object purchased for a customer, or a charge such as shipping.

The advantage of setting up items for reimbursement is that you can use them on estimates and purchase orders. Also, you can use them to calculate a total from a quantity and rate or price.

When you set up an item for reimbursement in QuickBooks Pro, you should mark the checkbox that allows you to track purchases and sales separately. When you record the purchase of the item, you mark the item as billable to the customer or job. Later, you can transfer the billable item to an invoice. (See "Charging for actual time and costs" on page 193.)

In QuickBooks, on the other hand, you cannot make items billable when recording purchases.

> **Note:** **Invoicing for reimbursable expenses.** For information about invoicing for reimbursable expenses in QuickBooks, see "Reimbursable expenses in QuickBooks" on page 194. For information on invoicing for reimbursable expenses in QuickBooks Pro, see "Reimbursable time and costs in QuickBooks Pro" on page 195.

To learn about...	Search the Help index for...
Turning on the preference for tracking reimbursed expenses as income	sales, preferences
Setting up items in QuickBooks Pro for reimbursable expenses	■ items, reimbursable ■ subcontractors, service items for

Tracking sales and customer payments

This section describes the different options for tracking sales, recording payments, and tracking what customers owe you.

How to track sales and payments	**182**
Charging for actual time and costs	**193**
Making changes while tracking sales	**198**
Repeating similar transactions	**200**
Managing what customers owe you	**201**

If you are not sure which options are best for your business, see "How QuickBooks can track your income" on page 171.

How to track sales and payments

Cash sales

To record a sale in which the customer pays in full and doesn't owe you money, you should record a cash sales receipt (which you can print if you want).

You do not have to receive payment in cash in order to record a cash sales receipt. It works equally well with a payment by check, credit card, or debit card. All that matters is that you have received payment for the sale, so you need to record the payment as well as the sale.

Recording a cash sales receipt does the following:

- It tracks what you sold (that is, the service or product) so you can analyze your sales on reports and graphs and keep track of inventory (if your business sells inventory).

- It tracks the sales tax, if any, you collected and increases what you owe for sales tax.

- It either deposits the amount from the sale in your bank account or records the money with other undeposited funds. (You specify in the window what QuickBooks should do with the money.)

If all you want is a summary of the total services or products for a day or week, you can enter the summary directly on the cash sales receipt form. (If you don't need to track the services or products, and you don't collect sales tax, don't use a cash sales receipt. Simply enter the payments as a deposit into your checking account.)

To record what you sold and received full payment for, use the Enter Cash Sales window.

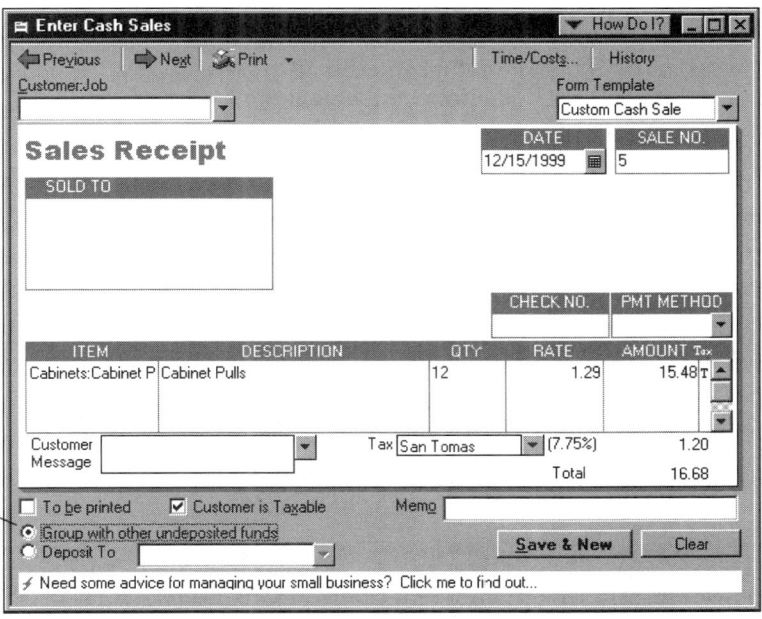

The Customer:Job field can be blank on a cash sales receipt.

Specify where to record the proceeds from the sale:

- Group with other undeposited funds (for deposit later).
- Or, deposit directly in the account specified.

The cash sales receipt does not require a customer name. You can leave it blank or use a generic name such as "Counter Sales," "Cash Customer," or "Daily Sales Summary."

payment item

A type of item on your Item list. You can set up a different payment item for each method of payment.

Use payment items on cash sales receipts only when you need to show two or more kinds of payments on the same receipt.

You enter a sale or summary of sales by entering one or more items from your Item list. If the items are taxable, QuickBooks calculates the correct sales tax and adds it to your sales tax liability.

You can print the form as a receipt to give to the customer if you wish.

If a summary cash sales receipt covers payment by more than one method (for example, checks and credit card charges), you can show the breakdown by using a different payment item for each method. (Otherwise, you don't have to enter any payment items; QuickBooks knows you have received payment.)

To learn about...	Search the Help index for...
Creating a cash sales receipt to record both a sale and its payment	cash sales
Creating a daily sales summary form that you can fill in with quantities and amounts	sales, summary
Tracking sales tax collected on cash sales	• sales tax, applying to sales • sales tax, tracking how much you owe
Tracking daily overages or shortages	overages
Printing a cash sales receipt	receipts

Estimates and proposals

In QuickBooks Pro, you create estimates or proposals using the Create Estimates window.

The estimate window displays the cost of each item and the markup, but only the customer's price prints (unless you customize your estimates differently).

To create an invoice based on this estimate, click Create Invoice.

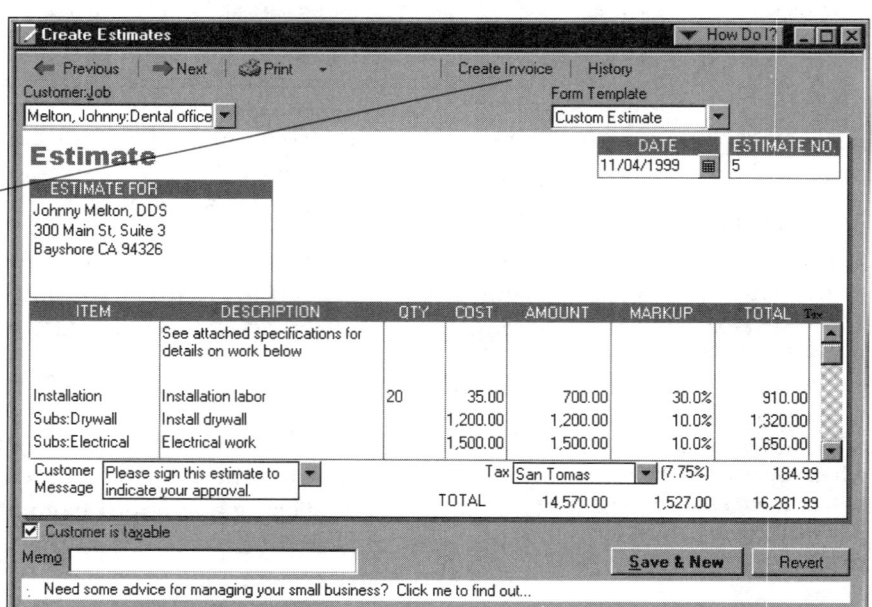

Because estimates represent only potential sales, they do not affect any income accounts or any account balances.

CHAPTER 11 Tracking income

QuickBooks Pro allows only one estimate for each job, or for each customer that does not have any jobs.

Tip: **To create alternative proposals for the same job, set up a separate job for each proposal.** For example, call them Family Room 1, Family Room 2, and Family Room 3. If one is accepted, you can delete the other two estimates and their jobs, and then rename the remaining job.

To learn about...	Search the Help index for...
Preparing estimates (or proposals) (Pro only)	estimates, creating
Marking up the cost of items on estimates (Pro only)	estimates, markups on
Printing an estimate (Pro only)	estimates, printing
Displaying a list of estimates (Pro only)	estimates, list of

Invoices

You create invoices using the Create Invoices window. On the other hand, if you already have an estimate for the same customer or job, you can create an invoice directly from the estimate.

This invoice design is based on the Intuit Service Invoice template, one of several preset invoice design templates you can choose.

You can also create your own custom design. See Chapter 7, *Creating a professional image*, beginning on page 77.

Some fields shown here do not print. You can customize what displays onscreen and what prints.

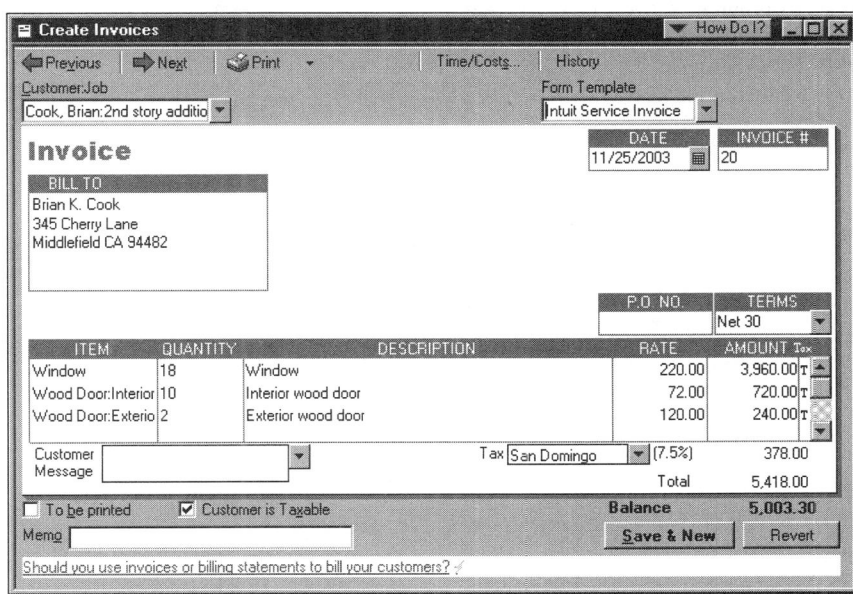

Tracking sales and customer payments | 185

Note: **You cannot have more than one job on a single invoice.** If you create a job for a customer (so you can track multiple jobs for the customer separately), then you should associate each sale with both the customer name and the job name. If you do simultaneous jobs for a customer and want to present the customer with detail for all the jobs on a single statement, consider using statement charges *instead of* invoices. See "Statement charges" on page 187.

In QuickBooks Pro, if you are set up to create progress invoices from an estimate, you can display and print additional detail about the estimate and the previous invoices based on the same estimate.

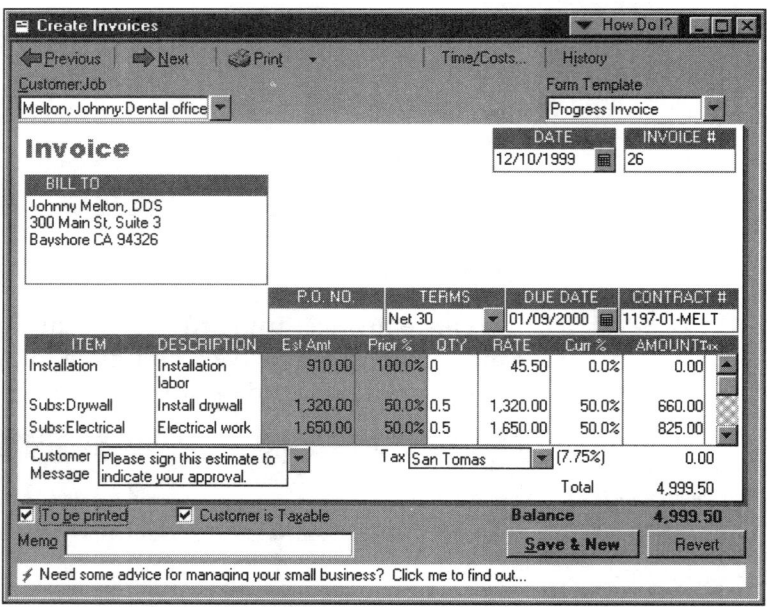

A progress invoice has columns that compare the estimate amounts with the amounts previously invoiced and the amount on the current invoice.

You can customize what displays and what prints on your progress invoices.

When you create a progress invoice from an estimate, you can base it on a percentage of the estimate or on selected items (or different percentages).

In his contracting business, Frank invoices for only 90% at the completion of a job. He invoices for the final 10% (the retainage) later.

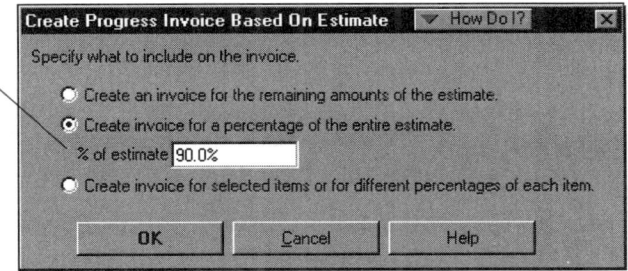

To learn about...	Search the Help index for...
Creating an invoice from an accepted estimate (QuickBooks Pro only)	invoices, basing on estimates
Invoicing in phases from a single estimate (QuickBooks Pro only)	progress invoicing
Preparing invoices that are not based on an estimate	invoices, creating
Adding billable time or costs to an invoice	expenses, billing to a customer
Adjusting the sales tax QuickBooks calculates on an estimate or invoice	sales tax, applying to sales
Recording back-ordered items	pending sales
Printing one or more invoices	invoices, printing
Displaying a register that shows all invoices	accounts receivable, register
Displaying a register that shows all invoices, statement charges, or payments for a particular customer or job	customers, registers for

Statement charges

You enter statement charges for a customer and job directly in a register that looks like a checkbook register. The register shows previous statement charges and payments, as well as the current balance, for the customer or job.

Tracking sales and customer payments | 187

If you choose a job name as well as a customer name in the **Customer:Job** field, the register shows sales transactions for that job alone.

QuickBooks fills in the Billed Date and Due Date after you print a statement that includes the charge.

You enter a new statement charge on the register's first blank line.

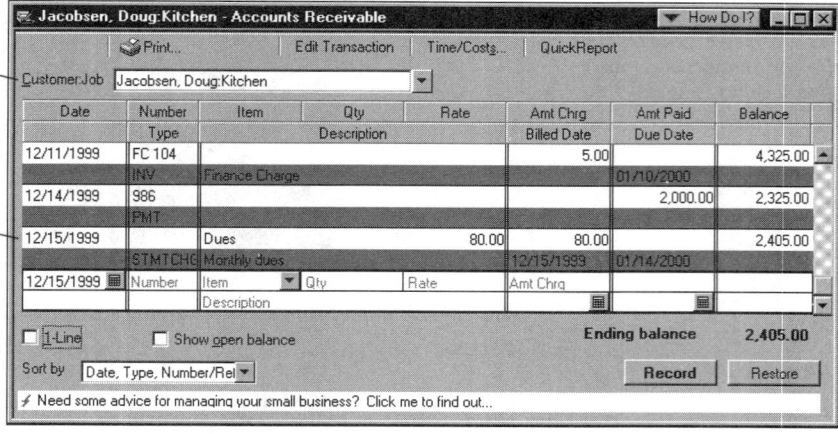

To learn about...	Search the Help index for...
Recording individual charges that will be listed on a statement	statements, entering charges

Statements

A QuickBooks statement prints information already recorded. You cannot edit what is on a statement. A statement covers a time period and shows the previous balance, new activity, and the new balance.

If you record statement charges, the statement contains the date, description, and amount of each charge. And, if you customize your statement to add columns for quantity and rate, the statement has the quantity and rate of each charge. When you print the statement, QuickBooks sets the date of expected payment for each new statement charge (based on the payment terms you set up for the customer).

On the other hand, if you record invoices, the statement contains only the date, invoice number, and total for each invoice.

- A *billing statement* is a statement that shows new statement charges. See page 176 for an example.

- A *reminder statement* is a statement that shows only the previous and new balances and the dates and amounts of recent payments, invoices, and credit memos. See page 174 for an example.

Tip: Do people pay you regularly, without receiving statements? For example, do you have to keep track of who has paid the monthly condo fee? You can do this by recording statement charges and printing statements but not sending them. You must print the statement in order to make QuickBooks set the date for when the charges on it are due.

To learn about...	Search the Help index for...
Creating, previewing, and printing statements	statements, printing

Receiving and depositing payments

The Receive Payments window is used to record payments and specify what they are for. You need to use it not only when you have actually received payment for invoices or statements but also when you need to apply any credit to any charge or refund for a customer.

If you track jobs as well as customers, you must choose both the customer name and job name in the **Customer:Job** field.

The Receive Payments window shows transactions for only one job.

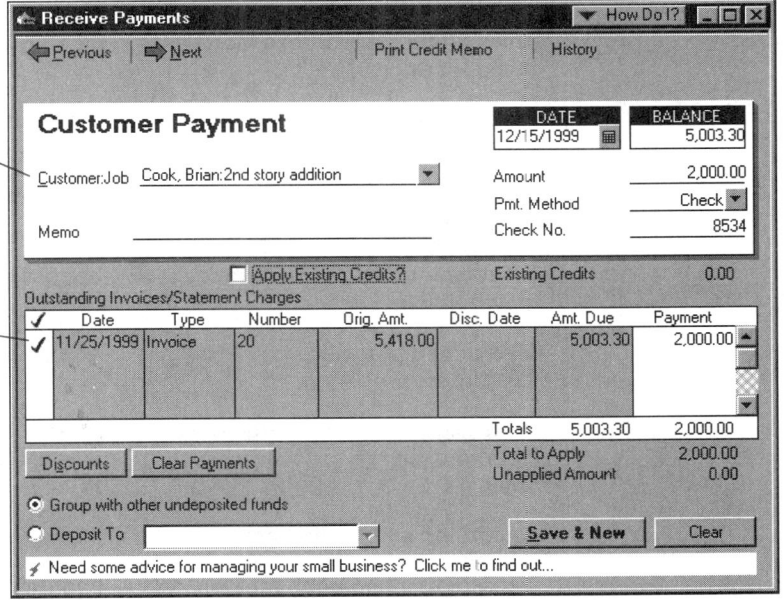

The checkmark next to the invoice tells QuickBooks to apply the payment to the invoice.

QuickBooks has a preference that determines whether or not it should automatically apply payments to the oldest invoices or charges first.

If you track separate jobs for customers, you can apply a payment to only one job at a time.

If one payment check covers several jobs, you must apply the amount for each job separately. (To deposit all the parts of the payment in a single deposit to your bank account, specify that each part be deposited with other undeposited funds.)

If you use the QuickBooks Merchant Account Service to authorize credit card payments, choose Accept Credit Card Payment from the Customers menu and then choose Process Credit Card Payments to authorize and record a transaction.

To indicate that you are keeping the payment in a "cash drawer" until you are ready to deposit it, choose "Group with other undeposited funds." To identify similar types of payments so you can deposit them all together, use the **Pmt. Method** field to label the payment.

To learn about...	Search the Help index for...
Recording customer payments received and applying them to outstanding invoices or statement charges	■ receiving payments, on invoices ■ receiving payments, on statements
Accepting credit card payments through the QuickBooks Merchant Account Service	merchant account service
Applying a discount for early payment	discounts, for early customer payments
Depositing undeposited customer payments	deposits, bank or checking account
Printing a list of the customer payments in a deposit	deposit slips
Handling a bounced check from a customer	bounced checks
Assessing a finance charge or late payment charge for overdue payment	finance charges, assessing on overdue invoices and statements
Recording an overpayment	overpayments
Recording a bad debt after a customer has failed to make payment	bad debts

Down payments, advance deposits, and retainers

If you receive payment before performing a service or providing a product, the way to track the payment depends on your type of business.

To learn about...	Search the Help index for...
Recording down payments received in advance of a sale	down payments
Recording and applying retainers (other than legal retainers)	retainers
Recording and applying legal retainers	law firms (handling retainers, client monies, and trust accounts)

Returns and refunds

To record the return of an item you sold, fill in the Create Credit Memos/Refunds window. Items on a credit memo reduce the sales income for those items.

In the Create Credit Memos/Refunds window, you can:

- Record the return of items.
- Click Refund to create a refund check to pay a customer to whom you owe money.

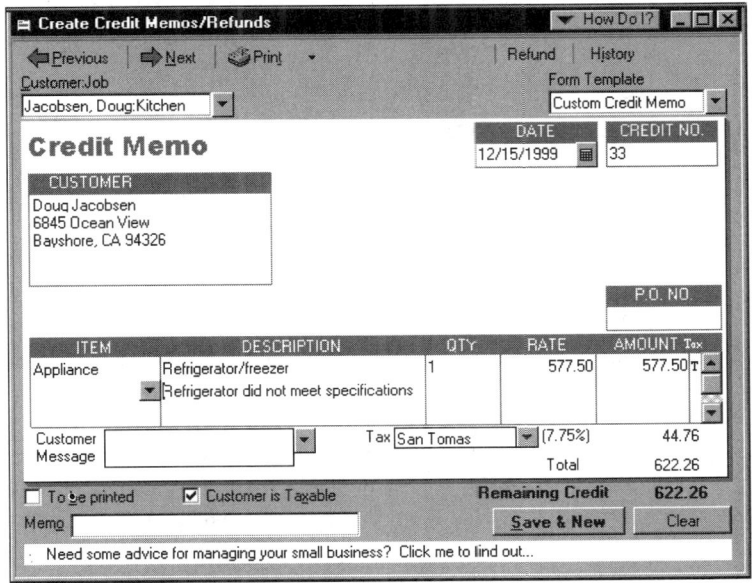

A credit memo reduces what the customer owes you. If the customer has already paid in full, the credit memo makes the customer's balance negative in the Customer:Job window. That is, you now owe the customer money.

Tip: **If there are no returned items (for example, if a customer simply overpays), you don't need to create a credit memo.** If you recorded a payment that was higher than what the customer owed, you already owe the customer money.

If you owe a customer money either as a result of a credit memo or an overpayment, you can issue a refund check.

To create a refund check, click Refund in the Create Credit Memos/Refunds window. QuickBooks fills out a refund check for you to record and print.

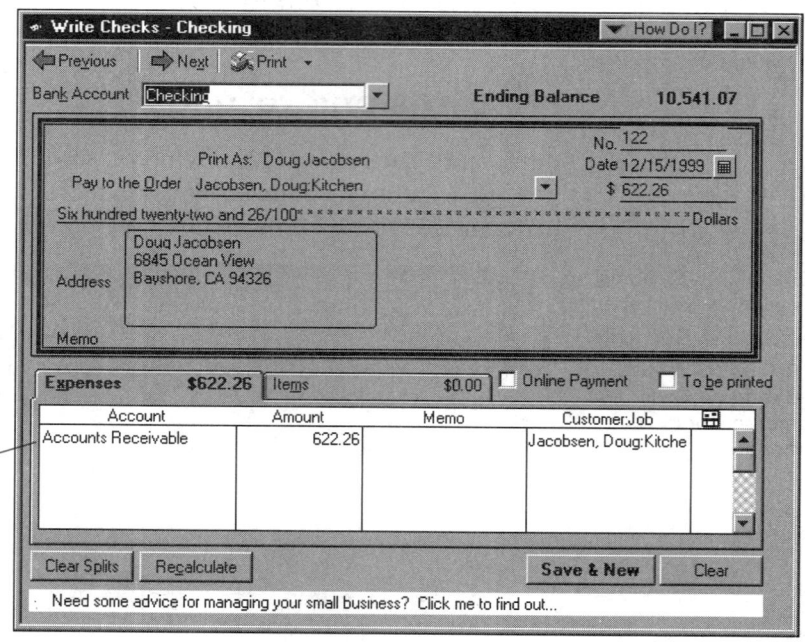

When you click Refund in the Create Credit Memos/Refunds window, QuickBooks fills in the Write Checks window with information from the credit memo.

A refund to a customer is assigned to the Accounts Receivable account, so that it can increase the customer's negative balance to zero.

If the customer paid by credit card and you issued a credit card refund, you can enter a payment item with a negative amount right on the credit memo for the refund. Then the credit memo has a zero total. The negative payment item reduces the balance of the bank (or Undeposited Funds) account you associated with the payment item.

If the customer owes you money (for the same job, if you track jobs) after you record a credit memo, simply wait until you receive a payment from the customer. Then, in the Receive Payments window, apply the new payment to the credit memo as well as to the appropriate invoices or statement charges.

To learn about...	Search the Help index for...
Recording returned items	credit memos, creating
Writing a refund check	refunds
Recording credit card refunds	refunds

Charging for actual time and costs

Charging your customer for the actual time and costs for a job is a two-step process:

1 Track the time and costs, assigning them to the specific job.

2 Transfer the time and costs to a sales form (with or without a markup) or to the register for the job (like the one on page 188).

The following table shows what you must do to track time or costs so that you can charge for them.

To track...	You must...	See...
All expenses incurred for the job (QuickBooks only) Miscellaneous costs incurred for this job (costs you prefer not to record by using items) (QuickBooks Pro only)	Record a bill, check, or credit card charge, using the Expenses tab to identify the accounts and amounts for other costs incurred for this job.	■ "Paying bills" on page 257 ■ "Using checks" on page 265 ■ "Using credit cards" on page 267
Time billable to this job (QuickBooks Pro only)	Record hours spent on this job, using the Timer, the Stopwatch, or entering time manually into QuickBooks. ■ Assign the hours to the service item that should be used on the invoice. ■ To show the service date for each time entry on the invoice, customize the invoice to add a Service Date column. ■ Be sure to mark the hours as billable.	■ "Setting up and using the Timer" on page 315 ■ "Using the Stopwatch to time an activity" on page 323 ■ "Entering time manually into QuickBooks" on page 324

To track...	You must...	See...
Subcontracted services, products, materials, and other charges billable for this job (QuickBooks Pro only)	Record a bill, check, or credit card charge, using the Items tab to identify goods and services purchased for this job. Be sure to mark these items as billable.	■ "Items for reimbursable costs in QuickBooks Pro" on page 125 ■ "Paying bills" on page 257 ■ "Using checks" on page 265 ■ "Using credit cards" on page 267

Reimbursable expenses in QuickBooks

When you have billable expenses in QuickBooks and are ready to invoice for them, click the Expenses button on an invoice for the customer or job. (If you are using QuickBooks Pro, see "Reimbursable time and costs in QuickBooks Pro" on page 195.)

QuickBooks displays the Choose Reimbursable Expenses window. It shows the expenses you have marked billable but have not yet billed to this customer or job. In this window you mark which billable expenses to add to the invoice.

This window is in QuickBooks only, not QuickBooks Pro.

To hide a markup on an invoice, be sure to select this checkbox.

For a percentage markup, add a % sign after the number. QuickBooks prefills your preset markup percentage if you set one up in sales and customer preferences.

Most people use an income account for markup.

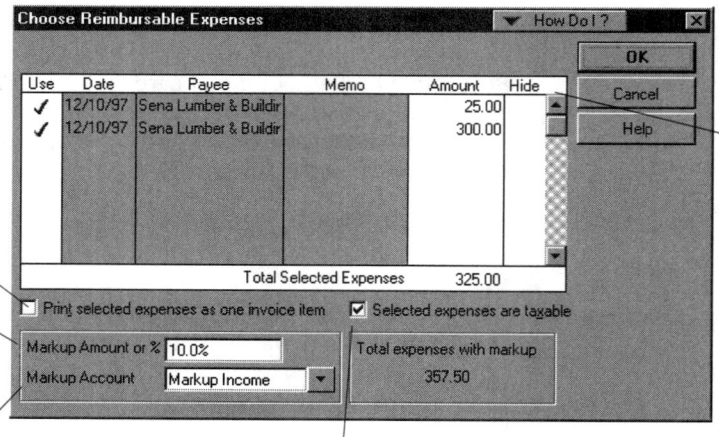

Click the **Hide** field only if you do not want ever to charge this customer for the expense. (The bill is unaffected.)

To make the marked expenses taxable on the invoice, select this checkbox.

After you click OK in the window, QuickBooks puts all the marked expenses on the invoice.

Note: You can set up so that QuickBooks assigns income for a reimbursed expense to an income account. If you don't do this setup, the income cancels the original expense in the expense account. See "Setting up to track reimbursed expenses as income" on page 180.

Reimbursable time and costs in QuickBooks Pro

In QuickBooks Pro, when you click the Time/Costs button on an invoice for a customer or job, it displays a window with three separate tabs, one for billable items, billable expenses, and billable time.

On the Items tab, you mark which billable items to add to the invoice.

This window shows all billable but not-yet-billed time and job costs for this particular job.

Each of the three tabs displays the dollar total for the lines that have a mark in the **Use** field. These amounts will be added to the invoice.

To use all lines on this tab, click Select All. To unmark all lines, click Clear All (the button name changes).

Select this checkbox to print only the overall total and a general description for the group of marked items on all three tabs.

To print an overall total but no detail for one tab alone, mark the lines on only one tab, select the checkbox, and click OK.

Time tab displays only if time tracking is on.

Click the **Hide** field only if you do not want ever to charge this customer for the item. (The bill is not affected.)

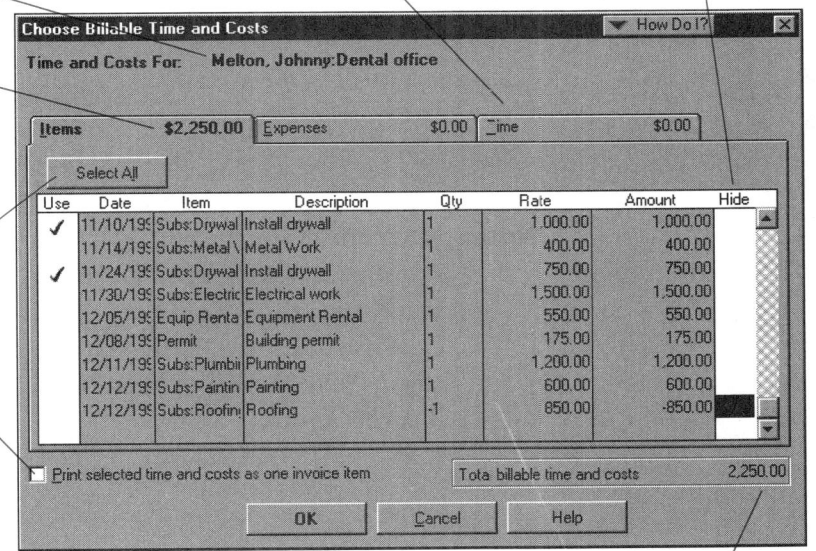

The **Description** and **Rate** fields show the sales description and rate for each item from the item setup. They may differ from the purchase description and rate.

This is the total amount for marked items on all three tabs.

On the sales form, QuickBooks Pro uses the sales price, not the cost, for each inventory part and for each resale non-inventory part, subcontracted service, and reimbursable other charge item. You can change the price on the sales form. If you set up the item with a sales price of 0.00 because costs vary, be sure to enter a sales price on the sales form.

On the Expenses tab of QuickBooks Pro, you mark which billable expenses to add to the invoice. You may add a markup to your actual expenses.

For a percentage markup, add a % sign after the number. QuickBooks Pro prefills your preset markup percentage if you set one up in sales and customer preferences.

Most people use an income account for markup.

To make the marked expenses taxable on the invoice, select this checkbox.

To hide the markup on an invoice, be sure to select this checkbox.

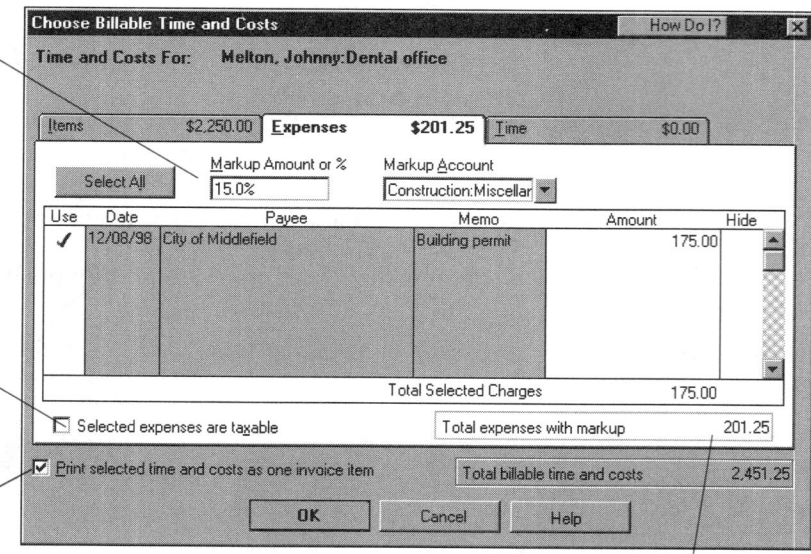

This total includes the markup.

Note: You can set up so that QuickBooks assigns income for a reimbursed expense to an income account. If you don't do this setup, the income cancels the original expense in the expense account. (Your net income is the same in either case.) See "Setting up to track reimbursed expenses as income" on page 180.

Finally, on the Time tab of QuickBooks Pro, you mark which billable time to add to the invoice.

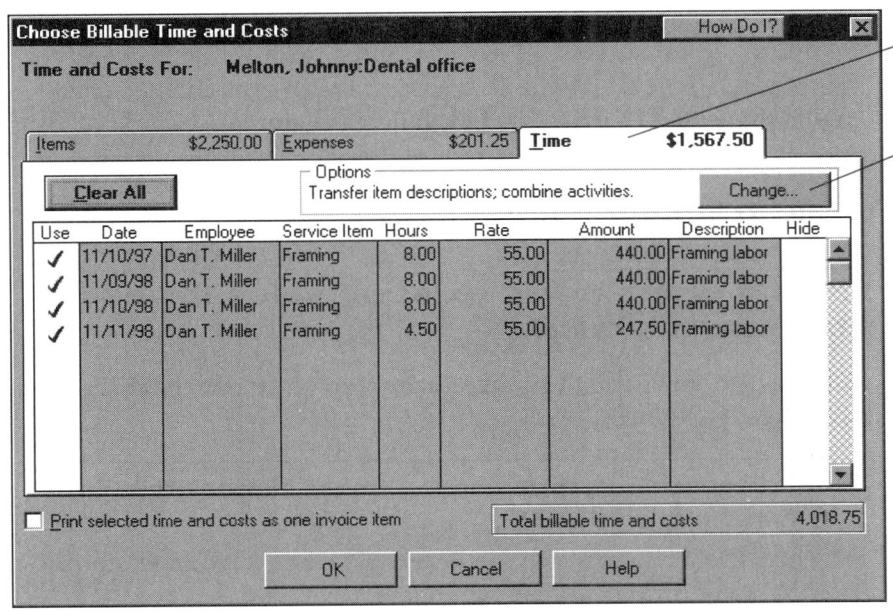

The Time tab shows all time that is billable for this job but has not yet been billed.

Click Change to specify the following:

- Whether to copy your time notes or the description of the service item into the **Description** field of the sales form.

- Whether to show each activity as a separate line or to combine all activities for the same service item.

The rates shown are the rates set up for each service item.

In this window and on the sales form, QuickBooks Pro uses the hourly rate for the service item you assigned to the activity, not the payroll rate of the employee. If the service item has the subcontractor checkbox marked, QuickBooks Pro uses the sales price. You can change the rate on the sales form.

To change how QuickBooks Pro groups and describes time activities on the sales form, click Change.

After you click OK in the window, QuickBooks Pro puts all the marked time and costs on the invoice. If you return to the window *before* recording the invoice, the items already on the invoice have an invoice symbol in the Use field.

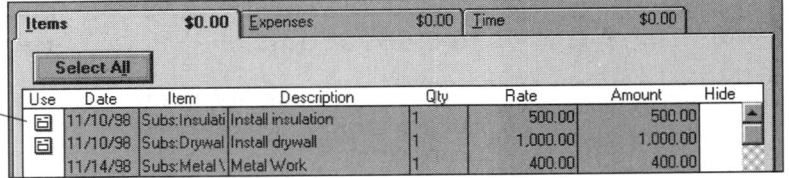

The invoice symbol in the **Use** field indicates that the item has already been added to the invoice.

Tracking sales and customer payments | 197

You can put given job costs on a sales form only once.

If you record a sales form that has actual job costs on it and then discover you made a mistake, the actual job costs you used previously are no longer available to use again. The only way you can reinstate such costs is to go to the original record (that is, weekly timesheet, single activity, bill, check, or credit card charge). Click the Billable field to make the cost billable again.

Making changes while tracking sales

Finding or changing existing sales forms or statement charges

QuickBooks allows you to change a sales form or statement charge you have already recorded.

Don't change sales forms or statement charges to record payments received later.

To enter the payments, use the Receive Payments window, not the original sales form or statement charge.

If the form was among the last ones you recorded, you can move to previous forms in the window where you entered the form by clicking the Previous button.

The easiest way to find a statement charge or an older invoice or credit memo is to scroll through the customer register. You can sort the register by date, amount, number, and so on.

Cash sales receipts are either in your bank account register or in the register for undeposited funds, depending on how you specified what to do with the payment received. Even if you have already deposited the cash receipt payment with other undeposited funds, the cash sales receipt remains in the register for undeposited funds. The register will also have the subsequent deposit.

To learn about...	Search the Help index for...
Finding and viewing statement charges or older invoices for a customer	customers, registers for

To learn about...	Search the Help index for...
Finding and viewing cash sales receipts for which payments were deposited with other undeposited funds	Undeposited Funds account

Correcting the application of a payment

After you have recorded a payment, you may discover that you should have applied it to different invoices or statement charges. (Or you may have failed to apply it at all.) You can edit the payment and apply it correctly.

If the payment was originally with other undeposited funds and you subsequently deposited the funds, you must delete the payment from the deposit before you can edit the payment. After correcting the application of the payment, be sure to edit the deposit and add the corrected payment to it to keep your bank balance correct.

To learn about...	Search the Help index for...
Correcting a customer payment that is already recorded	receiving payments, fixing misapplied
Editing a deposit of undeposited funds to delete or add a payment	deposits, editing

Voiding or deleting a sales transaction

QuickBooks allows you to void or delete a sales transaction, although you would not want to do either if you have already recorded a payment for it.

You can delete a sales form altogether from QuickBooks; however, there may be better alternatives.

- If you want complete records of all sales, you may want to void a sales form instead of deleting it.

- Don't delete an invoice or receipt if you made an error on the invoice. Just correct the error on the original form and reprint it.

- Don't delete an invoice if you've already applied a payment to it. If a customer cancels an order on which you have received some payment, your records will be clearer if you create a credit memo to reverse all or part of a sales transaction.

To learn about...	Search the Help index for...
Voiding or deleting a sales transaction	■ transactions, voiding ■ transactions, deleting
Reversing all or part of a sales transaction with a credit memo	credit memos, creating

Repeating similar transactions

Making a copy to use later

If you need to create similar estimates, invoices, cash sales receipts, or statement charges, you can make a copy to use later or for a different customer. Then you don't have to start from scratch.

QuickBooks calls making a copy *memorizing*. You can memorize estimates, invoices, or cash sales receipts without specifying a customer name.

Statement charges work slightly differently. You must memorize a customer or job name with the statement charge. You might memorize a statement charge if you wanted to repeat the same charge, say, every month. If you have similar charges for different customers, you must memorize each one separately.

Scheduling repeated transactions

When you memorize any transaction, you can set up a schedule to record the same transaction again and again. For example, if your organization charges members a monthly fee, you can schedule memorized statement charges for each member. You can specify whether you want QuickBooks to enter the charges automatically or to remind you that it's time for you to enter them.

Starting from a copy

QuickBooks calls starting from a copy of a transaction *recalling*. You can recall any transaction that has already been memorized, and can make changes on the recalled transaction. For example, if you recall an invoice with no customer name, you'd add the correct name and perhaps add or delete some items.

To learn about...	Search the Help index for...
Making a copy of estimates, invoices, or cash sales receipts	memorized transactions, creating
Setting up for automatic entry of regular charges you assess	automatic transaction entry
Grouping memorized transactions so they are all entered at the same time	memorized transactions, grouping together
Using a copy of a transaction	memorized transactions, using

Managing what customers owe you

When you keep track of how much a customer owes you—your accounts receivable, also called A/R—it's very important to keep track of *which* invoices or statement charges have been paid and which are still unpaid. You do this by recording each customer payment in the Receive Payments window and specifying what the payment is for. Then QuickBooks can tell you what is overdue.

Tip: **Would you like to know how to get customers to pay their bills faster?** Customers who pay late or not at all can be a problem for any business. QuickBooks can help you manage your accounts receivable, use A/R reports effectively, establish a credit policy, and devise a strategy for collecting overdue bills. For information on these topics, choose Decision Tools from the Company menu, and then choose Manage Your Receivables.

Connecting related transactions

The most important thing to remember when tracking accounts receivable is to make sure that related transactions are connected within QuickBooks.

- When a customer makes a payment after receiving one or more invoices, you have to tell QuickBooks which invoices the payment is for.

- When a customer makes a payment after receiving a statement with details of statement charges, you have to tell QuickBooks which statement charges the payment is for.

- If a customer makes a down payment ahead of time and you write an invoice after doing the work, you have to tell QuickBooks that the invoice has been partially paid by the down payment.

- If a customer overpays, you have to tell QuickBooks that you are applying the credit to an unpaid invoice, to an unpaid statement charge, or to a refund check.

- If you write a credit memo for some returned items, you have to tell QuickBooks that you are applying the credit to an unpaid invoice, to an unpaid statement charge, or to a refund check.

QuickBooks considers invoices and statement charges still open and due until you connect them to a payment (or credit). If you don't make the connections, a customer can seem to have a zero or negative balance and yet have overdue invoices or statement charges.

To learn how to record the various kinds of customer payments, see "Receiving and depositing payments" on page 189.

Viewing all accounts receivable transactions

Besides the accounts receivable reports and graphs, QuickBooks has an accounts receivable register. This register, like a checkbooks register, shows every transaction that affects how much people owe you. It includes all invoices, payments, credit memos, statement charges, and finance charges. In addition, each customer register shows the accounts receivable transactions for that customer.

The **Number** field shows invoice and statement charge numbers, FINCHG for finance charges, or check numbers for customer payments.

QuickBooks records invoice or statement charge amounts in the **Amt Chrg** field, and payment amounts in the **Amt Paid** field.

The **Type** field shows whether the transaction was an invoice (INV), a statement charge (STMTCHG), a credit memo (CREDMEM), a payment from a customer (PMT), or a customer discount (DISC).

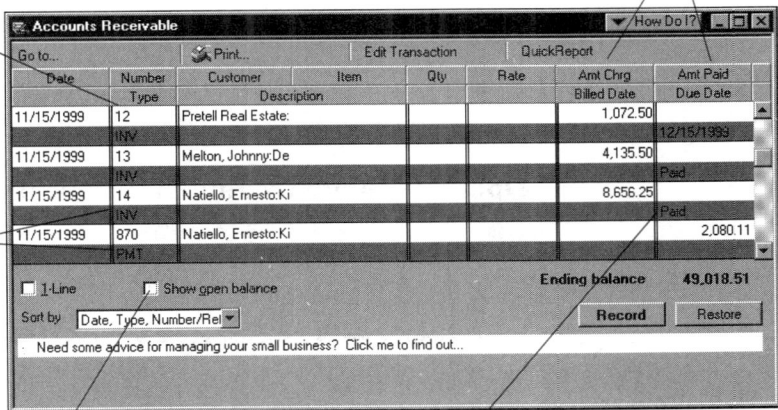

Select **Show open balance** to show the amount still due for invoices and billing statements.

When a customer pays an invoice or billing statement, QuickBooks replaces the date in the **Due Date** field with the word "Paid."

The Ending balance shows the total amount you are owed (unpaid invoices minus any unused customer credit).

Tracking sales and customer payments

The one-line view of the A/R register displays many more transactions in one window. You can use this view when you want to see more transactions with less detail.

To see the one-line view, select **1-Line**.

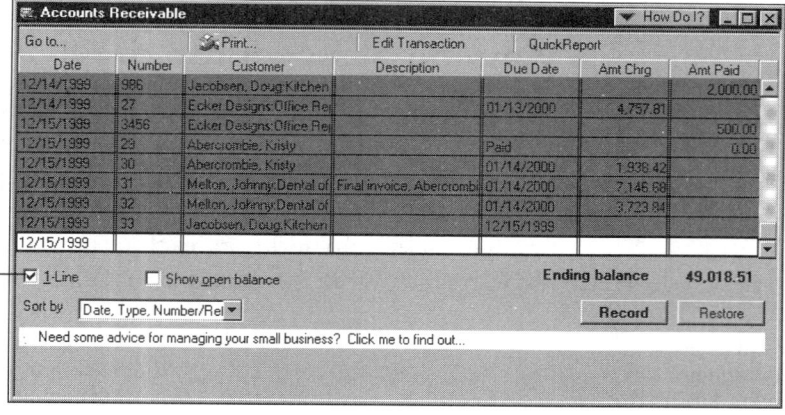

When you select a transaction in the accounts receivable or customer register, you can click Edit to display the window for the transaction and see detail.

Tip: Do you need to find the payments for a specific invoice? Select the invoice in the register. Then, from the Edit menu, choose Transaction History. You'll see a list of all the payments for this invoice.

To learn about...	Search the Help index for...
Viewing the accounts receivable register or a customer register	■ accounts receivable, register ■ customers, registers for
Displaying a list of payments for a particular invoice	invoices, payments toward

Getting information about sales and what people owe you

This section contains:

Which items or customers bring in the most income?	**205**
How do my actual costs and income so far compare to the estimate for the total job?	**207**
Are my customers paying me on time?	**208**
Other reports about sales and accounts receivable	**210**

Which items or customers bring in the most income?

QuickBooks and QuickBooks Pro provides valuable sales information about items or customers through graphs and reports.

For example, Paula runs a shop that sells handmade crafts. She sells a lot of inexpensive items and fewer expensive items, but she doesn't know which types of items contribute the most to the shop income.

She can find out quickly by creating a sales graph that is a pie chart breaking down her sales income by item.

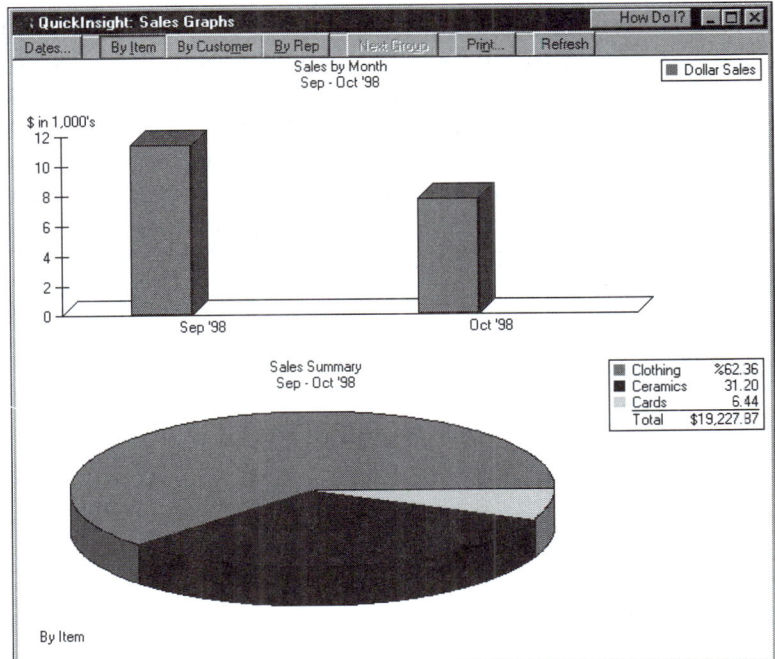

The bar graph shows sales income from all items by month for the fiscal year.

The pie chart shows the percentage of sales income from each item for the entire fiscal year.

If she prefers a report with quantities and dollar amounts by item, she runs a sales by item summary report. The report has a separate line for each item, including subitems, whereas the pie chart does not show subitems.

This report summarizes sales by item for the period specified. It includes sales reported on the following:

- Invoices
- Cash sales receipts
- Statement charges
- Returns on credit memos

Items are grouped by item type (for example, inventory part).

Subitems of the same item (for example, cabinets) are grouped together.

Sales by Item Summary
September through October 1998

03/26/98

	Qty	Amount	% of Sales	Avg Price
Parts				
Ceramics	240	6,000.00	31.2%	25.00
Cards				
Art	137	548.00	2.9%	4.00
Commercial	463	689.87	3.6%	1.49
Total Cards		1,237.87	6.4%	
Clothing				
Caps	137	1,370.00	7.1%	10.00
T-shirts	531	10,620.00	55.2%	20.00
Total Clothing		11,990.00	62.4%	
Total Parts		19,227.87	100.0%	
TOTAL		**19,227.87**	**100.0%**	

If she wants to see a report that lists each individual sale for each item, she can run the sales by item detail report.

Jack, is more interested in a breakdown of his income by customer than by item. He does a lot of small jobs for three big clients. He can compare income from these clients by customizing the pie chart of sales (page 205) to be by customer instead of by item. In addition, he can run a report of sales by customer to see dollar amounts by customer, broken down by job. He can even add columns to the report to compare this period's income with last period's or with the year-to-date income.

How do my actual costs and income so far compare to the estimate for the total job?

When Frank does a remodeling job for a client, he likes to compare the actual costs and income so far with his estimate for the total job. He runs a job estimates vs. actuals detail report for that job.

The job estimates vs. actuals detail report for a job is available only in QuickBooks Pro.

The report breaks down amounts first by item type and then by item.

You can choose to have additional columns for $ Difference or % Difference.

12/15/98	**Job Estimates vs. Actuals Detail for Ecker De...**			
	All Transactions			
	Est. Cost	Act. Cost	Est. Revenue	Act. Revenue
Parts				
Lumber				
Rough	745.00	1,200.00	819.50	1,445.00
Trim	175.00	175.00	192.50	350.00
Total Lumber	920.00	1,375.00	1,012.00	1,795.00
Total Parts	920.00	1,375.00	1,012.00	1,795.00
Service				
Framing	440.00	0.00	528.00	660.00
Removal	210.00	478.85	252.00	532.00
Subs				
Drywall	475.00	450.00	522.50	450.00
Insulating	1,000.00	800.00	1,100.00	900.00
Painting	600.00	600.00	660.00	600.00
Plumbing	1,500.00	700.00	1,650.00	700.00
Total Subs	3,575.00	2,550.00	3,932.50	2,650.00
Total Service	4,225.00	3,028.85	4,712.50	3,842.00

Are my customers paying me on time?

Carol sends out many invoices every month and needs to know how much of the total amount owed is current and how much is past due.

The accounts receivable graphs give her the big picture of what her customers owe.

The bar graph shows whether your customers are overdue on their payments and how late they are.

The first bar is for the current period (not overdue).

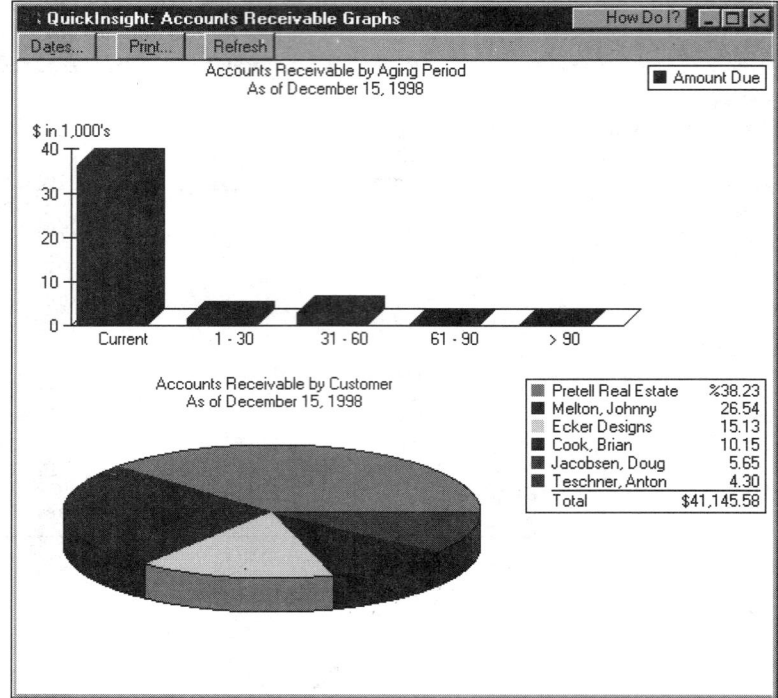

The pie chart shows you which customers owe you the most.

Place the mouse pointer over any bar, pie slice, or name in the legend, and hold down the right mouse button. QuickBooks shows the exact dollar amount for each bar, slice, or name.

To see dollar amounts, Carol runs an A/R aging summary, which breaks down the amount due by customer and job as well as by aging period.

From an A/R aging summary report, you can learn which customers are overdue on their payments.

The balance in the **Current** column is not yet overdue. The balance in the **1-30** column is one to 30 days past due.

12/15/98	A/R Aging Summary As of December 15, 1998					
	Current	1 - 30	31 - 60	61 - 90	> 90	TOTAL
Cook, Brian						
2nd story addition	3,003.30	0.00	0.00	0.00	0.00	3,003.30
Kitchen	466.69	5.95	700.00	0.00	0.00	1,172.64
Total Cook, Brian	3,469.99	5.95	700.00	0.00	0.00	4,175.94
Ecker Designs						
Office Repairs	6,226.11	0.00	0.00	0.00	0.00	6,226.11
Total Ecker Designs	6,226.11	0.00	0.00	0.00	0.00	6,226.11
Jacobsen, Doug						
Kitchen	2,245.00	80.00	0.00	0.00	0.00	2,325.00
Total Jacobsen, Doug	2,245.00	80.00	0.00	0.00	0.00	2,325.00
Melton, Johnny						
Dental office	10,918.25	0.00	0.00	0.00	0.00	10,918.25
Total Melton, Johnny	10,918.25	0.00	0.00	0.00	0.00	10,918.25
Pretell Real Estate						
155 Wilks Blvd.	1,072.50	5.65	2,239.00	0.00	0.00	3,317.15
75 Sunset Rd.	12,412.18	0.00	0.00	0.00	0.00	12,412.18
Total Pretell Real Estate	13,484.68	5.65	2,239.00	0.00	0.00	15,729.33

When Carol wants to phone some past due customers, she runs a collections report. The collections report lists past-due invoices and statement charges, as well as names and phone numbers for contacting delinquent customers.

The collections report lists all invoices (or statement charges) that are past due. It even has the customer's phone number so you can call easily.

12/15/98	Collections Report As of December 15, 1998						
Type	Date	Num	P. O. #	Terms	Due Date	Aging	Open Balance
Cook, Brian							
Kitchen							
Brian							
415-555-2248							
Brian (work number)							
415-555-0220							
Invoice	10/15/98	4		Net 30	11/14/98	31	700.00
Total Kitchen							705.95
Total Cook, Brian							705.95
Jacobsen, Doug							
Kitchen							
Doug or Linda							
415-555-4411							
Invoice	10/23/98	5		Net 30	11/22/98	23	75.00
Invoice	12/10/98	FC 104			12/10/98	5	5.00
Total Kitchen							80.00
Total Jacobsen, Doug							80.00

Tip: If you prefer to mail a collection letter and you have Microsoft Word 97 (or higher), QuickBooks Pro provides a variety of customizable letters. You can show overdue amounts without having to retype your QuickBooks data. For more information, see "Writing letters" on page 441.

Other reports about sales and accounts receivable

The onscreen Help gives descriptions of all the reports about sales, estimates, and accounts receivable, as well as instructions on how to create each one.

To learn about...	Search the Help index for...
Finding the report you want using the QuickBooks Report Finder	reports, finding
Reports and graphs about what you have sold or provided, as recorded on cash sales receipts, invoices, statement charges, and credit memos	■ sales, reports about ■ sales, graphs of
Reports about estimates, including comparisons with actual costs and revenues (QuickBooks Pro only)	estimates, reports about
Reports about sales by sales reps on your Sales Rep List	sales, reports about
Reports and graphs of all income, not just sales income	■ profit and loss reports ■ income and expense graph
Reports and graphs about what people owe you and what is overdue	accounts receivable, reports about
Specifying whether QuickBooks should calculate aging on accounts receivable reports and graphs from the due date or the transaction date	aging

CHAPTER 12

Working with vendors

Tracking vendor information	212
Setting up vendors	215
Using vendor names and managing your Vendor list	217
Reports about vendors	220

Why should I enter vendors in QuickBooks?

The Vendor list in QuickBooks allows you to record information about your vendors (the people or companies from whom you buy goods and services or owe taxes), and track your related accounts payable and 1099-MISC information. You can also create reports and print mailing labels based on your Vendor list. With the Vendor Detail Center, you can get valuable insight on each of your vendors.

Tracking vendor information

How can the Vendor Detail Center help manage my business?

The Vendor Detail Center lets you easily view and analyze vendor-related data. You can tailor the type of information displayed to your particular needs, and take action if necessary.

QuickBooks displays alerts to help keep you up to date with important business information, as well as new QuickBooks features and services.

Get key information such as a list of a vendor's payments.

You can easily access relevant QuickBooks forms so that you can act on the vendor information displayed. For example, if you're viewing outstanding purchase orders, you can easily display associated forms.

QuickBooks displays tips and helpful information.

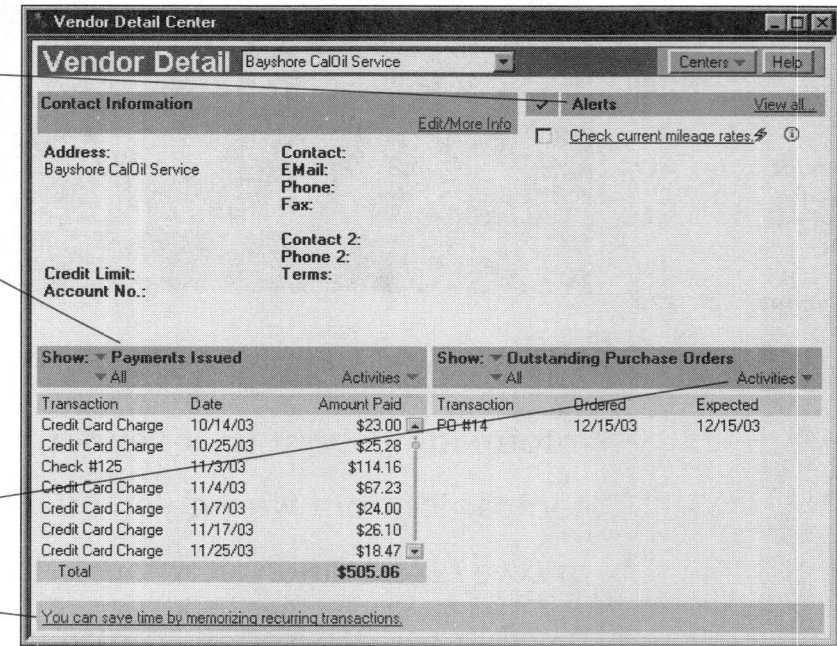

To learn about...	Search the Help index for...
Using centers in QuickBooks	centers
Managing alerts	alerts, managing

How much information should I add for each vendor?

For most vendors, you'll want to add the basic information such as the vendor name, address, and phone number; but you can also add account and terms information, categorize your vendors by types (that you define), create custom fields to track information important to your business, and add notes about conversations, products, or other information about this vendor.

QuickBooks prints this information in the **Memo** field of checks that pay bills from this vendor. Or, it sends it with online payments.

You can classify your vendors by type.

This field tracks bill aging and tells you when payment is due.

If you file a 1099-MISC form for this vendor, fill in the **Tax ID** field and select the checkbox.

[New Vendor dialog screenshot showing fields: Vendor "Boswell Insulation", Address Info / Additional Info tabs, Account, Categorizing and Defaults with Type "Subcontractors", Terms "Net 30", Credit Limit, Tax ID "22-1234567", Vendor eligible for 1099 checkbox, Custom Fields, Define Fields button, Opening Balance 5,000.00 as of 12/15/1999, OK, Cancel, Next, Vendor is inactive]

If you use Symantec ACT! or Microsoft Outlook contact management software to manage vendor data, you can transfer basic vendor information (such as name, address, phone, and so on) from your contact manager to QuickBooks Pro and vice versa. See Chapter 23, "Sharing QuickBooks Pro information with your contact manager" on page 438.

To learn about...	Search the Help index for...
Transferring information from your contact manager to QuickBooks	contact management, synchronizing names with a contact manager

Defining custom fields for vendors

To track additional information about your vendors, you can define up to seven custom fields. You might want to define fields for:

- Web site addresses
- Pager numbers
- Customer service numbers
- Hours open (for example, 9:30 - 5:30)

After you add custom fields, you can customize your forms to include these fields. You can also display and filter for customized field data in your reports.

Tracking vendor information | 213

Categorizing vendors by type

By setting up and using vendor types, you can create reports and send special mailings based on a specific vendor group.

For example, a construction business might set up the following vendor types:

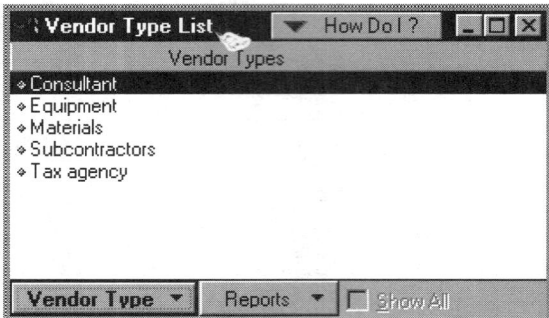

Information you may want to set up for different kinds of vendors

Besides entering the name, address, and phone number for your vendors, use the following table for ideas on additional information that might be useful.

Vendors	Comments	Information you may want to set up
Product suppliers and service companies	N/A	■ Account number ■ Terms ■ Credit limit ■ Product or service information using the notepad
Financial institutions	Financial institutions are considered vendors because they provide services and products (such as loans and credit cards) that you repay.	■ Account number ■ Terms ■ Contact names
Tax agencies	Tax agencies are considered vendors because you owe them money.	Use the notepad to track information about conversations with tax staff.

Vendors	Comments	Information you may want to set up
Contractors, subcontractors, consultants, agents, brokers	These people provide a service for which you owe money, but they are not employees.	■ Tax ID ■ "Vendor eligible for 1099" ■ Pager or cell phone number using a custom field.
Utilities, phone companies, landlords	Besides entering the main phone number for these vendors, consider adding custom fields for pager, customer service, or emergency phone numbers.	Define fields for one or more of the following: ■ Pager or cell phone number ■ Customer service phone number ■ Emergency phone number

Setting up vendors

> **Note:** You may have already set up some of your vendors with the EasyStep Interview.

What to set up	Comments	Search the Help index for...
Vendor types (optional)	Use this feature to classify your vendors by the type of service they perform or the items they sell. After you add all your entries to the vendor types list, you can select the appropriate type for each vendor you add.	vendor types
Custom fields for vendors	Use these fields to record additional information about the vendor. Once you've set up the custom fields for one vendor, the fields will appear for all vendors.	vendors, custom fields for

What to set up	Comments	Search the Help index for...
Vendors	If you plan to track accounts payable, you must enter information about the vendors you work with.	vendors, adding
	■ Payment terms The Terms drop-down list is located on the Additional Info tab of the New Vendor window. When you enter a bill from this vendor, QuickBooks uses the terms to calculate when the bill is due.	terms for payment
	■ Credit limit (optional) The Credit Limit field is located on the Additional Info tab of the New Vendor window. Enter the credit limit that your company has with this vendor. QuickBooks warns you when you are about to exceed the limit.	vendors, adding
	■ Tax ID field and 1099 checkbox The Tax ID field is located on the Additional Info tab of the New Vendor window. Fill in the Tax ID field if you send 1099-MISC forms to the vendor. Then select the 1099 checkbox.	1099s
	■ Opening balance Enter the amount you owed this vendor as of your QuickBooks start date.	■ opening balances, entering for accounts receivable and accounts payable ■ historical transactions
Account to track vendor discounts (Optional)	If you receive discounts for early payment, you can set up an expense account called "Vendor Discounts." Because discounts reduce your expenses, this type of account is sometimes called a contra-expense account.	accounts, adding to your chart of accounts

Using vendor names and managing your Vendor list

Using vendors in QuickBooks

As you create purchase orders, enter bills, and use other forms, you'll choose your vendor from the vendor drop-down list.

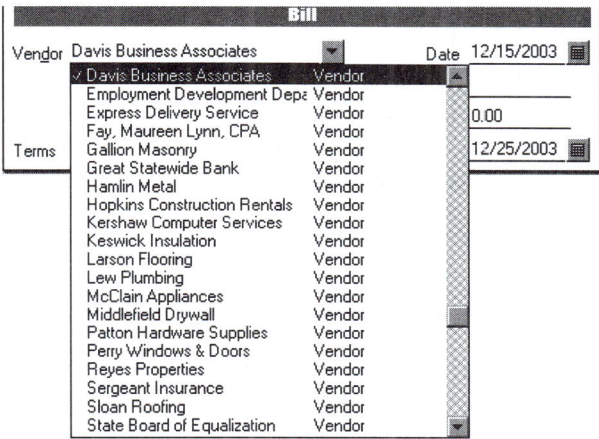

If you discover that a vendor is missing from the list, you can enter it in the **Vendor** or **Name** field and add it at this time.

Managing your Vendor list

The Vendor list displays helpful information at a glance:

- Name of each vendor
- Current balance you owe each vendor

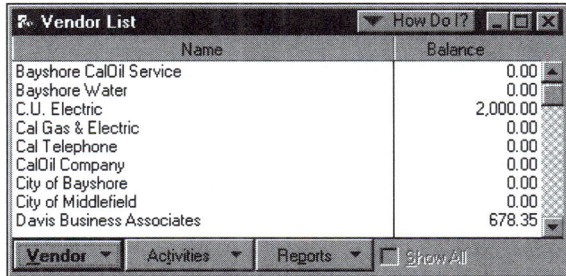

Managing your Vendor list includes updating your vendors' records to keep the information current. It also includes making little-used or no-longer used vendors inactive. By managing your list in this way, you make the list much easier to work with.

To learn about...	Search the Help index for...
Displaying the Vendor list	vendors, list of

Editing vendors

You can edit a vendor record at any time to update vendor information.

To learn about...	Search the Help index for...
Editing vendors	vendors, editing information for

Hiding vendors

If you haven't used a vendor for a long time, you can make the vendor inactive. QuickBooks keeps the information associated with that vendor, but hides the vendor from the Vendor list and from any vendor drop-down lists. You do not need to change or delete any transaction that uses the vendor. You can make the vendor active again at any time.

To learn about...	Search the Help index for...
Making vendors inactive	vendors, hiding and showing
Making inactive vendors active	vendors, hiding and showing

Merging vendor records

If you have duplicate vendor records stored in your Vendor list, you can use the merge feature to combine the duplicate records into one record.

For example, if your Vendor list included both "BayShore Water" and "BayShore Water Co" you'd want to merge them.

To learn about...	Search the Help index for...
Merging vendor records	merging, list entries

Deleting vendors

If you add a name to your Vendor list by mistake, you can delete the vendor. QuickBooks allows you to delete a vendor only if there are no transactions associated with the vendor.

To learn about...	Search the Help index for...
Deleting vendors	vendors, deleting

Adding notes

The vendor notepad provides a place to record important conversations and product information. You can access the notepad from the Add/Edit Vendor window or anytime you are viewing a transaction related to the vendor. You can also create To Do notes to remind you of a vendor-related task, such as placing an order or making a phone call.

To learn about...	Search the Help index for...
Using the vendor notepad	vendors, notes about
Creating To Do notes	To Do notes

Contacting your vendors by mail

You can use your QuickBooks data in conjunction with prewritten Microsoft Word letters to mail your vendors change of address notifications, requests for credit applications, and other messages.

To learn about...	Search the Help index for...
Using your QuickBooks data with Microsoft Word letters	letters using QuickBooks data in Microsoft Word

Reports about vendors

You can run reports to get information about all your vendors or information about a specific vendor. These reports answer questions about outstanding balances, unpaid or paid bills, or late charges for overdue bills.

> **Note:** *In addition to reports, you can use the Vendor Detail Center to get vendor-related information.* See "How can the Vendor Detail Center help manage my business?" on page 212.

Am I in danger of paying late charges for any of my bills this month?

The A/P aging detail report shows you unpaid bills, grouped and subtotaled by aging period. It also shows how many days a bill is overdue, which would depend on when you received the bill and the payment terms you have set up with the vendor.

Rock Castle Construction
A/P Aging Detail
As of December 15, 1998

Type	Date	Num	Name	Due Date	Aging	Open Balance
Current						
Bill	11/15/98		Perry Windows & ...	12/15/98		810.00
Bill	11/30/98		C.U. Electric	12/15/98		1,500.00
Bill	11/17/98		Patton Hardware S...	12/17/98		325.00
Bill	11/20/98		Perry Windows & ...	12/20/98		5,925.00
Bill	11/20/98		Timberloft Lumber	12/20/98		1,960.00
Bill	12/05/98		Hopkins Construct...	12/20/98		550.00
Bill	11/24/98		Middlefield Drywall	12/24/98		1,200.00
Bill	12/11/98		Lew Plumbing	12/26/98		1,200.00
Bill	12/01/98		Fay, Maureen Lyn...	12/31/98		250.00
Bill	12/01/98		C.U. Electric	12/31/98		500.00
Bill	12/05/98	7893	Wheeler's Tile Etc.	01/04/99		1,250.00
Bill	12/12/98		Washuta & Son Pa...	01/11/99		600.00
Bill	12/12/98		Patton Hardware S...	01/11/99		810.00
Total Current						**16,880.00**
1 - 30						
Item Receipt	11/18/98		Perry Windows & ...			2,325.00
Bill	11/05/98		Washuta & Son Pa...	12/05/98	10	2,000.00
Item Receipt	12/05/98		Patton Hardware S...			3,459.20
Bill	11/24/98		Keswick Insulation	12/09/98	6	900.00
Credit	12/12/98	CR-1...	Sloan Roofing			-850.00
Bill	11/13/98		Sloan Roofing	12/13/98	2	5,700.00
Bill	11/28/98		Lew Plumbing	12/13/98	2	700.00
Bill	11/14/98		Hamlin Metal	12/14/98	1	950.00
Bill	11/14/98		Timberloft Lumber	12/14/98	1	3,075.00
Total 1 - 30						**18,259.20**

How can I see a list of unpaid bills for each vendor?

The unpaid bills detail report shows which vendors you still owe money and lists your unpaid bills for each vendor. It also lists item receipts and unapplied bill credits. To see all the transactions that affect your balance with each vendor, run the vendor balance detail report. It shows payments as well as bills, item receipts, and bill credits.

Didn't I pay my wholesaler last month?

To answer this question, you could either run a QuickReport for the vendor or an open balance report for the vendor. Both reports show detail about a specific vendor rather than all the vendors you work with. See "QuickReports: reports at your fingertips" on page 406.

What's my vendor's phone number?

Instead of always opening the vendor's record, you can print a vendor phone list.

To learn about...	Search the Help index for...
Creating reports about vendors	vendors, reports about
Customizing reports	report customization

CHAPTER 13

Inventory

Is QuickBooks inventory right for my business?	224
Setting up for tracking inventory	228
Working with QuickBooks inventory	233
Getting information about your inventory	244

Should I use QuickBooks to track my inventory?

If you purchase goods for resale, keep them in inventory, and then sell them, QuickBooks can help you track the current quantity and value of your stock. In addition, QuickBooks can handle the accounting associated with buying, holding, and selling inventory.

QuickBooks is not designed to handle certain kinds of inventory. Before you begin to set up inventory in QuickBooks, read the first section of this chapter carefully to determine whether QuickBooks is suitable for your inventory tracking needs.

Is QuickBooks inventory right for my business?

This section helps you decide whether to use QuickBooks to track your inventory.

Which types of inventory can I track in QuickBooks?	224
What QuickBooks inventory can do for you	226

Which types of inventory can I track in QuickBooks?

inventory

The most common kinds of inventory are merchandise or stock in trade; raw materials; work in process; finished products; and supplies that physically become a part of the item intended for sale.

(From the IRS *Tax Guide for Small Business*)

QuickBooks inventory is designed for retail and wholesale businesses that buy items ready for resale. If your inventory meets *all* the following guidelines, you can track it successfully in QuickBooks:

- You purchase and hold multiple copies of the same items. That is, your inventory is not made up of one-of-a-kind items.

- The value of your inventory is based on the purchase price of each item. You do not add any labor or repackaging that increases its value.

- You actually sell all or most of your inventory. You do not simply use it up in the course of your business.

- You keep items in stock rather than ordering just what you need for a specific job.

- When you sell items from inventory, you want to track the quantities sold in the same units as you track the quantities purchased. For example, if you buy three types of jam in jars and sell a gift basket with a jar of each type, you want to track the quantity of jars sold, not the quantity of gift baskets.

- You are willing to track the value of your inventory according to the average cost method. (See "How QuickBooks calculates the value of your inventory" on page 242.)

Here are some instances in which QuickBooks inventory is probably not suited to your business:

- You have a manufacturing business, and your inventory includes products that you create from different components or materials.

- You stock items that are all unique from one another (for example, antiques, rare coins, gemstones, or items that must be tracked by serial numbers).

- Your inventory consists of items you rent or lease out, rather than sell, to customers.
- You sell items on consignment, so you do not own the items you sell.
- You need to fill orders for back-ordered items automatically as soon as you receive the new shipment.
- You rely on a point-of-sale scanning system to update your inventory.
- You want to track the stock of items you purchase for use in your work (for example, office supplies).
- You need to value your inventory by LIFO (last in, first out) or FIFO (first in, first out).

If you're not sure whether to use QuickBooks to track your inventory

If you are really not sure, it's safest not to use the inventory feature.

You can set up items that are *not* inventory items for things you purchase, things you sell, or both. QuickBooks calls such items *non-inventory part*s (although they do not have to be a part of anything else). See "Types of QuickBooks items" on page 119.

Here are some advantages of using non-inventory parts instead of inventory parts:

- If you decide you have inventory that QuickBooks can track, you can change a non-inventory part into an inventory part. However, you cannot change an inventory part into a non-inventory part, nor can you delete an inventory part that is used in any QuickBooks transaction.
- Because QuickBooks doesn't keep track of how many non-inventory parts you have on hand, you can use them for raw materials or components or anything you do not sell directly.
- You can use non-inventory parts with generic descriptions for one-of-a-kind items you sell (for example, a ring or an antique dresser). You can edit the description or sales price right on the sales form. Using generic non-inventory parts keeps the quantity of items on your list of items from drastically increasing.

Should I be using QuickBooks if it can't track my inventory?

Ultimately, the answer depends on how much you need your inventory tracking to be integrated into your accounting software.

Many businesses use QuickBooks for the basic flow of money in and out of the business. They either make periodic accounting entries to show the value of inventory on their books or simply track their inventory in a separate program (such as a spreadsheet).

Talk it over with your accountant to see whether you can use Quickbooks for everything but your inventory.

What QuickBooks inventory can do for you

If you have the kind of inventory that QuickBooks can track, here are some advantages of using the inventory feature:

- You can see at a glance how many items are in stock and how many are on order.
- Every time you receive more items, QuickBooks automatically updates the value and quantity of your inventory of those items. If the items had been on order, QuickBooks reduces the number on order.
- QuickBooks warns you if you try to sell more of an item than you have in stock.
- QuickBooks warns you if you are running low on a certain item and need to reorder.
- When you sell inventory, QuickBooks tracks the cost of the goods you are selling and the income you receive. It also automatically updates the value and quantity of your inventory of those items.

This diagram shows the basic process of tracking inventory in QuickBooks.

Tracking inventory

Setting up for tracking inventory

This section helps you set up your inventory.

List for setting up for inventory tracking in QuickBooks	228
Accounts for tracking inventory	230
Setting up inventory items	230
Tips for setting up inventory items	231

Tip: **The level of detail you use while setting up your inventory items and accounts determines the level of detail in your reports.** Take some time to determine the level of detail you'd like to track. See Chapter 4, *Organizing data effectively,* beginning on page 39.

List for setting up for inventory tracking in QuickBooks

If you are doing this setup as part of setting up your business in QuickBooks, the goal is to set up your inventory as of your QuickBooks start date. (See "Setup tasks" on page 24.) Then enter all purchases and sales of inventory as part of the process of entering all historical transactions between your start date and today.

If your business is already set up in QuickBooks but you are just beginning to purchase inventory, you are starting with zero quantities. After setting up items you plan to purchase, you are ready to enter purchase orders, purchases, and sales from now on.

What to set up	Comments	Search the Help index for...
(If you collect sales tax) Turn on and set up sales tax if you have not already done so.	If your sales tax is set up first, you can indicate which inventory items are taxable when setting them up.	sales tax, setting up
Turn on the preference for using inventory.	QuickBooks automatically turns on this preference if you use the EasyStep Interview to create your company and indicate that you plan to track inventory.	preferences, inventory

What to set up	Comments	Search the Help index for...
Create one or more income accounts for tracking income from sales of inventory.	QuickBooks automatically creates two other accounts you need: ■ Inventory Asset, an asset account for the value of your inventory ■ Cost of Goods Sold, an account for tracking the cost of items you sell See "Accounts for tracking inventory" on page 230.	accounts, adding to your chart of accounts
Gather the quantity and value for each inventory item you had on hand as of your QuickBooks start date.	You need correct opening quantities and values to set up your inventory items in QuickBooks.	inventory, value of
Set up inventory items by adding them to your Item list.	If you did not have any stock of an item on your QuickBooks start date, enter zero for the quantity on hand and value as of that date. QuickBooks will start calculating the cost of goods sold from the first time you begin purchasing the items to sell.	inventory, items
Turn on preference to track expenses by customer and job. (QuickBooks only)	QuickBooks Pro is automatically set up to track expenses by customer and job. By turning on this preference you will be able to track inventory you purchase for a particular customer and job on a purchase order.	"Preference to track expenses by customer and job (QuickBooks Pro only)" on page 148.
Enter purchase orders for any items currently on order.	You do not have to enter purchase orders that were received in full between your start date and today.	inventory, ordering
Enter all purchases and sales of inventory between your QuickBooks start date and today.	To bring your quantities and values up to date, you must enter these prior purchases and sales.	■ inventory, receiving ■ inventory, selling

Accounts for tracking inventory

When you set up inventory items on your Item list, you need to associate each item with three different accounts.

QuickBooks automatically sets up the first two accounts for you. Simply indicate that you want to track inventory (either in the EasyStep Interview or in the purchases and vendors preferences). Then set up an inventory item.

- **Inventory Asset account:** QuickBooks uses this "other current asset" type account to track the current value of your inventory.

  Although most businesses need only one such account, you may set up additional other current asset accounts for inventory if you wish.

- **Cost of Goods Sold account:** QuickBooks uses this "cost of goods sold" type account to track the cost to you of the items you have sold. On your chart of accounts, this account is below your income accounts but above your expense accounts. On a profit and loss statement, QuickBooks subtracts the total cost of goods sold from your total income to provide a gross profit before expenses.

  Although most businesses need only one such account, you may set up additional cost of goods sold accounts if you wish.

- **One or more sales income accounts:** You need one or more income accounts to track the income from the resale of inventory. You can associate all or most of your inventory items with the same income account. The number of income accounts you have depends on how much detail you need to see on your profit and loss statements. For guidelines and tips, see Chapter 4, *Organizing data effectively,* beginning on page 39.

Setting up inventory items

If you track inventory, the Inventory Part item type allows you to keep track of how many items remain in stock after a sale, how many items you have on order, your cost of goods sold, and the value of your inventory.

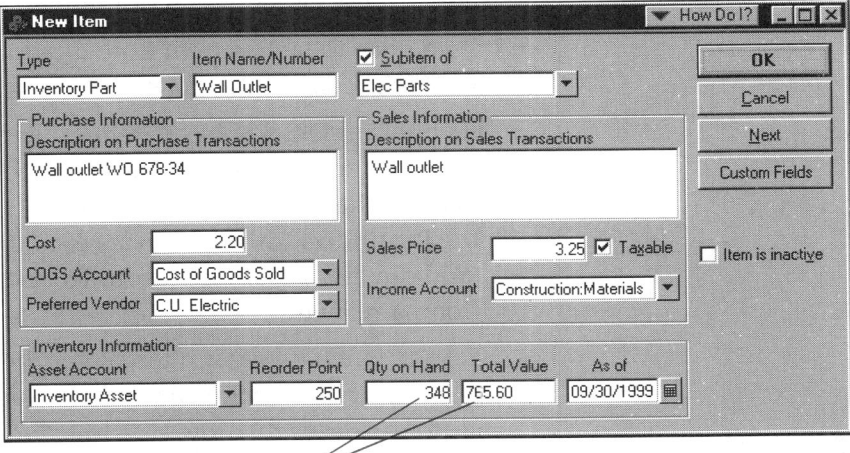

Enter the price you usually pay for this item in the **Cost** field.

Enter the price you charge for this item in the **Sales Price** field.

Enter the quantity on hand and value as of your QuickBooks start date.

Choose an **Income Account** for tracking income when you sell the item.

Setting up subitems or group items

If you have a long list of inventory items, you can organize your list by setting up items for general types of items, such as garden tools. Then you can set up subitems for the items you actually sell (such as shears, trimmers, and spades).

Tip: **The item you set up for the general type must be an inventory part itself.** Subitems must be of the same item type as the parent item. You can make the quantity and value of the parent item zero because you do not buy or sell it.

If you sell or purchase groups of inventory items as one unit, set up group items to represent the entire unit. This makes it easy to enter the unit on purchase orders, purchase forms, and sales forms. However, QuickBooks tracks the inventory of the individual items in the group, not the inventory of the group item itself. Also, the price of the group must be the sum of the prices of the individual items. (You can include an item for a discount or additional charge.)

Tips for setting up inventory items

- Set up an item for each kind of good you have on hand. Do not try to use the same item for products that have different values (aside from price fluctuations).

- You can use either names or numbers for items.
- If you like to buy an item from a certain vendor, enter that vendor's name in the **Preferred Vendor** field.
- If you want QuickBooks to remind you to order more of an item, fill in the **Reorder Point** field. When the quantity on hand for that item reaches this amount, QuickBooks reminds you to reorder on the Reminders list that appears each time you start QuickBooks. (You can also access the Reminders list by choosing it from the Company menu.)
- For the purchase description, enter the information the vendor needs to know. For the sales description, enter the information the customer needs to know.
- You can use custom fields to provide additional description for your items, such as color, size, or finish of the item.

Once you use an inventory item, you cannot delete it or change it to a different type of item.

Before setting up inventory items and using them, be sure that QuickBooks inventory is right for your type of business. If you record purchases or sales of an inventory item, you will not be able to delete the item unless you delete all transactions for the item. As long as the item is on your Item list, you cannot set up a new item of the same name but different item type. (However, you can hide unwanted items so you don't see them on your list.)

To learn about...	Search the Help index for...
Setting up inventory items	inventory, items
Setting up subitems	subitems
Setting up group items	items, grouped together

Working with QuickBooks inventory

This section helps you order, record receipt of, and enter sales of your inventory.

Ordering inventory items	233
Receiving inventory items	234
Buying inventory items over the counter	236
Selling inventory items	238
Managing your inventory	239
Inventory and your QuickBooks accounts	242

Ordering inventory items

You can write purchase orders for inventory items and send them to your vendors. Or, you can record purchase orders to track orders made by phone.

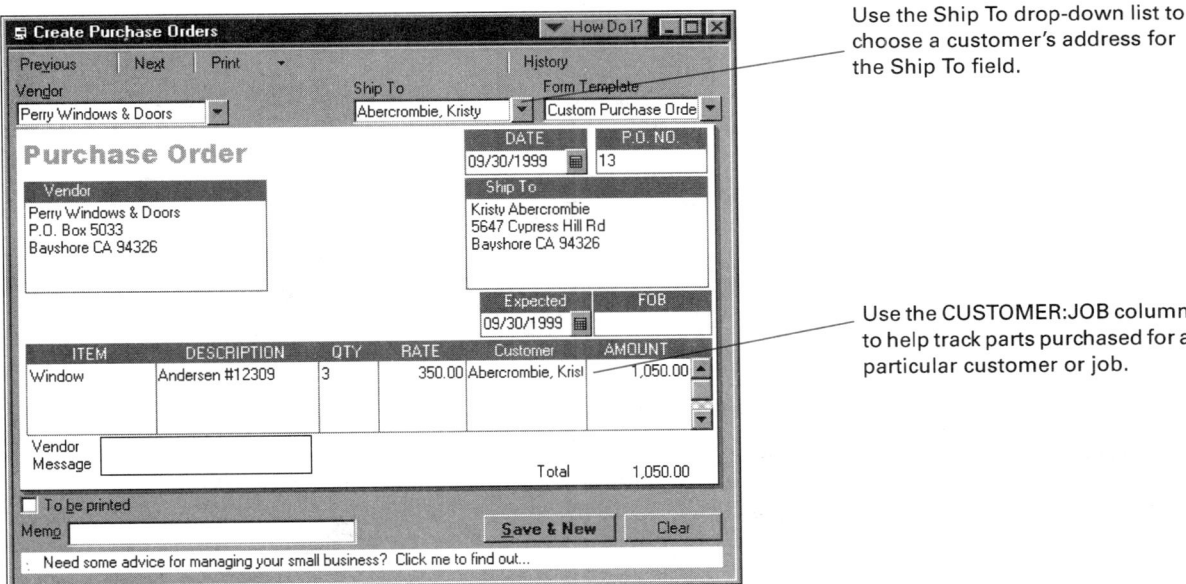

Use the Ship To drop-down list to choose a customer's address for the Ship To field.

Use the CUSTOMER:JOB column to help track parts purchased for a particular customer or job.

When you record a purchase order for inventory items, QuickBooks tracks the status of the items you have on order. There is no effect on any of your accounts.

Tip: To see a list of outstanding purchase orders, choose **Purchase Orders List from the Vendors menu.** The list is alphabetical by vendor.

To learn about...	Search the Help index for...
Filling out a purchase order for inventory	inventory, ordering
Viewing inventory items on order	inventory, reports about
Viewing items on order for a particular customer or job	purchase orders, reports about

Receiving inventory items

QuickBooks provides several ways to record the receipt of items. No matter which way you use, QuickBooks always increases the quantity on hand for each inventory item you receive.

If you receive items with a bill

If you receive items with a bill, use the Enter Bills window to record the items received.

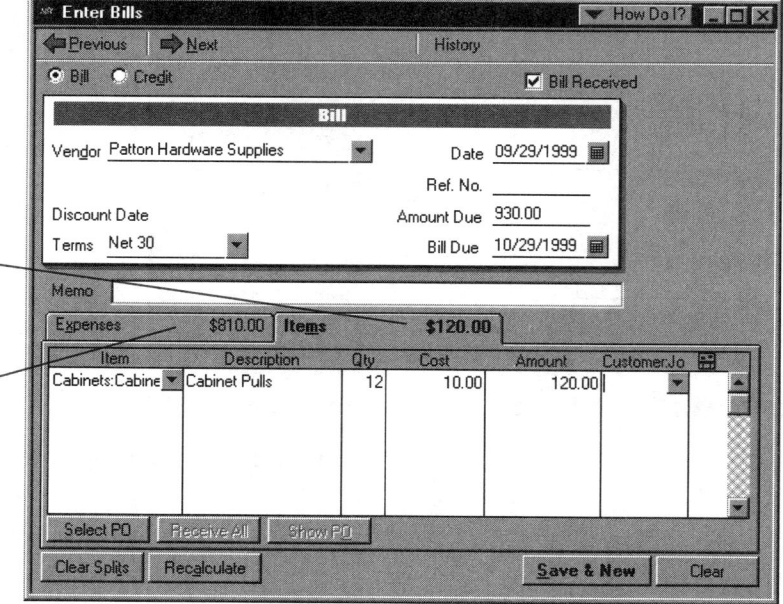

Record the items on the Items tab of the bill (shown in front in this example).

If you have additional expenses (such as freight charges), record them on the Expenses tab of the bill.

If you have recorded a purchase order for the items, you can receive against that purchase order. When you enter the vendor name on the bill, QuickBooks checks to see if open purchase orders exist for that vendor. If there are, it lets you record which items you have received against one or more open purchase orders.

If you receive items before the bill arrives

If you receive items without a bill, use the Create Item Receipts window to record the fact that they arrived. Later, when you receive the bill, you can turn the item receipt into a bill.

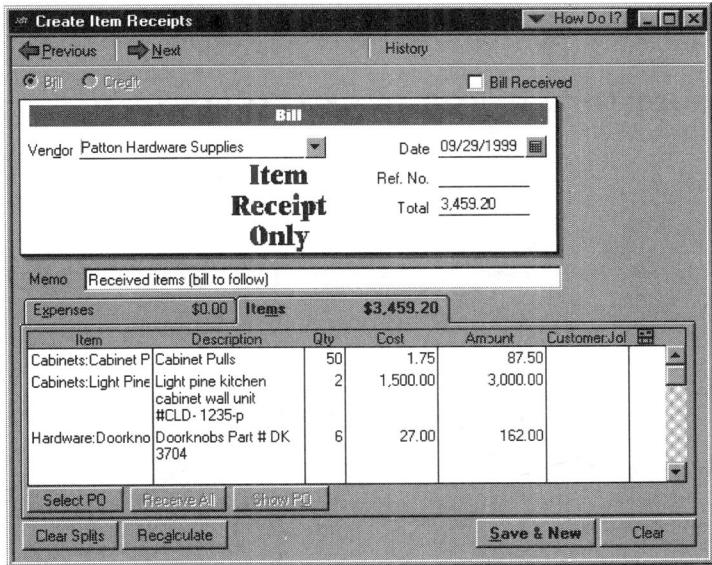

When you record an item receipt, QuickBooks increases the quantity and value of your inventory.

If you have recorded a purchase order for the items, you can receive against that purchase order just as you can for a bill.

When you receive the bill for items received earlier

When you indicate that you want to enter a bill for items received earlier, QuickBooks asks for the vendor name and then displays all item receipts for that vendor. When you choose the appropriate item receipt, QuickBooks displays a bill that matches items on the item receipt.

If the actual costs are different from what you expected, you can edit them on the bill. QuickBooks automatically adjusts the value of your inventory.

You can also add miscellaneous expenses on the Expenses tab of the bill.

To learn about...	Search the Help index for...
Recording items received with or without a bill, and entering the bill when it comes	receiving inventory
Paying bills	bills from vendors, paying

Buying inventory items over the counter

When you pay for and receive items on the spot, you record the items and payment in one step.

Paying with a check or cash

If you pay by check or cash when buying inventory items over the counter, use the Write Checks window to enter the purchase.

If you wrote a check, the **Bank Account** field should show your checking account.

If you paid cash, the **Bank Account** field should show the QuickBooks bank account you set up for petty cash.

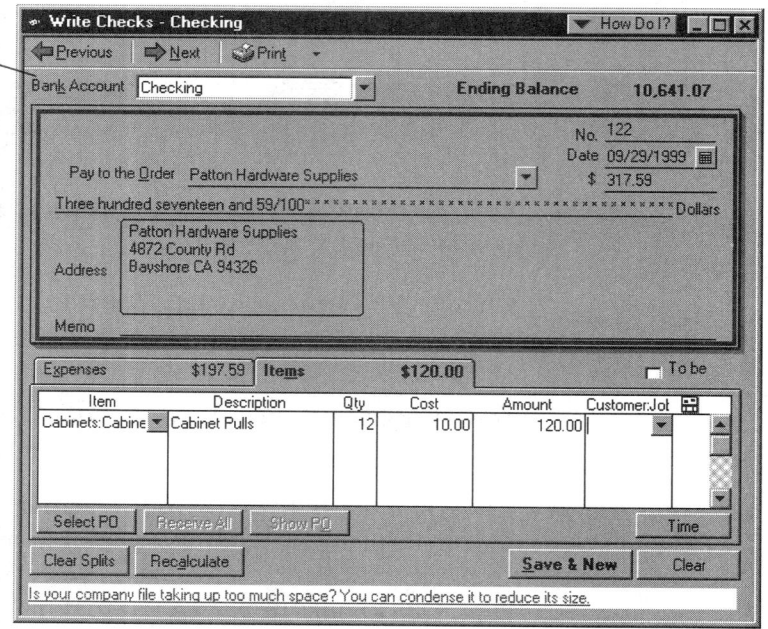

236 | CHAPTER 13 Inventory

Paying with a credit card

If you pay by credit card when buying inventory items over the counter, use the Enter Credit Card Charges window to enter the purchase.

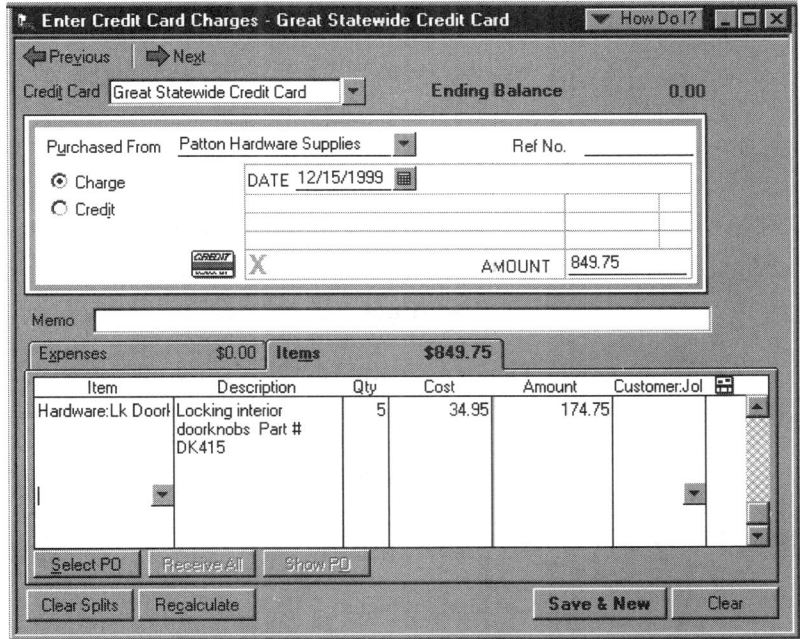

Always use the Items tab (not the Expenses tab) on the Write Checks or Enter Credit Card Charges window.

The Items tab distinguishes inventory items from standard business expenses and allows QuickBooks to increase the quantity and value of your inventory.

To learn about...	Search the Help index for...
Recording a check or cash purchase	checks, writing for expenses and items
Recording a credit card purchase	credit cards you use, transactions, entering and editing

Selling inventory items

You record the sale of inventory items the same way you record any sale in QuickBooks. See "How to track sales and payments" on page 182.

When you sell items from inventory, QuickBooks does the following:

- It tracks how many items remain in stock after the sale.
- It enters a line in your Inventory Asset account register for each item sold, and it reduces the value of your inventory by the number of items sold times the average cost per item.
- It increases your sales income by the amount of each line item.
- It increases your cost of goods sold by the result of the quantity sold times the average cost of each item.

Tip: **You can add shipping charges to a sales form.** You need an "other charge" type of item for the shipping charges. (See "Types of QuickBooks items" on page 119.) Then add this item to the sales form along with the inventory items you are selling.

To learn about...	Search the Help index for...
Creating invoices	invoices, creating
Creating packing slips	packing slips
Recording cash sales	cash sales
Receiving payments	inventory, selling

Tracking back orders and layaways

Depending on your needs, you can track backorders and layaways in one of two ways in QuickBooks.

- Enter invoices and mark them as pending. You can then get reports on backorders or layaways by customer. You can also record any down payments or prepayments. However, pending invoices do not affect your inventory quantities on hand (because a pending invoice is not a sale). You may inadvertently record a sale of an item you have already set aside as a layaway.
- Or, enter postdated invoices (that is, invoices with dates some time in the future). Postdated invoices do reduce your inventory. They

do not affect your income on reports as long as the reporting period doesn't extend into the invoice dates.

To learn about...	Search the Help index for...
Creating a pending invoice	pending sales

Managing your inventory

Managing your inventory includes such tasks as viewing items you have on hand and on order, recording returns to vendors or from customers, and updating your inventory quantities.

QuickBooks keeps track of how many of each item you have in stock or on order, and warns you if you try to sell something you don't have.

When you record inventory returns to a vendor or from a customer, QuickBooks adjusts the amount you owe the vendor or the amount the customer owes you. It also adjusts the quantity on hand and value of your inventory.

When you record changes to your physical inventory, QuickBooks automatically updates the value of your inventory.

Viewing quantities on hand and on order

View the quantities on hand and on order in several ways:

- To view all quantities on hand, display your Item list. (See the illustration on page 119.)

- To view the reorder points, quantities on hand and on order, and average weekly sales of each item, create a stock status by item report. See "Which items do I need to reorder?" on page 244.

- To view a list of purchase orders and quantities still on order for one item, create an item QuickReport. See "Which purchases and sales affected my quantity on hand?" on page 245.

Returning inventory to a vendor

If you return items to a vendor, you must enter a bill credit to make QuickBooks reduce your inventory of those items. Enter a bill credit regardless of whether you have received a bill and regardless of whether you have paid for the items already.

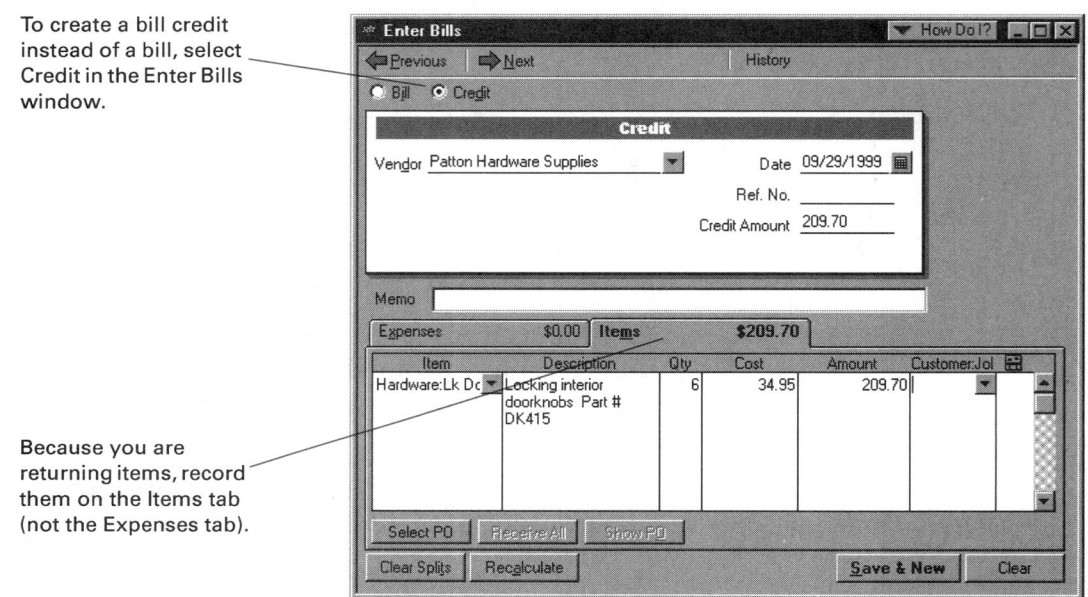

To create a bill credit instead of a bill, select Credit in the Enter Bills window.

Because you are returning items, record them on the Items tab (not the Expenses tab).

Tip: Enter the bill credit in addition to the original item receipt, bill, check, or credit card charge that includes the items you are returning. When you are ready to pay the bill, apply the bill credit to the full bill in the Pay Bills window. If you have already paid for the items, apply the bill credit against another bill from the vendor or against a refund you receive.

Receiving returns from a customer

When you receive returns from a customer, you enter a credit memo. (See the illustration on page 191.) The credit memo reduces the sales income for the returned items and reduces the cost of goods sold. In addition, it increases the inventory asset account by the same amount and increases the quantity in inventory. QuickBooks doesn't recalculate the average cost of the returned items.

Adjusting inventory

Many companies that have inventory take a physical inventory every 6 to 12 months, often at the end of their fiscal year. For help with taking inventory, print the physical inventory worksheet (an inventory report). The worksheet shows each item name and description, preferred vendor, and quantity on hand, and has blank lines on which you can record the physical count.

Although QuickBooks automatically adjusts your quantities after every purchase and sale, you may need to adjust them yourself from time to time for reasons such as breakage, theft, shrinkage, or fire. If you know about changes to your physical inventory, you should record those changes as they happen rather than at year end.

When you adjust your quantity on hand, QuickBooks assumes that the average cost of the item remains the same and adjusts your inventory value accordingly. If needed, QuickBooks lets you adjust the value of your inventory.

For example, after doing a physical inventory, you find you have seven fewer shirts than you thought you had. You decrease your quantity. QuickBooks then asks you which account you would like to attribute this shrinkage to for your profit and loss statement. As you reduce the quantity, you reduce your inventory asset amount and increase your expense.

To learn about...	Search the Help index for...
Viewing quantity on hand	inventory, reports about
Viewing items on order	inventory, items
Returning items to a vendor	inventory, returning
Receiving returns from a customer	returns, recording
Taking a physical inventory	inventory, taking stock of
Adjusting quantity on hand	Inventory, adjusting

Inventory and your QuickBooks accounts

As you use QuickBooks to do everyday tasks like receive items, write invoices, and enter cash sales, QuickBooks automatically updates the accounts associated with your inventory.

When you receive inventory, you affect at least two accounts:

- Your inventory asset account increases in value by the cost of the items you have received.
- If you haven't paid for the items, your accounts payable balance increases. If you paid by check, your bank balance decreases. If you paid by credit card, your credit card balance increases.

When you sell inventory, you affect several accounts:

- QuickBooks automatically calculates the cost of the items you sold. (For details, see "How QuickBooks calculates the value of your inventory" following.) This cost shows up on your profit and loss statement in your cost of goods sold (COGS) account.
- Income from the sale of the item shows up on your profit and loss statement in an income account. As long as you charge more than the cost of the items, you are increasing your gross profit.
- Your inventory asset account decreases in value by the cost of the items you have sold.
- For cash sales, your bank account or your account for undeposited funds increases. For invoiced sales, your accounts receivable balance increases.

How QuickBooks calculates the value of your inventory

QuickBooks uses the average cost method for valuing your inventory rather than other methods such as LIFO (last in, first out) or FIFO (first in, first out).

That is, QuickBooks calculates the average cost of an inventory item (equal to the total value of the items currently in stock divided by the number of items in stock).

When you purchase more of the same items, the value of the inventory increases by the purchase cost. Purchasing more items may change the average cost per item.

When you sell some items, the value of the inventory decreases by the average cost per item multiplied by the number of items sold. Selling items does not change the average cost per item.

How QuickBooks calculates cost of goods sold

The cost of goods sold (COGS) is the expense to your business of goods you have sold from inventory. QuickBooks calculates the cost of goods sold for an item as the average cost of the item at the time of sale multiplied by the quantity sold.

On your chart of accounts and your profit and loss statement, the cost of goods sold account is below your income accounts but above your expense accounts. Although most people need only one cost of goods sold account, you can set up additional accounts. QuickBooks uses the account assigned to the inventory item in the Edit Inventory Item window.

When you sell goods, you are also realizing income. The difference between the income and the cost of goods sold is your profit on the sale.

Getting information about your inventory

This section includes the following topics:

How can I print a price list of my items?	**244**
How do I find out about items I've ordered for a customer?	**244**
Which items do I need to reorder?	**244**
What is the current value of my inventory by item?	**245**
What is my profit on the items I sell?	**245**
Which purchases and sales affected my quantity on hand?	**245**
Other reports about inventory items	**246**

Inventory reports provide a picture of your inventory status. You can run reports showing quantities on hand and when to reorder. You can also run reports showing the total value of your inventory or the profitability of certain items.

How can I print a price list of my items?

The price list includes not only your inventory items but also your service, non-inventory part, other charge, and discount items. For each item, it lists the item name, description, price or rate, and preferred vendor.

How do I find out about items I've ordered for a customer?

If you specify customers and jobs on purchase orders, you can use the open purchase orders by job report to find out which items are still on order for your customers. Use Show All to see all purchase orders for customers. This report includes the source name (vendor) and delivery date for the items.

Which items do I need to reorder?

The inventory stock status by item report presents information to help you reorder items low in stock. It shows the item name, description, preferred vendor, reorder point, quantity on hand, quantity on order, and expected receipt date.

If the quantity on hand plus the quantity on order is on or below the reorder point, a checkmark warns you to reorder the item.

The report also shows the average sales per week of each item (the quantity of sales for the whole period covered by the report divided by the number of weeks in the period). This value helps you estimate when your current stock will be depleted.

What is the current value of my inventory by item?

The valuation summary report shows the item name, description, unit price, quantity on hand, average cost, asset value, percent of total inventory value, sales price, retail value, and percent of total retail value of each inventory item.

What is my profit on the items I sell?

In QuickBooks Pro only, there is an item profitability report that shows the actual cost, actual revenue, and difference (gross profit) for each item you sell. If you want to see your profit as a percentage, customize the report to add a column for percentage difference.

Which purchases and sales affected my quantity on hand?

The QuickReport for an inventory item shows the opening and ending quantity on hand for the item for the period of the report. It also lists every transaction (purchase, sale, or quantity adjustment) that has affected quantity on hand since the beginning of the time period (usually this fiscal year to date).

In addition, this report shows a list of purchase orders for this item for the time period and the quantities still on order.

Other reports about inventory items

Other reports about inventory items include inventory stock status by vendor, a physical inventory worksheet, and sales and purchase reports based on items.

To learn about...	Search the Help index for...
Finding the report you want with the QuickBooks Report Finder	reports, finding
Creating a report about inventory items	inventory, reports about
Creating a QuickReport about an inventory item	items, reports about
Creating a report on profitability by item (QuickBooks Pro only)	items, reports about
Creating a sales report by item or customer	sales, reports about
Creating a purchase report by item or vendor	purchases, reports about

CHAPTER 14

Tracking and paying expenses

Ways to track and pay expenses in QuickBooks	248
Setting up to track and pay expenses	255
Using A/P to track and pay expenses	256
Paying bills immediately (non-A/P)	264
Mixing business and personal funds	271

How should I track the money I spend?

Tracking expenses in QuickBooks means tracking any money you spend on anything relating to your business. These can be services you purchase, items you plan to keep in inventory for resale, fixtures that will become capital assets of your business, office supplies, coffee filters, desks, computers, cleaning services, plant rental or subcontractor services. Basically, any time money leaves your business, you must decide how you want to track it.

Tip: **Keep supporting documents—sales slips, paid bills, receipts, and canceled checks.** If the IRS ever needs to see your records, you must be able to document all your expense deductions.

Ways to track and pay expenses in QuickBooks

This section contains the following information:

Tracking expenses	**248**
Paying for expenses	**251**
Paying for expenses on the spot	**252**
Paying bills at a later time	**253**

Tracking expenses

By account

The expense accounts you set up to track expenses will determine the level of detail you have on your reports regarding your expenses.

For example, a construction firm may want to capture the information about job expenses using the four subaccounts as shown below, but lump all office supplies into one account.

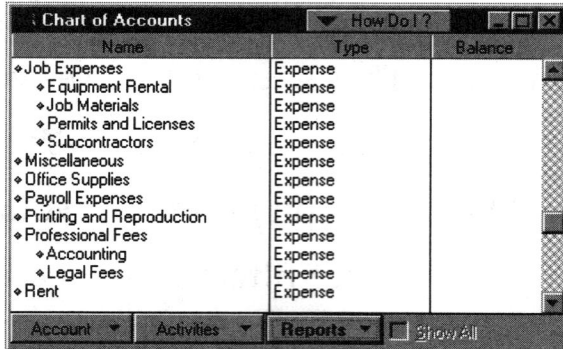

An advertising agency, though, may want to track more detail on its office supplies.

Tax implications

You may want to model your expense accounts after the tax lines that appear on the tax forms you file. For example Schedule C (Profit and Loss from Business) includes the following tax lines:

(line) 8 - Advertising

(line) 9 - Bad debts from sales or services

(line) 10 - Car and truck expenses

If you file this form, you'll want to set up at least one QuickBooks expense account to track "Car and truck expenses," but you could also choose to have subaccounts for this expense area.

Note: **If you designate your tax lines for your expense accounts you can simplify your income tax reporting.** See "Setting up income tax tracking" on page 300.

By class

While you must have some expense accounts set up for your business, classes are optional, but provide another way to track and look at your expense (and income) information.

For example, you may want to track the income and expenses for each partner in your law firm. You would set up your Class List as follows and then for each transaction (invoice, expense, and so on) specify the appropriate class.

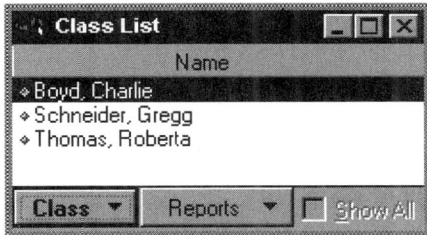

For more information about classes, see "Tracking income and expenses with classes" on page 47.

By customer (and job)

Some businesses using QuickBooks find it useful to track customer information and related job information, parts ordered, and costs.

For example, a construction company may do several jobs for one customer and may want to track the expenses (and income) for them separately.

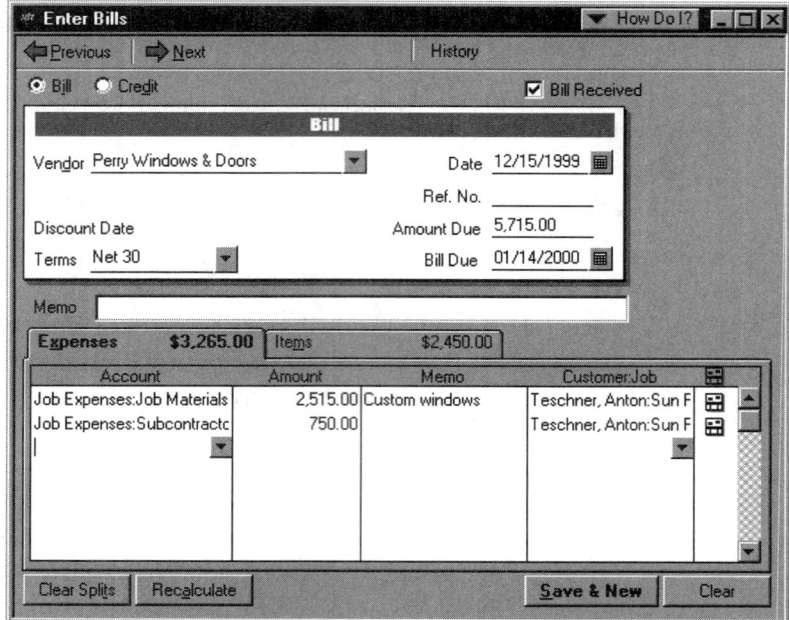

Use the Customer:Job column to track the expenses for a customer, and in this example, a specific job.

You can track the parts you order for a particular customer and job on a purchase order. You'll continue tracking the parts (and the customer:job information) when you receive them and enter the bill (or item receipt).

For more information about customers, see Chapter 10, *Customers and jobs,* beginning on page 141.

Summary of expense accounts, classes, and customers

If you assign the amount of the bill to various expense accounts, customers, jobs, and classes in the detail area of the form or register, your reports will accurately reflect how much you spend within each expense account, for each customer or job, and within each class you have set up.

By purchase order

QuickBooks purchase orders can help you track inventory parts. At any time, you can see items you have on order and when they're due to be received. For more information about inventory parts, see Chapter 13, *Inventory,* beginning on page 223.

If you are a QuickBooks Pro user, you can also order non-inventory parts, services you order from subcontractors, and other charge items on a purchase order if you set up these items with both an income and an expense account, reflecting that you both buy and sell these items. For more information about these types of items, see Chapter 9, *Items—your services, products, and more,* beginning on page 113.

Paying for expenses

Situation	How to record in QuickBooks	Comments	See...
You purchase an item or service and must pay for it on the spot.	Enter the expense as a check, credit card, or petty cash transaction.	These could include costs of dining out, office supplies, highway tolls, and expenses incurred at the post office.	"Paying bills immediately (non-A/P)" on page 264
You receive a bill and want to track and pay it using accounts payable (A/P).	Enter the bills as soon as you receive them and be reminded of when they are due.	Using A/P can help you pay on time and help you forecast your cash flow. You'll also be able to easily find out: ■ Which vendors you owe money to and how much you owe them; ■ If you've paid a certain bill; ■ If any of your payments are overdue, including which ones and by how much; ■ How much you spent with each vendor last quarter.	"Using A/P to track and pay expenses" on page 256
You receive a bill and want to pay it immediately.	Pay for the expense with a check, credit card, or cash.	It's a simple way to handle paying your bills.	"Paying bills immediately (non-A/P)" on page 264

Ways to track and pay expenses in QuickBooks

Situation	How to record in QuickBooks	Comments	See...
You purchase an item for your business but pay for it with a personal check or credit card.	We recommend setting up a liability account to track these expenses. You would enter these types of expenses directly in the account's register.	Consider opening business checking and credit card accounts to make your expense reporting simpler for tax purposes.	"Mixing business and personal funds" on page 271
You want to use online payment.	You can enter bills or write checks in QuickBooks as you usually do. Your online transactions are automatically stored in an "outbox" until you're ready to send them.	For information about scheduling payments, see page 256.	"Using online payment" on page 253 and "Setting up online payment" on page 256
You handwrite your checks.	Enter the check information in the check window or register.	On the Write Checks window, you'll need to make sure you clear the **To be printed** checkbox and that the **No.** field has the same number as the check you write.	"Using checks" on page 265.

Paying for expenses on the spot

All businesses incur some expenses that involve immediate payment, such as costs for travel and dining out, and office supplies. For these payments, you'll want to update the appropriate QuickBooks register or form with the expense information.

For example, if you paid for a business lunch with a credit card, enter the expense on the Enter Credit Card Charges window or in the appropriate credit card register, choosing the appropriate expense account.

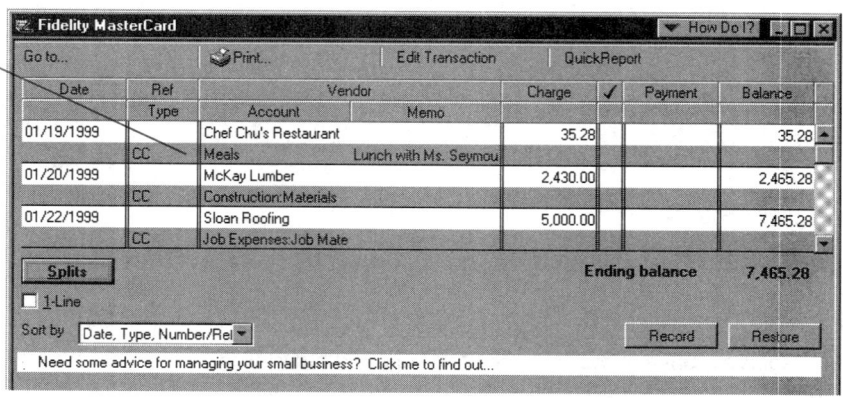

Paying bills at a later time

accounts payable

The record of outstanding bills a business must pay. Called A/P for short.

You can track and pay bills you receive through the mail by using the QuickBooks **accounts payable (A/P) feature** or by **simply paying bills as you receive them** with a check, a credit card, or cash.

Note: You should use just one method to avoid duplicating payments.

Using online payment

Whether you use A/P or not, you should consider using the QuickBooks online payment feature. Online payment works with any U.S. account with check-writing privileges. You can:

- Pay anyone, from the electric company to your janitorial service.
- Send remittance information on an online payment check voucher.
- Create online payment instructions for one or more payments, and then send all your instructions in one connection.
- Schedule a payment, up to a year in advance, to arrive on a certain date.
- Inquire about online payments, and cancel them if the need arises.

    Note: For more information on online payments, go to www.quickbooks.com.

How Your Bills Get Paid

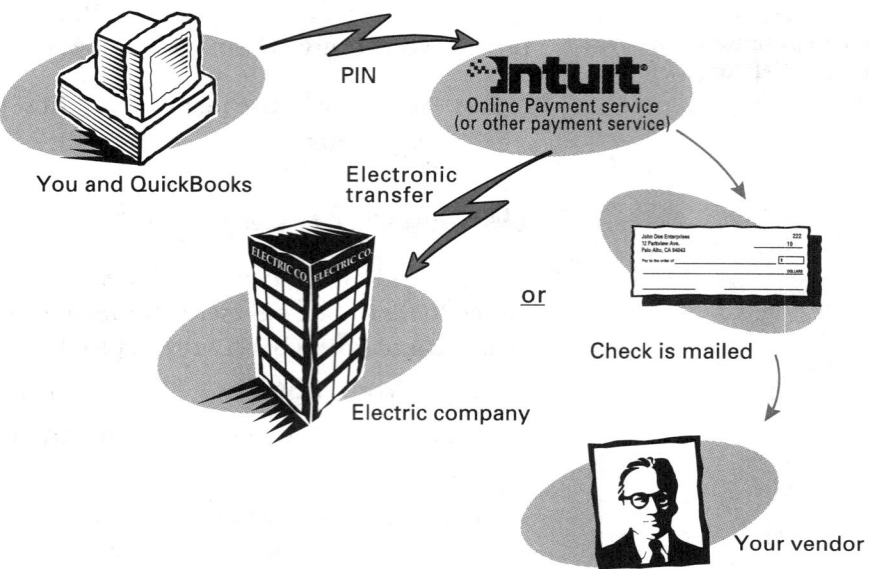

Note: You cannot send paychecks, payroll liability payments, or sales tax checks using online payment.

Delivery date information

Depending on your financial institutions payment processing model, you may be able to specify a delivery date for your online payments. If you can enter a delivery date, QuickBooks calculates the payment delivery date based on the type of online payment that the payee is set up to receive. However, because processing times can vary, it's a good idea to enter a delivery date that's a few days before the due date.

- If the payee is set up to receive an electronic funds transfer (EFT), the financial institution transfers the money directly from your account to the payee on the payment date you designate.

- If the payee cannot receive EFTs, the payment processor prints a check that includes the account number the payee uses to identify you. The processor then sends the check to the payee via U.S. mail.

The number of business days needed for processing the payment is the *lead time*. QuickBooks will calculate the necessary lead time at the time you enter the payment.

Setting up to track and pay expenses

Task	Comments	Search the Help index for...
Decide your bill paying scheme.	**Important**. Once you decide whether you'll use A/P tracking or just pay bills as they arrive, you'll want to use the method consistently to avoid duplicate payment of bills!	bills from vendors, paying vs. tracking
Add additional accounts to the chart of accounts as needed.	The Accounts Payable account is automatically added to your chart of accounts the first time you enter a bill. QuickBooks uses this account to track the money your business owes to others. When you enter a new bill, or pay off outstanding bills, QuickBooks records the transaction in the register for your Accounts Payable account.	■ accounts, adding to your chart of accounts ■ accounts, online ■ petty cash account
Set your checking-related preferences.	Company-wide checking preferences include whether to print account names on voucher checks and whether to warn about duplicate check numbers.	preferences, checking
Set up your printer for check printing.	None	entries under: printing checks
Set the preference for whether to automatically recall the last transaction for a vendor.	When this preference is on, QuickBooks automatically recalls the last bill or check for a vendor when you enter the vendor name on a new bill or check.	automatic transaction entry
If you want to order services or goods, turn on the preference for using purchase orders and inventory.	Even if you don't track inventory, turn on this preference if you want to issue purchase orders to subcontractors and other vendors.	purchase orders, turning on
Set up the Reminders preferences.	You can designate how many days in advance you want to be reminded of due bills and if you want to see a summary or a detailed list of due bills.	preferences, reminders

Setting up online payment

Action	Comments	Search the Help index for...
Setting up online payment	See "Setting up online banking (account access and payment)" on page 99.	online payments, setting up
Setting up online payees	Online payees can be anyone to whom you need to send payments. Employees cannot receive online paychecks, but they can receive other types of online checks. The **Account Number** field number is used by the payee to identify you. It is printed on the check so a payee can apply your payment to the correct account. If you do not have an account number, enter a note or message to your payee.	payees for online payment
Scheduling online payments	You can schedule payments up to 12 months in advance using the date fields on the Write Checks and Pay Bills windows and on your checking register. For example, you may want to schedule the payment of your monthly rent check. Using the Write Checks window, you enter the appropriate information and a **Delivery Date** of 06/30/00. Click Next when done. Now enter the same information for next month's rent payment changing the **Delivery Date** to 7/31/00, and so on. You'll then need to send these online payments. **Important:** The balance of your checking register will be affected.	online payments, scheduling

Using A/P to track and pay expenses

This section contains the following information:

Paying bills	**257**
Applying a vendor's discount	**259**
Handling bills you receive regularly	**261**

Editing bills and payments	**261**
Sending an online payment inquiry	**261**
Deleting bills and payments	**262**
Viewing an A/P transaction history	**262**
Entering and applying credits from vendors	**263**
Receiving items with a bill	**263**
Accounts payable reports	**263**

Paying bills

If you track your accounts payable, paying bills in QuickBooks is essentially a two-step process. You enter the bills in one window and pay them later using a different window. The following steps provide the general work flow:

1 Enter bills in the Enter Bills window as soon as you receive them. This keeps your cash flow reports up to date, and you won't run the risk of setting bills aside and forgetting about them.

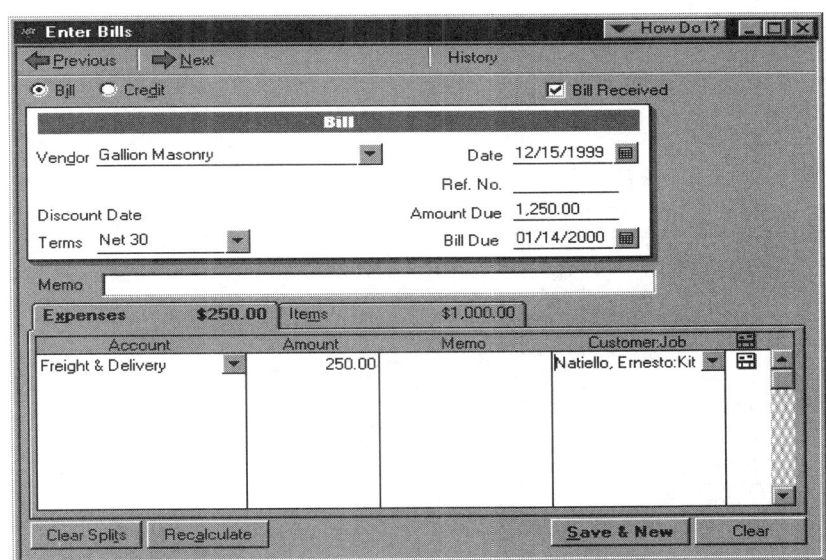

The Expenses tab is used to enter purchases assigned to an expense account. You can also enter shipping charges or tax not associated with any one item.

The Items tab is for entering items you've purchased with or without a purchase order.

You can enter bills directly into the Accounts Payable register instead of using the Enter Bills window. However, if you want to receive a bill or items against a purchase order, use the Enter Bills window.

2 You will be prompted by the Reminder window when bills are due. (If you didn't set up this feature up, see the checklist on page 255.)

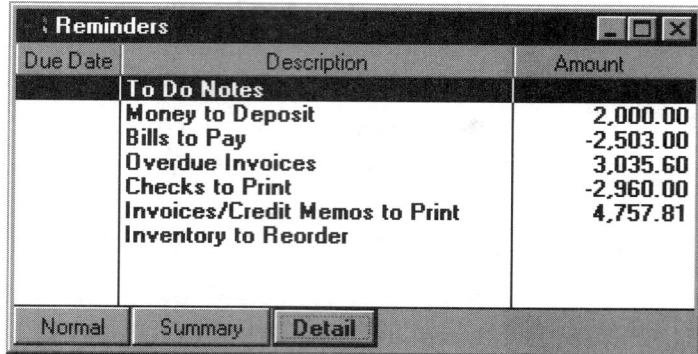

3 Indicate which bills to pay in the Pay Bills window and which payment method (online payment, check, or credit card) to use. If you don't see a bill you expected to pay, check the "Show bills due on or before" date field. See also "Applying a vendor's discount" on page 259.

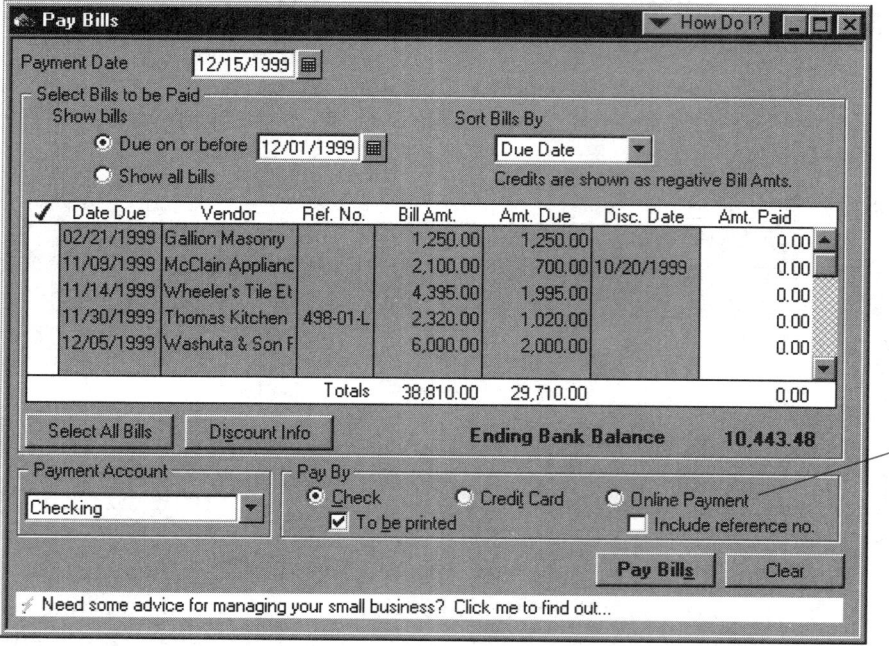

This option appears only if you enabled online payment

If you want to include an invoice number or other remittance information, click **Include reference no.**

4 **The Pay Bills window writes the checks for you.** You either print them or send instructions online if you are using online payment.

CHAPTER 14   Tracking and paying expenses

To learn about...	Search the Help index for...
Entering bills	bills from vendors, entering
Paying bills	bills from vendors, paying
Online payment of a bill	bills from vendors, online payments
Going online	online banking, sending
Recording and paying late-payment charges	late payments to vendors
Printing checks	printing checks

Applying a vendor's discount

You can apply a vendor's discount from the Pay Bills window.

- If you entered a vendor's payment terms when you set up the vendor or designated terms on the Enter Bills window, QuickBooks calculates the discount for you. You can change the amount of the discount as needed.

- If you don't specify a vendor's payment terms, calculate the discount manually and enter it in the Discount Information window (see page 260).

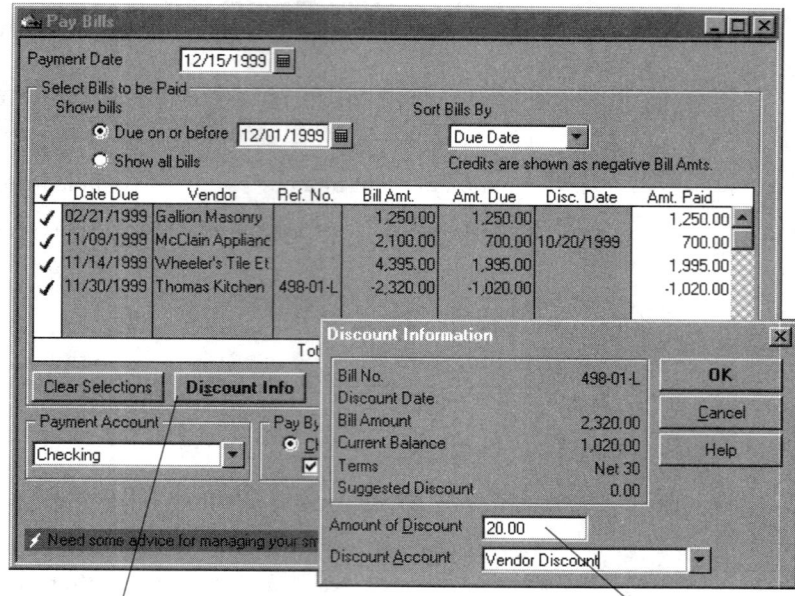

Click the Discount Info button from the Pay Bills window to enter the discount.

You can accept the prefilled discount amount or enter another one. When you click OK, the discount is subtracted from the amount you owe.

To learn about...	Search the Help index for...
Creating an expense account to track your vendor discounts	accounts, adding to your chart of accounts
Applying a vendor's discount	discounts, from vendors
Payment terms	payments you make, terms
Setting up a reminder to pay bills	bills from vendors, reminding yourself to pay

Handling bills you receive regularly

In your business, you probably receive the same bills every month. For example, you may receive phone and utility bills or make loan payments and pay rent at the same times each month. You can memorize these bills and have QuickBooks re-enter them at the intervals you specify.

To learn about...	Search the Help index for...
Memorizing bills	bills from vendors, memorizing

Editing bills and payments

You can edit any bill or payment transaction except online payment transactions. Even if you've already paid a bill, you can edit its amount.

If you reduce the bill amount, QuickBooks creates a credit with the vendor you overpaid. If you increase the bill amount, QuickBooks considers the bill not fully paid until you pay the additional amount.

To learn about...	Search the Help index for...
Editing bills	bills from vendors, editing
Editing payments	payments you make, editing

Sending an online payment inquiry

With QuickBooks, you can send messages to any financial institution at which you have accounts enabled for online banking. You can inquire about the status of a specific payment, and you may choose to send a message with the inquiry.

To learn about...	Search the Help index for...
Online payment inquiries	online payments, inquiring about
Online banking messages	online banking, messages about

Deleting bills and payments

You can delete any bill or payment transaction. If you delete a bill that you have already paid, QuickBooks creates a credit with the vendor. If you delete a payment, the bill or bills it was paying will have unpaid balances.

To learn about...	Search the Help index for...
Deleting bills	bills from vendors, deleting
Deleting payments	payments you make, deleting

Viewing an A/P transaction history

A transaction history shows transactions related or linked to the one you selected, so you can move easily to any related transaction. For example, from a bill, you can see any of the payments that paid the bill.

The following table describes the transaction history QuickBooks shows for different types of transactions.

Transaction type	History shows these related transactions, in chronological order
Bill	Payments made on the bill Discounts Purchase Orders
Payment	Bills to which your payment was applied
Credit with a vendor	Bills to which your credit was applied
Item receipt	PO's against which the items were received

To learn about...	Search the Help index for...
Viewing the history of a transaction	transaction history

Entering and applying credits from vendors

Use the Enter Bills window to enter a credit from a vendor. Simply change the Bill setting to Credit. You can easily apply any credit you have with a vendor in the Pay Bills window.

To learn about...	Search the Help index for...
Credit from a vendor	vendors, credit from

Receiving items with a bill

When you receive items with a bill, you can record their receipt and enter the bill at the same time. This feature allows you to associate the items received with the purchase order you entered when ordering them. See also "Receiving inventory items" on page 234.

To learn about...	Search the Help index for...
Receiving items with a bill	inventory, receiving

Accounts payable reports

Accounts payable reports can answer questions such as these about your business:

- Which vendors do I owe money to?
- Which of my bills are more than 30 days past due?

QuickBooks has preset A/P reports that give you information about your unpaid bills. You can calculate the aging for the A/P reports and graphs from the due date or the transaction date.

You can filter each preset report so that it shows only the information you want to see. You can also customize each report so that it looks the way you want onscreen and on paper.

Report	Description
A/P aging summary	Shows aging status of unpaid bills in accounts payable, subtotaled by vendor.
A/P aging detail	Lists each unpaid bill, grouped and subtotaled by aging period. Shows how many days a bill is overdue.

Using A/P to track and pay expenses | 263

Report	Description
Unpaid bills detail	Lists each unpaid bill, grouped and subtotaled by vendor.
Vendor balance summary	Shows unpaid balances for each vendor.
Vendor balance detail	Lists each transaction for a vendor, subtotaled by vendor. Total for a vendor equals that vendor's unpaid balance.

For more information about reports, see Chapter 19, *Tracking your progress with reports and graphs,* beginning on page 397.

Reporting online payments

You'll need to create a custom summary report to report your online activities. After you create the report, you may want to save the settings for future use. See "Saving report settings" on page 405 for more information.

To learn about...	Search the Help index for...
Creating a report of online payments	online payments, reports about

Paying bills immediately (non-A/P)

This section contains the following information:

Using checks	**265**
Using credit cards	**267**
Using cash to pay for expenses	**269**
Tracking a vendor's discount	**270**
Mixing business and personal funds	**271**

For bills you pay immediately, you'll use check and credit card windows that emulate familiar paper forms. You can also enter these types of transactions in the account's register. For cash purchases, you enter the expense in your petty cash register.

Using checks

If you are not tracking your bills with the accounts payable feature, you can simply write a check when the bill is due. The following steps provide the general work flow:

1 Write the check for the expense using the Write Checks window.

If you are using online payment and you want to include an invoice number or other remittance information, select **Transmit Memo**. A check voucher is printed with the information entered in the **Transmit Memo** field.

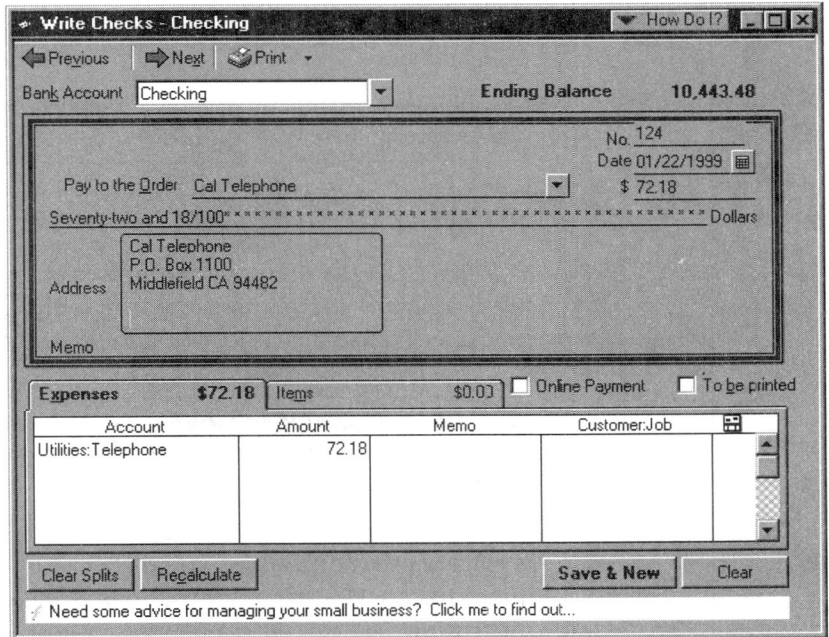

The Expenses tab is used to enter purchases assigned to an expense account. You can also enter shipping charges or tax not associated with any one item.

The Items tab is for entering items you've purchased with or without a purchase order.

You can write a check directly into the check register instead of using the Write Checks window. However, if you want to pay for an expense connected with a purchase order use the Write Checks window.

2 Either print the checks or send them online if you are using online payment. (If you write checks by hand, you'll need to clear the **To be printed** checkbox on the Write Checks window and make sure the **No.** field has the same number as the check you write.)

To learn about...	Search the Help index for...
Writing checks	checks, writing for expenses and items
Printing checks	entries under: printing checks
Online payment of a bill	bills from vendors, online payments
Going online	online banking, sending
Changing information on a check you've recorded	checks, editing

Voiding or deleting checks

Voiding a check changes the amount of the transaction to zero, but keeps a record of the transaction in QuickBooks. If you stop payment on a check or a check is lost, you may want to void it rather than delete it.

Deleting a check removes the transaction from QuickBooks. Once a check is deleted it cannot be recovered.

If you are using online payment, choose Cancel Payment from the Edit menu to cancel a payment that has already been sent to the financial institution.

Note: **This will not stop a payment that has already been issued.** To stop a payment you must contact your financial institution.

To learn about...	Search the Help index for...
Voiding checks	checks, voiding or deleting
Deleting checks	checks, voiding or deleting
Canceling an online payment	online payments, canceling a payment

Handling bills you receive regularly

If you repeatedly write similar checks, such as rent or insurance payments, you can save time by memorizing the checks.

To learn about...	Search the Help index for...
Memorizing checks	checks, memorizing

Using credit cards

If you are not tracking your bills with the accounts payable feature, you can simply use your credit card to pay for a bill when it's due. The following steps provide the general work flow:

1   Enter the credit card charge in the Enter Credit Card Charges window.

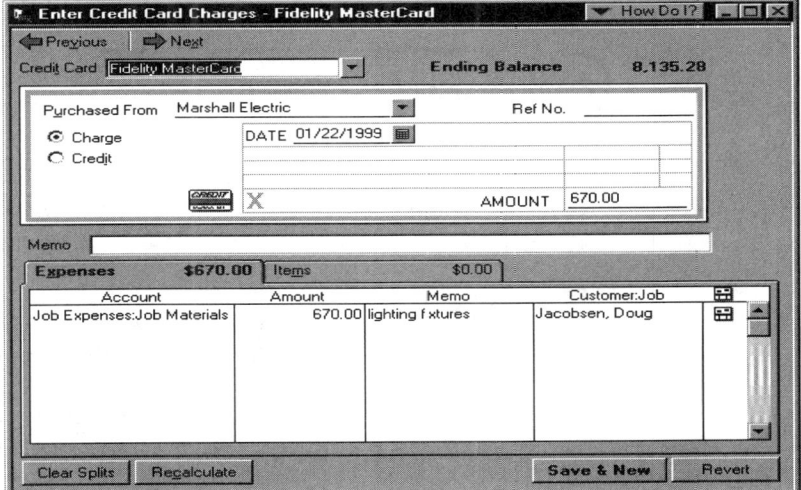

The Expenses tab is used to enter purchases assigned to an expense account. You can also enter shipping charges or tax not associated with any one item.

The Items tab is for entering items you've purchased with or without a purchase order.

You can enter charges directly into the credit card register instead of using the Enter Credit Card Charges window. However, if you want to pay for a bill connected to a purchase order, use the Enter Credit Card Charges window.

2   If you are using online payment, send the payment instructions online. Otherwise, call or visit the company and give them your credit card number.

To learn about...	Search the Help index for...
Entering or editing a credit card charge	credit cards you use, transactions, entering and editing
Online payment of a bill	bills from vendors, online payments
Going online	online banking, sending

Voiding or deleting a credit card entry

Voiding a charge changes the amount of the transaction to zero, but keeps a record of the transaction in QuickBooks.

Deleting a charge removes the transaction from QuickBooks. Once a charge is deleted it cannot be recovered.

To learn about...	Search the Help index for...
Voiding a charge	credit cards you use, voiding or deleting a charge
Deleting a charge	credit cards you use, voiding or deleting a charge

Handling merchandise you return that was paid for with a credit card

If you return merchandise for which you receive credit, you'll need to enter this amount into the credit card account's register or in the Enter Credit Card Charges window. Make sure to assign the credit to the appropriate expense account, class, and customer:job.

To learn about...	Search the Help index for...
Credit card refunds	credit cards you use, credits

268 | CHAPTER 14 Tracking and paying expenses

Using cash to pay for expenses

If you pay for expenses with cash, enter the transaction in your petty cash register.

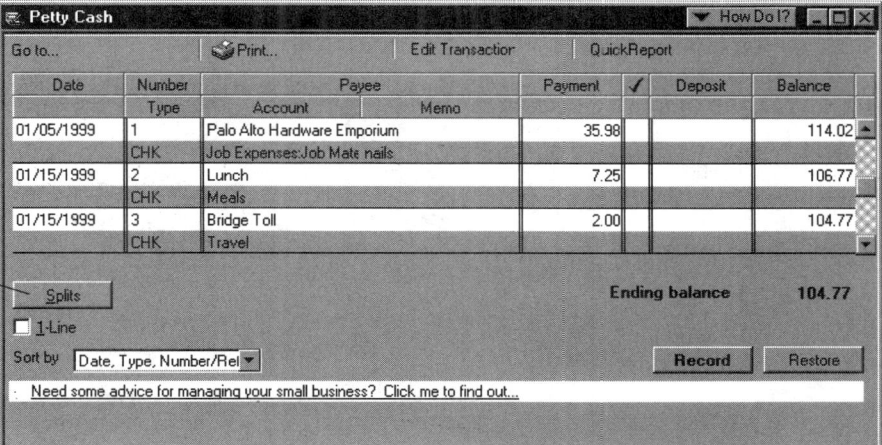

To enter class and customer:job information, click Splits.

To learn about...	Search the Help index for...
Entering cash expenses	cash account, handling expenses
Handling ATM withdrawals in QuickBooks	ATM withdrawals

Tracking a vendor's discount

You can record a vendor's discount as a negative expense to your Vendor Discount expense account on the appropriate form.

Note: The total amount of the check cannot be negative.

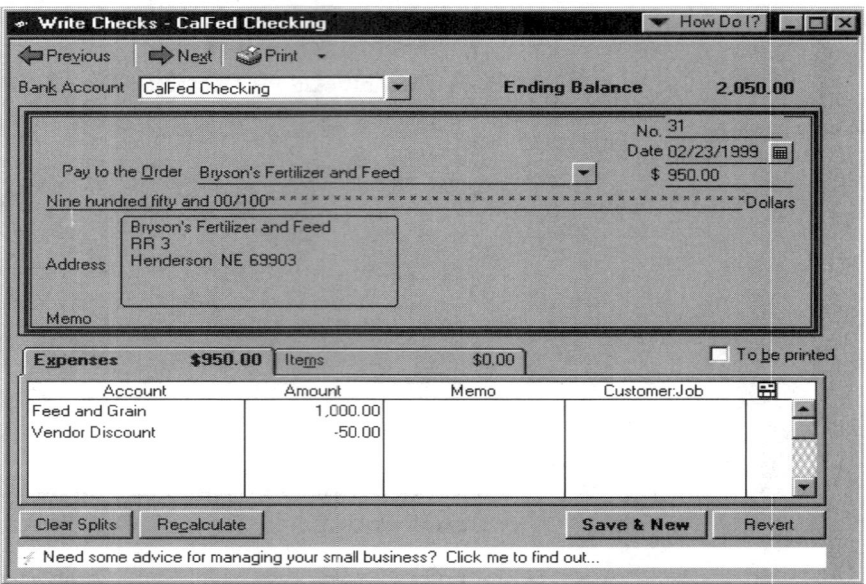

To learn about...	Search the Help index for...
Creating an income account to track your vendor discounts	accounts, adding to your chart of accounts

Mixing business and personal funds

You should keep your business account separate from your personal checking account. -

IRS publication 583, "Starting a Business and Keeping Records"

You should have checking and credit card accounts that are business-only accounts. In fact, the IRS recommends opening a business checking account as one of the *first* things you do when starting a new business. But from time to time you may find it convenient to pay for a business expense with your personal credit card or check, or pay for a personal expense with your business check or credit card.

For owners or partners

The owner's or partner's equity account can track both business expenses you pay for with personal funds and personal expenses paid for with business funds.

Note: **If you track your personal finances in Quicken or in a separate QuickBooks company file, you have to enter the purchase in that file as well.** This section is about recording the purchase in your QuickBooks business file.

Paying for business expenses with personal funds

Enter these business expenses directly in the owner's or partner's equity account register as an increase.

In the Account field, enter the appropriate expense account.

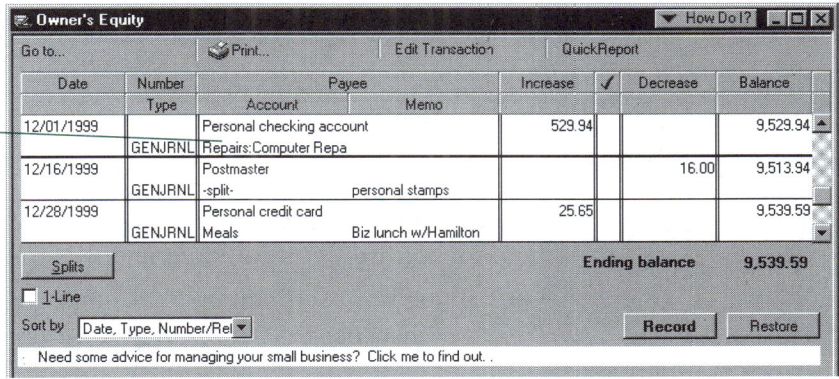

Owners or partners can take a draw (write a check) at any time to reimburse themselves.

To learn about...	Search the Help index for...
Creating an owner's draw	owner's draws

Paying for personal expenses with business funds

If you pay for personal expenses with business funds, enter the transaction in the appropriate QuickBooks window (Write Checks, Enter Credit Card Charges, Petty Cash Register) using the owner's or partner's equity account. This will decrease the equity in that account.

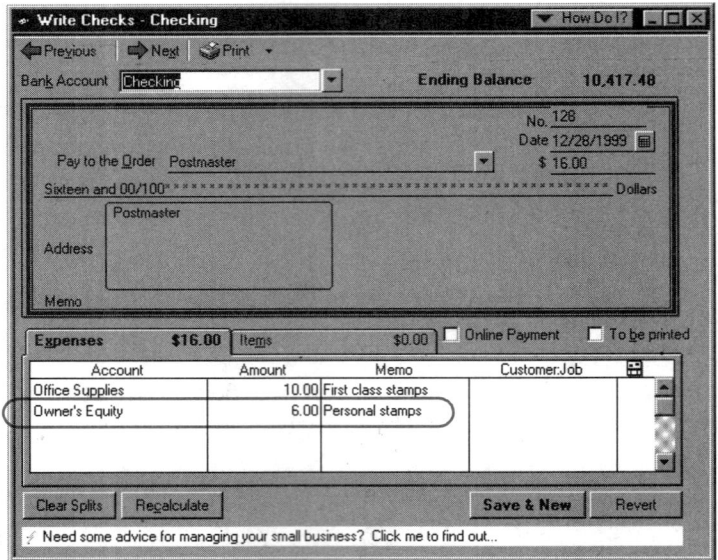

For employees

To reimburse an employee who has paid for a business expense with personal funds, you can do one of the following:

- If you want to reimburse the employee at the time you record the expense, use the Write Checks window.

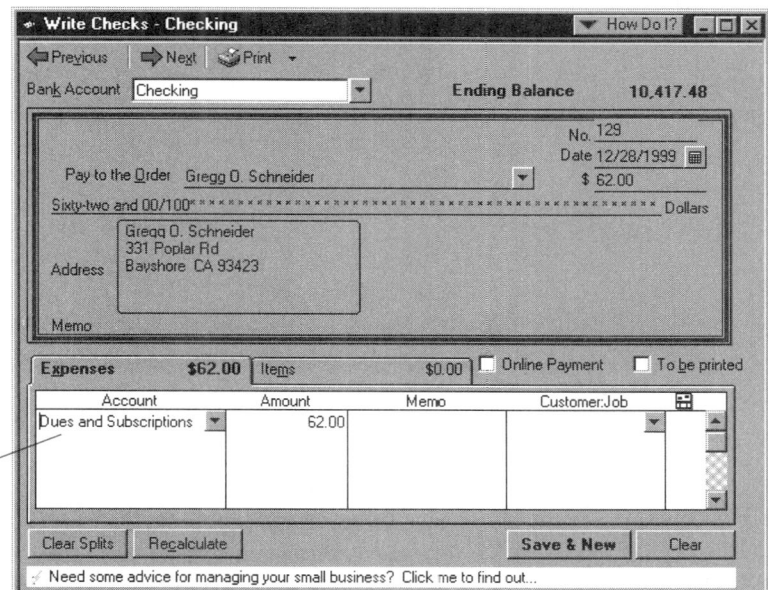

Enter the appropriate expense account in the Account field.

- If you want to reimburse the employee later, enter the expense in an Other Current Liability account as an increase.

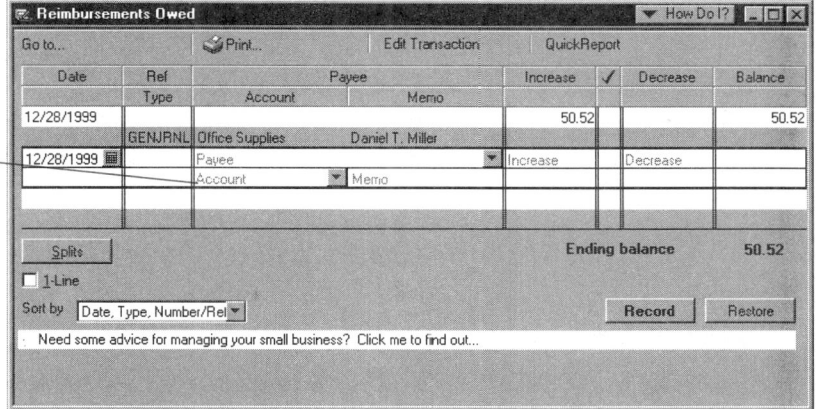

Enter the expense account in the Account field and the employee's name in the Memo field.

When you reimburse the employee, use the Write Checks window. In the Account field, enter the Other Current Liability account, not the expense account, so that the reimbursement check reduces the amount owed.

Tip: Use the To Do Notes feature to keep track of whom you owe!

CHAPTER 15

Tracking and paying sales tax

How QuickBooks tracks sales tax	276
Setting up sales tax	280
Tracking and paying sales tax	286
Getting reports about sales tax	294

How can I collect and pay the right amount of sales tax?

The sales tax feature of QuickBooks helps you determine how much sales tax to collect on each sale, as well as how much you may need to pay when it is due.

This chapter does not intend to be exhaustive on the subject of sales taxes. Tax laws and regulations change frequently and their application can vary widely based on the specific facts and circumstances involved. Users are responsible for consulting with their own professional tax advisors concerning their business's specific tax circumstances.

This chapter is about tracking the sales tax you collect from customers, not the sales tax you pay to your vendors.

If you don't collect any sales tax for the services you provide or the products you sell, you don't need to set up sales tax in QuickBooks.

If you need to track the exact sales tax you paid on purchases, you can set up an expense account for sales tax. Most people simply include the sales tax they pay vendors as part of the overall cost of the purchase.

How QuickBooks tracks sales tax

Your sales tax rates and tax districts   **277**
Do I need to group individual sales taxes in QuickBooks?   **279**

Keeping track of the sales taxes you have to collect from customers and pay to a tax agency can be a challenge. Some of the things you sell may be taxable while others may not be. Certain customers must be taxed, while sales to others are nontaxable. In addition, different sales may require different taxes. You may even have to collect more than one tax on a sale.

Fortunately, QuickBooks can help you automate your sales tax tracking. You can enter sales quickly and easily, and you'll have more accurate information about the sales taxes you've collected when it comes time to pay.

Take the time to set up your sales tax carefully and methodically. Then it will be easy to apply the right sales tax to each sale so you will have a better idea of how much sales tax you owe.

The following diagram illustrates the basic steps you perform when tracking sales tax in QuickBooks.

Tracking sales tax

Setting up sales tax

Set up tax rates and tax agencies.

- State tax 8.0%
- Sales tax board

Indicate who and what is taxable.

 Customer is taxable

 Taxable item

Collecting sales tax

QuickBooks calculates appropriate sales tax on each taxable sale.

Sales forms

Paying sales tax

Pay what you owe.

Checks to tax agencies

Your sales tax rates and tax districts

You collect sales tax for one or more particular sales tax districts. For example, when Stacy sells from her store or makes deliveries within the county, she collects sales tax for the county she is in. If she makes deliveries in the next county, she collects for that county.

For each tax district, you have to tell QuickBooks the tax rate and the name of the agency you pay.

QuickBooks stores the information about your sales tax on your Item list. The Item list has a type of item called a sales tax item, designed exclusively for sales tax. If your rates change, you can update them by editing the relevant sales tax items.

You may be thinking that the Item list is a strange place for sales tax information. Remember that some QuickBooks items are for the services and products you sell, while others are for various calculations on sales forms (subtotals, discounts, credits for payments). Sales tax is just another calculation on a sales form.

Every state with sales tax has a different sales tax structure, so it's hard to generalize. Check with your own state and local sales tax agencies to find out their rules.

The following table describes different sales tax situations you may be dealing with.

Situation	What to use in QuickBooks	See...	Search the Help Index for...
All taxable sales are in a single tax district.	Sales tax item set up for your tax district	"If your business collects only one tax for one agency" on page 282	sales tax, items
Taxable sales are in two or more tax districts, and you must report sales by district. **Example:** You must report sales by county.	A different sales tax item for each tax district. ■ The districts can be for the same tax agency. ■ The districts can have the same tax rate.	"If your business collects sales taxes based on location" on page 282	sales tax, items
You collect a combination of sales taxes on one sale, and you pay the taxes to different tax agencies. **Example:** You pay a statewide tax to one tax agency and a city tax to a different agency.	Sales tax group item that is made up of two or more sales tax items (one for each tax agency)	■ "Do I need to group individual sales taxes in QuickBooks?" on page 279 ■ "If your business collects a combination rate" on page 283	sales tax, tax assignments

Situation	What to use in QuickBooks	See...	Search the Help Index for...
You must report sales that are nontaxable because they are outside your state or tax district.	Zero-rate sales tax item set up for out-of-state sales	▪ "If you report nontaxable sales to out-of-state customers" on page 283 ▪ "Which customers are subject to sales tax?" on page 284	sales tax, out-of-state customers
You must report sales that are nontaxable because the customer is purchasing for resale.	Zero-rate sales tax item set up for sales to resellers	▪ "If you report nontaxable sales to resellers" on page 284 ▪ "Which customers are subject to sales tax?" on page 284	sales tax, zero-rate
You don't need to report why a sale is nontaxable but you want to make sure the customer is not charged for sales tax.	Simply set up the customer to be nontaxable. QuickBooks automatically reports such sales as nontaxable for your most common sales tax.	"Which customers are subject to sales tax?" on page 284	customers, sales tax for

Do I need to group individual sales taxes in QuickBooks?

If you collect a sales tax that is a combination of separate sales taxes, QuickBooks allows you to group the separate taxes together and apply a rate that equals the total of the separate rates.

You may not need to divide your tax into parts in QuickBooks even if the actual tax is a combination of rates. For example, in California, the tax in a county is usually a statewide rate plus some additional taxes levied by the county or a special district. But in QuickBooks, you can simply set up a sales tax item for each county for which you collect sales tax. All sales taxes collected for one county are paid to the same tax agency, and the tax form helps you calculate what you owe for each separate tax.

On the other hand, if you sometimes collect a combination of taxes paid to separate tax agencies, you need to track the taxes separately. For example, suppose you have a county rate plus an additional city rate. In QuickBooks you should set up separate sales tax items (on your Item list) for the county and city taxes. Then you set up a type of item called a *sales tax group* to combine the county and city items. For sales in the city, subject to the combination, you apply the sales tax group item. For sales in the county but outside the city, you apply the county's sales tax item.

Setting up sales tax

This section contains the following topics:

If your business collects only one tax for one agency	**282**
If your business collects sales taxes based on location	**282**
If your business collects a combination rate	**283**
If you report nontaxable sales to out-of-state customers	**283**
If you report nontaxable sales to resellers	**284**
Which customers are subject to sales tax?	**284**
Which items are subject to sales tax?	**285**
How do I specify when my sales tax is payable?	**286**

The following checklist helps you get ready to track sales tax in QuickBooks.

If you set up your company using the EasyStep Interview and indicated you tracked sales tax, you may have already completed some of these tasks.

What to set up	Comments	Search the Help Index for...
Add tax agency name or names and information to your Vendor list.	QuickBooks uses this information on the sales tax payment check it writes to each sales tax agency. To print your tax ID number on your payment check, enter it in the Account Number field on the Additional Info tab of the New or Edit Vendor window.	vendors, adding
Turn on sales tax.	Only the QuickBooks Administrator can turn on sales tax.	sales tax, turning on
Set company-wide preferences for payment frequency and how sales tax is owed.	You must set these preferences when you turn on sales tax, but you can change them later.	sales tax, preferences for

What to set up	Comments	Search the Help Index for...
Indicate the sales tax to prefill when setting up a new customer or starting to enter a new sale.	You must set this choice for "most common sales tax" when you turn sales tax on, but you can change it later.	sales tax, preferences for
Indicate whether to print the letter "T" next to taxable amounts on sales forms.	None	sales tax, preferences for
Set up each additional sales tax or component of sales tax as a sales tax item on your Item list.	Most businesses don't need to do this. For more information, see "If your business collects sales taxes based on location" on page 282 and "If your business collects a combination rate" on page 283.	sales tax, items
To track nontaxable sales, set up a zero-rate sales tax item for each reason (such as out-of-state, resale).	For a zero-rate item, you don't have to specify a tax agency to pay (because there's no tax to pay).	sales tax, zero-rate
If sales tax has components paid to different tax agencies, set up one or more sales tax groups.	See "If your business collects a combination rate" on page 283.	sales tax, tax assignments
Indicate which existing items on the Item list are taxable.	When you turn on sales tax, Quick-Books asks whether to make all existing non-inventory and inventory parts taxable. From now on, when you create a new item, it will automatically be taxable unless you clear the Taxable checkbox in the New Item window.	items, editing information

Setting up sales tax | 281

If your business collects only one tax for one agency

Most businesses collect only one sales tax for one agency. This is the easiest situation to set up. You need the following:

- The sales tax agency must be a vendor on your Vendor list. Be sure you have entered the agency's address and your sales tax account number, so QuickBooks can print checks with this information.
- You need a sales tax item on your Item list for your sales tax. Your sales tax rate is the rate for this item.
- If you need to report nontaxable sales to out-of-state customers, you need an additional sales tax item for out-of-state sales. See "If you report nontaxable sales to out-of-state customers" on page 283.
- If you need to report nontaxable sales to wholesalers or resellers, you need an additional sales tax item for resale. See "If you report nontaxable sales to resellers" on page 284.

If your business collects sales taxes based on location

If you deliver, visit customers, or have multiple sales offices, you may need to charge different sales taxes depending on the location of the sale. QuickBooks handles this easily if you do the following:

- For each different sales tax agency you pay, you must have a vendor on your Vendor list. (You need only one agency if you pay all your sales tax to the same agency.)
- For each different sales tax you collect, you need a sales tax item on your Item list. (If you have to report sales and tax by county or district, you need a separate sales tax item for each, even if the rate is the same.)
- If you need to report nontaxable sales to out-of-state customers, you need an additional sales tax item for out-of-state sales. See "If you report nontaxable sales to out-of-state customers" on page 283.
- If you need to report nontaxable sales to wholesalers or resellers, you need an additional sales tax item for resale. See "If you report nontaxable sales to resellers" on page 284.

- Be sure your customers are set up with the correct sales tax item assigned. Then when you record a new sale to a customer, QuickBooks automatically uses the correct sales tax item.

If your business collects a combination rate

If you collect more than one tax, payable to different agencies, on the same sale but you want to charge your customers one overall tax amount, here is what you must do:

- For each different sales tax agency you pay, you must have a vendor on your Vendor list.
- For each single tax you collect and pay, you need a sales tax item on your Item list.
- For each combination rate you collect, you need a sales tax group on your Item list. A sales tax group includes two or more single taxes set up as sales tax items. The rate for the group is the total of the rates for the items in the group. Group tax items allow QuickBooks to track and report taxes separately, but display them as one combined amount to customers.
- If your most common sales tax is a combination, be sure that the sales tax group item is shown as the most common sales tax in the sales tax preferences. Then new customers and new sales will automatically have the combination rate.

If you report nontaxable sales to out-of-state customers

If you have to report sales that would be taxable had they not been to out-of-state customers, you need to have a zero-tax sales tax item that you can use to identify the out-of-state sale. Then the sales tax liability report will have a separate line showing total nontaxable sales to out-of-state customers.

If you set up sales tax through the EasyStep Interview, your Item list already has a sales tax item called Out of State. This sales tax item has a 0% tax rate and no tax agency.

If you turn on sales tax after setting up your company file, you have to set up this sales tax item yourself. Give it a name you can recognize (such as Out of State) and be sure the tax rate is 0%.

If you report nontaxable sales to resellers

If you need to identify and report nontaxable sales to resellers, set up a sales tax item called Resale with a 0% tax rate. Then the sales tax liability report will have a separate line showing total nontaxable sales to resellers.

Which customers are subject to sales tax?

After you've set up information about your sales tax, you have to indicate which customers are subject to sales tax. For example, you may sell to retail customers who pay tax and to wholesale customers who are exempt from tax. When you set up or edit customer information, you specify whether the customer is taxable.

When you indicate that a customer pays sales tax, you specify *which* sales tax (if you collect more than one). Then when you write a sales form and fill in the customer name, QuickBooks knows which tax (if any) to apply. (If the taxability of a sale changes for a special case, you can always change it right on the sales form.)

If a customer does not pay sales tax and you have to report *why* any sales are not taxable, then choose a zero-rate sales tax item in addition to saying the customer is not taxable. For example:

- If the customer is out-of-state, choose the Out of State tax item. (See "If you report nontaxable sales to out-of-state customers" on page 283.)

- If the customer buys for resale, choose your Resale tax item. (See "If you report nontaxable sales to resellers" on page 284.)

If you don't have to report the reasons sales are not taxable, assign your most common sales tax. As long as you say the customer is not taxable, QuickBooks doesn't charge sales tax. On reports, it includes sales to nontaxable customers with sales of nontaxable items to taxable customers.

Tip: **You can customize the customer phone list report to show the taxability and tax item of all your customers.** Create the report and then customize it by adding columns for Taxable and Tax Item. If any customer has the wrong taxability, double-click it on the report to display its Edit Customer window. Then click the Additional Info tab and edit the sales tax information.

Which items are subject to sales tax?

Your sales forms may contain some items that are taxable and some that are not. As part of the information about the items on your Item list, you have to specify whether the item is usually taxable. The actual tax can vary with the customer and the circumstances of the sale.

When QuickBooks calculates the sales tax on a sale, it includes only the items marked as taxable and ignores the others. You must make sure to have the correct taxability for each item.

Tip: **The item listing report shows the taxability of all your items.** Check this report to make sure your items are set up correctly. You can customize the report to remove columns you don't need to see. If any item has the wrong taxability, double-click it on the report to display its Edit Item window. Then clear or select the **Taxable** checkbox.

How do I specify when my sales tax is payable?

In some states, you owe sales tax on all sales that occurred before a specified date. In other states, you owe sales tax on only those sales for which you have received payment.

You can set a company-wide preference in QuickBooks that specifies on which sales you owe sales tax. QuickBooks uses this preference to calculate how much tax you owe.

In addition, you can set a company-wide preference about how often your sales tax becomes payable. QuickBooks uses this preference to calculate the ending date of sales on which you now owe sales tax. It also uses this preference for the time period covered by the sales tax liability report.

If you collect more than one sales tax, and they differ in which sales they cover or how often you have to pay, don't worry. You can change the preferences any time.

Tracking and paying sales tax

This section contains the following topics about tracking and paying the sales tax you collect on sales.

Applying sales tax to an invoice or cash sale	**287**
Special tax situations	**289**
Keeping track of how much sales tax you owe	**291**
Paying sales tax	**292**
Changing information about your sales tax	**293**

Once you have set up sales tax correctly, QuickBooks automatically adds the correct sales tax to each sale and tracks how much you owe. In addition, if you enter a credit memo for the return of taxable items, QuickBooks reduces the sales tax you owe.

When it's time to pay sales tax, you can use a window that lists all unpaid sales tax for sales through a specified date (such as the end of last month). You tell QuickBooks which taxes to pay, and it writes the check or checks.

There is a report that gives you information you may need in filling out sales tax forms, such as the total gross sales, the taxable sales, and the nontaxable sales. (See "What is the breakdown of my sales tax, taxable sales, and nontaxable sales by sales tax district?" on page 294.)

QuickBooks keeps track of all the sales tax you have collected, all the sales tax you have paid, and your current sales tax liability in an account it sets up for you. This account, called Sales Tax Payable, is a current liability account on your chart of accounts. Your balance sheet always shows the total amount of sales tax you owe.

Applying sales tax to an invoice or cash sale

QuickBooks automatically calculates the tax on a sale if you've done the following (see "Setting up sales tax" on page 280):

- Set up a sales tax item on your Item list for each sales tax you collect
- Assigned the appropriate sales tax to each customer
- Specified which of the items on your Item list that you sell are taxable

QuickBooks cannot track sales tax for statement charges.

If you enter any taxable items directly in a customer register, QuickBooks cannot add sales tax to them. If you collect sales tax, you must enter the sale on a cash sales receipt or invoice.

When you enter a sale to an existing customer, QuickBooks applies the tax you have assigned this customer to items you've marked taxable (shown with a "T" on the sales form). It displays the tax name in the **Tax** field at the bottom of the sales form. Next to the tax name it displays the rate and amount.

If the sale is to a new customer (or no customer), QuickBooks automatically fills in your most common tax in the **Tax** field at the bottom of the sales form. However, you can choose a different tax from your list of tax items.

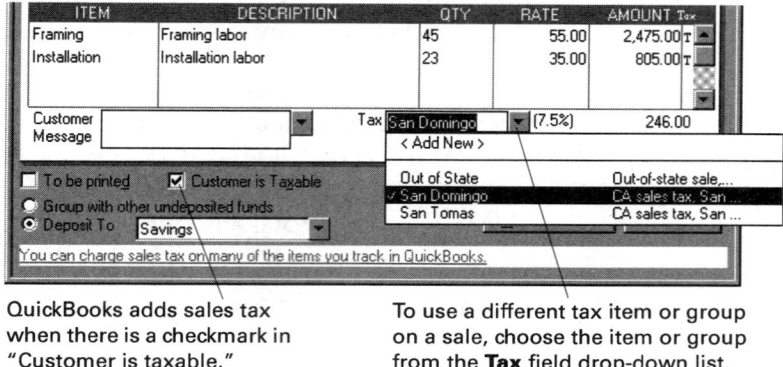

QuickBooks adds sales tax when there is a checkmark in "Customer is taxable."

To use a different tax item or group on a sale, choose the item or group from the **Tax** field drop-down list.

You can change an item's taxable status on a sales form by clicking the Tax column. However, if the item should always have the opposite status, change the status on the item itself. (See "Which items are subject to sales tax?" on page 285.) If the item is normally taxable, but this customer does not have to pay sales tax, then clear the **Customer is taxable** checkbox on the sales form. See the following section ("Nontaxable sales").

ITEM	DESCRIPTION	QTY	COST	AMOUNT	MARKUP	TOTAL	Tax
Framing	Framing labor	45	55.00	2,475.00		2,475.00	T
Installation	Installation labor	23	35.00	805.00		805.00	T

Click a "T" to remove it (make an item nontaxable); click in the Tax column after the amount to make a "T" appear (make an item taxable).

Nontaxable sales

QuickBooks does not add any sales tax for items that are not taxable (that is, items that have no "T" in the Tax column). If the customer is taxable, but none of the items on a particular sale is taxable, leave the sales tax item in the **Tax** field, so that the sale is reported as a nontaxable sale for the correct district(s).

If you generally collect sales tax but never tax a particular customer, be sure the customer is set up as nontaxable. See "Which customers are subject to sales tax?" on page 284. Note that even if the customer is nontaxable, you can assign a sales tax item in order to track the amount of nontaxable sales for each reason (out of state, resale).

On the other hand, if the customer is usually taxable but does not have to pay sales tax on this particular sale, simply clear the **Customer is taxable** checkbox at the bottom of the sales form. If you use special sales tax items to track the reason a customer is exempt from sales tax, choose the appropriate sales tax item in the **Tax** field. See "If you report nontaxable sales to out-of-state customers" on page 283 and "If you report nontaxable sales to resellers" on page 284.

Special tax situations

You may need to change the sales tax that QuickBooks automatically applies when you have an unusual sale. The following table gives examples of special tax situations and how you can handle them.

Special tax situation	How to handle in QuickBooks	Result
Sale to out-of-state or resale customer.	Choose your Out of State or Resale zero-rate sales tax item for the sale.	QuickBooks records the sale as nontaxable. On the sales tax liability report, it totals the sale with other nontaxable sales for the same sales tax item.
Some items on a sale are taxed at one rate, some at another rate.	You should do all of the following: ■ Create a placeholder 0.00% tax item to put in the **Tax** field, because you can't record a sale with the **Tax** field empty. ■ List items taxed at the same rate together. ■ Add a subtotal item after each set of same-rate items. ■ On the line after each subtotal of same-rate items, enter the appropriate sales tax item in the **Item** field.	QuickBooks includes the taxable items subtotaled above each tax line item in that tax line item's gross sales and taxable sales. Nontaxable items included in the subtotal above each tax line item are included in that tax item's gross sales and nontaxable sales.

Special tax situation	How to handle in QuickBooks	Result
All taxable items on a sale are taxable at one rate; some items are taxable at an additional rate.	You should do all of the following: ■ In the **Tax** field, enter the tax item for all taxable items. ■ List all items taxable at the additional rate together. ■ Add a subtotal item after this set of items. ■ On the line after the subtotal item, enter the sales tax item for the additional rate in the **Item** field.	All taxable items are included in taxable sales for the tax item in the **Tax** field. Items with the additional tax are included in taxable sales for the tax line item.
QuickBooks cannot calculate tax the way you need it calculated (for example, for tiered taxes).	You should do all of the following: ■ Create a placeholder 0.00% tax item to put in the **Tax** field, because you can't record a sale with the **Tax** field empty. ■ If you need to report both nontaxable and taxable sales, add a subtotal item after all the items on the sales form. Otherwise, list all taxable items together and add a subtotal item after them. ■ On the line after the subtotal, enter a sales tax item in the **Item** field. ■ Select and type over the amount of the tax, using an amount you calculate yourself.	QuickBooks reports the amount you type in as the amount of tax you owe your tax agency for the sale. Taxable sales and nontaxable sales amounts are based on the taxable and nontaxable amounts included in the subtotal above the tax line.
Shipping and handling are taxable in your state.	Set up another charge item called "Shipping and Handling" and mark it as taxable.	QuickBooks calculates tax on shipping and handling, because you've marked it as taxable.

Keeping track of how much sales tax you owe

Each time you enter a sale that includes sales tax, QuickBooks tracks the tax information in your Sales Tax Payable account. You can view the sales tax liability you are accruing by displaying the Sales Tax Payable register.

The Sales Tax Payable register shows all sales tax transactions for all sales tax districts.

These two transactions are for a payment to the state collection agency for two different sales tax districts.

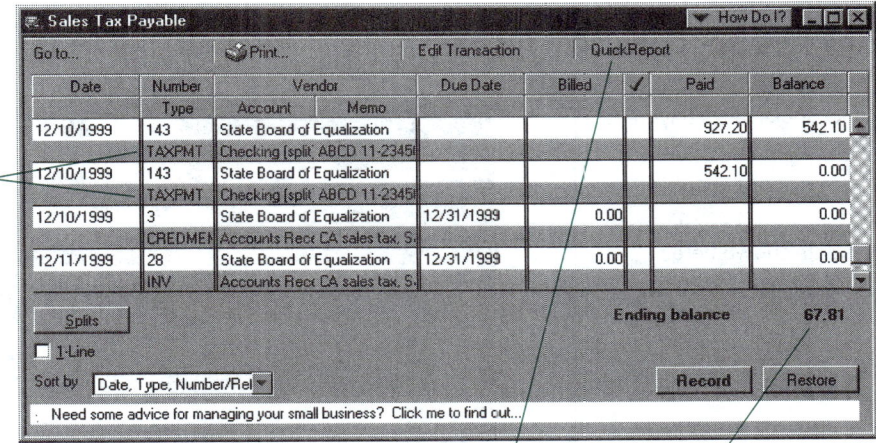

To see a list of all transactions involving a particular tax agency, select a transaction involving that agency; then click QuickReport.

This is the total of all unpaid sales tax.

Note: QuickBooks tracks all sales tax amounts in the same Sales Tax Payable account. If you need to know how much you owe for each sales tax collected, use the sales tax liability report (see "Getting reports about sales tax" on page 294) or the Pay Sales Tax window (see "Paying sales tax" on page 292). Also, the register shows the total unpaid sales tax, even if it is not yet due.

To learn about...	Search the Help index for...
Displaying the register for the Sales Tax Payable account	sales tax, register
Viewing a vendor QuickReport of all transactions for a particular sales tax agency	report types, sales taxes
Adjusting the amount of sales tax owed, either during initial company setup or to correct an error	sales tax, adjusting your liability

Tracking and paying sales tax | 291

Paying sales tax

Use the Pay Sales Tax window to do the following:

- View how much you owe for each sales tax you collect, through the date shown in the **Show sales tax due through** field of this window

- Have QuickBooks write or record a payment check to your tax agency or agencies.

QuickBooks takes payment from the account shown here.

You owe sales tax through the date shown here.

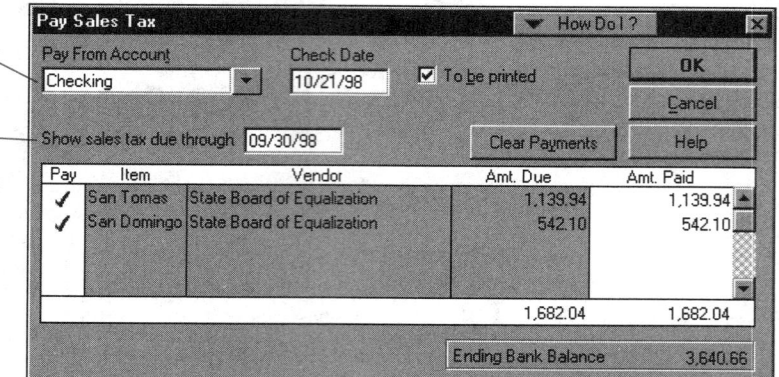

Use the Pay Sales Tax window even if you don't print checks.

The only way QuickBooks can keep track of how much sales tax you have paid is for you to use the Pay Sales Tax window. If you don't print checks from QuickBooks, just clear the **To be printed** checkbox in the window. (In your bank account register, you can edit the check number if QuickBooks entered a check number different from the one you used.)

QuickBooks automatically displays the unpaid tax owed through the end of your last sales tax period. You can change the date QuickBooks uses by indicating whether you pay monthly, quarterly, or annually in the company-wide sales tax preferences. See "How do I specify when my sales tax is payable?" on page 286.

Similarly, QuickBooks calculates the tax you owe on either a cash basis (that is, as of when you receive payment) or an accrual basis (as of the date of the sale), depending on how the sales tax preferences are set.

If you actually owe less tax than shown because you receive a discount or have a tax credit you have not yet entered, you must first enter the discount or credit directly in the Sales Tax Payable register. Then you must "pay" it in the Pay Sales Tax window. (Because it reduces the total tax you owe, it has a negative sign in the window.)

When you record a payment through the Pay Sales Tax window, QuickBooks writes one check to each vendor you are paying. It updates your Sales Tax Payable account with the payment information. It also reduces the balance in the bank account you specify to use for the payment.

To learn about...	Search the Help index for...
Paying sales tax	sales tax, paying
Changing the company's sales tax period or cash vs. accrual basis for paying sales tax	sales tax, accounting basis
Applying a discount to the amount of sales tax owed	sales tax, adjusting your liability
Recording a sales tax credit from the sales tax agency	sales tax, adjusting your liability
Editing the check number of a sales tax payment check written by hand	registers, editing entries

Changing information about your sales tax

You can change any of the following for a sales tax item that is set up to track a particular sales tax:

- Tax rate
- Name (displayed on your Item list, in the **Item** field of sales forms, and in reports)
- Description (displayed and printed in the **Description** field of sales forms)
- Choice of tax agency to whom you pay sales tax
- (For sales tax group items) Which sales tax items are part of the group

When you change a rate, new transactions will use the new rate. However, transactions already recorded will keep the old rate.

Tip: **To change information about the tax agency, edit the agency on your Vendor list.** The agency is set up as a QuickBooks vendor. The Vendor list has information about the vendor address and your tax account number.

To learn about...	Search the Help index for...
Changing sales tax information	items, editing information

Getting reports about sales tax

What is the breakdown of my sales tax, taxable sales, and nontaxable sales by sales tax district?

In QuickBooks, the preset sales tax liability report shows a breakdown of your sales tax and sales by sales tax district (that is, sales tax item).

When you use a zero-rate sales tax item on out-of-state sales, the report separates these nontaxable sales from other nontaxable sales.

Rock Castle Construction
Sales Tax Liability Report
November 1997

12/15/97

	Total Sales	Non-Taxable Sales	Taxable Sales	Tax Rate	Tax	Sales Tax Payable As of Nov 30, '97
State Board of Equalization						
Resale	3,850.00	3,850.00	0.00	0.0%	0.00	0.00
San Domingo	27,245.50	20,017.50	7,228.00	7.5%	542.10	1,606.20
San Tomas	28,873.41	21,590.00	7,283.41	7.75%	564.46	927.20
Total State Board of Equalization						2,533.40
No tax vendor						
Out of State	2,475.00	2,475.00	0.00	0.0%	0.00	0.00
Total (no tax vendor)						0.00
TOTAL						**2,533.40**

For each sales tax item recorded on a sales form or sales tax payment, the report lists the following:

- Total sales (both taxable and nontaxable) during the report period

    If your sales tax is set up as owed only for paid sales, the report shows sales with payment dates during the report period.

- Total nontaxable sales

- Total taxable sales
- Sales tax rate (currently)
- Amount of sales tax for the taxable sales
- Amount of tax you owed as of the end date of the report period

    The amount of tax owed includes amounts that may have been accrued before the beginning date of the report. Furthermore, because the report does not examine tax payments made after the ending date, you may no longer owe this tax amount. To see whether you still owe this amount, use the Pay Sales Tax window (page 292).

If you collect sales tax for different tax districts but pay the tax to the same tax agency, the report subtotals all the taxes for the same agency. Similarly, if you collect a group of separate taxes payable to the same agency, the report subtotals the taxes in the group.

If you need to report the sales total for nontaxable, out-of-state sales, the best way to track such sales is through a zero-rate sales tax item called something like "Out of State." Then your report will have a separate line for out-of-state sales. (See the example in the report illustrated.)

QuickBooks displays your sales tax liability report on an accrual basis unless you changed the setting to cash basis in your sales tax preferences. For information about the difference between cash basis and accrual basis for this report, see "How do I specify when my sales tax is payable?" on page 286.

If you send out billing statements that list statement charges, the sales tax liability report includes all your statement charges with nontaxable sales. (QuickBooks does not track any sales tax on statement charges, even for items that are normally taxable.)

Tip: **To see a list of sales tax amounts collected and tax payments for a particular sales tax district, create an item QuickReport for the sales tax item.** A QuickReport for a sales tax item lists each sales form with that item on it and the amount of tax collected. You can double-click to display the actual sales form. The report also lists each payment for that sales tax item.

To learn about...	Search the Help index for...
Creating a report that shows sales tax collected and owed and the taxable and nontaxable sales for a period	report types, sales taxes
Understanding the sales tax liability report	report types, sales taxes
Creating an item QuickReport that lists each sale and payment for a particular sales tax district	report types, sales taxes

CHAPTER 16

Gathering income tax information for the IRS

Figuring it all out	298
Setting up income tax tracking	300
Reporting income tax information	302
Handling assets	304
Handling 1099-MISC forms	307

How can QuickBooks save me time in filing my tax forms?

You can use QuickBooks to collect and report tax-related income and expense information to help you fill out your tax forms. For a complete tax preparation tool, consider TurboTax® for Business. You can transfer your QuickBooks data to this program to give you a head start in tax preparation.

This chapter does not intend to be exhaustive on the subject of taxes.

Tax laws and regulations change frequently and their application can vary widely based upon the specific facts and circumstances involved. Users are responsible for consulting their own professional tax advisors concerning their specific tax circumstances.

For information on payroll (employment) taxes, see "Paying payroll taxes and liabilities" on page 386. For information about sales tax, see Chapter 15, *Tracking and paying sales tax,* beginning on page 275.

297

Figuring it all out

The good news for small business owners who need to figure out their taxes—you are not alone! There are experts, programs, books, and software designed to help you pay your taxes. We offer a few suggestions here.

Consulting tax experts

- First and foremost, contact the Internal Revenue Service (IRS) for information for small business owners. For more information, contact your local IRS office or visit their Web site at **www.irs.gov**.

- You may want to talk to a tax accountant to find out how to take advantage of recent tax changes. Review the Professional Advisor's Program at **www.quickbooks.com** to find a QuickBooks-savvy tax advisor in your area. (Not all Professional Advisors are tax advisors.)

- Check out software products such as TurboTax for Business (**www.intuit.com/turbotax**), which walks you through paying your business taxes and includes information and publications. A bonus—you can import your QuickBooks data into TurboTax products.

Keeping current with tax information

Even if you rely on a tax expert to complete your forms and keep abreast of tax changes for you, we recommend that you also keep current with tax information. You know your business better than anyone, and only you can make the decision to take advantage of new tax changes.

For example, recent tax changes include the following:

- The self-employed health insurance deduction is 45% for 1998 and 1999.

- The maximum capital gains rates for *most* capital assets held more than 12 months are 10 percent, 20 percent, and/or 25 percent. Beginning in the year 2001, the 10 percent capital gains rate will be lowered to 8 percent and the 20 percent rate will be lowered to 18 percent for assets held more than five years after December 31, 2000.

Stay informed with links to the Internet

Tax alerts in QuickBooks can take you directly to places such as the IRS Web site (**www.irs.gov**) for timely information, or to the TurboTax site (**www.turbotax.com**) for the latest in tax software and electronic filing.

To learn about...	Search the Help index for...
QuickBooks alerts	alerts, about

What QuickBooks can do for you

QuickBooks can help you track your income tax, your payroll (employment) taxes, and your 1099 information.

QuickBooks tracks	Output created
Income tax information, including information for schedules A, B, C, E, F, H, K-1; forms 1040, 1065, 1120, 1120S, 990, 990-PF, 990-T, 4835, 2106, 2119, 8829. This list is not exhaustive. Your options will vary depending on your business entity.	Prints a report detailing all the tax lines for various schedules and forms that you designated when you set up your accounts and company information.
1099-MISC income form information For more information, see "Handling 1099-MISC forms" on page 307.	Prints on the 1099 forms you provide.
Payroll information for W-2, W-3, 940s, and 941s. Beginning in the tax year 2000, you can prepare forms 940 and 941 and other federal and state payroll tax forms on a Web site accessed from within QuickBooks (if you have an internet connection and a subscription to the QuickBooks Basic Payroll service).	Prints on the W-2 and W-3 forms you provide. Prints government-approved 940 and 941 forms.

Figuring it all out | 299

Other taxes you may need to pay

Depending on your business situation, you may need to pay other types of taxes.

- Self-employment tax

    The IRS guidelines specify that if you are self-employed, you must pay social security and Medicare tax that would otherwise be picked up by your employer. Some professions may be exempt from paying these taxes under certain conditions.

- Excise (luxury or sin) taxes

    According to the IRS, small businesses affected by excise taxes include, but are not limited to cigar shops, wineries and breweries, stores that sell imported perfumes, imported electronics (containing ODCs) or guns, and trucking firms.

Contact the IRS for more information.

Setting up income tax tracking

QuickBooks can track the information you need to report on your income tax forms and help you save time and tax preparation fees.

The following table highlights the income tax tracking information. You may have entered this information during setup using the EasyStep Interview (in the General and Income & Expenses sections). If you ever need to change this information, use the Help Index references.

Task	Comments	Search in the Help Index for...
Change the first month of your company's income tax year. This could be by calendar year or fiscal year.	You must be consistent from year to year.	company, changing information about
Change the income tax form you use for your company.	**Important:** If you change the tax form you use, all associations between accounts and tax lines are reset to <unassigned>. You'll need to reassign the appropriate tax lines.	■ income taxes, changing the form you file ■ accounts, tax lines

Task	Comments	Search in the Help Index for...
Enter your federal identification number.	■ If you are a sole proprietor who has no employees and who files no excise or pension tax returns, you can use your **social security number** as your identification number. Otherwise, you must have an **employer identification number (EIN)** if your business fits any of these situations: (1) you are a corporation or partnership; (2) you pay wages to one or more employees; (3) you file pension or excise tax returns. To apply for an EIN, call 1-800-TAX-FORM.	■ company, changing information about
Choose a tax line for each appropriate account in your chart of accounts.	Normally balance sheet accounts do not have a tax line. You may want to add accounts to more closely match your tax forms.	■ accounts, tax lines ■ accounts, adding to your chart of accounts

Why are tax line assignments important?

If you assign tax lines to your accounts you can:

- Transfer your income tax data from QuickBooks to one of Intuit's TurboTax products

- Get accurate tax reports, which keep you abreast of your tax situation and help you prepare your income taxes (if you're doing your taxes by hand)

The way you set up accounts and their tax line assignments depends on whether you used the preset chart of accounts, added accounts to the preset chart of accounts, or set up your own chart of accounts. Other unique situations may also apply. Search the Help index for more information.

If you change the tax form you use, all associations between tax lines and accounts are reset to <unassigned>.

You'll need to reassign the appropriate tax lines.

Setting up income tax tracking | 301

To learn about...	Search the Help index for...
Setting up accounts to track income tax-related income and expenses	income taxes, setting up for

Make sure that you have the latest tax information

Use TurboTax to always have the latest tax information: Intuit provides an updated list of tax forms (the BUSTAX.SCD file) in all TurboTax products for Windows and TurboTax for Business. If you use QuickBooks for Windows, install the *latest* version of TurboTax to update your income tax form information.

Reporting income tax information

The QuickBooks income tax summary report shows the total amount associated for each tax line you specified in your accounts. If you fill out your tax forms by hand, you can print the income tax summary report and use it to aid you in completing your tax forms. Or, to make income taxes even simpler, you can easily transfer your tax information to one of Intuit's TurboTax products. See "Transferring income tax information to TurboTax" on page 304.

Getting the numbers you need to file your income taxes

Whether you fill out your income tax forms by hand or transfer your QuickBooks data to one of Intuit's TurboTax products, you'll want to complete the following steps to make sure your numbers are correct.

- Check and correct tax line assignments. The accuracy of the income tax summary report depends on whether each tax-related account has the right tax line assignment.

- Check that the amounts in your income tax summary report are correct.

- Calculate your sales and returns.

- Calculate the total of your purchases.

To learn about...	Search the Help index for...
Checking tax line assignments to ensure the accuracy of your income tax summary report	income taxes, filling out tax forms
Checking the amounts distributed to various accounts	income taxes, filling out tax forms
Calculating sales and returns	income taxes, calculating sales and returns
Calculating the total of your purchases	income taxes, calculating purchases

Income tax summary report

The income tax summary report shows the amount associated with each tax line for the tax form you specified during setup.

```
               Rock Castle Construction
                   Income Tax Summary
                        Dec 31, '98
Sch C
   Gross receipts or sales              ▶ 116,454.79  ◀
   Other business income                      105.92
   Bad debts from sales/services                33.99
   Car and truck expenses                      255.10
   Insurance, other than health              2,025.00
   Interest expense, other                     534.15
   Legal and professional fees                 250.00
   Office expenses                             170.71
   Rent/lease vehicles, equip.                 850.00
   Rent/lease other bus. prop.               2,400.00
   Repairs and maintenance                       0.00
   Utilities                                   216.25
   Wages paid                               19,780.38
   Other business expenses                   1,145.00
   Labor, cost of goods                     40,099.00
   Materials/supplies, COGS                 24,046.74
   Other costs, COGS                           700.00
   Tax Line Unassigned (balance sheet)      24,054.39
```

Income tax detail report

The income tax detail report shows the individual transactions and the total associated for each tax line you specified in your accounts.

Make sure the reporting preference is set to the accounting method you use for tax reporting: Accrual or Cash.

From the Edit menu, choose Preferences, then Reports & Graphs, and then click the Company Preferences tab.

Transferring income tax information to TurboTax

If you use the current TurboTax for Windows or TurboTax for Business to prepare your taxes, you can import your QuickBooks tax data into the tax software. Once you've set up QuickBooks accounts with the correct tax line assignments, QuickBooks tracks your tax-related income and expenses automatically throughout the year.

Note: QuickBooks 2000 and QuickBooks Pro 2000 will work only with TurboTax, TurboTax for Business, and ProSeries for tax year 1999.

To learn about...	Search the Help index for...
Transferring tax information from QuickBooks to your tax software	TurboTax

Handling assets

Buying assets

Entering the purchase of a business asset in QuickBooks is the same as entering the purchase of any good or service (see "Paying for expenses" on page 251), except that you assign the purchase to an asset account rather than to an expense account. You may want to set up additional accounts to track depreciation.

To learn about...	Search the Help index for...
Buying an asset	assets, purchasing
Adding an asset account	accounts, assets
Using a loan to pay for an asset	assets, loans to pay for

Handling depreciation of assets

Current tax laws note that you can get back some of your cost of certain property by taking tax deductions for its depreciation. You can depreciate property (buildings, equipment, vehicles, patents, copyrights, and so on) if it meets these criteria:

> *It must be used in business or other income-producing activity; it must be something that wears out, decays, gets used up, becomes obsolete, or loses value from natural causes; and it must have a useful life that you can determine, and the useful life must be longer than one year.*

\- IRS Publication 946, *How to Depreciate Property*

To track depreciation **for tax purposes,** it is important to consult your tax advisor or the IRS. IRS depreciation publications are available on the Internet at **www.irs.gov**.

Note: If you simply want to track depreciation so that your financial statements are more accurate, choose Decision Tools from the Company menu.

To learn about...	Search the Help index for...
An example of depreciation	depreciation
Using a loan to pay for an asset	assets, loans to pay for
Setting up depreciation accounts	depreciation, accounts to track
Entering a depreciation transaction	depreciation, transactions

Selling assets at a gain or loss

Refer to IRS Publication 544, Sales and Other Dispositions of Assets, for more information. Of particular interest may be section 4, "Ordinary or Capital Gain or Loss for Business Property."

If you sell a fixed asset for more than or less than its value on your company books you need to account for the difference. You can add an account (Other Income type) called Capital Gain/Loss so that gains or losses will appear on your profit and loss statement. (Losses will be negative.)

For example, suppose you bought a truck for $15,000 a few years ago. You have depreciated it to $8,000, but you are able to sell it for $9,000. Thus, you have a capital gain of $1,000 on the sale. You want your records to show that you no longer own the asset, so its current value on your books should be zero, but you also need to track your capital gain on the sale in your Capital Gain/Loss account.

To learn about...	Search the Help index for...
Selling a fixed asset	assets, selling fixed

Theft or loss of a fixed asset

A fixed asset may be destroyed, stolen, or condemned and you may receive an insurance settlement or other property as payment. The IRS refers to this as **involuntary conversion** and states that,

> *Gain or loss from an involuntary conversion of your property is usually recognized, for tax purposes. You report the gain or deduct the loss on your tax return for the year you realize it.*
>
> - IRS Publication 544, *Sales and Other Dispositions of Assets*

For more information, consult the IRS or your tax advisor.

To learn about...	Search the Help index for...
Recording the theft or loss of an asset	assets, recording theft or loss

Handling 1099-MISC forms

The IRS requires certain 1099-MISC forms of all businesses that make or receive payments. The IRS uses these forms to verify that the recipient has included your payment as income on his or her income tax form.

You must give a copy of each information return you file to the recipient or payer.

Setting up to track 1099-MISC information

Tasks	Comments	Search in the Help Index for...
Setting up for reporting payments on 1099-MISC forms	None	1099s
Setting up vendors (recipients)	You must: ■ Enter the address in the correct format ■ Enter the federal identification number in the Tax ID field ■ Select the "Vendor is eligible for 1099" checkbox	vendors, adding

Verifying amounts and printing 1099-MISC forms

Before you print your 1099-MISC forms, you should verify information that you'll report to the IRS. After you print your 1099-MISC forms, QuickBooks displays 1096 summary information at the bottom of the window. (It does not print Form 1096.)

To learn about...	Search the Help index for...
Verifying 1099 thresholds, vendors, accounts, and amounts	1099s
Printing 1099s	1099s

Why doesn't my 1099 report have anything on it?

There may be several reasons:

- Your vendors may be on the Other Names lists (the report looks for them on the Vendor list). Change them to vendors.
- You haven't selected the "Vendor eligible for 1099" checkbox for your vendors. Go to the Additional Info tab in the Edit Vendor window, and select this checkbox.
- You haven't selected accounts for tracking 1099-related expenses. Go to the Company Preferences tab after selecting the Tax: 1099 Preference icon, and then set up accounts.
- Your threshold amounts for 1099s forms may be out of date. Call the IRS at 800-TAX FORM to get the current threshold amounts.
- The date range for the 1099 report isn't correct. (These reports automatically show 1099 information for the last calendar year.) Change the date range of the report.
- You entered a bill in the last calendar year and pay taxes in the current calendar year.

CHAPTER 17
Time tracking

Should I track time?	310
Setting up QuickBooks for tracking time	314
Setting up and using the Timer	315
Using the Stopwatch or entering time manually	323
Tasks you can do with time data	325
Reports about time	330
Installing the Timer	335
Quick Reference Sheet for the QuickBooks Pro Timer	338

How can I base payroll or invoices on time worked?

Time tracking, available only in QuickBooks Pro, allows you to track hours worked by yourself, employees, or subcontractors. You can make the time billable for specific jobs. And you can transfer time to paychecks and regular checks.

QuickBooks Pro provides time-tracking capability to suit your needs:

- The Stopwatch: When you're working in QuickBooks and want to take a stopwatch approach (that is, turn on a timer, work, and then stop the timer), use the Stopwatch on the Time/Enter Single Activity window.

- The QuickBooks Pro Timer: The Timer is a separate program that runs on Windows on any computer. Because it's separate, you can distribute copies of the Timer to people who don't have access to QuickBooks, such as employees and subcontractors. Then you can merge their time data into the QuickBooks company file.

- You can also enter time data manually into QuickBooks in the Weekly Timesheet window or Time/Enter Single Activity window.

Should I track time?

This section contains the following topics:

Should I make time billable?	**310**
Should I track time for subcontractors?	**311**
How much detail should I track for time activities?	**311**
Choosing a method to track time	**313**

Tracking time can help you make better decisions about work capacity, future hiring needs, and employee productivity.

Furthermore, if you track the time you, your employees, or your subcontractors spend on each job, you'll be able to do the following:

- Invoice customers based on the number of hours of work done for them.
- Automatically fill in hours on paychecks.
- Track payroll costs by job, class, or type of work.
- Report hours worked by person, job, or type of work.

    For example, see "How many hours did each person work?" on page 330.

- Track billable versus non-billable time.

Should I make time billable?

billable

The status of time worked (or a purchase) for a particular customer or job that allows QuickBooks to charge the customer for the time (or purchase).

After you put the time or purchase on a sales form, QuickBooks marks it non-billable, so you won't charge twice for the same thing.

When you record time worked for a particular customer or job, one option is to mark it as billable. Then when you invoice the customer, you can add the billable time to the invoice with a few clicks.

If the work done by employees is billable to customers, it becomes billable as soon as you record the time in QuickBooks. It doesn't matter whether you have paid the employees yet.

In some businesses you may want to track time without making it billable. For example, if you agree to do a job at a fixed price, you would not invoice for time.

You may still want to track the time so you can decide after completing the job whether you set the right price.

Also, you can track sick and vacation time, which is normally not billable.

Should I track time for subcontractors?

Most businesses don't need to track time for subcontractors, with a few exceptions:

- On time reports, you want to see all time for a particular job, whether for an employee, a subcontractor, or an owner.

    Glenn's construction company has only one employee now. By tracking time worked by subcontractors, he'll know what to expect when he has employees doing this type of work in the future.

- You want to track subcontractor time independently of the time subcontractors report on the bills they submit to you.

    Jill gives subcontractors copies of the Timer program and asks them to return time data to her weekly so she can track how many hours have been spent on her project long before she receives the bills.

How much detail should I track for time activities?

activity

A QuickBooks term for work tracked by the time tracking feature.

You track time based on activities. Each activity needs, at a minimum, the following to describe it:

- Name of person who did the work
- Date the work was done
- Time spent doing the work

The level of detail you include when tracking an activity depends on whether or not it's billable and how much detail you want in your reports.

Describe an activity by specifying ...	Comment
Name of person who did the work	Required.
Date the work was done	Required; each activity can be for only one date.
Time spent doing the work	Required. (If you use the Timer or the Stopwatch to time an activity, they fill in the time spent.)
Customer (and job) the work is for	Required only if you plan to invoice for the time. Even if you don't invoice for the time: ■ Allows you to report on hours worked by customer and job. ■ Allows you to track payroll expenses by customer and job.
Type of work (described by a service item from the Item list)	Required only if you plan to invoice for the time. Even if you don't invoice for the time: ■ Allows you to report on hours worked by type of work. ■ Allows you to track payroll expenses by type of work.
Whether time is billable	Time must be billable if you plan to invoice for the time.
Class	If your company does class tracking, you can do the following: ■ Filter time reports by class. ■ If you are set up to split payroll expenses by class, you can assign classes to employee time. Then you can automatically track all payroll expenses by class.

Choosing a method to track time

QuickBooks Pro comes with a separate Timer program that can run on a computer regardless of whether QuickBooks is on the computer. You have a choice between tracking time via the Timer and then transferring the time data to QuickBooks, using the Stopwatch on the Time/Enter Single Activity window, or entering time data directly into QuickBooks manually on the Weekly Timesheet window or the Time/Enter Single Activity window.

Situation	How to track time	See...
You want to use a stopwatch approach to time tracking (in which you turn on a timer, work, and then stop the timer).	Use the Stopwatch on the Time/Enter Single Activity window in QuickBooks (Pro version only).	■ "Setting up QuickBooks for tracking time" on page 314 ■ "Using the Stopwatch to time an activity" on page 323
You want people who don't have access to your QuickBooks company data file to track their own time.	Distribute copies of the QuickBooks Pro Timer to these people, and have them give you their time data.	■ "Setting up QuickBooks for tracking time" on page 314 ■ "Installing the Timer" on page 335 ■ "Setting up and using the Timer" on page 315 ■ "Quick Reference Sheet for the QuickBooks Pro Timer" on page 338
You (and others in your company) have access to your QuickBooks company data file and want to enter time data after the work is done.	You and they can enter the time data manually into QuickBooks (Pro version only) either on a weekly timesheet or as separate activities one at a time.	■ "Setting up QuickBooks for tracking time" on page 314 ■ "Entering time manually into QuickBooks" on page 324
Employees submit paper timesheets.	One person can enter everyone's time data directly into QuickBooks (Pro version only) on a weekly timesheet for each person.	■ "Setting up QuickBooks for tracking time" on page 314 ■ "Entering time manually into QuickBooks" on page 324

Setting up QuickBooks for tracking time

This section contains the following topics:

List for preparing QuickBooks to track time	**314**
Setting up to use time tracking with payroll	**315**

List for preparing QuickBooks to track time

The following list is for tasks you must do in QuickBooks to prepare for tracking time.

 A QuickBooks user must do this preparation before Timer users can set up their own Timers.

What to set up	Comments	Search the Help index for...
Turn on time tracking and indicate the first day of your work week.	The weekly timesheet starts with the day of the week you specify.	preferences, time
On the Customer:Job list, names of customers and jobs for which time will be tracked.	If you don't plan to track time by customer or job, you don't need these names on the list now.	▪ customers, adding new ▪ jobs, adding new
On the Item list, names of service items that describe the types of work that will be tracked	Service items are required only if you make the time billable to a customer or job.	service items, setting up
Names of all people whose time will be tracked. Each name must be on one of the following lists in QuickBooks: ▪ Employee ▪ Other Name (for owners and partners) ▪ Vendor (for subcontractors)	If you plan to use time tracking to help with payroll for any employees, you must also set up payroll information for those employees. See: ▪ "Setting up to use time tracking with payroll" on page 315 ▪ "Setting up employees" on page 361	▪ employees, adding ▪ other names, list of ▪ vendors, adding
On the Payroll Item list, names of hourly or salary wage items to be used when paying employees for time tracked	Required only if you will track time for employees.	▪ hourly wages ▪ salaries
On the Class list, names of classes that apply to the work that will be tracked	Class tracking is completely optional.	classes, adding

Setting up to use time tracking with payroll

As part of the payroll setup for employees, be sure to select the checkbox "Use time data to create paychecks" on the employee's Payroll Info tab.

☑ Use time data to create paychecks

Paychecks will automatically have the employee's time data (including job, class, type of work, sick, and vacation) for the period covered by the paycheck. QuickBooks keeps track of your payroll expenses for hourly or salaried gross pay, employer taxes, and other payroll overhead by job, class, and type of work.

Setting up and using the Timer

This section contains the following topics:

How the Timer works with QuickBooks	**315**
Setting up the Timer	**316**
Using the Timer	**318**
Importing Timer data into QuickBooks	**322**

How the Timer works with QuickBooks

The QuickBooks Pro Timer is designed to track and record time data for export to QuickBooks Pro. Use it when you want to gather time data from people who don't have access to QuickBooks.

Note: If you simply want to time an activity in QuickBooks—not gather time data from others—use the Stopwatch on the Time/Enter Single Activity window instead of the Timer. See "Using the Stopwatch to time an activity" on page 323.

You can make copies of the Timer program to give to other people whose work you want to track in QuickBooks. Photocopy and distribute the two-page Quick Reference Sheet on page 338 and page 339 for those users.

Note: **If you distributed the Timer program that came with QuickBooks Pro 6.0 or QuickBooks Pro 99, you should replace those copies with the Timer program that comes with QuickBooks Pro 2000.** The newer version of the Timer can update data files created by the earlier version.

The following flowchart shows the relationship between QuickBooks Pro and the Timer.

The two programs share information as follows:

- QuickBooks Pro exports lists, such as the Customer:Job list.
- The Timer imports those lists.
- The Timer exports data about time activities.
- QuickBooks Pro imports the time data and makes it part of the company data file.

Setting up the Timer

Before you can set up the Timer, you must first install it. Also, be sure to do all the tasks on the task list in the next section.

Task list for setting up the Timer

The following task list for setting up the Timer shows whether the QuickBooks user or the Timer user has to do the task (in case they are not the same person).

Task	Which user and which Help index?	Search the Help index for...
Export QuickBooks lists for Timer into an IIF file and give file to Timer user.	QuickBooks	Timer, exporting lists to
Prepare Timer install disks (if Timer user is unable to use QuickBooks CD-ROM or QuickBooks install disks).	QuickBooks	Timer, creating disks for
Install the Timer on the user's computer.	See "Installing the Timer" on page 335.	N/A
Create a Timer data file for the QuickBooks company file that will use the time data.	Timer	data files, creating for the Timer (search the Timer Help)
Import the QuickBooks lists in the IIF file into the Timer data file.	Timer	lists, importing from Quick-Books (search the Timer Help)
Name the person whose work will be recorded in this Timer file.	Timer	default user (search the Timer Help)

Exporting lists from QuickBooks Pro

The first step in getting the Timer ready to use is to prepare a file with the information the timer needs in order to work with QuickBooks Pro. The Timer must describe activities using the same names that are on the lists in QuickBooks.

Information Timer needs	Source in QuickBooks
Names of possible Timer users	Employee, Vendor, and Other Names lists
Names of customers and jobs (if time will be billable to a customer or job)	Customer:Job list

Information Timer needs	Source in QuickBooks
Type of work that the customer may be invoiced for (if time will be billable)	Service-type items from the Item list
Names of QuickBooks classes (if time will be assigned to classes)	Class list

If the Timer will be used on another computer, the exported list file should be either on a 3.5-inch disk or on a network that both computers can access.

To learn about...	Search the Help index for...
Preparing a file of information from QuickBooks lists, for use by the Timer	Timer, exporting lists to

Using the Timer

After you have done the tasks described in "Setting up QuickBooks for tracking time" on page 314 and in "Setting up the Timer" on page 316, you are ready to track time with the Timer.

Recording activities in the Timer

You can use the Timer either to time and record an activity while you are doing it or to record it after you have done it.

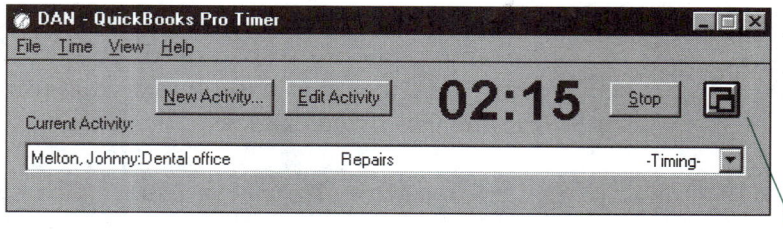

You can run the Timer in a very small window (as at the left) or in a larger window (above) that shows detail and provides menu access.

Click this button to switch between minimal size and full size.

The first time you do an activity for a given customer, job, and type of work, you have to set up the activity in the Timer. For the amount of detail you should include in an activity, see "How much detail should I track for time activities?" on page 311.

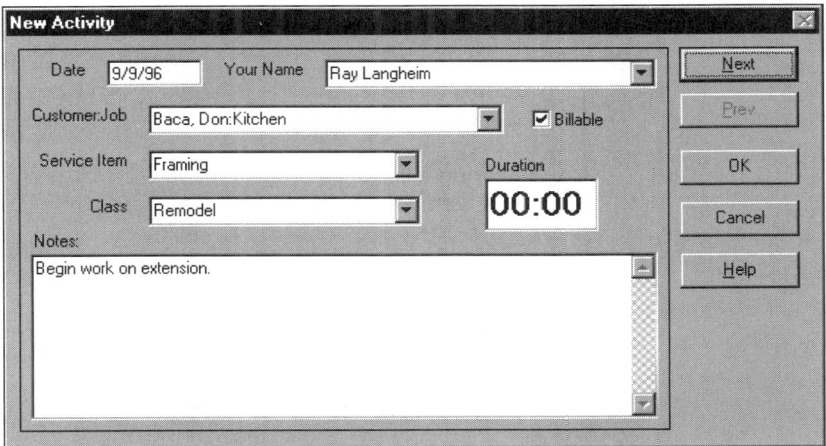

If you have previously set up an activity for a given customer, job, and type of work, you can choose the activity from a drop-down list and use it as a template for the new day's work instead of setting up a similar activity for the new day.

You can add a note while timing an activity or after completing it.

To learn about...	Search the Timer Help (not the QuickBooks Help) index for...
Timing an activity while you are doing it	■ activities, setting up for timing ■ activities, timing
Recording an activity after doing it	activities, entering time for manually
Recording notes about an activity	activities, adding notes to

Viewing and editing recorded activities

You can view a list of all recorded activities. You cannot print this list (or anything else in the Timer). However, after you export time data to QuickBooks, the QuickBooks user can print the list of activities.

To learn about...	Search the Timer Help (not the QuickBooks Help) index for...
Viewing a list of all recorded activities within a specified date range	activities, viewing data about
Changing information about a recorded activity	activities, editing data about
Deleting a recorded activity	activities, deleting the record of

Viewing and changing customer information

When you import lists from QuickBooks, you import customer contact information as well as customer names.

You can add a new customer name to use when describing an activity. However, you cannot add a job for a new or existing customer. The Help topic suggests what to do instead.

If a customer is on the list imported from QuickBooks, or if you already exported Timer data using the customer, you cannot change information about the customer. Instead, the QuickBooks user must change the information and give you an updated list file.

To learn about...	Search the Timer Help (not the QuickBooks Help) index for...
Viewing contact information about a customer	customers, contact information for
Adding, editing, or deleting a customer	■ customers, adding ■ customers, editing ■ customers, deleting

Sharing Timer information with QuickBooks

You need to export your recorded activities to an IIF file that QuickBooks can import.

Also, from time to time, you will need to update the lists in your Timer data to make them match those in the QuickBooks company file. The QuickBooks user must prepare the updated list file and make it available for importing into the Timer.

For a diagram of how data moves between the Timer and QuickBooks, see "How the Timer works with QuickBooks" on page 315.

To learn about...	Search the Timer Help (not the QuickBooks Help) index for...
Copying (exporting) activities to an IIF file that QuickBooks can read	activities, exporting to QuickBooks
Updating the Timer's lists of customers, jobs, service items, and classes to match changes in the QuickBooks file	lists, updating

Managing Timer data files

You can back up a Timer data file. You must restore a backup copy before you can open it in the Timer.

You can reduce the file size by using the Condense feature. The Condense feature in the Timer, unlike the one in QuickBooks, does not remove or consolidate any information.

If you track time for more than one QuickBooks company, you must have separate Timer data files.

To learn about...	Search the Timer Help (not the QuickBooks Help) index for...
Backing up your Timer data onto a 3.5-inch disk or your hard disk	data files, backing up
Restoring a backup of Timer data so you can use or view it	data files, restoring from a backup disk

Setting up and using the Timer | 321

To learn about...	Search the Timer Help (not the QuickBooks Help) index for...
Reducing the size of your Timer file	data files, condensing to save disk space
Creating a new Timer data file to use with a different QuickBooks company file	data files, creating for the Timer
Switching to the Timer data file for a different QuickBooks company	data files, opening

Importing Timer data into QuickBooks

After the Timer user exports the data from the Timer into an IIF file (see "Sharing Timer information with QuickBooks" on page 321), you can import the data into the QuickBooks company file.

> When you've finished importing the Timer data, you should check the Timer import detail report (available only from the Import Summary window) to ensure that QuickBooks has assigned the correct payroll item to each activity.

When you've finished importing the Timer data, you should check the Timer import detail report (available only from the Import Summary window) to ensure that QuickBooks has assigned the correct payroll item to each activity.

In addition to activities, QuickBooks imports any items on lists (that is, names, service items, classes) that are not currently on the corresponding QuickBooks lists. You can view reports of the imported list items.

The time reports in QuickBooks report on all activities, including those imported from the Timer. To create a report similar to the Timer import detail report, you can customize a time by job detail report to add columns for payroll item and import date.

To learn about...	Search the QuickBooks Help index for...
Importing Timer data from the IIF file into the QuickBooks company file	Timer, importing timed activities from
Viewing a report of the imported Timer activities or the imported items on lists	Timer, reports about imported activities
Editing an imported activity in QuickBooks	time, entries
Viewing a report on activities exported to or recorded in Quick-Books	time, reports about

Using the Stopwatch or entering time manually

This section contains the following topics:

Using the Stopwatch to time an activity	323
Entering time manually into QuickBooks	324

Using the Stopwatch to time an activity

Use the Stopwatch on the Time/Enter Single Activity window in QuickBooks Pro when you want to time an activity—simply start the Stopwatch, work, and stop it when you've completed the work.

Once recorded, the time shows up in both this window and in the Weekly Timesheet window.

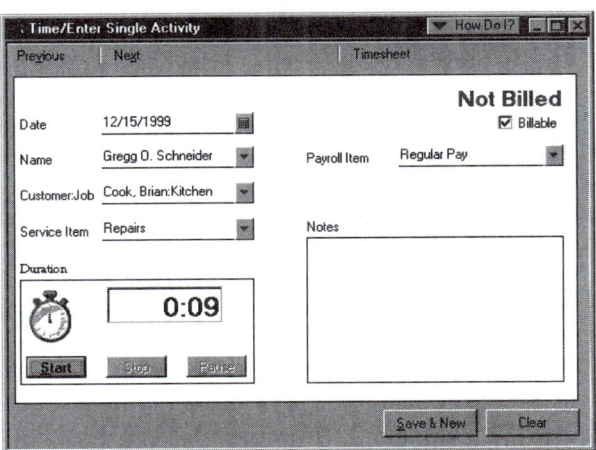

To see how much detail to include when you time an activity, see "How much detail should I track for time activities?" on page 311.

Entering time manually into QuickBooks

If you want to enter time data a week at a time and you generally don't enter a lot of detailed notes about your activities, use the Weekly Timesheet window to enter time data manually.

On the weekly timesheet, the far-right column has symbols that indicate whether the time is billable, not billable, or already billed.

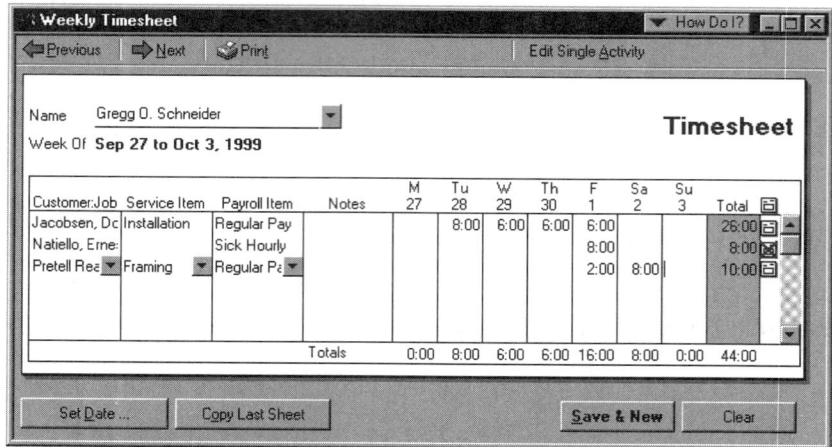

If you tend to enter a lot of detailed notes about your activities or prefer to enter time data as you complete each activity, use the Time/Enter Single Activity window.

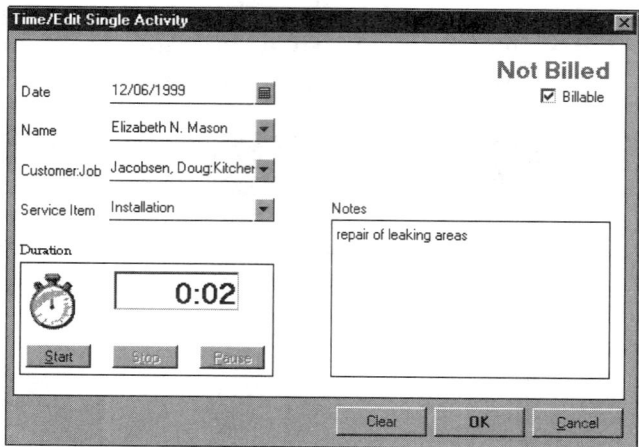

When you fill in and record a Time/Enter Single Activity window, you can later view the information on a weekly timesheet. Conversely, when you fill in and save a weekly timesheet, you can view Time/Enter Single Activity windows that each show the work on one job on one day. The two are simply different views of the same data, similar to views of individual checks versus your check register.

To learn about...	Search the Help index for...
Filling out a weekly timesheet	timesheets
Entering details for a single activity	single activity entries
Using the Stopwatch to time an activity	Stopwatch

Tasks you can do with time data

This section contains the following topics:

Viewing, editing, and printing time data	**325**
Using time data with payroll	**326**
Paying nonemployees for time	**326**
Charging customers for time	**328**
Costs of work and invoicing for work	**329**

Viewing, editing, and printing time data

In addition to creating reports about time data (see "Reports about time" on page 330), you can view, print, and edit time data as follows:

- View a timesheet for one person's work during a particular week.
- Print timesheets (each with one person's work for one week or part of a week).
- View the full text of the note entered for a particular activity.
- Edit time data.

To learn about...	Search the Help index for...
Viewing and printing timesheets	timesheets
Adding notes about an activity to an invoice	invoices, time and cost

To learn about...	Search the Help index for...
Adding notes about an activity to a time report	time, reports about
Editing time data	time, entries

Using time data with payroll

QuickBooks automatically transfers time data when you create paychecks for employees who are set up for transferring time data. That is, it fills in the number of hours for each payroll item for salary or hourly wages included in the time data for the payroll period.

If customers or jobs, service items, or classes are assigned to an employee's time activities, this detail is also included. For example, out of 40 hours altogether, 19 may be assigned to Job A, 11 to Job B, and the remaining 10 hours to Job C. QuickBooks then splits the payroll expenses for this employee according to how you assigned the time.

Paying nonemployees for time

When you have time data for someone who is not an employee—an owner, partner, or vendor—you may want to write a check based on the time worked. QuickBooks can transfer time data for a specified date range to a check. That is, it can fill in the number of hours worked and the rate for that type of work.

If the person is on your Employee list and is set up for transferring time data to paychecks, then the person's paychecks are always based on the time worked. For further information, see Chapter 18, *Payroll*, beginning on page 341.

Tip: **If you need to report payments for time worked on Form 1099-MISC, be sure the person is set up as a vendor.** Always use the vendor name when you track time and when you pay the person. Then when it's time to print 1099-MISC forms, QuickBooks will report the correct amount paid.

To learn about...	Search the Help index for...
Setting up an owner or partner	owners partners, setting up
Adding a name to the Vendor list	vendors, adding
Editing an employee name	employees, editing

Service items for the time data

If you plan to transfer time to a check, the time data should have a service item assigned. QuickBooks uses the rate for purchases of the service item when calculating how much to pay a nonemployee for the hours worked.

Service items for owner or partner time

When you pay an owner or partner, the payment is a draw against equity, rather than an expense to the business. Therefore, you need to have at least one service item that affects the person's equity account when used in payments to the person. This service item should not be used for vendors.

When tracking time for an owner or partner, assign the time to a service item set up to track costs in the person's equity account.

Service items for vendor time

When you pay a vendor, the payment is an expense to the business. Therefore, you need to have at least one service item that affects an expense account when used in payments to the person. This service item should not be used for owners or partners.

When tracking time for a vendor, assign the time to a service item set up to track costs in an expense account.

To learn about...	Search the Help index for...
Setting up a service item for services with both costs and income	service items, billing work by sub-contractors or owners

Transferring time to a check

When you pay someone not on your payroll for time worked, use the Write Checks window.

QuickBooks alerts you if there is time data for the payee for dates after the end date of the period for the last-time payment to this payee. If you answer that you want to pay for time, you can specify the date range of the time to pay for. Then QuickBooks prefills the Items tab of the check with the service item, customer and job (if any), rate, number of hours, and amount.

To learn about...	Search the Help index for...
Writing a check to pay a nonemployee for time worked	time, paying nonemployees for

QuickBooks does not track whether time is paid for.

If you pay for time and then edit the time data (or import data from the Timer), QuickBooks does not track which time has been paid for and which has not. All it tracks is the end date of the last payment for time.

If you always pay for time dated after the end date of the last payment, you will not pay for the same time twice. Otherwise, print a time by job detail report and mark the activities you are paying for.

Charging customers for time

You can transfer time data to invoices and statement charges as long as the time data has a customer:job and service item and is currently marked as billable.

When you're writing an invoice, you can display the unbilled time worked for the job and select which time to include. (See "Charging for actual time and costs" on page 193.) When you record the invoice, QuickBooks Pro marks the time you selected as billed, so you won't bill for it again by mistake. (You can also charge for time as a statement charge instead of writing an invoice.)

To learn about...	Search the QuickBooks Help index for...
Transferring time to invoices and statement charges	■ invoices, time and cost ■ statements, time and cost
Making time billable again if you billed for it mistakenly	time, making billed time billable again

Costs of work and invoicing for work

When you record time, you are not recording any costs. To record costs, you have to take additional action. The following table shows how you record costs for time worked. The table also shows what you have to do to invoice customers for work.

When work is done by ...	You record the cost of the work when you ...	To be able to invoice for the work, you have to ...
Employees	Pay the employees.	Make the time billable.
Subcontractors (vendors)	Enter bills from the subcontractors (or write checks or enter credit card charges for the work).	On the bills, checks, or credit card charges, make the items or expenses billable. OR Track the time and make the time billable.
Owners or partners	If you pay owners and partners for time worked, the payment is a draw against the person's equity. It is not an expense and therefore does not affect the net profit.	Make the time billable. OR Write a check to pay for the time worked, and make the items on the check billable.

Because recording time has no direct effect on costs, the reports about time show hours but they don't show costs.

If you enter bills for subcontractors or if you pay subcontractors, owners, or partners for time worked, you must guard against making their work billable twice.

Don't make both time and the payment for that time billable.

- If you make a subcontractor's bill for time worked billable, you can invoice for the subcontractor's charges from the Expenses or Items tab (the same one you used on the bill) of the Choose Billable Time and Costs window. (This is the recommended method. See "Charging for actual time and costs" on page 193.)

- If you pay a subcontractor, owner, or partner for time worked by using the Write Checks window, you can make the service items on the check billable. Then you can invoice for the time from the Items tab of the Choose Billable Time and Costs window.

- If you make the time itself billable, you can invoice for the time from the Time tab of the Choose Billable Time and Costs window.

- If you make both the time and the bill or payment billable, you are in danger of invoicing the customer twice for the same work.

Reports about time

This section contains the following topics:

How many hours did each person work?	330
How much time did we spend on each job?	332
How much time did we spend on each type of work?	333
Is there a detailed list of each time activity?	333

How many hours did each person work?

The time by name report shows hours worked (or tracked as sick or vacation time) subtotaled first by the name of the person who performed the work and then by customer and job.

Note: Time reports do not show costs. If you're looking for payroll hours and costs, including hours and costs of sick and vacation time, use the payroll summary report.

	Time by Name	
12/15/98	October 1 through December 15, 1998	
		◇ Oct 1 - Dec 15, '98 ◇
Dan T. Miller		
	Abercrombie, Kristy:Remodel Bath...	16.00
	Cook, Brian:2nd story addition	32.00
	Cook, Brian:Kitchen	88.00
	Ecker Designs:Office Repairs	56.00
	Jacobsen, Doug:Kitchen	24.00
	Melton, Johnny:Dental office	20.50
	Natiello, Ernesto:Kitchen	40.00
	Pretell Real Estate:155 Wilks Blvd.	59.50
	Pretell Real Estate:75 Sunset Rd.	▶ 80.00 ◀
	No job assigned	8.00
Total Dan T. Miller		424.00
Elizabeth N. Mason		
	Teschner, Anton:Sun Room	120.00
Total Elizabeth N. Mason		120.00

For sick or vacation time, there may be no customer or job.

Jessica wants to see hours worked by each person broken down by job. She clicks Customize on the time by name report buttonbar. From the **Formats** drop-down list, she chooses Time by Name by Job.

In the **Formats** field, you can choose among five ways to subtotal the time by name report.

If you mark one of these three checkboxes, the checkboxes to its right become available as additional options.

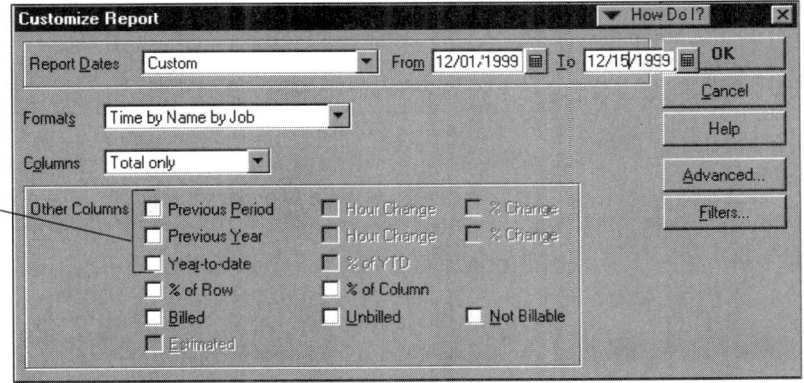

Alan wants to see separate columns for billed, unbilled, and not-billable hours. He clicks Customize on the time by name report buttonbar. In the Other Columns area, he selects Billed, Unbilled, and Not Billable.

Dru wants to compare time worked by each person during the same time period last year. She clicks Customize on the time by name report buttonbar. From the **Formats** drop-down list, she chooses Time by Name Only. In the Other Columns area, she selects Previous Year.

Reports about time | 331

Mehrdad wants to see a list of all activities for one person in order by date. He clicks Customize on the time by name report buttonbar. From the **Formats** drop-down list, he chooses Time by Name Only. In the revised report, he places the pointer over the hours for the particular person and double-clicks to display a list of all activities for that person.

How much time did we spend on each job?

The time by job summary report shows hours worked, subtotaled first by customer and job and then by service item.

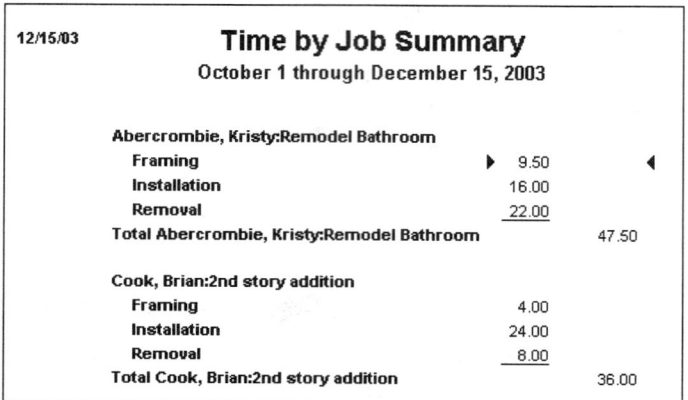

For sick or vacation time, there may be no customer or job. Time with no customer or job is at the bottom of the report (not shown in this example).

For each job, Rina wants to see hours worked by each person instead of the hours worked by service item. She clicks Customize on the time by job report buttonbar. From the **Formats** drop-down list, she chooses Time by Job by Name.

On a report showing time by job by item, David wants to compare estimated hours with hours actually worked. He clicks Customize on the time by job summary report buttonbar. In the Other Columns area, he selects Estimated. (The estimated hours appear on the report only if the estimate date is within the date range of the report.)

How much time did we spend on each type of work?

The time by item report shows hours worked subtotaled first by service item and then by job.

12/15/98	**Time by Item**	
	October 1 through December 15, 1998	
		◇ Oct 1 - Dec 15, '98 ◇
Framing		
	Abercrombie, Kristy:Remodel Bathroom ▶	9.50 ◀
	Cook, Brian:2nd story addition	4.00
	Cook, Brian:Kitchen	24.00
	Ecker Designs:Office Repairs	16.00
	Jacobsen, Doug:Kitchen	32.00
	Melton, Johnny:Dental office	20.50
	Natiello, Ernesto:Kitchen	16.00
	Pretell Real Estate:155 Wilks Blvd.	51.50
	Pretell Real Estate:75 Sunset Rd.	134.00
	Teschner, Anton:Sun Room	82.00
Total Framing		389.50
Installation		
	Abercrombie, Kristy:Remodel Bathroom	16.00
	Cook, Brian:2nd story addition	24.00
	Cook, Brian:Kitchen	94.00
	Ecker Designs:Office Repairs	16.00
	Jacobsen, Doug:Kitchen	42.00
	Pretell Real Estate:155 Wilks Blvd.	16.00
Total Installation		208.00

For each service item, the report has subtotals by job.

For sick or vacation time, there may be no service item. Time with no service item is at the bottom of the report (not shown in this example).

For each service item (type of work), Amy wants to see hours worked by each person instead of the hours worked by job. She clicks Customize on the time by item report buttonbar. From the **Formats** drop-down list, she chooses Time by Item by Name.

Is there a detailed list of each time activity?

The time by job detail report lists each time activity (work recorded for a single person, customer:job, date, and service item) and shows whether it is billed, unbilled, or not billable.

The report is grouped and subtotaled first by customer:job and then by service item. Each activity is on a separate line, whether you entered it on a weekly timesheet, entered it in the Time/Enter Single Activity window, or imported data from a Timer file.

You can add a column for payroll item, class, or notes by customizing the report.

Within one job, activities are grouped by the service item assigned to the activity.

To QuickZoom to the Time/Enter Single Activity window for any activity on the report, place the mouse pointer on the activity and double-click.

```
09/30/99                    Time by Job Detail
                          October through December 1999
             ◊  Date   ◊     Name      ◊ Billing Status ◊   Duration    ◊

          Cook, Brian:2nd story addition
             Framing
         ▶   12/04/98    Gregg O. Schneider    Billed             4.00 ◀
             Total Framing                                        4.00

             Installation
             12/07/98    Dan T. Miller         Unbilled           8.00
             12/08/98    Dan T. Miller         Unbilled           8.00
             12/09/98    Dan T. Miller         Unbilled           8.00
             Total Installation                                  24.00

             Total Cook, Brian:2nd story addition                28.00
```

Vacation and sick hours are likely to be among time activities not associated with any customer or job. Activities with no customer:job are at the bottom of the report (not shown here).

Mariseth wants to add a column that shows the payroll item associated with each activity. She clicks Customize on the time by job detail report buttonbar. In the **Columns** field, she selects Payroll Item.

Jay wants to view time for a single employee. He clicks Filters on the time by job detail report buttonbar. He selects the **Name** filter, and chooses the name of the employee.

To learn about...	Search the Help index for...
Finding the report you want with the QuickBooks Report Finder	reports, finding
■ Creating a report that shows hours worked by each person (time by name report)	report types, time
■ Creating a report that shows time spent by job (time by job summary report)	
■ Creating a report that shows time spent by type of work (time by item report)	
■ Creating a report that lists details of each time activity (time by job detail report)	
Creating a payroll summary report after paying employees to show the cost of work done	payroll, reports about

Installing the Timer

You can run the Timer on a computer that has the following hardware and software:

- 486 PC (or higher) with a minimum of 8 MB (megabytes) of RAM (random access memory); 16 MB is recommended.
- Hard disk with at least 8 MB of free disk space (plus space for your data file)
- Windows version 3.1 or higher (including Windows 95, 98, and NT 4.0)
- VGA monitor, SVGA monitor, or better

There are two ways to install the Timer, depending on what is available:

Situation	What to use to install	See...
The Timer user has access to the CD-ROM for QuickBooks Pro.	CD-ROM	"Installing the Timer from the CD-ROM" below
The Timer user does not have access to the CD-ROM for QuickBooks Pro.	A set of Timer install disks created by the QuickBooks Pro user	■ "Creating install disks for the Timer" on page 336 ■ "Installing the Timer from 3.5-inch disks" on page 336

Installing the Timer from the CD-ROM

You can circulate the QuickBooks Pro CD-ROM to others in your company who want to install the Timer without installing QuickBooks.

To install the Timer from the CD-ROM:

1 Close all Windows applications, including QuickBooks. Also turn off virus protection programs.

2 Insert the CD-ROM in your CD-ROM drive.

3 In Windows 95, 98, or NT 4.0: In the window that opens automatically, click Other Installation Options and choose the option for installing the Timer.

In Windows 3.1: From the File menu of Program Manager, choose Run. In the Run window, type

d:\timer\install.exe

and click OK. (If your CD-ROM drive is not drive D, substitute the correct drive letter.)

4 Follow the onscreen instructions. If you have an earlier version of the Timer program, we recommend that you install the Timer in the same folder as the earlier version.

5 After installing the Timer, remove the CD-ROM from your drive.

Creating install disks for the Timer

If you have the QuickBooks Pro CD-ROM, it contains a file you can use to create a set of 3.5-inch install disks to give to a person who needs the Timer.

To learn about...	Search the Help index for...
Using the CD-ROM to create a set of install disks for the Timer	Timer, creating disks for

Installing the Timer from 3.5-inch disks

To install the Timer from 3.5-inch install disks:

1 Close applications that are running on your computer so that the install process can update files that may be shared by other programs.

2 Place the first Timer install disk in your 3.5-inch disk drive.

3 In Windows 3.1, from the File menu of Program Manager, choose Run. In Windows 95, 98, or NT 4.0, click the Start button and then choose Run.

4 Type **a:install** if you're installing from Drive A (or type **b:install** if you're installing from Drive B); click OK to continue.

5 Click Next to display the Choose Timer Directory window.

6 In the Choose Timer Directory window, check that the suggested drive and folder (or directory) are where you want to install the Timer program.

To change the drive or folder (or directory), click Browse and enter a different path. Then click OK.

7 Click Next to display the Select Program Folder window.

8 In the Select Program Folder window, click Next to continue.

9 Confirm that the settings are correct and click Next to begin installing.

When the Install program asks for the next disk, follow the onscreen directions.

10 You must restart your computer before starting the Timer for the first time. In the Setup Complete window, indicate whether or not you want to restart your computer now. Then click Finish.

Don't forget to remove the last disk and store all disks in a safe place.

Quick Reference Sheet for the QuickBooks Pro Timer

The QuickBooks Pro Timer is designed to track and record time data for use with QuickBooks Pro.

- The Timer can track how long it takes to perform an activity. Click the Start button when you begin the activity and click the Stop button when you stop work.
- Alternatively, you can enter the time worked after you have done the work.

How the Timer works with QuickBooks Pro

- The Timer needs to import a file of lists that was created by QuickBooks Pro.
- Then you can use the Timer to record activities.
- Finally, you can export a file of activity data for QuickBooks Pro to import.

Installing the Timer from 3.5-inch disks

1 Insert the first Timer install disk in your 3.5-inch disk drive.

2 In the Run window of Windows 3.1, Windows 95, 98, or NT 4.0, type **a:install** (or **b:install**) and click OK.

3 Follow the onscreen instructions.

Starting the Timer

- In Windows 95, 98, or in NT 4.0, click Start, then Programs, then QuickBooks Pro, and then Timer.
- In Windows 3.1 Program Manager, double-click the Timer icon in the QuickBooks Pro program group.

Creating and setting up a Timer file

1 In the Open Timer File window (displayed the first time you start the Timer), choose Create New Timer File and click OK.

2 Enter the filename and location, and click OK.

3 From the File menu of the Timer, choose Import QuickBooks Lists.

4 Select the name of the IIF file you need to import. You may have to change the drive and folder (or directory). Click OK.

The person who works with QuickBooks Pro must make this IIF file available to you.

5 From the File menu of the Timer, choose Preferences and then Default Name.

6 Choose your own name from the drop-down list.

7 If your time is always billable to a customer or job, select the checkbox.

8 Click OK.

9 Fill in the fields you need and click OK.
For help with this window, click Help.

Setting up an activity to time

1 In the main Timer window, click New Activity.

2 Fill in the fields you need and click OK.

Timing an activity

1 If the activity you want to time is not already in the Current Activity field, choose it from the drop-down list.

- If you choose from Today's Activities, the Timer will add time to the time already shown for today.
- If you choose from Activity Templates, the Timer will start with zero time.

2 To start timing, click Start (or Resume).

3 To stop timing, click Stop.

Entering time manually

1 Choose the activity from the Activity Templates section of the drop-down list in the Current Activity field.

If the activity is not on the list, set it up first.

2 When the activity is in the Current Activity field, click Edit.

3 In the Edit Activity window, change the date if you did not perform the work today.

4 In the Duration field, enter the time.

You may enter time in any of the following formats:

- Hours and minutes (for example, 01:30)
- Hours as decimals (for example, 1.5)
- Hours as fractions (for example, 1 1/2)
- Number of minutes (for example, 90)

No matter which format you use, the Timer displays hours and minutes when you tab out of the field.

5 Click OK to record the activity and its time.

Shrinking the Timer

- Click the Resize button (to the right of the Start button).
- To make the timer full size again, click the Resize button on the shrunken Timer.

Exporting Timer data for QuickBooks

1 From the File menu of the Timer, choose Export Time Activities.

2 In the Export Activities window, change the date through which to export all unexported activities if the date is not correct.

3 Click Export.

4 In the Create Export File window, specify a name, drive, and folder (or directory) for the IIF file you are creating.

5 Click OK.

Using the Timer's Help system

For onscreen help while using the Timer, press F1 or choose Help for this Window from the Help menu.

To find out how to use other Timer features (such as, entering notes or viewing your activity data), choose Help Contents from the Help menu.

This page should be copied and distributed to persons using the QuickBooks Pro Timer.

CHAPTER 18

Payroll

An overview of QuickBooks payroll	342
How QuickBooks payroll works	348
Setting up payroll	354
Managing payroll and employee information	371
Running payroll and paying taxes	379
Getting information about your payroll	393

Should I use QuickBooks to track my payroll?

Paying employees can be a big responsibility. You have to keep track of hours, salaries and wages, social security numbers and dependents, vacation and sick time, bonuses and advances, as well as company payments to government and private pension plans. It's not surprising that many businesses let their bookkeeper or accountant deal with payroll.

An overview of QuickBooks payroll

With QuickBooks, you can manage your payroll quickly and easily. When you hire an employee, you simply enter the personal and salary information into an employee record. Keeping track of an employee's time and allocating it to different customers or jobs is just as easy.

When it's time to create your paychecks, just choose which employees to pay—QuickBooks remembers the hours worked, calculates wages, deducts taxes, figures employer contributions, writes the paychecks, and prints them.

A subscription to one of the QuickBooks Payroll Services—either Basic Payroll or Deluxe Payroll—allows QuickBooks to use the most current tax information available to automatically calculate your federal and state payroll taxes and to prepare tax forms. Each provides a different level of service that depends on your payroll needs.

Note: **Without a subscription to one of the QuickBooks Payroll Services, you'll need to calculate and enter your payroll tax deductions manually for each paycheck.** For information on the payroll services and your payroll options in QuickBooks, see "QuickBooks Payroll Services" on page 346, or choose Set Up Payroll Services from the Employees menu, then click Learn About Payroll Services.

If you don't use the payroll feature in QuickBooks

If you have employees, you must track payroll. You can do it yourself, or use an accountant or bookkeeper, a payroll service, QuickBooks, or a combination of these methods.

If you decide not to use the QuickBooks payroll feature to pay your employees, you still need to have employees on your Employee list to track the checks that you write to them.

By default, the QuickBooks payroll feature is turned on. When you turn the payroll feature off, however, the Employee list has only very basic information about each employee—including name, address, phone number, social security number, hire and release dates, and any other custom information you define.

What the payroll feature in QuickBooks can do for you

QuickBooks can perform many different payroll tasks, including calculating wages and taxes, managing compensation and liabilities, and processing payments for both employees and payroll tax agencies.

Some tasks have additional requirements, such as a subscription to one of the QuickBooks Payroll Services—Basic Payroll or Deluxe Payroll.

QuickBooks payroll feature can:	Additional requirements
Calculate payroll amounts	
■ Calculate wages for each pay period.	None
■ Calculate hours worked, year-to-date totals for all employees, and shows this information on payroll reports.	None
■ Calculate amounts for, and prints on, Forms W-2 and W-3.	None
■ Calculate federal, state, and selected local taxes for the United States, including the District of Columbia and Puerto Rico. **Note:** This edition of QuickBooks doesn't calculate taxes for Guam, the Virgin Islands, American Samoa, or Canada.	Basic Payroll subscription **or** Deluxe Payroll subscription
■ Prepare and print federal payroll tax Forms 940 and 941.	**Note:** Deluxe Payroll prepares and files these forms for you.
■ Observe wage base limits for taxes	Basic Payroll subscription **or** Deluxe Payroll subscription

An overview of QuickBooks payroll

QuickBooks payroll feature can:	Additional requirements
Manage compensation, liabilities, and data	
■ Handle all kinds of compensation: salary, hourly (including overtime), commission, or a combination.	None
■ Track sick or vacation time.	None
■ Track Advanced EIC payments, company loan repayments, 401(k), deductions, tips, union dues, bonuses, car expenses, and many other nonstandard payroll items.	None
■ Use time data or allows you to specify hours worked for each job and class to allocate payroll expenses.	QuickBooks Pro
■ Track your company's liability to the government, insurance companies, and other agencies.	None
■ Observe annual limits you set for deductions and company-paid benefits.	None
■ Record employee details such as pay and commission rates, social security number, and tax exemptions.	None

QuickBooks payroll feature can:	Additional requirements
Process employee and tax agency payments	
■ Create your paychecks with earning, deductions, and year-to-date detail provided on the voucher (if you use voucher checks), or on a separate paystub that is automatically created and can be printed for your employees.	None
■ Pay employees on a daily, weekly, biweekly, semimonthly, monthly, quarterly, or yearly basis.	None
■ Allow you to specify extra taxes or deductions in addition to the standard federal and state taxes, and apply them to employees.	None
■ Create checks to pay your company's payroll liabilities.	None

Note: If you need to file Form 1099-MISC for an independent contractor, set up the person as a vendor in QuickBooks. **Employees cannot receive 1099-MISC forms.** See "Information you may want to set up for different kinds of vendors" on page 214 for more information.

QuickBooks Payroll Services

QuickBooks Payroll Services provide two levels of service—Basic and Deluxe. Both allow QuickBooks to use the most current tax information and forms available to calculate your taxes. Deluxe Payroll provides additional features, however, that help take the worry out of processing your payroll. Each service is subscription-based and requires that you have the following:

- an Internet connection
- a valid subscription to the service

    You can subscribe to the payroll services from QuickBooks. First, however, set up your company payroll as instructed in "Setting up payroll" on page 354 and register your QuickBooks software.

Without a subscription to one of the QuickBooks Payroll Services, you'll need to calculate and enter your payroll tax deductions manually for each paycheck.

The following sections describe features provided with each service.

QuickBooks Basic Payroll

Basic Payroll lets you process your own payroll with the confidence that your federal and state tax tables will be updated with the latest payroll withholding regulations. For a monthly fee, a subscription to Basic Payroll can do the following:

- Download regular payroll updates via the Internet as tax regulations change throughout the year.
- Use QuickBooks to automatically calculate taxes on paychecks.

    Note: Without a subscription to Basic Payroll, QuickBooks will continue to provide earnings, additions, and non-tax deductions.

- Prepare and print federal payroll tax forms.
- (For an additional fee) Deposit your employees' paychecks directly into their bank accounts. (Two bank accounts per employee.)

    Note: With QuickBooks 2000, the Basic Payroll service replaces the Tax Table Service. If you upgraded from an earlier version of QuickBooks and subscribed to the Tax Table Service, you must subscribe to Basic Payroll to continue getting payroll updates. You can apply the remainder of your Tax Table Service subscription to your Basic Payroll subscription and get a 60-day free trial period.

QuickBooks Deluxe Payroll

Deluxe Payroll is a more comprehensive solution that includes calculating your payroll to making your federal and state tax deposits from your payroll expense accounts. For a monthly fee, Deluxe Payroll provides most of the features of Basic Payroll, plus the following:

- Makes your federal and state payroll tax deposits from your payroll accounts.
- Prepares and files federal and state payroll tax forms required for your company.
- Prepares and delivers to you Forms W-2 for your employees and files Form W-3 for your company at the end of the year.
- Provides a toll-free number for technical support and help with setting up your payroll in QuickBooks.

To learn about...	Search the Help index for...
Using a payroll service other than QuickBooks Payroll Services	payroll services, other than Intuit
If you are set up for QuickBooks payroll, but don't want to use the QuickBooks Payroll Services	payroll taxes, calculating without a payroll service subscription
If you have employees, but aren't using QuickBooks payroll	payroll, not using
Signing up for QuickBooks Basic Payroll	Basic Payroll service, signing up
Signing up for QuickBooks Deluxe Payroll	Deluxe Payroll service, signing up
What you need to do to add the optional direct deposit feature	direct deposit, in Basic Payroll direct deposit, in Deluxe Payroll

How QuickBooks payroll works

This section contains the following information:

The importance of payroll items	**348**
Payroll expense and liability accounts	**349**
How QuickBooks tracks company-paid taxes and benefits	**353**

The importance of payroll items

When you create any kind of payroll transaction in QuickBooks—whether it's a paycheck, a payroll tax payment, or an adjustment at setup time or later—QuickBooks expresses the transaction in terms of payroll items.

Payroll items are a unique feature in QuickBooks. There are payroll items for compensation, taxes, other additions and deductions, and employer-paid expenses. QuickBooks uses payroll items to track individual amounts on a paycheck and accumulated year-to-date wage and tax amounts for each employee. You can assign these payroll items to different accounts as needed.

QuickBooks identifies payroll transactions by their use of payroll items:

- Payroll reports include only transactions that use payroll items.

- Payroll liability balances are based on transactions that use payroll items.

- Employee year-to-date amounts are based on transactions that use payroll items.

When you indicate you want to use payroll, QuickBooks creates the Payroll Item list with some standard payroll items. You can add payroll items to this list.

To learn about...	Search the Help index for...
Payroll items	payroll items, defined

Payroll expense and liability accounts

When QuickBooks adds your initial payroll items, it also adds two accounts to your chart of accounts:

- Payroll Expenses (an expense account)
- Payroll Liabilities (an other current liability account)

To keep your balance sheet and your profit and loss statement accurate, QuickBooks associates the appropriate account or accounts with each payroll item.

Whenever you create a new payroll item, QuickBooks helps you assign it to the correct account or accounts by prefilling the account name to use. Of course, you can use a different account if you like.

It is also correct for some types of payroll items (such as a deduction that is a loan repayment) to be associated with an account other than an expense or a liability account.

To learn about...	Search the Help index for...
Payroll Liabilities account	payroll liabilities, account
Payroll Expenses account	payroll, expenses account

Payroll items associated with expenses

Expenses are the amounts you record and pay as they occur. Common company payroll expenses include gross pay, company-paid payroll taxes, and company-paid benefits for employees.

For all payroll expenses, we suggest using the Payroll Expenses account. Whenever you run your payroll, QuickBooks keeps track of your company's expenses for each employee. You can then see totals for these expenses on the payroll summary report and on the profit and loss statement.

Keeping track of expenses by customer and job, class, and service item

You can break down company-paid payroll expenses not only for salaries and hourly wages, but also for:

- Company-paid payroll taxes
- Additions, commissions, and company contributions if the "Track Expenses By Job" checkbox is selected in the setup wizard for the individual payroll item.

QuickBooks prorates the company-paid expenses for an employee in the same proportions as you prorated the dollar amounts of the employee's earnings.

Tracking expenses by customer and job

Some businesses like to see which customers and jobs create the most expense or work for them. If you want to keep track of all payroll expenses by customer or job, you need to do the following:

- If you are not using QuickBooks Pro, turn on the accounting preference for Customer:Job tracking. (In QuickBooks Pro, Customer:Job tracking is always on.)
- Turn on the following payroll and employee preference: "Report all payroll taxes by Customer:Job and Service Item."
- On every payroll item for a commission, addition, or company contribution, select the checkbox for "Track Expenses By Job."
- On each paycheck you write, associate every salary or hourly wage with the correct job or jobs.

Tracking expenses by class

If your business is a nonprofit organization that needs to do fund accounting, you may want to keep track of expenses by class. To track payroll expenses by class, do the following:

- Turn on "Use class tracking" in the accounting preferences.
- Turn on the following payroll and employees preference: "Report all payroll taxes by Customer:Job, Service Item, and Class."
- On every payroll item for a commission, addition, or company contribution, select the checkbox for "Track Expenses By Job."
- Depending on the payroll and employee preference you choose, assign one class to an entire paycheck, or assign a separate class to each earnings payroll item on a paycheck.

Tracking expenses by service item (QuickBooks Pro only)

Some businesses keep track of expenses by service item. To track payroll expenses by service item, do the following:

- Turn on the payroll and employee preference for "Report all payroll taxes by Customer:Job and Service Item."
- On every payroll item for a commission, addition, or company contribution, select the checkbox for "Track Expenses By Job."
- Set up employee to "Use time data to create paychecks."
- On each paycheck you write, associate every Customer:Job with the correct Service Item.

To learn about...	Search the Help index for...
Keeping track of payroll expenses by customer and job, or class, or service item	payroll, tracking expenses

Payroll items associated with liabilities

Liabilities are the amounts you owe but have not yet paid. For each type of payroll liability, QuickBooks suggests using the Payroll Liabilities account.

When you do your payroll, QuickBooks calculates how much you owe for each tax, deduction, or company contribution payroll item and records it in this liability account. With each paycheck you write, the balance of the liability account increases.

When you pay your payroll taxes or other payroll liabilities with the Pay Liabilities window, QuickBooks decreases the balance of the liability account.

Some payroll items simply deduct amounts from the employee's paycheck. For example, federal and state income tax withholding reduce the amount the employee receives, but are not expenses to the company. When you write the paycheck, your company is temporarily keeping these taxes, but you will turn them over to the government shortly. In the meantime, you have a tax liability. Payroll items for deductions are usually assigned to the Payroll Liabilities account.

Combinations of expenses and liabilities

Some payroll items are a combination of liabilities and expenses. For example, federal unemployment (FUTA) tax creates an additional tax liability and is a company expense at the same time. Payroll items for company-paid taxes and company contributions are usually assigned to both a liability account and an expense account.

Customizing payroll accounts

You may change the names of the payroll liability account and payroll expense account that QuickBooks provides. If you use numbered accounts, you may change the account numbers QuickBooks provides.

You can also use subaccounts of Payroll Liabilities to see more detail on your balance sheet for payroll liabilities, and subaccounts of Payroll Expenses to see more detail on your profit and loss statement of your payroll expenses.

For example, corporations may need to report expenses for officer salaries separately from those for non-officer salaries.

To learn about...	Search the Help index for...
Adding new accounts	accounts, adding to your chart of accounts
Editing account information	accounts, editing information about
Subaccounts	subaccounts

How QuickBooks tracks company-paid taxes and benefits

QuickBooks tracks company-paid taxes with each paycheck you write. It also allows you to track company-paid benefits with each paycheck through company contribution payroll items.

Here are some advantages of tracking company-paid taxes and company-paid expenses with the paycheck:

- You always have a record of how much tax you owe at any time, so you can plan to have the cash to pay it.

- For taxes (such as federal unemployment) that have an earnings cap, you can see when QuickBooks reaches the cap for an employee and stops accruing additional tax liability.

- When you track company-paid benefits with a paycheck, you can track the total cost to the company for each employee. The total cost equals compensation plus company-paid taxes plus company-paid benefits.

QuickBooks doesn't print information about company-paid taxes and company-paid expenses on voucher paychecks. On paystubs it prints information about company-paid expenses only if they are taxable. However, payroll reports show all these expenses and liabilities.

Setting up payroll

The amount of time it takes to set up your payroll information in QuickBooks varies depending on the size of the company. Setting up consists of the following steps:

1 Set up your payroll data in QuickBooks.

- Payroll items—see "Setting up your payroll items" on page 358
- Employees—see "Setting up employees" on page 361
- Year-to-date amounts—see "Summarizing amounts for this year to-date" on page 364
- Federal —an EIN is a nine-digit number issued by the IRS, and is required to pay your payroll taxes.

    An EIN is also required by the QuickBooks Payroll Services (both Basic Payroll and Deluxe Payroll) to process your payroll and your payroll liabilities.

    If you don't have an EIN, you can request one by contacting the IRS and obtaining Form SS-4. Call 1-800-TAX-FORM or refer to IRS Publication 15, *Circular E, Employer's Tax Guide*.

    For information on adding an EIN to your company information in QuickBooks, see "Changing company information" on page 425.

2 Sign up for one of the QuickBooks Payroll Services—either Basic Payroll or Deluxe Payroll. **QuickBooks cannot compute payroll taxes or process payroll tax forms unless you have a subscription to a payroll service.**

Both Basic Payroll and Deluxe Payroll ensure that you have the most current tax information available, even with mid-year tax changes from federal and state tax agencies. For information about the QuickBooks Payroll Services, see pa ge346.

Note: Beginning with QuickBooks 2000, the Basic Payroll service replaces the Tax Table Service. For information about upgrading to one of the payroll services, see pag e346.

3 Use the Payroll & Employee preferences to specify the following:

- Which payroll features to use
- How you want to sort your employee list
- What prints on the paycheck and its voucher

4 Protect your company's payroll data from unauthorized access by setting up user permissions. For information about restricting access to your company file, see "Setting up users" on page 63.

To learn about...	Search the Help index for...
Setting up payroll	payroll setup, required information
Signing up for the QuickBooks Payroll Services	payroll services, description of services Basic Payroll service, signing up Deluxe Payroll service, signing up
Getting payroll updates	tax tables
Setting payroll preferences	preferences, payroll
Setting user permissions for payroll	permissions

QuickBooks 2000 does not work with QuickPay or QuickPayroll.

If you've been doing your payroll with either QuickPay or QuickPayroll, and plan to use payroll with QuickBooks 2000, you'll need to set up your payroll in QuickBooks. Follow the instructions in Chapter 2 of the *Installation and Conversion Guide*.

Setting up payroll   355

Information you need before you start	Where to find it
Company	
Pay period frequency or frequencies.	Your accountant or company records
State or states for which you file payroll taxes.	Your accountant or company records
Start date for payroll.	Your company records
Federal EIN. **Note:** An EIN is required if you are signing up for one of the QuickBooks Payroll Services.	Your company records, IRS Publication 15, Circular E, Employer's Tax Guide, or the Internal Revenue Service
Tax information	
State employer tax ID number or numbers.	Your accountant or state tax agency
State unemployment tax (SUI) rate(s) for employer and/or employee.	Your accountant or state tax agency
State disability tax (SDI) rate or rates. **Note:** As of 1999, this applies to the following states: HI, NJ, and NY. If the rate is the same for everyone in your state, QuickBooks already knows it.	Your accountant or state tax agency
Local income taxes that you withhold or pay on behalf of your employees. **Note:** This applies only in a selected number of states.	Your accountant or local tax agency
Whether you qualify for the federal unemployment (FUTA) tax credit.	IRS Publication 15, Circular E, Employer's Tax Guide, your accountant, or the Internal Revenue Service
Compensation, benefits, and other paycheck items	
Which types of compensation you pay employees and officers: hourly wages, salaries, and/or commissions.	Your accountant or company records
Types of deductions from net pay that you withhold. ■ Examples include: union dues, repayments of employee loans or advances, health or life insurance paid by the employee, deductions for pension plans.	Your accountant or company records
Types of additions to pay you add to a paycheck. ■ Examples include: bonuses, travel expenses, employee loans, tips.	Your accountant or company records
Types of company contributions (that is, company-paid expenses) you need to track with each paycheck. ■ Example: health or life insurance paid by the company.	Your accountant or company records

Information you need before you start	Where to find it
Employees	
Employee names, addresses, and social security numbers.	Employees' social security cards
Employee withholding setup.	Employees' Forms W-4 and equivalent state forms
Current employee wages/salaries, additions, deductions, and company contributions.	Paychecks, reports, or payroll ledger
Sick and vacation time policies and hours accrued.	Paychecks, reports, or payroll ledger
Year-to-date amounts	
■ Quarterly and pay period summaries of employee payroll amounts from the beginning of this calendar year to your start date. ■ Paychecks from your start date to today.	Payroll service, accountant, payroll ledger, or paystubs
■ Quarterly and pay period summaries of payroll liability payments from the beginning of this year to your start date. ■ Payroll liability checks from your start date to today.	Payroll service, accountant, or payroll ledger
Direct deposit (an optional feature of Basic Payroll and Deluxe Payroll)	
For each employee: ■ Bank account numbers ■ Routing numbers	Employees' direct deposit request forms

Setting up payroll | 357

Setting up your payroll items

When you create any kind of payroll transaction—whether it's a paycheck, a payroll tax payment, or an adjustment at setup time or later—QuickBooks expresses the transaction in terms of payroll items.

There are payroll items for compensation, taxes, other additions and deductions, and employer-paid expenses. QuickBooks uses payroll items to track individual amounts on a paycheck and accumulated year-to-date wage and tax amounts for each employee.

QuickBooks creates a Payroll Item list with some standard payroll items. You can add payroll items to this list. The names of the payroll items are what you'll see on paychecks and in payroll reports. You can change any of these names.

Note: QuickBooks provides preset options for the taxability of a payroll item, which are based on the most current information from the IRS and other tax agencies. We recommend that you retain the preset taxability of a payroll item, as it is unlikely that it would need to change.

Depending on your company's payroll, you may need to set up additional payroll items of the following types.

Situation	Select this type in payroll item setup
Your company has salaried employees whose annual salary is independent of the number of hours actually worked for regular pay, sick pay, and vacation pay.	Wage, and then Salary Wages
Your company has employees whose pay is based on the number of hours worked for regular pay, sick pay, and vacation pay.	Wage, and then Hourly Wages
Your company has officers whose annual salary is independent of the number of hours actually worked for regular pay, sick pay, and vacation pay.	Wage, and then Salary Wages
Your state requires income tax withholding from the employees' paychecks.	State Tax, and then State Withholding

Situation	Select this type in payroll item setup
Your company and/or employees are in any of the following locations (as of 1999) that collect disability insurance (SDI) based on employee wages: CA, HI, NJ, NY, RI; or Puerto Rico. This tax may be paid by the company and/or employee.	State Tax, and then State Disability
Your state collects unemployment insurance (SUI) based on employee wages. This tax may be paid by the company and/or employee.	State Tax, and then State Unemployment
You need to pay other taxes (state, county, city, or district) based on employee wages. These taxes may be paid by the company and/or employee.	Other Tax
You need to deduct an amount from gross or after-tax pay for employees. Examples include union dues, loan repayments, employee-paid insurance, and employee deductions for pension or 401(k).	Deduction
You need to add an amount to gross or after-tax pay (net pay) for employees. An example is a bonus.	Addition
Some (or all) of your employees are paid by commission.	Commission
Your company makes contributions to employee benefits, such as health or life insurance or a 401(k) plan.	Company Contribution

To learn about...	Search the Help index for...
Changing the name of payroll items	payroll items, editing
State taxes automatically created in QuickBooks	state, taxes
Method QuickBooks uses to calculate taxes	payroll, calculations

To learn about...	Search the Help index for...
Adding payroll items for state taxes	payroll items, adding
Adding payroll items for local and other taxes	payroll items, local and other taxes
Adding other payroll items	payroll items, adding

Common payroll items:
- Adoption assistance
- Advance against salary
- Award
- Charity donations
- Deductions for MSAs
- Deductions for retirement plans
- Dependent care
- Distributions from a nonqualified plan
- Elective 457(b) plan
- Employee loan
- Employer contributions to MSAs
- Employer contributions to retirement plans
- Flexible spending plans
- Garnished wages
- One-time compensation
- Life/health insurance
- Piece work
- Miscellaneous local or other tax withheld
- Moving expenses
- Repayments of employee loans
- Sick pay reimbursement
- Taxable fringe benefits
- Tips
- Travel advance
- Union dues

Examples of payroll items

Visit the following Web site for examples of how to set up common payroll items in QuickBooks:

http://www.intuit.com/quickbooks/help/payitems.html

This site provides current information about the types of payroll items you can add in QuickBooks, the taxability of the different payroll items, and additional information you should be aware of. For example, to set up a payroll item for employee bonuses you'll need the following information before you enter it into QuickBooks:

Type of information you need...	For example...
Payroll item name	Bonus
Item type	Addition
Tax tracking	Compensation
Additional information	To suppress payment of regular salary on a bonus check, delete the salary item in the Preview Paycheck window. (Select it and press Ctrl+Del.)

The list on the left shows other types of sample payroll items available on the Web site. This site is updated with new information from time-to-time, so you may want to check the site when you create new payroll items in QuickBooks.

Setting up employees

According to the IRS, "anyone who performs services for you is your employee if you can control what will be done and how it will be done." The IRS has information on how to determine whether an individual providing services is an independent contractor or an employee. See IRS Publication 15, *Circular E, Employer's Tax Guide*, or visit the IRS Web site at **www.irs.gov**.

Generally, people in business for themselves are not employees. If your company is incorporated, corporate officers who work in the business are employees.

Note: **If you need to file Form 1099-MISC for an independent contractor, set up the person as a vendor in QuickBooks. Employees cannot receive 1099-MISC forms.** See "Information you may want to set up for different kinds of vendors" on page 214 for more information.

To set up employees for payroll, do the following:

- (Optional but recommended) Set up the employee defaults.
- Add employees to your Employee List, or add payroll information for employees already on your Employee list.

Entering standard employee information

The employee defaults help you set up payroll for several employees quickly. You enter payroll information that most employees have in common. Don't worry if there are a few exceptions—you can change them on an individual basis whenever you need to. Any changes you make to these defaults will show up every time you enter information for a new employee.

The Employee Defaults window resembles the Payroll Info tab of the New/Edit Employee window. You can set up the following information as employee defaults:

- Salary or wage payroll items (with or without rates)
- Pay period
- Class, if you're using classes to track your employees (see Chapter 4, *Organizing data effectively*, beginning on page 39)
- Whether you want to use time data to create checks (QuickBooks Pro only)
- Additions, deductions, and company contributions that appear on paychecks

    Note: The order in which you enter payroll items in the Addition, Deductions, and Company Contributions table can affect the amount QuickBooks calculates for each item and for taxes. For information about the order in which to enter these payroll items, refer to QuickBooks onscreen Help.

- Whether your employees are covered by a qualified pension plan (Deluxe Payroll users only)
- Taxes—Federal, State, Other/Local
- Sick and vacation time

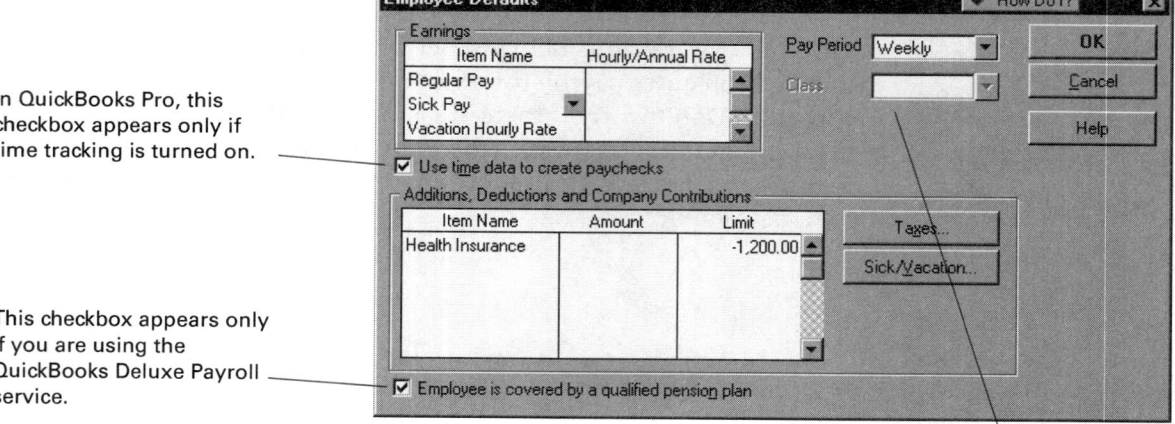

In QuickBooks Pro, this checkbox appears only if time tracking is turned on.

This checkbox appears only if you are using the QuickBooks Deluxe Payroll service.

The **Class** field is available only if you have class tracking turned on.

To learn about...	Search the Help index for...
Setting up the employee defaults	employee defaults, creating
Determining the order in which you add payroll items to the Employee Defaults window	employee defaults, order of payroll items in

Adding employees

If you've already set up your employee defaults, QuickBooks can prefill much of the information when you start to set up individual employees.

The Employee list contains the names of all your employees. When you add a new employee to the list (or edit information for an existing employee), the first window you see has three tabs:

- Address Info
- Additional Info
- Payroll Info

You'll need payroll items for all the taxes you enter, as well as for other payroll information. If you have not already set up all the payroll items you need, QuickBooks gives you a chance to add them as you work.

Each of your employees needs to fill out a Form W-4 and its state equivalent to tell you what filing status they will use and how many personal exemptions they will claim. You can get blank forms from the IRS and state agencies.

To learn about...	Search the Help index for...
Adding employees	employees, adding
Setting up payroll information for existing employees	employees, payroll information about
Categorizing employees by class	employees, grouping by department or location
Types of employees	employees, types
How the order of payroll items affects amounts on your employee's paychecks	paychecks, affecting amounts

Summarizing amounts for this year to-date

If you start using QuickBooks for payroll after you've already issued paychecks earlier in the current calendar year, you need to:

- Enter year-to-date information to summarize payroll transactions from January 1 through your QuickBooks start date.

  For a discussion of start dates, see "Setup tasks" on page 24.

- Enter payroll transactions (paychecks and liability checks) for the period between your QuickBooks start date and today.

After you've entered this information, QuickBooks updates your year-to-date amounts as it issues paychecks during the remainder of the calendar year and keeps your payroll tax amounts correct.

You must enter two types of information: year-to-date summaries for each employee and year-to-date summaries of payments of payroll taxes and other liabilities. A wizard helps you enter the year-to-date information.

Note: **Skip this section if your company has not issued any paychecks earlier in the current calendar year.** You are ready to start writing paychecks.

To enter year-to-date amounts:

- From the Employees menu, choose Enter YTD Amounts.

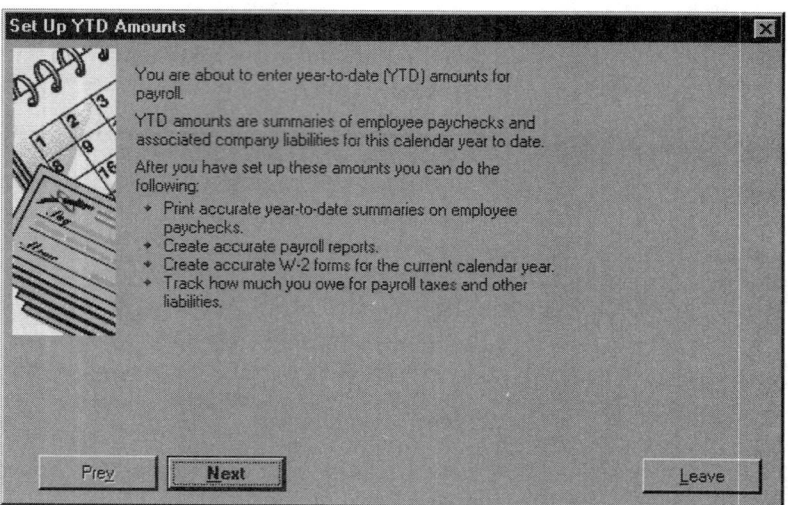

Year-to-date summaries for each employee

You must enter summaries of earnings, taxes, and other amounts for each individual employee (both current and former) you paid during the current calendar year from January 1 through your start date.

For each employee, you must enter both taxes withheld *and taxes that are a company expense,* as long as you owed them as a result of the employee's earnings. For example, you must enter federal and state unemployment tax summaries for each employee, as well as employee taxes.

QuickBooks collects year-to-date information on a quarter-by-quarter basis. We recommend that you use this same method to organize your year-to-date information before you begin entering year-to-date summaries. This organizational method will help you if you plan to subscribe to the Deluxe Payroll service, because the service also collects this information on a quarter-by-quarter basis.

When you select an employee and click Enter Summary, QuickBooks displays each payroll item you entered in that employee's record.

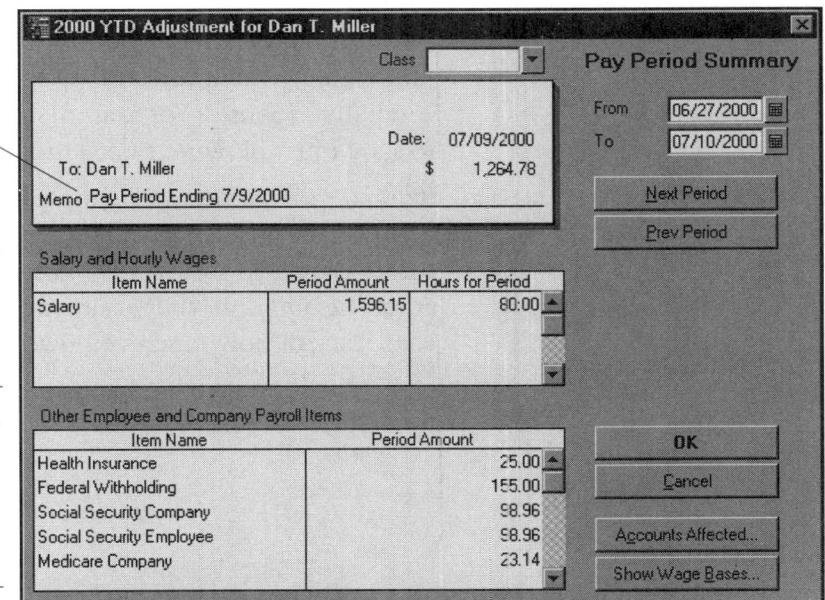

Enter summaries for the period specified here.

In this area, enter totals for salary or hourly wages paid during this period.

Enter hours worked during the period, if you want hour totals for reports. QuickBooks displays a message if hours are required for your state.

In this area, enter totals for all other earnings, withholdings, and company-paid taxes or payroll expenses for this employee. Include taxes regardless of whether you have paid them.

To insert an item, press Ctrl+Insert. You can skip over items not used in this period.

Setting up payroll

- In the Other Employee and Company Payroll Items area, leave the Period Amount field blank if there was no amount for a payroll item during this period.

- In the Salary and Hourly Wages area, enter payroll items for sick and vacation time taken during this period. You should enter sick and vacation hours and their corresponding wage amounts. Do not include these hours and wage amounts in your totals for regular salary or hourly wages.

- Add payroll items for one-time-only payroll amounts, such as bonuses, that occurred during this period. You must enter anything that affects compensation or payroll taxes. You do not have to enter non-payroll adjustments such as reimbursements for office supplies.

- Enter an amount for the employee or company portion of social security and Medicare. When you enter one portion, QuickBooks fills in the other portion for you, because the amounts should match. QuickBooks uses the separate amounts to track totals for employee withholding; it uses both portions to track your total tax liability.

- You must enter all tax liabilities created because of the compensation paid, even if the taxes were paid later and even if they were company expenses. For example, if the compensation was subject to state unemployment tax, enter the amount of tax.

- If you decide to track company-paid expenses such as insurance as a payroll expense for each pay period, you must enter amounts for the employee in this window. Later, in the wizard, you must also enter the amounts you've already paid, so that QuickBooks can keep track of how much you owe.

Wage bases

For every tax payroll item in the lower half of the YTD Adjustment window for an employee, QuickBooks tracks the wage base for reports and for the W-2 form. You can view the wage bases by clicking the Show Wage Bases button.

wage base

The total amount of employee wages or earnings on which a payroll tax is calculated.

QuickBooks calculates the wage base for a tax as follows:

- First, it totals all salary, hourly wages, and commissions.
- Then it adds to gross those additions and company contributions that affect gross and are subject to that specific tax.
- Finally, it subtracts from gross those deductions that are deducted prior to calculating that specific tax.

If the total exceeds the maximum annual earnings limit for this tax, the wage base equals the maximum earnings limit. If you entered amounts for earlier periods this year, QuickBooks counts the wage base from the earlier periods towards the maximum. For example, if the FUTA wage limit is $7,000 and you paid an employee $5,000 in each of the first two periods, the wage base for FUTA for the second period is $2,000.

To learn about...	Search the Help index for...
Entering YTD amounts for employees	year-to-date amounts, employee
Wage bases	wage base

Year-to-date summaries of payments of payroll taxes and other liabilities

Note: If your company has not made any payments for payroll taxes or other liabilities incurred during this calendar year, you can skip this section.

For this adjustment, you'll need to know how much you paid for each of the following:

- Each payroll tax (whether withheld or paid as a company expense)
- Each deduction paid (employee-paid dental insurance, for example)
- Each company contribution you paid (company-paid health insurance, for example)

This adjustment is just for payroll liabilities you paid. It is not for expenses (such as salaries, bonuses, or hourly wages) paid directly to employees.

Enter the date you made the liability payment.

Enter the ending date of the period you are summarizing.

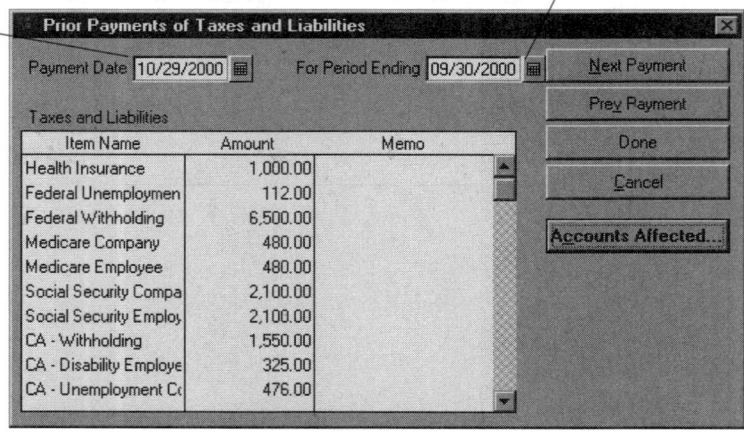

To learn about...	Search the Help index for...
Entering YTD liability payments	year-to-date amounts, liability payments
Checking YTD amounts	payroll checkup

Checking your payroll data

Because QuickBooks bases new payroll transactions on existing data, it's extremely important that you enter all of your payroll data into QuickBooks accurately. To help you make sure that your payroll data and year-to-date transactions are accurate, QuickBooks provides you with several options.

Running Payroll Checkup

Payroll Checkup is a diagnostic tool within QuickBooks that helps you verify your current setup by scanning your payroll data for any discrepancies.

When you change the taxability of a payroll item, enter year-to-date information, or subscribe to Deluxe Payroll, a prompt appears recommending that you run the Payroll Checkup to verify new or modified entries against your current payroll setup. Results appear on a separate page, which you can print and use to verify your payroll data.

Note: **Running the Payroll Checkup doesn't verify whether or not your payroll data is set up correctly.** It compares your wage base and tax amount totals with your current payroll setup in QuickBooks and summarizes any discrepancies.

To run Payroll Checkup:

1 From the Employees menu, choose Run Payroll Checkup. A wizard guides you through the checkup process.

2 Review the results in the Payroll Checkup Results page and determine whether or not you need to modify your payroll data. Refer to the Solutions section of the page for guidance.

Do not delete any zero-tax amounts resulting from the Payroll Checkup.

While scanning your payroll data, the Payroll Checkup may make some wage base adjustments, which can take some time and result in some zero-tax amounts. QuickBooks marks these adjustments by adding "Payroll Checkup" to the Memo field for the payroll item. Do not delete any payroll items with a zero-tax amount if "Payroll Checkup" appears in the Memo field.

Making sure that your data is complete

After you set up your payroll information in QuickBooks, you should make sure that it is complete.

Procedure	Comments	Search the Help index for...
Review your Employee list.	The Employee list should include names of all employees on your payroll at any time during the current calendar year.	employees, reports about lists, printing
Review your Payroll Item list.	The Payroll Item list should list everything you need to track on a paycheck.	payroll, reports about lists, printing
Review an employee contact list report.	The employee contact report should include all employees.	employees, reports about
Review your payroll summary for all employees for this entire calendar year.	You should be able to match the amounts for payroll items with the amounts for payroll accounts on prior payroll reports.	employees, reports about
Review your payroll liabilities as of December 31 of **this** year.	You should be able to match the amounts for payroll items with the amounts for payroll accounts on prior liability reports.	payroll, reports about

Managing payroll and employee information

As your business grows and changes, you will probably find it necessary to add or remove payroll items from your list, hire (and sometimes release) employees, track additional information about your payroll, and modify your payroll service.

This section contains the following information:

Changing payroll item information	**371**
Changing employee information	**374**
Setting up employees for direct deposit of paychecks	**378**

Changing payroll item information

By default, the Payroll Item list is organized by payroll item type. Earnings items (for yearly salaries, hourly wages, and commissions) are at the top of the list. You can re-sort the list, if you'd like, by clicking a button in the column header.

To view your payroll items:

- From the Employees menu, choose Payroll Item List.

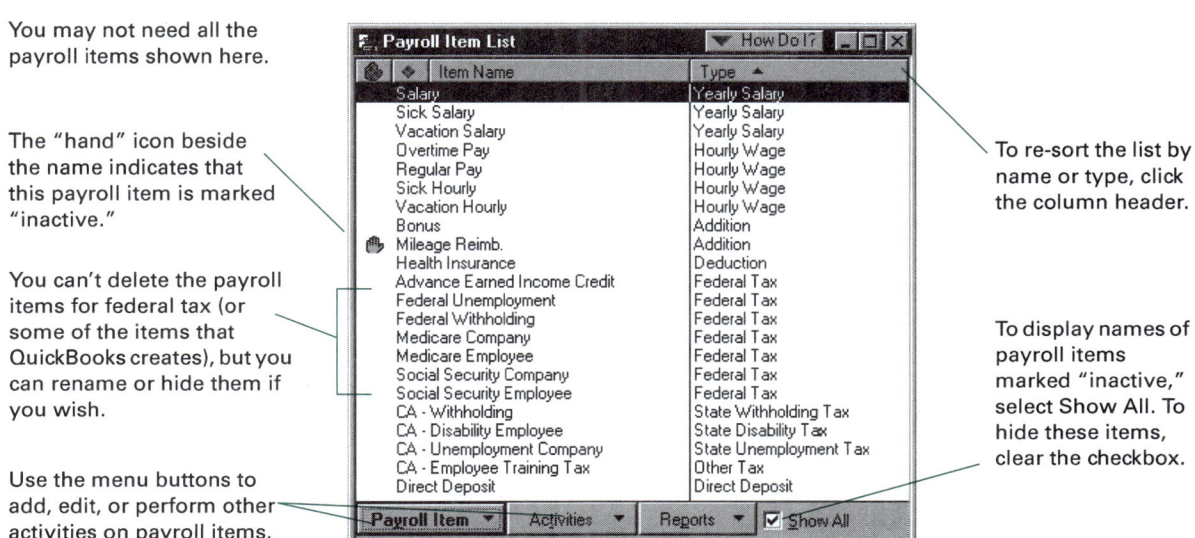

You may not need all the payroll items shown here.

The "hand" icon beside the name indicates that this payroll item is marked "inactive."

You can't delete the payroll items for federal tax (or some of the items that QuickBooks creates), but you can rename or hide them if you wish.

Use the menu buttons to add, edit, or perform other activities on payroll items.

To re-sort the list by name or type, click the column header.

To display names of payroll items marked "inactive," select Show All. To hide these items, clear the checkbox.

You can use the same item for many employees. For earnings, local taxes, and all other non-tax items, you can always customize the amount or percentage in the setup window for each employee.

You can change the information for existing payroll items, although you probably do not want to change the tax tracking or taxability of an item. You may want to change a payroll item for the following reasons, for example:

- Your state unemployment tax rate changes.
- You realize that you're eligible for the federal unemployment (FUTA) credit.
- Your accountant wants you to assign an item to a different account.

To learn about...	Search the Help index for...
Changing payroll item information	payroll items, editing

What the changes affect

Changes you make to payroll items affect the new checks you write, and certain changes can also affect how payroll amounts are classified historically on tax forms, reports, and check details. When existing items are changed, the change appears on payroll tax forms and the check detail.

Employee information and existing checks are affected when you change any of the following information for payroll items:

- Payroll item name
- Account assigned (liability and expense)
- Tax tracking (such as Compensation or Reported Tips)

Changing the following information affects future paychecks only:

- State unemployment or state disability tax rates
- Eligibility for federal unemployment (FUTA) credit
- Taxes affected (for additions to or deductions from gross pay)

Deleting, removing, or merging payroll items

You can delete a payroll item from the Payroll Item list if:

- It is not currently used in the employee default setup.
- It is not currently used in any employee record or payroll transaction.

Instead of deleting the payroll item, you can hide it on your Payroll Item list by making it *inactive*. Mark inactive those payroll items you used in the past but no longer need to use.

When you make a payroll item inactive, QuickBooks keeps the information associated with that payroll item, but hides it on the Payroll Item list and removes it from any drop-down lists that use payroll items. You can make a payroll item active again at any time.

If you find that you are using two payroll items to track the same thing, you can combine the payroll items as long as they are of a similar type. This is true for all payroll items except for federal and state taxes. Merging payroll items is an irreversible operation.

Changing payroll item information while using the QuickBooks Deluxe Payroll service

If you're using Deluxe Payroll, you cannot change the tax tracking classification or taxability of payroll items that are reported on federal and state forms, because the service is filing your tax forms based on these items. If you need to change this information, call the number listed in the phone directory. Choose Phone Directory from the Help menu and click QuickBooks Deluxe Payroll.

You cannot merge a payroll item that is used by the service.

To learn about...	Search the Help index for...
Merging payroll items	lists, merging two entries
Hiding and showing inactive payroll items, or Making payroll items active	lists, hiding and showing entries
Deleting payroll items	payroll items, deleting

Changing employee information

Use the Employee list to store information about your employees, including each employee's name, social security number, address, and phone number. QuickBooks also provides a notepad on which you can make notes about an employee.

To view your employees:

- From the Employees menu, choose Employee List.

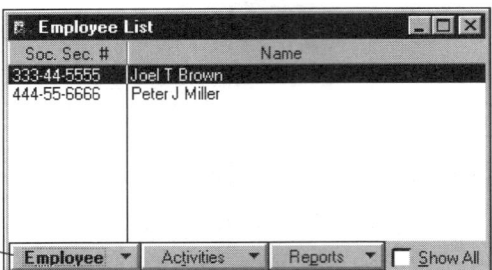

Use the menu buttons to add, edit, or perform other tasks for your employees.

To learn about...	Search the Help index for...
Viewing current information about an existing employee	employees, editing

Hiring and releasing employees

When you hire a new employee, simply add the employee to the Employee list. If you have set up your employee defaults (page 361), this information is copied from the defaults into your new employee record when you add the employee. Then, if you need to, you can change any of the information for this particular employee.

When an employee leaves the company, you need to enter the employee's release date in QuickBooks. When you enter a release date for the employee, QuickBooks displays the Deceased checkbox, which you should select if the employee is deceased. This status is shown on the employee's W-2 form.

Once you enter a release date in the employee's record, QuickBooks doesn't display the employee's name in the Select Employees To Pay window when the pay period end date is later than the release date. If the employee was paid during the current year, however, the employee's name will appear when you create W-2 forms for the year.

You can't delete a released employee if there are transactions associated with that employee. You can, however, hide the employee's name from your Employee list.

To learn about...	Search the Help index for...
Hiring a new employee	employees, adding
Releasing an employee	employees, releasing
Hiding the name of a released employee	employees, hiding and showing

Changing employee payroll information

You can change employee information whenever necessary. Changes in employee information affect all paychecks you write to this employee after you record the change. Changes you make to an employee's name, address, and social security number are reflected in existing paychecks, but do not affect any amounts on the paychecks.

The following types of information must be changed individually for each affected employee. Changing the payroll item doesn't affect existing employees:

- Annual limits for a deduction
- Rate or amount changes for a deduction addition, or company contribution
- Rate changes, if they vary by company, for a miscellaneous state or local tax

Tip: Change the information on the employee defaults first. Answer Yes to the question about changing it for all matching employees.

Changing employee information while using the QuickBooks Deluxe Payroll service

If you're using Deluxe Payroll, you cannot change an employee's tax-exempt status because the service prepares W-2 forms based on this information. If you need to change this information, call the number listed in the phone directory. Choose Phone Directory from the Help menu and click QuickBooks Deluxe Payroll.

To learn about...	Search the Help index for...
Changing information about an existing employee	employees, editing
Adding custom fields for an employee	employees, custom fields for
Giving an employee a raise	employees, raises
Adding notes for an employee	employees, notes about

Hiding, showing, or merging employees

You can hide an employee on the Employee list without deleting the name by making the employee *inactive*.

For example, one of your employees may be taking a six-month leave of absence. You can make the employee inactive instead of deleting him or her, since the employee will be returning to work.

When you make an employee inactive, QuickBooks keeps the information associated with that employee, but hides the employee's name on the Employee list and removes it from any drop-down lists that use employees. However, the employee's payroll figures still appear on payroll reports. You do not need to change or delete any transaction that uses the employee. You can make an employee active again at any time.

If you run a QuickReport and find that you have the same person on your Employee list twice (because of different spellings), you can merge the employee names. You can merge employee names only if there are no payroll transactions for either employee. Merging employee names is irreversible.

If you want to delete an employee: QuickBooks does not allow you to delete an employee if there are any transactions associated with the employee.

To learn about...	Search the Help index for...
Hiding and showing an inactive employee, or making employees active	employees, hiding and showing
Merging employee names	employees, merging two names
Deleting an unused employee	employees, deleting
Running a QuickReport for your employee list	employees, reports about

Contacting your employees by mail

In QuickBooks Pro only, you can use your QuickBooks data in conjunction with prewritten Microsoft Word letters to mail your employees notices about accrued vacation and sick time.

To learn about...	Search the Help index for...
Using your QuickBooks data with Microsoft Word letters	letters using QuickBooks data in Microsoft Word

Setting up employees for direct deposit of paychecks

Before you set up direct deposit, you must first sign up for one of the QuickBooks Payroll Services.

Direct deposit is an optional feature offered through the QuickBooks Payroll Services that enables you to directly deposit employee paychecks into their bank accounts. After you sign up for either Basic Payroll or Deluxe Payroll, the sign-up interview allows you to add bank account and routing information for your employees.

After you've signed up for the payroll service, QuickBooks automatically creates a new payroll item for direct deposit. This payroll item appears in the Payroll Item list (page 371) and in the Employee Summary area of the Preview Paycheck window shown on page 381.

You can modify your employee's bank account information by clicking the Direct Deposit button on the Payroll Info tab. QuickBooks displays the Direct Deposit window.

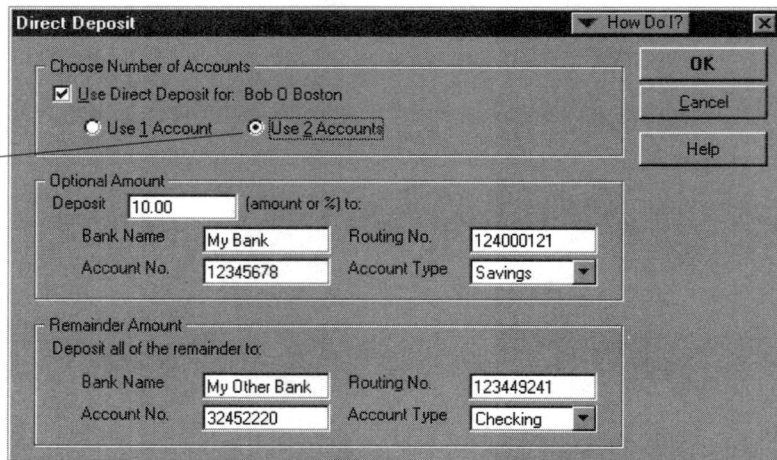

QuickBooks allows up to two bank accounts per employee.

To learn about...	Search the Help index for...
Setting up employees for direct deposit	direct deposit, setting up employees for
Adding the direct deposit feature to Basic Payroll or Deluxe Payroll	direct deposit, in Basic Payroll direct deposit, in Deluxe Payroll
Routing number formats	routing numbers

378 | CHAPTER 18   Payroll

Running payroll and paying taxes

This section contains the following information:

Paying your employees	**379**
Paying payroll taxes and liabilities	**386**
Filing your payroll tax forms	**388**
Adjusting the liability balance for a payroll item	**392**

Paying your employees

Before you begin writing paychecks, make sure that you've done the following:

- Gone online to get the latest payroll update, which includes the most current tax information available.

  Note: QuickBooks cannot compute payroll taxes unless you have a valid subscription to one of the QuickBooks Payroll Services. For information about the QuickBooks Payroll Services, see page 346.

- Set up your payroll items.
- Entered payroll information for your employees.
- Specified your payroll and employee preferences.
- Entered bank information for employees who want direct deposit.

To learn about...	Search the Help index for...
Getting payroll updates	tax tables, updating
Subscribing to the QuickBooks Payroll Service	payroll services, description of services
Setting up payroll items	payroll items, adding
Payroll information for employees	employees, payroll information about
Payroll and employee preferences	preferences, payroll
Setting up employees for direct deposit	direct deposit, setting up employees for

Selecting employees to pay

To select which employees you want to pay:

- From the Employees menu, choose Pay Employees. QuickBooks displays the Select Employees To Pay window.

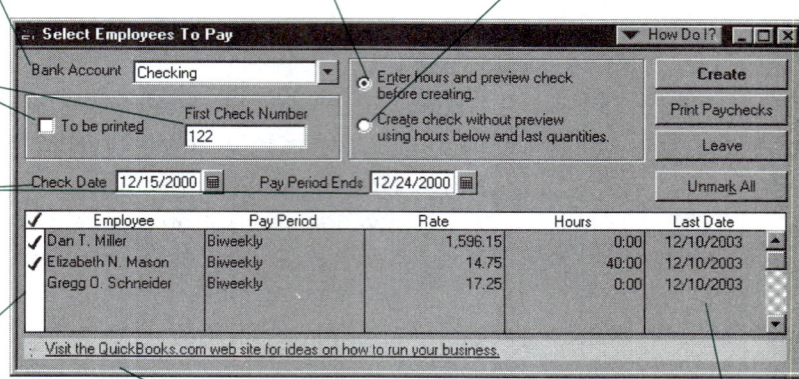

QuickBooks records the checks in this bank account.

If you have to enter hours worked, sick or vacation time, commission bases, or other variations from pay period to pay period, select this option.

If all your employees are salaried and are receiving their standard paycheck for this pay period, you may want to select this option.

If you print checks, select the checkbox. If you write checks by hand, clear the checkbox and enter the check number in the First Check Number field.

Though these fields default to today's date, you can specify a different check and pay period date on the paychecks.

QuickBooks creates a paycheck for each employee marked with a checkmark.

Click here for tips, advice, or information about using the payroll feature in QuickBooks.

When you create a check, this date changes to the latest pay period end date for this employee.

When you've finished selecting the employees to pay, click the Create button to display paycheck information about the first employee.

Tip: **You can pay employees in groups.** For example, first select all of your salaried employees whose paychecks you don't need to review, and pay them. Then select your hourly employees and preview paychecks so that you can enter their hours.

Previewing, adjusting, and creating paychecks

When you select "Enter hours and preview check before creating" in the Select Employees To Pay window, then click Create, QuickBooks displays the Preview Paycheck window.

If the employee receives hourly wages, enter or edit the number of hours worked at each rate. (QuickBooks Pro fills in the hours either from time data or from the last paycheck.)

If the employee receives a salary, you can enter hours to split the salary amount between jobs. However, QuickBooks calculates the total salary amount on the check from the pay period frequency and the annual salary.

If this is a bonus or commission check, you probably don't want sick or vacation hours to accrue for this employee. To prevent sick and vacation hours from accruing for this paycheck, select this checkbox.

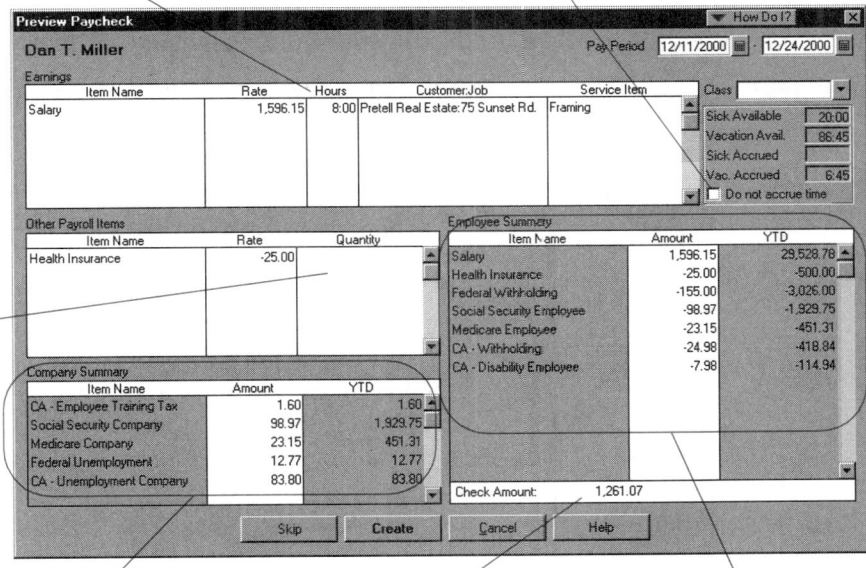

If a commission, addition, deduction, company contribution, or other tax is based on quantity, enter the quantity here.

The Company Summary shows company-paid taxes and contributions that do not affect the amount on the check.

The amount of the check.

The Employee Summary shows wages, commissions, withheld taxes, and other additions and deductions that print on the voucher of the employee's check.

In the Preview Paycheck window, you can do all of the following:

- View the amounts QuickBooks calculated for each payroll item (including gross earnings, taxes, and all other additions, deductions, and company contributions) for the paycheck.
- Enter or edit the number of hours worked.
- Enter sick or vacation hours, as well as prevent sick and vacation hours from accruing for this paycheck only.
- Enter the base quantity on which to calculate commissions and other additions or deductions based on quantity.
- Add or delete wage, commission, addition, deduction, or company contribution payroll items.
- Edit the amount for any payroll item.

  Note: You may not want to edit payroll items for flat-rate taxes. QuickBooks notices if your totals for certain flat-rate taxes are not correct for the year or quarter and fixes them automatically. If you're using Deluxe Payroll, you cannot change tax amounts except for state and federal withholding.

After you've entered all of your employees' paychecks and clicked Create, if you're using Deluxe Payroll or Basic Payroll with direct deposit, QuickBooks displays a message asking if you want to send your paychecks now. When you see this message, click OK to go online and send your paychecks to the payroll service.

When QuickBooks creates a paycheck, it does the following:

- Updates the pay period end date of the last check written for the employee, and removes the checkmark in the Select Employees To Pay window.
- Writes a paycheck for your employee made out for the net amount, showing the deductions in the voucher area.
- Increases or decreases accrued sick or vacation hours by the number of hours entered for the paycheck.

   If you selected the "Do not accrue" checkbox in the Preview Paycheck window, you prevent the sick and vacation hours from accruing on this paycheck only.

- Updates year-to-date balances for the employee.
- Records the check in your checking account register and reduces the account balance.

   If you are using the direct deposit feature of Basic Payroll or Deluxe Payroll, QuickBooks does not reduce the amount in your checking account register until you go online and send the paycheck to the service.

- Records an increase in each affected liability account, showing the extra liability resulting from the payroll transaction (for both employee paycheck deductions and company contributions).

   If you are using the direct deposit feature of Basic Payroll or Deluxe Payroll, QuickBooks increases your Direct Deposit Liabilities account, which returns to a 0.00 balance after you send your payroll.

- Updates and tracks your payroll expenses in expense accounts.
- Updates any other accounts you have assigned to any payroll items used in the payroll transaction.

To learn about...	Search the Help index for...
Previewing and adjusting paychecks	paychecks, checking amounts in

Running payroll and paying taxes | 383

Reviewing and correcting paychecks

After you've recorded a paycheck, you can review it at any time and make changes to it, if necessary.

QuickBooks also allows you to void or delete paychecks, although you should rarely need to do this:

- You may want to void a paycheck if there was a payroll error in a recent paycheck that your employee has not yet cashed.

  If the paycheck was in a previous quarter or year for which you've filed your payroll tax forms, you may have to refile these payroll tax forms when you void the paycheck and issue a new one. Consult your accountant for more information.

- You may want to delete a paycheck if it is a duplicate and you haven't printed it yet.

> **After you send an online check to the payroll service (Deluxe Payroll or Basic Payroll with direct deposit), you can change only:**
>
> - Memo
> - Check number
> - Print status / Cleared status (for reconciling)
> - QuickBooks bank account you wrote the check from
> - Expense and liability accounts affected (if you edit the payroll items)
>
> If you change a paycheck, the edited check information will be sent again to the service.
>
> You can void a paycheck that you've already sent to the service, which reduces your tax liabilities. However, if the paycheck was deposited directly to an employee's account, voiding the paycheck does not prevent the money from being transferred to the employee's account. You will need to get the money from the employee directly. You cannot delete a paycheck once you've sent it to the service.

To learn about...	Search the Help index for...
Editing existing paychecks	paychecks, changing
Voiding paychecks	paychecks, voiding
Deleting paychecks	paychecks, deleting

Printing paychecks and paystubs

You can print all your paychecks at one time, but you must print them separately from other checks. Paychecks use the same printer setup as your other checks in QuickBooks.

If you don't print your paychecks on voucher checks, you can print paystubs to provide your employees with the information that appears on a paycheck voucher. A printed paystub provides all the information required for a legal paystub including:

- Employee's full name, address, and social security number
- Pay period start and end dates
- Salary and hourly rate, hours, and amount of pay for the pay period
- Employee taxes
- Deductions from and additions to wages
- Taxable company contributions—such as the taxable portion of company-paid group term life insurance
- Federal and state allowances and exemptions
- (Optional) Sick and vacation time used and available
- Net pay
- Year-to-date amounts for the preceding items

Employees who are set up for direct deposit can receive an advice of deposit, which looks similar to a paycheck, but is non-negotiable.

To learn about...	Search the Help index for...
Printing paychecks	paychecks, printing
Printing paystubs	paystubs
Creating and printing direct deposit checks	paychecks, direct deposit

Paying payroll taxes and liabilities

You must have an EIN to pay your payroll taxes. For information about EINs and how to obtain one for your company, see page 354.

The QuickBooks Deluxe Payroll service makes your tax deposits directly from your payroll accounts.

If you are using Deluxe Payroll, the payroll service makes federal and state tax deposits for you from your payroll accounts. However, if you have liabilities to other vendors and agencies, such as insurance payments or local taxes, you will need to use the Pay Liabilities window to pay them.

When it's time to pay taxes or other payroll liabilities, QuickBooks shows you your current liabilities, lets you choose all or just some of them to pay, and creates checks to pay them. You can also add penalties, expenses, and discounts to these checks.

Always use the Pay Liabilities window to write checks for your liabilities and taxes.

Do **not** use the Write Checks window. If you do, QuickBooks does not update your outstanding balance, and your payroll reports will not be accurate.

To display the Pay Liabilities window:

1 From the Employees menu, choose Pay Payroll Liabilities.

   The Select Date Range For Liabilities window appears.

2 Enter the date range for the liabilities that you want to pay, then click OK.

You can modify this date range in the Pay Liabilities window.

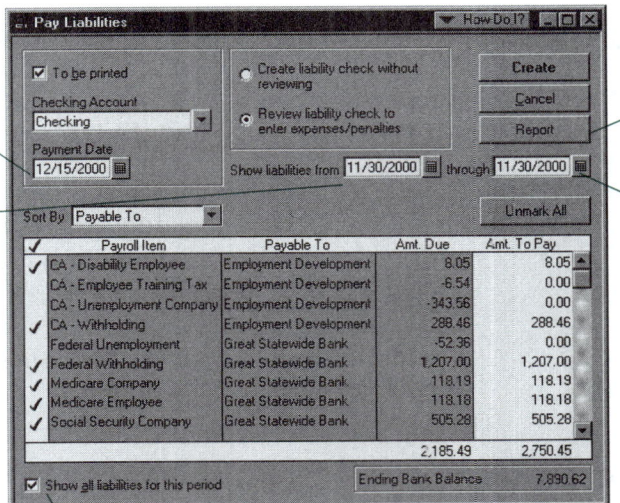

This is the date the transaction affects the checking account.

The window shows liabilities owed as of the end of last month that are not yet paid. Change these dates if you pay more than once a month.

QuickBooks writes a single check to each different payee for whom you mark payroll items to pay.

To add a name that is missing in the Payable To column of this window, edit the payroll item.

Click here to generate a Payroll Liabilities report for the specified period.

QuickBooks displays this date on the liability check as the paid-through date.

NOTE: If you are using Deluxe Payroll, federal and state taxes do not appear in this window.

Select this checkbox to show all payroll liabilities for the period, including any credits and zero amounts.

To learn about...	Search the Help index for...
Paying payroll liabilities and taxes	payroll liabilities, paying
Adding a name missing in the Payable To column (agency name)	payroll items, editing
Creating a report that shows your payroll liabilities	■ payroll, reports about ■ payroll liabilities, questions about
How payroll liabilities are calculated	payroll liabilities, calculating method in QuickBooks
Entering a discount for payroll liabilities	payroll liabilities, discounts
Entering a penalty for payroll liabilities	payroll liabilities, penalties
Entering a refund check for overpayment of payroll liabilities	payroll liabilities, refund check

Filing your payroll tax forms

QuickBooks helps you prepare federal payroll tax Forms W-2, W-3, 940, and 941.

Regulations for your type of business and geographic location may require you to complete and file other federal forms as well as state and local payroll tax forms. Always be sure to review the payroll regulations for your particular business to ensure you are in compliance.

Refer to the following sections for information about the different tax forms and what's required for QuickBooks to process many of these forms.

> **The QuickBooks Deluxe Payroll service files payroll tax forms for you.**
>
> If you are using Deluxe Payroll, the payroll service will prepare and file federal and state payroll forms required for your company.

Federal forms

This section describes various federal tax forms you'll need to file for your company and to prepare for your employees.

Form 941
(Employer's Quarterly Federal Tax Return)

Form 941 is a quarterly tax form on which you report federal income tax withheld, social security tax, Medicare tax, and advance earned income credit paid to employees. These amounts are usually based on total wages you pay out. However, the amounts may not exactly equal the amounts you've paid or withheld because of rounding errors.

If your amounts need to be adjusted, create a company liability adjustment instead of editing the amount on the Form 941. See "Adjusting the liability balance for a payroll item" on page 392.

Preparing Form 941 in QuickBooks. A wizard within QuickBooks helps you prepare your Form 941. The wizard parallels sections of an actual Form 941. You can print the form on blank paper.

To learn about...	Search the Help index for...
Preparing and printing Form 941	941s
How numbers are calculated on Form 941	941s
Creating a liability adjustment	payroll liabilities, adjusting

Form 940 (Employer's Annual Federal Unemployment (FUTA) Tax Return)

Form 940 is an annual tax form on which you report federal unemployment tax. This tax is generally based on total wages you pay out. Most employers are eligible for a FUTA credit. Check with your accountant or the IRS to see if you are eligible.

Note: QuickBooks does not create Form 940-EZ. The IRS will accept a Form 940 instead.

Preparing Form 940 in QuickBooks. A wizard within QuickBooks helps you prepare your Form 940. The wizard parallels sections of an actual Form 940. You can print the form on blank paper.

To learn about...	Search the Help index for...
Preparing, editing, and printing Form 940	940s
Receiving credit toward FUTA	FUTA credit

Forms W-2 and W-3

Form W-2 (Wage and Tax Statement) is the end-of-year form you send to each employee and submit to the Social Security Administration. Each form is for one employee and shows wages and taxes withheld for the year for that employee. Form W-3 (Transmittal of Wage and Tax Statements) is a summary of the W-2 forms you are submitting to the federal government.

Preparing Forms W-2 and W-3 in QuickBooks. QuickBooks prints Form W-2 and Form W-3 on preprinted forms you need to purchase. (QuickBooks cannot print the actual forms because the government requires a special ink on Forms W-2 and W-3.) You must review each W-2 form onscreen within QuickBooks before printing it.

For information on purchasing these forms from Intuit, visit the Web site at **www.intuitmarketplace.com**.

To learn about...	Search the Help index for...
Preparing and printing W-2 forms	W-2s
Preparing and filing W-3 forms	W-3s

State forms

Your state may require you to file payroll tax forms. Though you cannot prepare state forms within QuickBooks, you can generate reports that help you gather the information you need to prepare the forms.

Following are some of the QuickBooks' reports and features you can use to prepare your state payroll tax forms:

- **Payroll summary report.** You can use the payroll summary report to determine the wage base for a tax. To display the wage bases in the payroll summary report, double-click an amount on the report. A transaction by payroll item report appears and displays the wage base amount.

   To generate this report, choose Employees & Payroll from the Reports menu, then choose Payroll Summary.

- **Employee state taxes detail report.** This report lists wage information and state taxes withheld for each employee. To generate this report, choose Employees & Payroll from the Reports menu, then choose Employee State Taxes Detail.

- **Summarize your payroll data in a Microsoft Excel Workbook.** When you install QuickBooks, you copy an Excel workbook into your program folder. The workbook contains worksheets designed to capture payroll data required by most states when you file your state tax forms.

   To use this feature, you must have QuickBooks Pro and Microsoft Excel 97 (or later) installed on your computer. To access the Excel Workbook, choose Summarize Payroll Data in Excel from the Employees menu.

For more information about these reports, see the section starting on page 395.

To learn about...	Search the Help index for...
Filing state tax forms	state, taxes
QuickBooks reports that help you prepare your state tax forms	report types, payroll
Sending payroll data to the Microsoft Excel Workbook	Microsoft Excel, sending payroll data to

Adjusting the liability balance for a payroll item

If you are using the QuickBooks Deluxe Payroll service, you cannot adjust the liability balance for liabilities paid by the service (federal and state tax liabilities).

However, you can adjust the liability balance for local or other taxes not supported by the service and for benefit payments to a third party.

After you prepare a payroll tax form, you may discover that your balance for a liability payroll item (the amount you owe according to QuickBooks) needs to be adjusted. For example, you may have a small discrepancy due to rounding, or you may have failed to take the credit that reduces what you owe for federal unemployment (FUTA).

You can enter an adjustment at any time in the Liability Adjustment window.

Enter the date here that you want your payroll liability account to be affected.

A positive amount increases what you owe for the item. A negative amount reduces what you owe for the item.

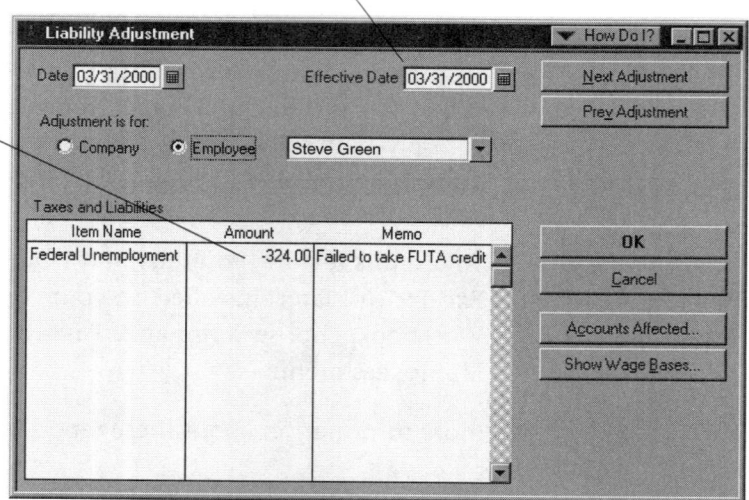

To learn about...	Search the Help index for...
Adjusting payroll liabilities	payroll liabilities, adjusting

392 | CHAPTER 18 Payroll

Getting information about your payroll

This section describes how reports and spreadsheet templates can answer questions about your company's payroll.

How much do I owe for payroll tax liabilities?	**393**
How much money do I spend on my payroll?	**394**
How can I tell if I'm withholding the correct tax amounts?	**395**
How can I get information for state payroll tax forms?	**395**
Other reports about employees and payroll	**396**

How much do I owe for payroll tax liabilities?

Joan wants to see how much she currently owes for each payroll tax for the current quarter. She knows if she has less than a $1,000 tax liability during the quarter, she can wait and make a payment when she files her Form 941.

She can find out quickly by creating a payroll liabilities report. The report shows liabilities incurred during the date range specified that are still unpaid.

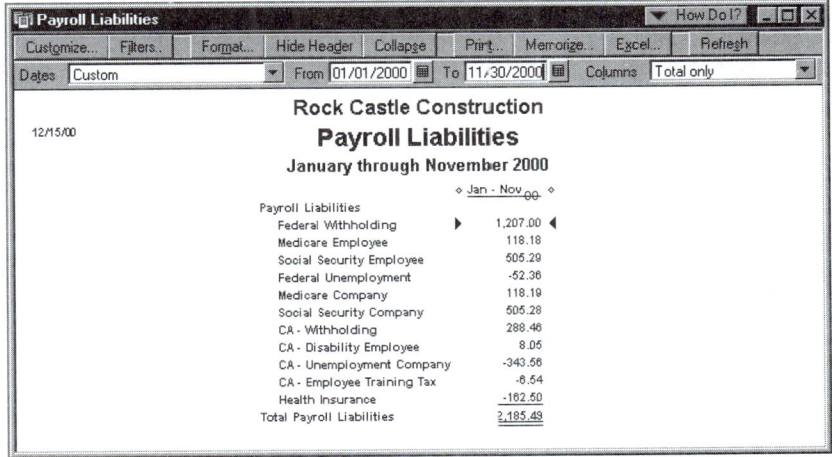

How much money do I spend on my payroll?

Bill likes to know how much money he should keep in his checking account when payday comes around twice a month. He runs a payroll summary report to see his payroll totals by employee and for the whole company for one payroll period.

You can change the date range to cover this year to date, last quarter, or any period you want.

The gross pay includes commissions and additions to gross.

The adjusted gross pay equals gross pay minus deductions from gross.

The net pay is the actual amount of money the employee(s) received. This amount is usually less than gross pay due to taxes withheld.

For taxes and company contributions, the amounts are liabilities accrued during the period, regardless of whether you paid them.

Rock Castle Construction
Payroll Summary
December 1 - 15, 2000

12/15/00

	Hours	Rate	Dec 1 - 15, '00
Employee Wages, Taxes and Adjustments			
Gross Pay			
Salary	80		1,596.15
Overtime Pay			0.00
Regular Pay	108		1,763.00
Sick Hourly	8		138.00
Vacation Hourly			0.00
Total Gross Pay			3,497.15
Adjusted Gross Pay			3,497.15
Taxes Withheld			
Federal Withholding			-401.00
Medicare Employee			-50.70
Social Security Employee			-216.82
CA - Withholding			-71.49
CA - Disability Employee			-9.50
Total Taxes Withheld			-749.51
Deductions from Net Pay			
Health Insurance			-12.50
Total Deductions from Net Pay			-12.50
Net Pay			2,735.14
Employer Taxes and Contributions			
Federal Unemployment			0.00
Medicare Company			50.70
Social Security Company			216.82
CA - Unemployment Company			0.00
CA - Employee Training Tax			0.00
Total Employer Taxes and Contributions			267.52

How can I tell if I'm withholding the correct tax amounts?

Tim wants to make sure that he's withholding the correct amount of tax from his employees' paychecks. He can generate the payroll item detail report to see each employee's wage base and withholding amount for a particular tax.

Rock Castle Construction
Payroll Item Detail
December 2000
12/15/00

Type	Date	Num	Name	Payroll Item	Wage Base	Amount
Federal Withholding						
Paycheck	12/11/2000	165	Dan T. Miller	Federal W...	1,596.15	-155.00
Paycheck	12/11/2000	166	Elizabeth N. Mason	Federal W...	590.00	-58.00
Paycheck	12/11/2000	167	Gregg O. Schne...	Federal W...	1,311.00	-188.00
Total Federal Withholding					3,497.15	-401.00
Medicare Employee						
Paycheck	12/11/2000	165	Dan T. Miller	Medicare E...	1,596.15	-23.14
Paycheck	12/11/2000	166	Elizabeth N. Mason	Medicare E...	590.00	-8.55
Paycheck	12/11/2000	167	Gregg O. Schne...	Medicare E...	1,311.00	-19.01
Total Medicare Employee					3,497.15	-50.70
Social Security Employee						
Paycheck	12/11/2000	165	Dan T. Miller	Social Sec...	1,596.15	-98.96
Paycheck	12/11/2000	166	Elizabeth N. Mason	Social Sec...	590.00	-36.58
Paycheck	12/11/2000	167	Gregg O. Schne...	Social Sec...	1,311.00	-81.28
Total Social Security Employee					3,497.15	-216.82

How can I get information for state payroll tax forms?

Robin wants to get a head start on preparing state payroll forms and needs detailed information about wages and state tax withholding for each employee. She can generate the employee state taxes detail report to see all state-related payroll items for each employee.

Rock Castle Construction
Employee State Taxes Detail
November 2000
12/15/00

Type	Date	Num	SSN/Tax ID	Payroll Item	Income Subject To Tax
Dan T. Miller					
Paycheck	11/13/2000	128	333-44-5555	CA - Withholding	1,596.15
Paycheck	11/13/2000	128	333-44-5555	CA - Disability Employee	1,596.15
Paycheck	11/13/2000	128	333-44-5555	CA - Unemployment Com...	1,596.15
Paycheck	11/27/2000	142	333-44-5555	CA - Withholding	1,596.15
Paycheck	11/27/2000	142	333-44-5555	CA - Disability Employee	1,596.15
Paycheck	11/27/2000	142	333-44-5555	CA - Unemployment Com...	1,596.15
Total Dan T. Miller					9,576.90
Elizabeth N. Mason					
Paycheck	11/13/2000	130	569-87-1234	CA - Withholding	619.56
Paycheck	11/13/2000	130	569-87-1234	CA - Disability Employee	619.56
Paycheck	11/13/2000	130	569-87-1234	CA - Unemployment Com...	619.56
Paycheck	11/27/2000	144	569-87-1234	CA - Withholding	590.00
Paycheck	11/27/2000	144	569-87-1234	CA - Disability Employee	590.00
Paycheck	11/27/2000	144	569-87-1234	CA - Unemployment Com...	590.00
Total Elizabeth N. Mason					3,628.68

Robin could also get a summary of her payroll data and display it in a Microsoft Excel Workbook that uses a specially prepared template installed with the QuickBooks (Pro only) software. Because the Workbook extracts payroll data requested by most states, she could also print and send the information with her state payroll tax forms.

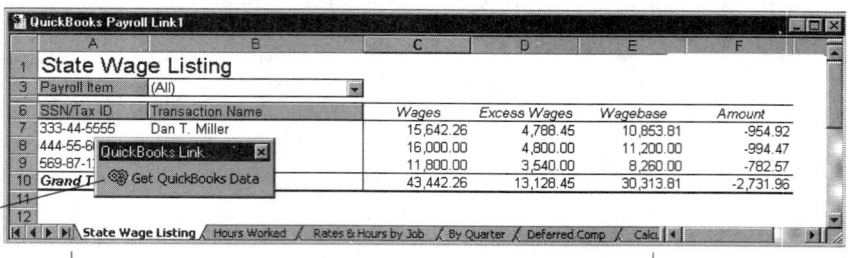

When you first open the Workbook, Excel uses sample data to set up the worksheets.

To import your payroll data from QuickBooks, click Get QuickBooks Data, then specify date filters and other options in the dialog box that appears.

This worksheet shows state wage information for each employee. To display additional information, click any of these tabs.

Microsoft Excel 97 (or later) is required.

Though you access this information from within QuickBooks, you must have Microsoft Excel 97 or later installed on your computer to display the Workbook.

Other reports about employees and payroll

QuickBooks' onscreen Help gives descriptions of all the reports about employees and payroll, as well as instructions on how to create them.

To learn about...	Search the Help index for...
Reports listing employees' names, phone numbers, social security numbers, addresses, federal and state filing status, and federal and state allowances	employees, reports about
Reports showing payroll transactions (paychecks and liability payments)	payroll, reports about
Filing state quarterly tax forms	state, taxes
Excel payroll templates	Microsoft Excel, sending payroll data to,

CHAPTER 19

Tracking your progress with reports and graphs

Setting up for reporting and graphing   398

Generating reports and graphs   399

How can I use reports in my business?

The purpose of any report or financial statement is to communicate information about your business—for you and others to get valuable insight into your company finances and performance and make informed decisions about a course of action.

QuickBooks provides a wide variety of preset reports and graphs designed to give you quick and easy access to your company's information. For example, besides a standard profit and loss statement, you also have five other variations of this report. In addition, you can create your own versions of reports, changing both the look and layout, as well as the scope of the information reported.

Setting up for reporting and graphing

What to set up	Comments	Search the Help Index for...
Select cash or accrual-based summary reporting	The IRS requires that certain business entities use the accrual method for tax reporting purposes. Please check with the IRS or your tax accountant to assess which method is appropriate for you. Regardless of the method you use for tax reporting, you can view most reports on a cash or accrual basis at any time by customizing the report when you create it. **Important:** The cash/accrual preference does not affect the 1099 reports (which are always cash based) or the sales tax reports.	■ accrual basis, changing reports to ■ sales tax, turning on
Set your aging preference	Aging is the tracking of due dates and amounts of outstanding invoices or your own unpaid bills. Because you can change the starting point for aging reports, you can age from the due date or from the transaction date.	aging
Choose your report and graph refresh option: ■ Refresh automatically ■ Prompt you to refresh ■ Don't refresh [automatically]	When a change to your data affects what you are viewing, QuickBooks automatically adjusts the report or graph if it can do so quickly. If QuickBooks can't make a quick adjustment, the only way to bring the report back into agreement with your data is to refresh the report or graph. Refreshing can be slow. If up-to-the-minute accuracy is unimportant to you, you may want to refresh reports and graphs at your own discretion instead of having QuickBooks refresh them automatically. All reports and graphs have a Refresh button that you can click at any time. This option can be uniquely set for each user.	refreshing reports and graphs

Generating reports and graphs

QuickBooks reports organize and summarize all the data you've entered.

The following report topics are available in this section:

Keeping your reported data accurate	**399**
Making preset reports work for you	**399**
Creating a report from scratch	**405**
Saving report settings	**405**
QuickReports: reports at your fingertips	**406**
Portraying your data with graphs	**407**
Investigating transactions or values on reports and graphs	**408**
Printing reports and graphs	**410**
Exporting the report to a Microsoft Excel spreadsheet	**410**

Keeping your reported data accurate

Your reported data can become inaccurate if new information is entered by you or another user. To make sure you have up-to-date, accurate data, click Refresh. For more information, see "Choose your report and graph refresh option:" on page 398.

Tip: If you need to run reports on a large company file while in multi-user mode, try to run them when other users are not using the company file. The reports will display faster and will not become inaccurate due to new data others may enter.

Making preset reports work for you

You can generate a preset report from several convenient places in QuickBooks, including the Report Finder (accessible from the Reports menu) and list displays, such as your Customer:Jobs list.

Finding the right report

With the Report Finder, you can quickly review and choose among the many preset reports that QuickBooks provides. To help you choose an appropriate report, the Report Finder displays a sample of each report, as well as a summary of what the report conveys about your business.

Choose a report category and view a general description of your choice.

The specific reports available to you are based on your report category selection.

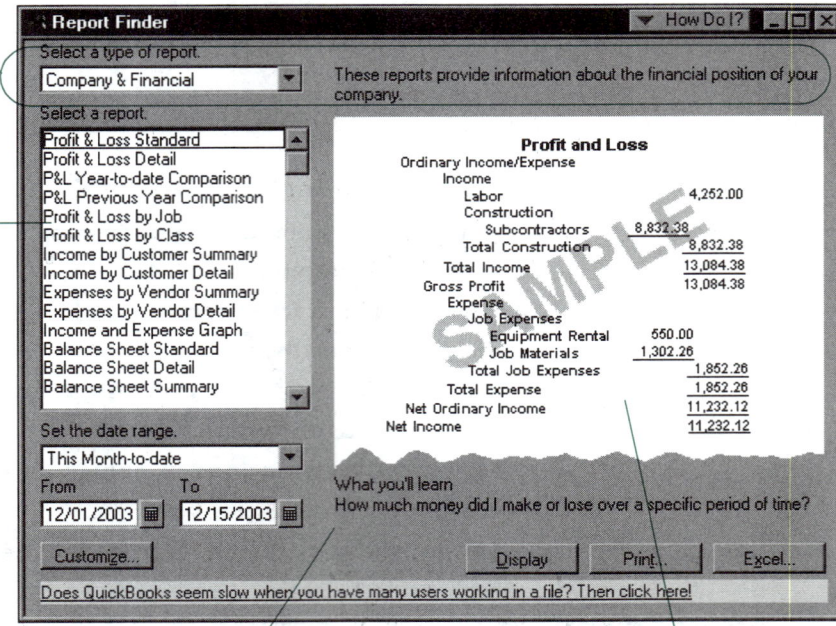

QuickBooks provides details about a report's content to help you decide whether the report is appropriate for your particular scenario.

View a thumbnail picture with sample data to get an idea of a report's content. You can customize a report before or after you generate it.

To learn about...	Search the Help index for...
Finding a report	reports, finding
Creating a report	reports, creating
Preset reports	report types, all

Customizing the look of the report

Most reports can be customized for unique presentation of your data. For example, you can do the following:

- Change the typeface (font)
- Adjust the width of a column
- Add or remove columns
- Change how numbers display

- Create or change subtotal groupings
- Change the sort order of transactions
- Change what displays in the report header and footer

The following examples show how one user decided to customize a report.

Nora at Rock Castle Construction clicked Customize to change the columns her report included.

Nora decided that the **Date** and **Num** columns were not crucial to her. All she wanted to see was the transaction type, due date, aging information, and the open balance for the vendor.

In the Customize Report window, she cleared the **Date** and **Num** columns

See the results on the following page.

After Nora removed the **Date** and **Num** columns, she also resized the **Type** column to make the report more readable.

In addition she used the Header/Footer option to remove the company name at the top of the report.

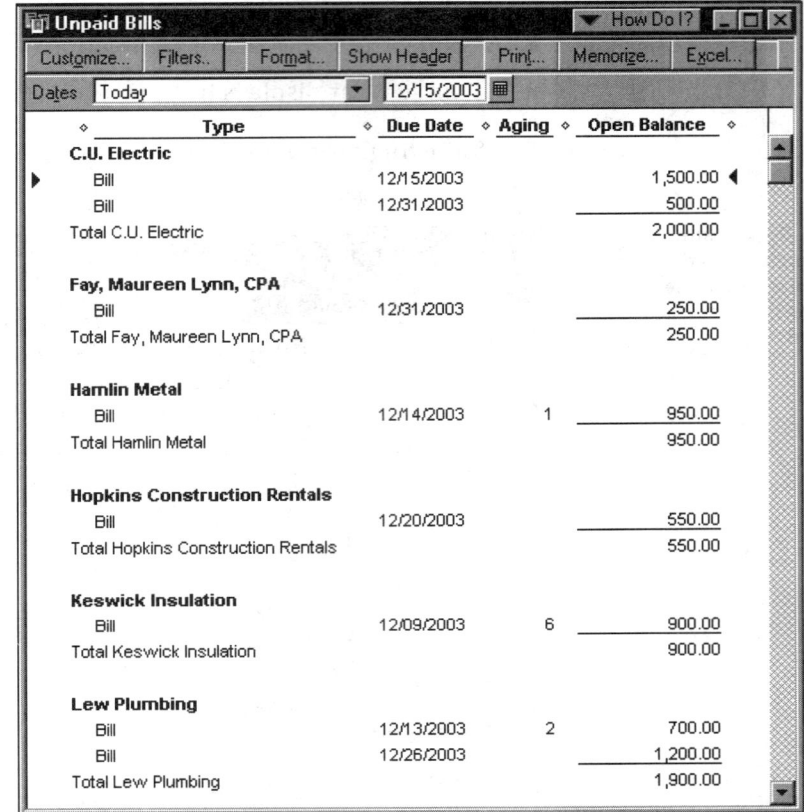

After you customize a report to your satisfaction, you can save your changes. See "Saving report settings" on page 405.

Tip: To change column titles or rearrange the order of columns, export the report to a Microsoft Excel spreadsheet. For further information, see page 410.

Changing the scope of the information in the report

Creating your own version of an existing report can also include *filtering* or changing the scope of the information that displays on a preset report.

For example, Nora at Rock Castle Construction wanted to see a Collections Report limited to commercial customers. She clicked the

Filters button in the buttonbar. From the Report Filters window, she selected Customer Type, then Commercial.

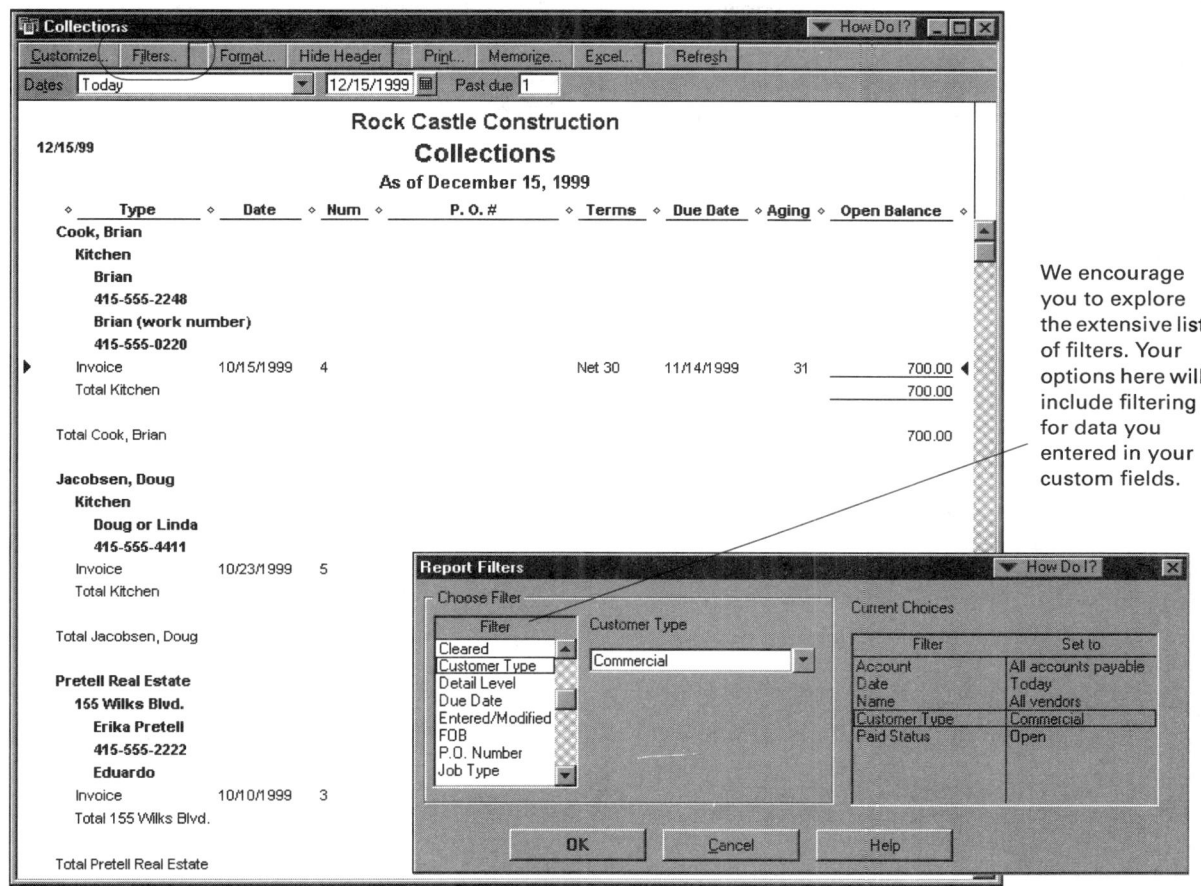

We encourage you to explore the extensive list of filters. Your options here will include filtering for data you entered in your custom fields.

Nora also changed the report's title (by accessing the Format window) to reflect the change in the report's scope.

Nora can choose to "memorize" this report to save her settings. See "Saving report settings" on page 405.

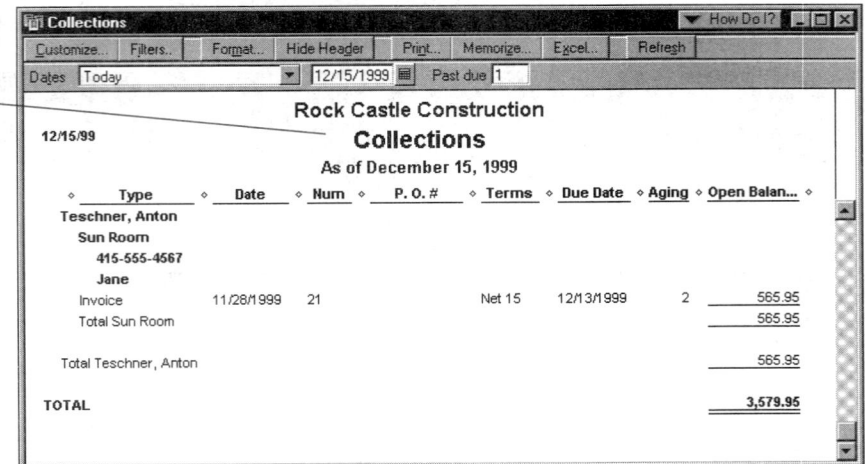

To learn about...	Search the Help index for...
Generating a report	reports, creating
Changing date ranges	reports, dates in
Customizing a report	report customization
Adjusting, adding, or deleting columns on a report	report customization, columns
Changing fonts	reports, fonts for
Tailoring the data in the report (filtering)	reports, changing the scope of
Changing headers and footers	report customization, headers

Creating a report from scratch

If QuickBooks doesn't provide a preset report with the information you need, you can create your own custom reports.

From the Reports menu, choose either Custom Summary Report or Custom Transaction Detail Report, depending on the level of detail you want as your starting point.

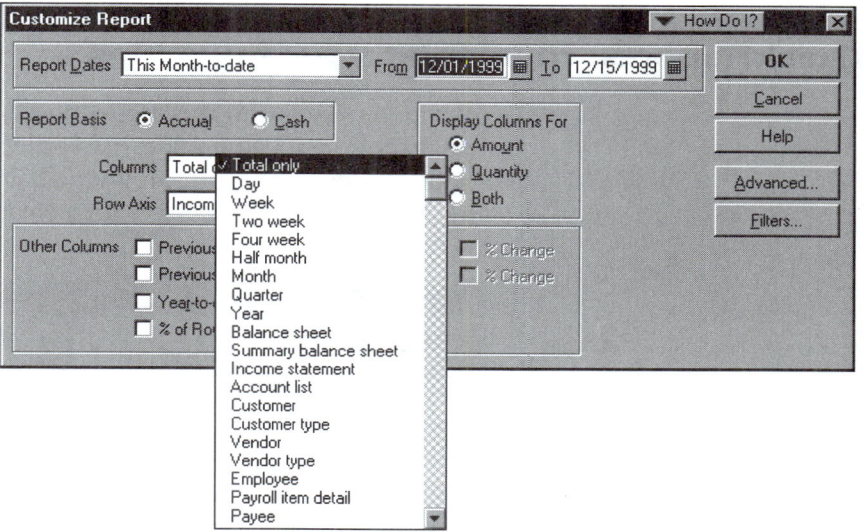

You can choose from a variety of reporting options (date ranges, accrual vs. cash) and information to report on by column and row. Choose the detail you want and click OK. You can create as many custom reports as you need.

Saving report settings

After you have customized or filtered a report, you may want to save the settings for future use. Saving report settings is called *memorizing*.

Memorizing the report saves all your customizing and filtering changes. It also saves the print orientation (portrait or landscape) of the report. The next time you generate a memorized report, QuickBooks recreates the format of the report, but uses your latest financial data.

When you memorize a report, QuickBooks adds it to the Memorized Report List. To display this list, from the Reports menu, choose Memorized Reports.

To learn about...	Search the Help index for...
Saving the settings of a customized report	reports, memorizing

QuickReports: reports at your fingertips

QuickReports display all the transactions you have recorded in QuickBooks for a specific list entry. For example, you can generate a QuickReport for an account on your Chart of Accounts list, like your savings account, or generate one for a customer, a vendor, for an item, and so on.

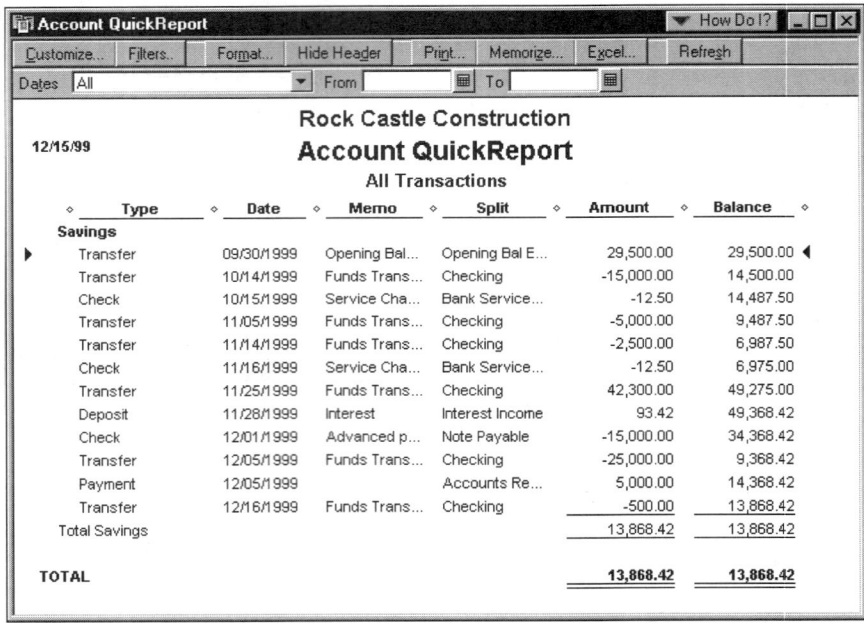

You can create a QuickReport from the Reports menu button on a list.

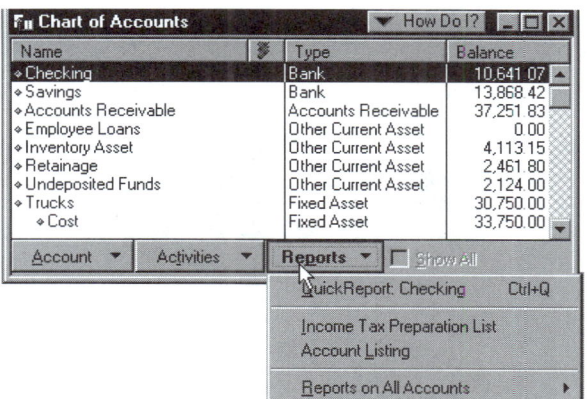

Portraying your data with graphs

QuickBooks can also display your company's data in bar graphs and pie charts. Graphs are helpful if you're looking for a visual summary of your company's finances.

QuickBooks provides six types of preset graphs: income and expenses, sales, accounts receivable, accounts payable, net worth, and budget vs. actual. Using these graphs you can:

- Analyze your income and expenses
- Study sales income
- Examine customer and vendor aging
- Determine changes in your net worth
- Develop better budgets

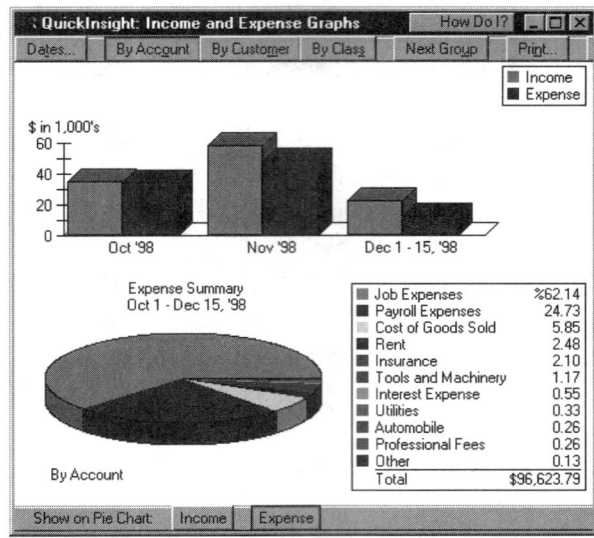

Most graphs you create cover the current fiscal year to date, unless you change the date range.

To learn about...	Search the Help index for...
Creating graphs	graphs, creating
Customizing graph appearance	graphs, customizing
Interpreting data on a graph	graphs, how to interpret

Investigating transactions or values on reports and graphs

From time to time, you may want to investigate a particular transaction or value on a report. You can do this easily by using QuickZoom, which is available on most reports. QuickZoom displays the original transaction or a report showing the transactions that contributed to that value. You can change values that are in error.

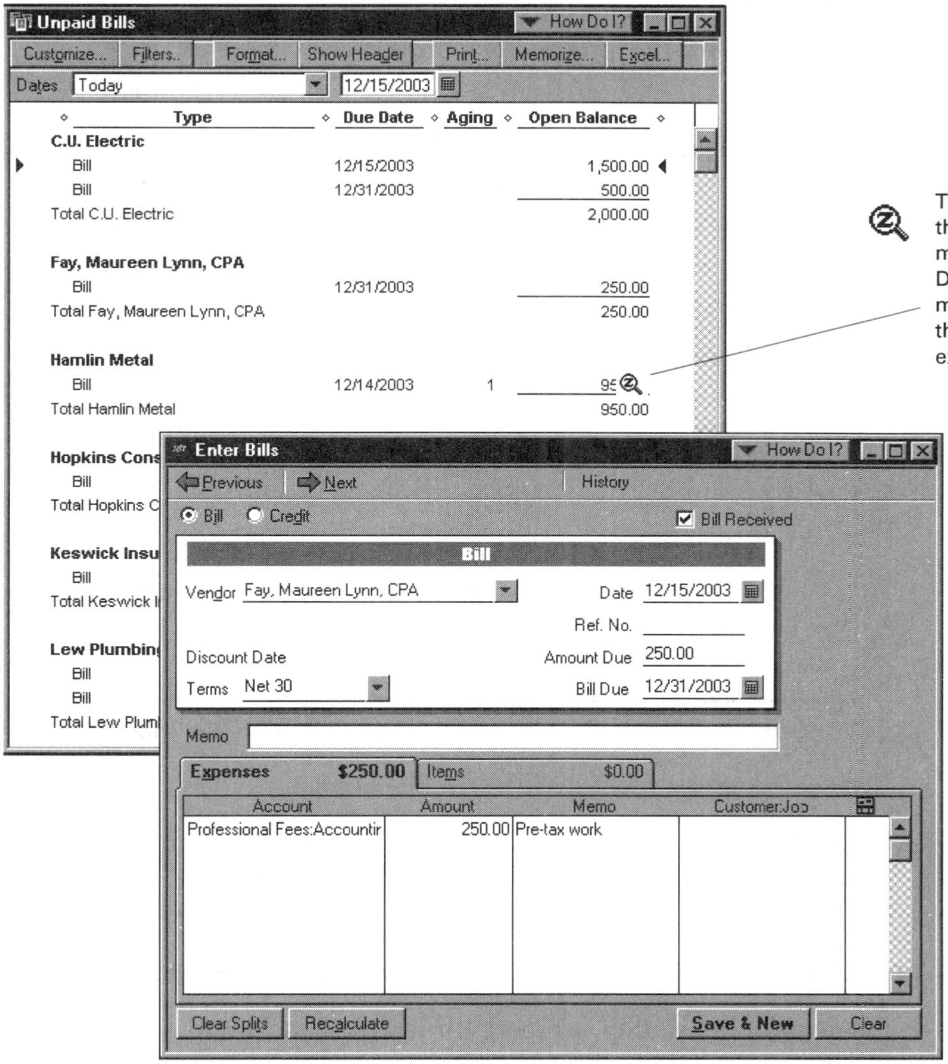

 The pointer changes to the QuickZoom magnifying glass. Double-click the magnifying glass on the value you want to examine.

To learn about...	Search the Help index for...
Using QuickZoom on summary reports	QuickZoom (Seeing the detail behind a summary amount)
Using QuickZoom on graphs	QuickZoom (Expanding detail in a graph)

Printing reports and graphs

When you print reports and graphs, you can choose to:

- Print in portrait (vertical) or landscape (horizontal) orientation
- Print in color (particularly useful for graphs)
- Control widows and orphans (prevent headings from printing near the bottom of a page or single lines at the top of a page) (reports only)
- Fit the report to __ page(s) wide (reports only)
- Have a page break after each major grouping (reports only)
- Print a range of pages (reports only)
- Enter the number of copies
- Change fonts and type size
- Change margins

You can also choose to preview the report before you print it. After you preview the report, you may want to make adjustments for greater readability and visual appeal.

To learn about...	Search the Help index for...
Printer setup	printer setup
Printing reports	printing, reports
Printing graphs	printing, graphs

Exporting the report to a Microsoft Excel spreadsheet

For greater flexibility in report formatting, data manipulation, and customization, you can export QuickBooks Pro report data to a Microsoft Excel spreadsheet.

For example, in Excel you can do the following:

- Take advantage of extensive filtering options
- Hide detail for some but not all groups of data
- Combine information from two different reports
- Experiment with "what if" scenarios
- Add comments

- Change the titles of columns
- Change the order of columns
- Save the report as a file you can e-mail to anyone with Excel
- Save a snapshot of the report data for future reference

The export feature allows you to preserve many QuickBooks report formatting features, such as fonts, colors, and formulas. At the same time, it allows you to take advantage of all the features of Excel.

Note: You must be using QuickBooks Pro and Microsoft Excel 97 or higher.

To learn about...	Search the Help index for...
Exporting a report to a Microsoft Excel spreadsheet (QuickBooks Pro only)	Microsoft Excel, exporting reports to

CHAPTER 20

Keeping on target with budgets

How can QuickBooks help me budget?	414
Reporting tools	415
Planning and setting up your budgets	417
Checking your progress against your budgets	418

Why should I budget?

Budgeting helps you plan for the future by setting goals for income and helping you monitor expenses.

How can QuickBooks help me budget?

QuickBooks creates budgets to track and report the specific information that you need to be successful.

Situation	What to do in QuickBooks	Reports
I want to create a comprehensive budget.	Create budgets for each income and expense account (projected amounts). Additionally, you can create budgets for your balance sheet accounts (projected ending balance).	■ Profit & Loss Budget Overview ■ Profit & Loss Budget vs. Actual ■ Balance Sheet Budget Overview ■ Balance Sheet Budget vs. Actual
I want to budget by project.	Create budgets for individual customers/jobs. For example, a construction company could set up budgets by: **Customer:job only** Barry Janzen:Addition **Or, by customer:job and accounts** Laurel Seymour:Cottage Income accounts ■ Labor ■ Materials ■ Subcontractors Expense accounts ■ Equipment Rental ■ Job Materials ■ Subcontractors	■ Profit & Loss Budget by Job Overview ■ Profit & Loss Budget vs. Actual by Job
I want to create a budget for each partner (or location, and so forth).	You can set up each partner as a class (see page 47) and then set a budget by class only or by class and accounts.	■ Profit & Loss Budget by Job Overview ■ Profit & Loss Budget vs. Actual by Job **Note:** These reports must be customized to include the class column.

Reporting tools

The strength of budgeting relies partly on your reporting tools. QuickBooks provides six preset budget reports and a budget graph. The reports are customizable.

Review these reports now to help you decide what type of information you want to receive when you budget.

Reports

Report	Description
For income and expense account budgets	
Profit & Loss Budget Overview	Shows budgeted amounts by month for each income and expense account for which you have set up a budget.
Profit & Loss Budget vs. Actual	Compares actual income and expenses with budgeted amounts by month. Shows difference in dollars and actual amount as a percentage of budgeted amount.
For customer and job budgets	
Profit & Loss Budget by Job Overview	Shows budgeted amounts by job for each income and expense account for which you have set up a budget for a job.
	If you haven't budgeted by account, but for a total for the customer:job, you will need to customize this report. (Click Customize in the report buttonbar. In the Columns field, choose a time period or Total only. From the Row Axis field, choose Customer:Job.)
Profit & Loss Budget vs. Actual by Job	Compares actual income and expenses for each job with budgeted amounts. Shows difference in dollars and actual amount as a percentage of budgeted amount.
For balance sheet account budgets	
Balance Sheet Budget Overview	Shows budgeted account balances by month for each balance sheet account for which you have set up a budget.

Report	Description
Balance Sheet Budget vs. Actual	Compares actual balances of balance sheet accounts with budgeted balances. Shows difference in dollars and actual balance as a percentage of budgeted balance.
For class budgets	
Profit & Loss Budget by Job Overview or Profit & Loss Budget vs. Actual by Job	You must customize these reports to add the class column. (From the Columns drop-down list on the report buttonbar, choose Class.)

Budget vs. actual graphs

The upper bar graph for budget vs. actual shows your company's actual net income less budgeted net income for each month. A monthly amount is favorable when the actual net income exceeds the budgeted net income.

The lower bar graph shows the six income or expense accounts that are the furthest from budget (either over or under).

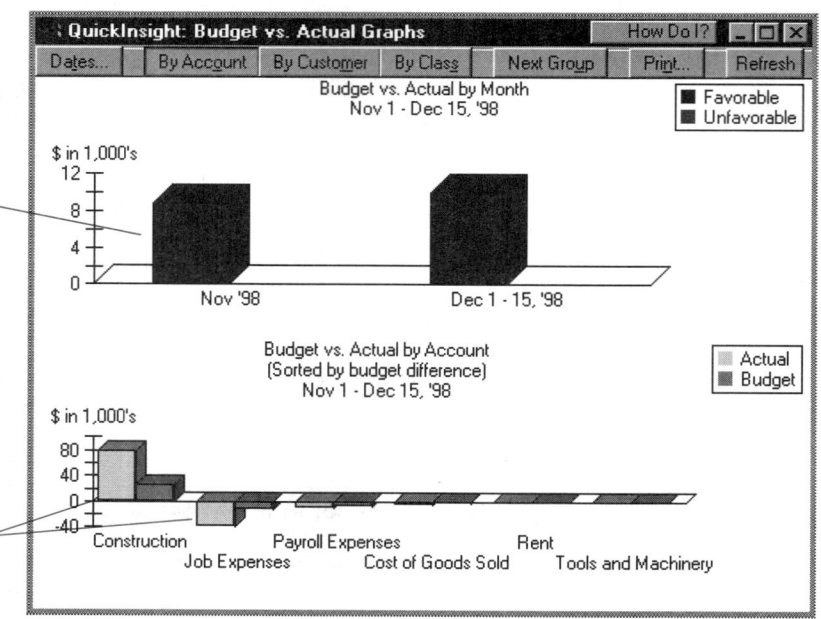

Use the buttonbar to display the data by customer or by class instead of by account.

When actual net income exceeds budgeted net income, the bar is above the x-axis. When actual is less than budgeted, the bar is below the x-axis.

Double-click a bar to see a bar graph of budget variance by account for that month.

Asset and income accounts have bars above the x-axis. Liability, equity, and expense accounts have bars below the x-axis.

Double-click a bar to see a bar graph of budget vs. actual by month for that account.

Planning and setting up your budgets

Task	Comments
Choose the budget reporting period.	Ideally, you'll want to set up account budgets at the beginning of your fiscal year, month by month. Even if an expense only occurs once during a yellow page ad), you'll still want to set a budget for it. Due to the cyclical nature of some businesses (catering or lawn service), you may find it more accurate to budget for only six or three months at a time.
Get all budget tools together.	- Printed copy of last year's end-of-the-year profit and loss statement - Printed copy of your QuickBooks Chart of accounts, Customer:job, and Class lists - Calculator
Review your prior year's profit and loss statements.	- Are you intending to increase sales or grow a certain area of your income? - Do you have areas of expense that seem out of proportion for the size of your business? - Do you have one-time purchases that you intend on making this year? (For example, a new computer system or company vehicle?)
For this fiscal year, determine the monthly budget numbers for each income and expense account (and/or customer:job, and/or class) and write it down on your accounts list.	- Some expenses are fixed for the year, such as office rent. - Variable expenses will include phone charges, office supplies, etc. - Don't forget to include your tax liability in your budget. Some expenses occur only once a year, such as the cost of a phone book ad or a permit.
Review the numbers and adjust as needed.	A good rule of thumb for beginners: underestimate your revenue; overestimate your expenses.

Task	Comments
Set up the budgets in QuickBooks.	For each account, customer or job, and class combination, you can create one budget per fiscal year. You can create as many separate budgets as you want within the same fiscal year as long as each budget applies to something different. In the Help Index see: **budgets, creating**.

Checking your progress against your budgets

At least once a month, you'll want to create budget reports to assess if you're on target. If you have grossly over- or underestimated a budgeted amount, you'll want to change it to be more accurate.

Tip: A good rule of thumb for beginners: underestimate your revenue; overestimate your expenses.

To learn about...	Search the Help index for...
Creating budget reports	budgets, reports about
Customizing budget reports	report customization
Creating a budget graph	budgets, graphs of
Printing a budget	budgets, printing
Changing a budget	budgets, editing
Deleting budgets	budgets, deleting

CHAPTER 21

Periodic tasks

Weekly tasks	420
Monthly tasks	421
Quarterly tasks	422
Year-end tasks	422
As-needed tasks	425

What should I be doing weekly, monthly, quarterly, and annually?

Certain tasks fall neatly into weekly, monthly, quarterly, and yearly time frames. You'll spend far less time on periodic tasks because QuickBooks pulls information together for you.

Weekly tasks

Your weekly tasks could include backup procedures, paying bills, and creating paychecks.

Task	Comments	Search the Help index for...
Making a backup copy of your QuickBooks company	Highly recommended!	backups
Creating your weekly paychecks	None	paychecks, entering
Paying bills due the following week	Use the Reminder feature to stay on top of bills.	■ bills from vendors, reminding yourself to pay ■ bills from vendors, paying
Printing any unprinted invoices, cash sales receipts, credit memos, statements, and mail	None	printing, sales forms
Creating a cash flow forecast report	Use this report to review your anticipated cash flow for the next few weeks.	cash flow forecast report

Tip: You can use the To Do notes and Reminders to keep tasks on track.

From the Company menu, choose To Do List.

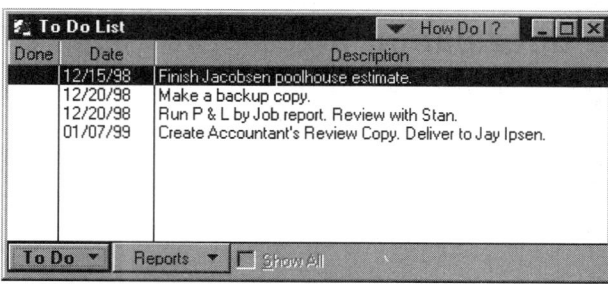

Monthly tasks

Monthly tasks include producing backup copies of your QuickBooks companies, paying taxes, and reconciling your credit card and checking accounts.

Task	Comments	Search the Help index for...
Making a backup copy of your QuickBooks company	Highly recommended! Keep this copy offsite, perhaps in a safe deposit box. This procedure safeguards you from losing valuable data in case of fire, flood, theft, or other disasters at your office.	backups
Paying your payroll taxes (this task may be weekly for you)	Check with the IRS and your state tax board to determine your schedule for payroll tax remittance.	payroll taxes, paying
Paying your sales tax	Check with your state and local tax boards regarding your sales tax liability and payment schedule.	sales tax, paying
Reconciling your checking and credit card accounts when you receive your statements	Don't let these pile up!	■ reconciling, bank statements ■ reconciling, credit card statements
Printing and mailing monthly reminder or billing statements to send to your customers	For a discussion on reminder vs. billing statements, see "If your customers owe you money or pay in advance" on page 172.	printing, statements
Printing a collections report	Use the report as a tool to contact customers with past due balances.	collections report
Creating a budget report to check how close you are to your budget	If you are grossly over or under budget, consider revising that particular budget.	budgets, reports about

Quarterly tasks

Quarterly tasks include paying taxes and reviewing profit and loss statements.

Task	Comments	Search the Help index for...
Paying sales tax due	Check with your state and local tax boards regarding your sales tax liability and payment schedule.	sales tax, paying
Filing Form 941 (Employer's Quarterly Federal Tax Return) and state withholding forms	None	■ 941s ■ payroll taxes, state forms
Creating a profit and loss statement and a balance sheet	None	■ profit & loss reports ■ balance sheet, reports

Year-end tasks

Year-end tasks include making any year-end entries, archiving last year's data, and gathering information for your tax forms. The great news for year end is that QuickBooks **does not require you to close your books!**

Not closing your books has two major advantages:

- You always have easy access to all your old data, including all transaction details.
- You can create comparison reports to compare this year with last year.

You can protect the prior year's transactions from accidental change by using a password.

What QuickBooks does at year end

QuickBooks reports reset your income and expense accounts at year end, so that you start the fiscal year reporting a zero net income. In your old bookkeeping system, you may have had to make such adjustments yourself.

Suppose, for example, that your net profit for the year was $50,000. A year-end balance sheet would show a line for net income of $50,000 in the equity section of the balance sheet.

At the beginning of the new fiscal year, QuickBooks increases your Retained Earnings equity account by the previous year's net income ($50,000 in this example) and makes your net income zero.

Making year-end accounting entries

Remember that every business has its own accounting requirements and bookkeeping practices.

1 Reconcile your checking accounts against your bank statements through the final month of the accounting year (such as December 2000).

2 Talk to your accountant about your year-end procedures.

- Consider using the Accountant's Review™ feature. This feature creates a special copy of your QuickBooks company file. While your accountant makes changes in this copy, you can continue working in your regular company file. After your accountant has made all the necessary changes, you then merge them into your master company file. See "Working with an accountant or advisor" on page 447 for more information.

- If your accountant is not familiar with QuickBooks, you'll need to find the reports your accountant would like to see, and ask for a list of "adjusting entries" for the year just ended.

3 Make the adjusting entries in your company file if your accountant hasn't already. (See "Making adjustments" on page 449.)

Safeguarding last year's data

Task	Comments	Search the Help index for...
Freezing the past year's transactions with a password after all adjustments have been made	You'll be able to view the earlier transactions as you normally do, but QuickBooks will ask for the password if you try to change them.	closing, an accounting period

Task	Comments	Search the Help index for...
Creating two backups labeled for the year	Keep one on your premises and one offsite.	backups
Archiving important paperwork	Clearly label all boxes and files and store in a secure location. See "Organizing your paper documents" on page 20 for details on the type of documents you'll want to archive.	None

Yearly tax forms

Here's how to use QuickBooks to gather information for yearly tax forms:

- For Form 1099-MISC, see "Handling 1099-MISC forms" on page 307.

- For Forms W-2 and W-3, see "Forms W-2 and W-3" on page 390. For Form 940, see "Form 940 (Employer's Annual Federal Unemployment (FUTA) Tax Return)" on page 389.

- For your business income taxes, run the income tax summary report and the profit and loss statement to assist you in filling out your forms. See "Reporting income tax information" on page 302.

As-needed tasks

Synchronizing QuickBooks Pro with your contact manager

How often you synchronize QuickBooks Pro and your Symantec ACT! or Microsoft Outlook contact management software depends on how frequently you add or update contact information. More specifically, the frequency depends on how often you change customer and vendor information and whether you want the data synchronized with QuickBooks and your contact manager. See "Sharing QuickBooks Pro information with your contact manager" on page 438.

The time required to complete the synchronization depends on the amount of information that needs to be updated in QuickBooks, your contact manager, or both.

Changing company information

You can change your company information at any time. From the Company menu, choose Company Information.

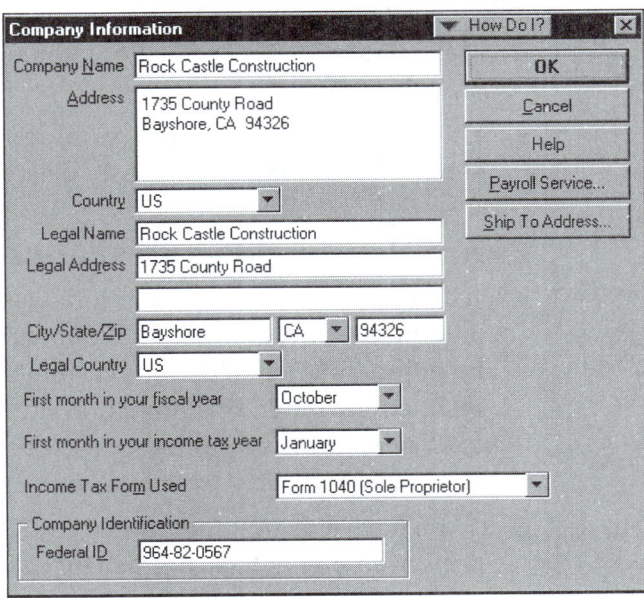

If you change the tax form you use, all associations between accounts and tax lines are reset to <Unassigned.> You will need to reset them appropriately.

	To learn about... Changing information about your company	**Search the Help index for...** company, changing information about

Condensing data

If your company file has grown too large, you can reduce its size by having QuickBooks condense the transactions for a period of time that you designate. When you condense data, you specify an ending date for the period of time you want to condense.

This has no effect on transactions dated *after* the ending date. For example, if your ending date is 12/31/99, all transactions dated 1/1/00 and later remain intact in your company file.

Of the transactions dated *on or before* the ending date, QuickBooks deletes and summarizes only those that have no effect on transactions dated after the ending date and where the transactions meet certain criteria (printed and reconciled.)

When you condense your company file, QuickBooks does two things:

- QuickBooks deletes transactions you no longer need to keep your records current.
- QuickBooks adds new transactions that provide monthly summaries of the transactions it deleted.

Examples of deleted transactions

- If an invoice has been paid in full, QuickBooks deletes the details and includes the amount in a summary transaction showing income accounts. Neither the customer name nor the items sold is retained. However, if an invoice is unprinted, unpaid, partially paid, or marked as pending, QuickBooks leaves the invoice in your file so you can apply payments to the invoice.
- If you have the audit trail turned on, QuickBooks removes transactions even if they have been changed, if they're dated before the ending date.
- If you have paid a bill for a reimbursable expense, QuickBooks deletes the bill regardless of whether you have invoiced the customer for the expense.

- If you have QuickBooks Pro, condensing deletes only those estimates that are dated on or before the ending date and that have a job status of Closed. If an estimate has any other job status (Pending, Awarded, In Progress, Not Awarded, or None), QuickBooks retains the estimate regardless of its date.

- If you have QuickBooks Pro, condensing deletes time data if it is marked as "billed" or "not billable" or if its job status is Closed. If you base your payroll on time data, you must also have paid your employees for the time. For example, if you billed your customer for the time but you have not yet paid your employee, QuickBooks does not delete the time data.

Note: QuickBooks does not condense any transactions that include inventory items.

Retained transactions

The following table gives examples of the situations that cause QuickBooks to retain transactions dated on or before your specified ending date.

Situation for which QuickBooks retains a transaction with earlier date	Example of retained transaction
The transaction has an open balance.	Unpaid, partially paid, or pending invoices, undeposited customer payments, unpaid bills, unused credit memos.
The transaction is linked to another transaction that has an open balance.	An undeposited customer payment that you applied to an invoice. Even though the invoice is paid, QuickBooks retains the invoice because it has a link to an open transaction (the undeposited payment).
The checking or credit card transaction is not marked as cleared.	Unreconciled transaction in a checking or credit card account.
The transaction is marked as "To be printed."	Any invoice, credit memo, sales receipt, or check that has a check mark in its "To be printed" checkbox.

Situation for which QuickBooks retains a transaction with earlier date	Example of retained transaction
The transaction is linked to a transaction in the current year.	

Summary transactions

The summary transactions that QuickBooks creates appear in the registers of your balance sheet accounts (Bank, Accounts Receivable, Accounts Payable, and so on). Each balance sheet account has one GENJRNL summary transaction for each month in which QuickBooks deleted transactions. The transaction amount is the total of the transactions that QuickBooks deleted for the month.

For a given month, the register may also show other transactions that QuickBooks did not delete. These are transactions that could be affected by transactions you have yet to enter.

When you open a register, you can spot the summary transactions by looking for GENJRNL in the Type field. To view a breakdown of amounts by account, select a GENJRNL transaction and click Edit. The General Journal Entry window shows the breakdown of amounts by account for ALL summarized transactions for this month.

Note: You cannot edit a GENJRNL summary transaction.

How condensing data affects your reports

Account balances

After you condense your data, you can still create reports that summarize financial activity for the period of time you condensed. For example, if you condense last fiscal year's data, you can still create profit and loss reports that compare last year's results to this year's. This is because QuickBooks adds summary transactions to your company file to preserve monthly account balances.

Transaction detail

After you condense your data, you won't be able to create reports that show daily detail for the period of time you condensed. This is because QuickBooks has deleted the individual transactions that would have provided the detail. In addition, you won't be able to create reports that show balances for individual customers or vendors over that period of time. As a result, the totals for sales revenue on sales tax liability reports will be incorrect. As a precaution, QuickBooks creates a backup file in case you need access to the deleted transactions later.

Cash basis reports

After you condense your data, you won't get an accurate cash basis report for data that includes a condensed time period. This is because QuickBooks has deleted the individual transactions that would have provided the information about whether transactions were paid. As a result, the totals will be incorrect.

How to condense a data file when you use one of the QuickBooks Payroll Services

If you process payroll using one of the QuickBooks Payroll Services, be aware of the following:

- You can condense data only for the previous calendar year and earlier. For example, to condense data from a previous year, such as 1999, choose December 31, 1999. You cannot condense data in the current year.

- **Deluxe Payroll service users only.** You must also start payroll for the current year before condensing data from previous years. To start payroll for the current year, write at least one paycheck and send payroll data to the service during the current year.

To learn about...	Search the Help index for...
Condensing your QuickBooks company file	condensing data
Restrictions for condensing data if you're using one of the QuickBooks Payroll Services	condensing data

As-needed tasks

CHAPTER 22

Updating QuickBooks

Updating your copy of QuickBooks — 432

> # How can I keep my software up to date?

To keep your copy of QuickBooks current, Intuit provides updates—including maintenance releases and new features—that you download from the Internet.

In this chapter, you'll learn how to keep your copy of QuickBooks up to date throughout the year.

Updating your copy of QuickBooks

This section contains the following information:

Getting updates from the Internet	**432**
Choosing an updating method	**433**
Installing a maintenance release and other updates	**435**
Sharing updates among multiple users	**436**

From time to time, Intuit provides updates to QuickBooks that are available for downloading from the Internet. These updates might be:

- A maintenance release, which Intuit creates when a problem is discovered and fixed after QuickBooks is delivered to customers.

    Note: **Maintenance releases are also available on CD-ROM.** To order a CD-ROM version, call the phone number for Intuit Direct Sales. Choose Phone Directory from the Help menu and click Intuit Direct Sales and Customer Service.

- A new feature.
- A new service.
- Timely information that is relevant to your business.

Getting updates from the Internet

Within QuickBooks, the Update QuickBooks window provides a convenient way to download updates from the Intuit server to your computer. To download an update, you must:

- Have a modem (baud rate of at least 28.8 recommended), or other means of connecting to the Internet.

- Be registered with at least one Internet Service Provider (ISP). You have an ISP if you subscribe to an online service.

With maintenance releases and a few other updates, you'll need to exit from QuickBooks to install the new information. See *Installing a maintenance release and other updates,* beginning on page 435. To display the Update QuickBooks window, choose Update QuickBooks from the File menu.

Choosing an updating method

From the Update QuickBooks window, there are two ways to update your copy of QuickBooks—automatically and immediately.

Updating QuickBooks automatically

With the automatic method, you identify the updates that you want to receive and QuickBooks downloads the necessary files to your computer transparently. QuickBooks downloads your updates in the background, with little impact on your computer's performance.

Automatic updating lets you interrupt your Internet connection or even close QuickBooks at any time without worrying about whether your updates have been downloaded. If you disconnect from the Internet while QuickBooks is in the process of downloading files, QuickBooks keeps track of the information that you want to receive. Once you reestablish an Internet connection, QuickBooks resumes the download at the point when it was stopped. Additionally, this worry-free updating method continues to work as long as you have an Internet connection. QuickBooks doesn't have to be running for you to receive updates.

You can easily navigate to any of the three pages related to the Update QuickBooks window by clicking here.

Click to specify which updates you want QuickBooks to download automatically.

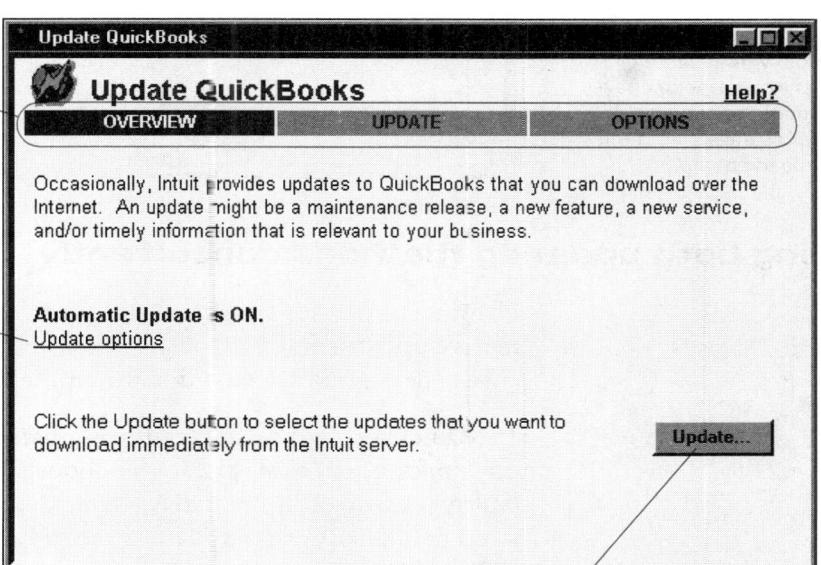

Click to select the updates you want and download them now. Also, click here to check the status of updates downloaded automatically and immediately.

Updating your copy of QuickBooks | 433

Updating QuickBooks immediately

The Update QuickBooks window also provides you with the flexibility to control when downloading takes place. You can choose to download updates immediately. QuickBooks begins the downloading process once you click Get Updates in the Update QuickBooks window. This contrasts with the automatic method, where QuickBooks downloads your updates during times when your Internet connection isn't being heavily used. The Update QuickBooks window provides information on the status of your download.

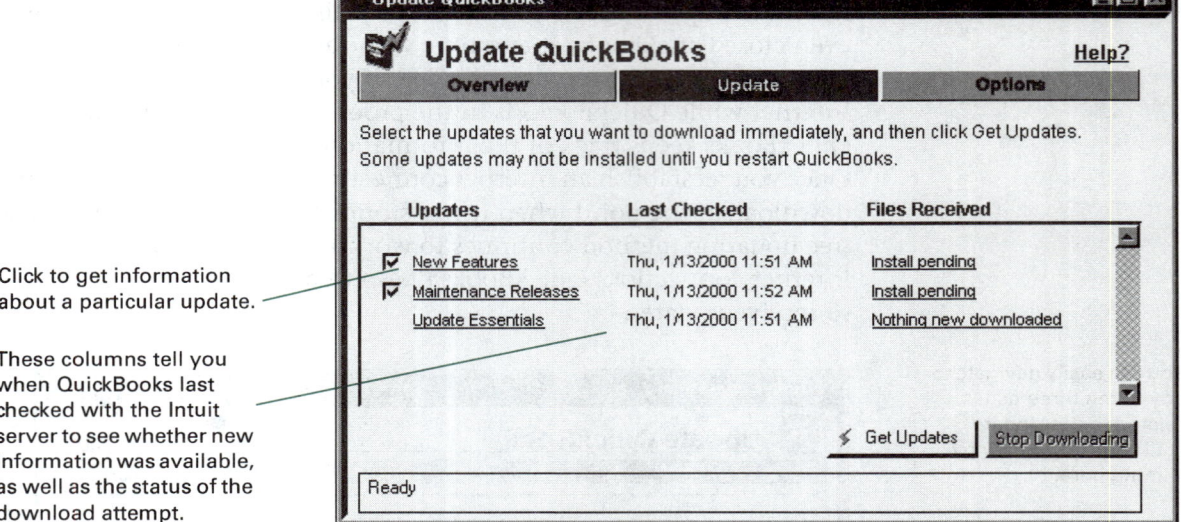

Click to get information about a particular update.

These columns tell you when QuickBooks last checked with the Intuit server to see whether new information was available, as well as the status of the download attempt.

Using both updating methods concurrently

Intuit recommends that you keep your copy of QuickBooks set to receive updates automatically. Keep in mind, though, that you can always download selected updates immediately, whenever you want.

The QuickBooks updating feature is efficient and downloads only new information. For example, if you choose to download an update (automatically or immediately), QuickBooks first checks to see if the latest data files for that update are already loaded onto your computer. If they are already present, QuickBooks doesn't download multiple copies.

To learn about...	Search the Help index for...
Updating QuickBooks	updating, QuickBooks
Choosing an updating method	updating, QuickBooks
Updating QuickBooks automatically	automatic update
Updating QuickBooks immediately	immediate update

Installing a maintenance release and other updates

In most cases, QuickBooks automatically installs updates once they're downloaded from the Intuit server to your computer. However, a maintenance release (also known as a patch) and a few rare updates require you to exit from QuickBooks before the new information goes into effect.

With these kinds of updates, QuickBooks displays a message box once you choose to exit the program. In the message box, click Yes to exit QuickBooks and install the update. If you click No, QuickBooks will close without installing the update.

If you are installing a maintenance release from a CD-ROM, simply insert the CD-ROM and follow the instructions provided.

To learn about...	Search the Help index for...
Installing an update in QuickBooks	installing, updates

Sharing updates among multiple users

QuickBooks lets you share updates in a multiple-user environment. This can be useful in situations where you want all users to share downloaded updates or where one or more users does not have Internet access.

QuickBooks helps facilitate the sharing of updates by automatically setting up a shared location in which updates are downloaded. Each user needs to open the shared data file (usually the company file), display the Update QuickBooks window, and turn on the Share Download option.

If any user in a multi-user environment downloads and installs a maintenance release (or patch), QuickBooks detects the latest version and prompts each of the users—as they exit the program—to install the new version. For example, Tom might download and install a maintenance release while Jane is currently paying bills. When Jane exits from QuickBooks, she sees a message telling her to install the latest version.

To learn about...	Search the Help index for...
Sharing updates in a multi-user environment	updating, QuickBooks

CHAPTER 23

Staying in touch with important contacts

Sharing QuickBooks Pro information with your contact manager	438
Creating reports about contacts	441
Writing letters	441
Printing labels and Rolodex cards	442
Making To Do notes	444

Can QuickBooks help me keep in touch with key contacts?

QuickBooks has many features that help you keep in contact with the people who are important to your business.

With these features, you can do the following:

- Share information between QuickBooks Pro and Symantec ACT! or Microsoft Outlook contact management software.
- Create reports about contacts on your Customer:Job, Vendor, Employee, and Other Name lists.
- Write and send letters (created in Microsoft Word) using data from your "names" lists (customers, vendors, employees, and other name).
- Make To Do notes that remind you of upcoming events or of tasks that you want to complete by a certain date.

Sharing QuickBooks Pro information with your contact manager

You can configure QuickBooks Pro so that your Customer:Job, Vendor, and Other Name lists share information with Microsoft Outlook 97 (or higher) and Symantec ACT! (versions 3.0.8 and 4.0.2) contact management software. You no longer need to enter names, addresses, and phone numbers twice in an effort to keep information in QuickBooks and your contact manager up to date. QuickBooks provides a way for you to transfer information between the two applications so that both are synchronized with each other.

Note: To find out the version number of your copy of Symantec ACT!, choose About ACT! from the Help menu in the Symantec ACT! application. If you have version 4.0, you can get a free update by visiting the Symantec Web site at **www.symantec.com** and going to the Service and Support area.

When synchronizing information with QuickBooks and Symantec ACT! or Microsoft Outlook, you have three options for transferring information:

- QuickBooks to contact manager
- Contact manager to QuickBooks
- QuickBooks to contact manager *and* contact manager to QuickBooks

Note: QuickBooks cannot accommodate the direct transfer of contact information from a personal digital assistant (such as a Palm Computing® or Microsoft® Windows CE device). To get contact information from your personal digital assistant (PDA) into QuickBooks, first export the PDA data into Symantec ACT! or Microsoft Outlook. At that point, you can synchronize QuickBooks with your contact manager.

Setting up and synchronizing QuickBooks with Symantec ACT! or Microsoft Outlook

Setting up for synchronization

Before you begin synchronizing, you must define the parameters for synchronization. During setup, you do the following:

- Choose which contact manager you want to synchronize with QuickBooks.
- Decide which direction you want to transfer information: From QuickBooks to contact manager? From contact manager to QuickBooks? Both ways?
- Select the QuickBooks lists that you want to synchronize with your contact manager. Because of the complex way in which QuickBooks handles employee information, your employee list is not available for synchronizing.
- Select the default method by which QuickBooks will resolve conflicts and discrepancies with your contact manager data.

Following the initial setup, you do not need to go through the setup process again unless you want to change your synchronization settings. To begin setup, choose Synchronize Contacts from the Company menu. Follow the instructions provided by the synchronization setup wizard.

Synchronizing QuickBooks and your contact manager

After completing the setup process, you can synchronize the information between QuickBooks and your contact manager at any time. During synchronization, QuickBooks identifies records where the information in QuickBooks and the contact manager do not match. At that point, you will have several options for resolving conflicts and discrepancies.

Depending on the number of contacts and the type of information you track for each one, the initial synchronization may take a fair amount of time. In most cases, the process will go faster when you synchronize in the future—unless you change the data in QuickBooks or the contact manager *and* change the synchronization settings each time you synchronize. The frequency with which you synchronize depends on how often you make changes to your contact information in either QuickBooks or your contact manager.

Note: **Only a subset of your contact manager information can be synchronized.** Contact managers store much more information about a contact than QuickBooks needs. However, you can synchronize the most vital contact information (including name, address, phone, and fax).

To learn about...	Search the Help index for...
Synchronizing QuickBooks with a contact manager	contact management, synchronizing names with a contact manager
Changing synchronization settings	contact management, synchronizing names with a contact manager
Transferring data from a personal digital assistant, such as a Palm Computing® or Microsoft® Windows CE device	personal digital assistants, synchronizing with QuickBooks
Fixing synchronization problems	contact management, synchronizing names with a contact manager

Creating reports about contacts

You can create reports that list the contact information you need to reach your key customers and vendors.

If you created custom fields such as pager numbers and hours of operation for your customers and vendors, you can customize the report to include this information as well.

List Report	Description
Customer contact list	Shows each customer's name, balance, phone and fax number, contact name, and billing address.
Vendor contact list	Shows each vendor's name, balance, phone and fax number, contact name, address, and account number.
Employee contact list	Shows each employee's name, phone number, social security number, and address
Other name contact list	Shows the name, address, phone and fax numbers, and contact for each name

To learn about...	Search the Help index for...
Creating custom fields for customers and vendors	custom fields, for customers, vendors, or employees
Creating list reports	report types, lists
Adding additional columns of data to list reports	report customization, columns

Writing letters

From time to time you may need to send a letter to a customer, vendor, or employee, or to a group of customers or vendors. With QuickBooks you can easily add the pertinent QuickBooks data (name, address, balance information, and so on) to a standard letter without having to retype it.

QuickBooks provides a number of business letters focusing on collections, news, and announcements. You can edit these letters as needed to suit your business and style of communication.

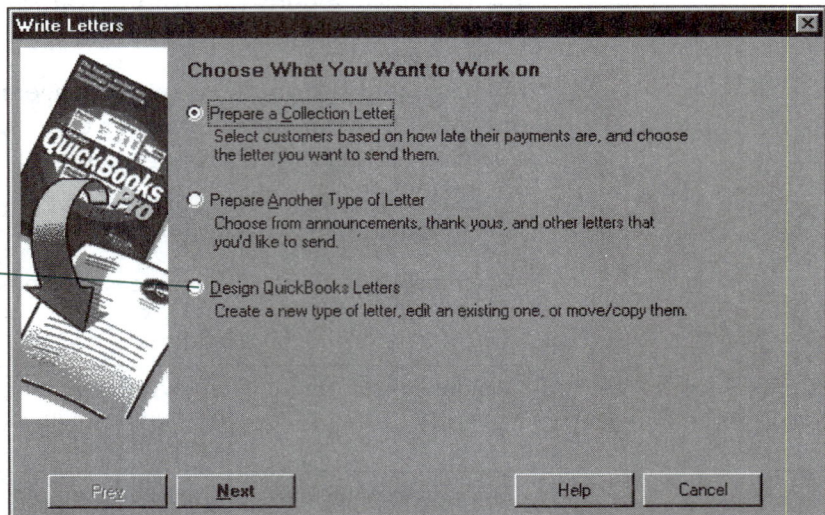

You can convert any existing letters you use to work with QuickBooks or design new ones.

Note: You must be using QuickBooks Pro 2000 and Microsoft Word 97 or higher.

To learn about...	Search the Help index for...
Getting your QuickBooks data into Microsoft Word	letters using QuickBooks data in Microsoft Word

Printing labels and Rolodex cards

You can print mailing labels and Rolodex cards for customers, vendors, employees, and others sorted by name or nine-digit zip code. You can select names according to criteria you set.

Choose whether to print mailing labels or Rolodex cards in the Printer setup window. Names and addresses print on mailing labels; names, alternate contact names, addresses, and phone numbers print on Rolodex cards.

Format	Description
self-adhesive labels	QuickBooks can print on a variety of Avery standard mailing labels. Click Help in the Label Printer Setup window for a list of supported label formats.
	For sheet-fed printers, the labels are arranged in columns of two or three on an 8.5-inch-wide backing.
	For continuous-feed printers, the labels are arranged in columns of one or two on an 8.5-inch-wide backing.
Rolodex cards	Prepunched card stock is designed for your computer's printer.
	QuickBooks can print on either 3-inch by 5-inch cards or on 2.25-inch by 4-inch cards.

To learn about...	Search the Help index for...
Choosing a format	mailing labels, choosing a format for
Sorting labels by zip code and printing labels and Rolodex cards	mailing labels, printing

Making To Do notes

You can enter notes to help keep track of phone calls you need to make, tasks that you want to complete by a certain date, or upcoming events, such as a lease expiration.

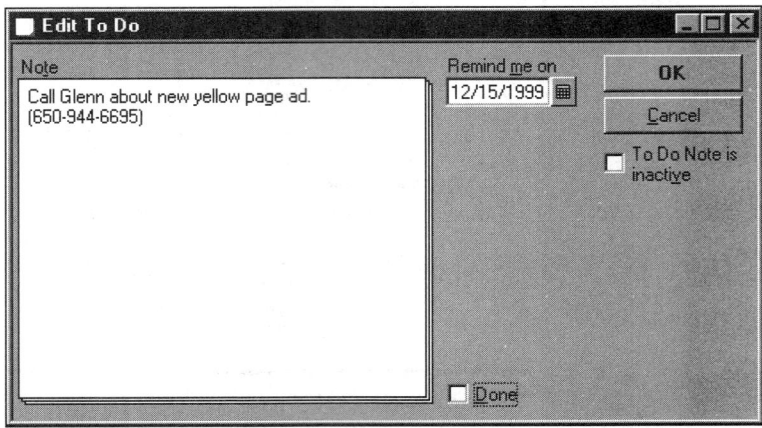

You can use the To Do list to look at your notes at any time, or use the Reminders list to see which notes are currently due when you start QuickBooks.

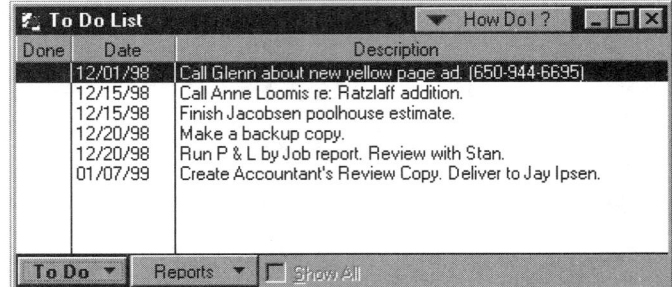

You can create a To Do notes report that shows the status, date, and description for each To Do note.

To learn about...	Search the Help index for...
Using To Do notes	To Do notes
Printing To Do notes	To Do notes
Creating a To Do notes report	To Do notes

Remind me!

You can use the QuickBooks Reminders list to display those tasks you need to take care of now or in the near future, including those tasks you list on your To Do notes.

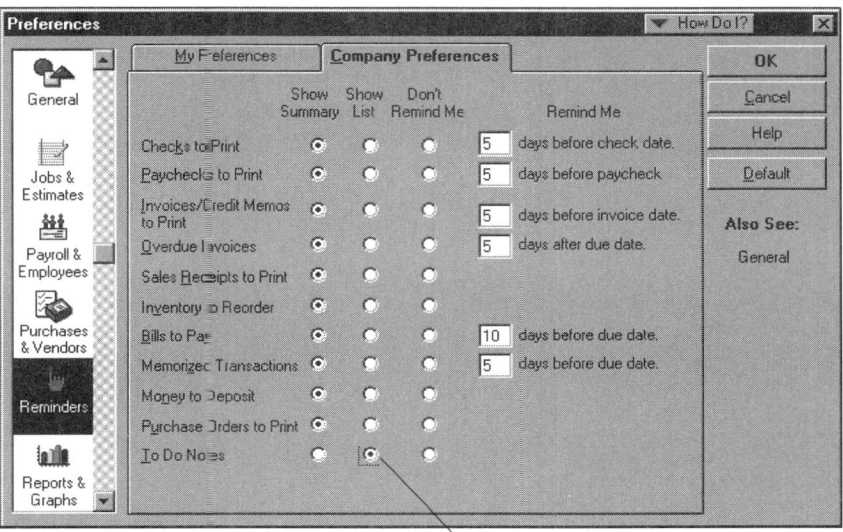

Set up your Reminder Preferences to Show List for your To Do notes so you'll see the individual note information.

To learn about...	Search the Help index for...
Using reminders	preferences, reminders

Making To Do notes | 445

CHAPTER 24

Working with an accountant or advisor

Working with an accountant who doesn't use QuickBooks	449
Working with an accountant who uses QuickBooks	450

How can I get help with my bookkeeping or computers?

From time to time, you may need advice that falls beyond the scope of what the QuickBooks documentation or technical support team can supply. In these situations you'll want to contact your accountant or other specialized professional.

After you find the right accountant, review the following table to determine which work situation best fits you and your business.

Note: To locate a QuickBooks Professional Advisor in your area, go to **www.quickbooks.com/support** and then click Professional Advisors.

Situation	What to do in QuickBooks	Comments	See...
Your accountant does not use QuickBooks and/or prefers working with hard copy printouts.	Print out all the reports and lists your accountant requests.	Later you'll need to enter into QuickBooks any adjustments recommended by your accountant.	"Working with an accountant who doesn't use QuickBooks" on page 449
Your accountant uses QuickBooks and would like to review your books "online" and make any necessary changes.	■ **Option 1:** You can allow your accountant to make changes to a copy of your QuickBooks company file called the Accountant's Review copy, and later merge this copy back into your master company file. This feature allows you to continue working in your master file while your accountant works in his or her copy.	Restrictions exist on what you and your accountant can change during the period when the Accountant's Review copy is out.	"Working with an accountant who uses QuickBooks" on page 450
	■ **Option 2:** If you have QuickBooks Pro and have set up multiple users, you can set up your accountant as a QuickBooks user and allow him or her to work onsite in the company file simultaneously (multi-user mode) with the rest of your staff.	Your accountant may want to conduct some operations that are allowed in single-user mode only.	"Option 2: Have your accountant work onsite" on page 453
	■ **Option 3:** If your accountant is not local and/or needs complete access to all areas of your company file, you can send him or her a backup copy of your company file.	**Proceed with caution!** As your accountant's copy will become your master company file when it's returned, any changes you make to your company file while it's out will be lost. You will need to reenter them in the new master file.	"Option 3: Give your accountant a backup copy" on page 453

Working with an accountant who doesn't use QuickBooks

Traditionally, accountants and business owners expect that there will be an exchange of paper (the books and supporting documents). If this is how you and your accountant expect to work, you'll need to coordinate the types of information you have to supply. This will depend on the type of task your accountant is performing for you.

For example, if your accountant is reviewing your books at year end, you may need to supply the following:

- Profit and loss statement
- Balance sheet
- General ledger report
- Journal report
- Trial balance

Making adjustments

Your accountant's review of your books may necessitate that you make adjustments to various accounts, such as adding the depreciation of a fixed asset. He or she may describe how to make these adjustments in terms of debits and credits. To add these adjustments in QuickBooks, you can use the General Journal Entry window.

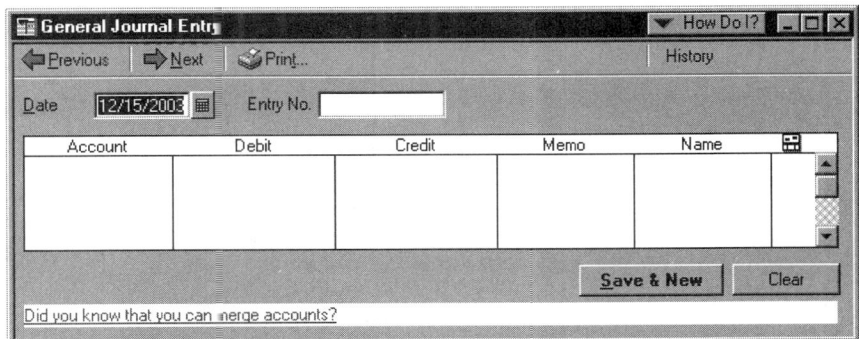

To learn about...	Search the Help index for...
Adding journal entries	general journal entries
Printing journal entries	printing, general journal entries

Working with an accountant who uses QuickBooks

Option 1: Use the Accountant's Review feature

The Accountant's Review™ feature of QuickBooks allows an accountant to make certain kinds of changes in a special copy of the company file. Meanwhile, you can continue to enter daily transactions in the original master file. After the accountant has made the changes, you merge them into the master company file.

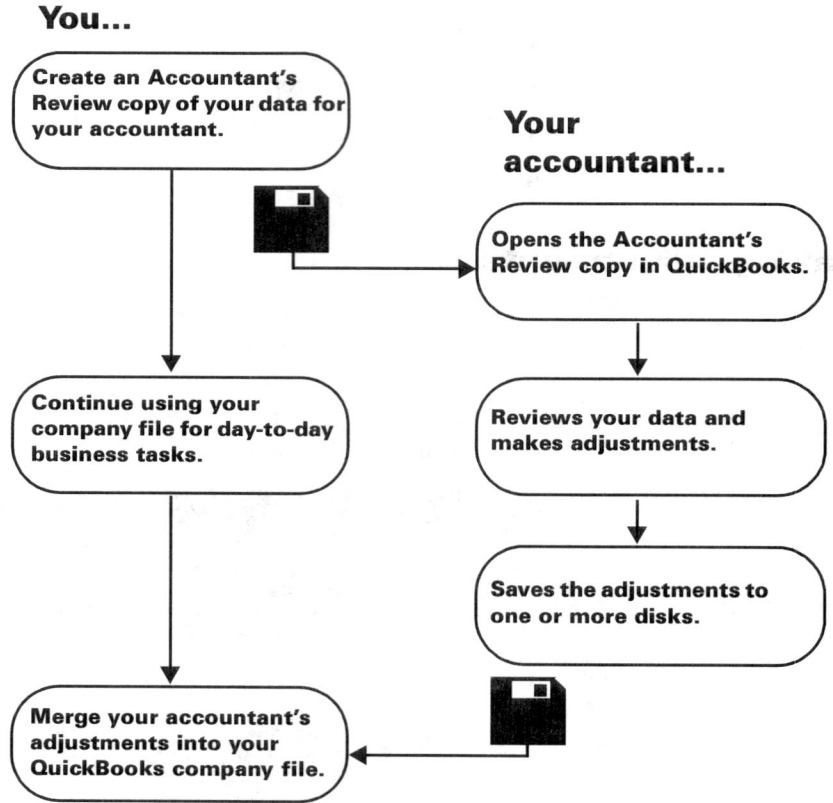

What can and can't be changed

The Accountant's Review feature may not be right for everyone. The accountant can make some kinds of changes but not others.

The advantage of using the Accountant's Review feature is that you can continue to work normally with your master company file (that is, the regular company file from which you make the Accountant's Review copy). After the accountant has made changes, you can merge the changes into your master file.

The following table shows what an accountant can and cannot do while using an Accountant's Review copy of your file, and any restrictions you have while this copy is out.

Note: If you have set up yourself or others as users, tell your accountant the user name and password of the QuickBooks Administrator. The accountant should enter this name and password when opening the Accountant's Review copy of your file.

Your accountant can...	Your accountant cannot...	You cannot...
■ View all existing transactions and lists	■ Enter transactions other than general journal transactions	■ Delete any items from lists
■ Add new items to the chart of accounts, Item list, Payroll Item list, To Do Notes list, Memorized Transaction list (general journal transactions only) To add inventory items, you must have this feature turned on. See page 230.	■ Memorize transactions other than general journal transactions	■ Reorganize lists (move items or make one item a subitem of another)
	■ Edit or delete existing transactions, including paychecks	
	■ Reorganize lists (move items, make one item a subitem of another)	
■ Edit existing account names and numbers	■ Rename accounts or items	
■ Edit existing payroll items	■ Make items inactive	
■ Edit account and tax information for existing items on Item list	■ Edit names of existing items on Item list	
■ Enter general journal transactions	■ Adjust payroll liabilities	
■ Reconcile new transactions	■ Enter or edit employee YTD payroll setup transactions	
■ Adjust inventory values or quantities	■ Export changes made to 941, 940, or W-2 forms	
■ Create reports	■ Export changes to preferences	
■ Change preferences temporarily	■ Memorize reports	
■ Create, adjust, and print 941, 940, and W-2 forms	■ Change a non-inventory part type to an inventory part type.	
■ Print 1099 forms	■ Merge new inventory part items with previous, existing inventory part items.	

Preparing an Accountant's Review copy

To learn about...	Search the Help index for...
Setting up your accountant as a user with all privileges. (Do this only if you have set up yourself or others as users.)	permissions
How to use an Accountant Review copy of your current company file	accountant's review copy

For accountants only: Working with an Accountant's Review copy

The file created from the master company file is a compressed version of a special type of company file. Before working with the file for the first time, you must decompress the file.

Note: If your client has set up users and passwords, you'll need to find out the user name and password assigned to you.

Once you have opened an Accountant's Review copy, it remains the current QuickBooks company unless you open a different company or you close the company. If you try to record a change that is not allowed, QuickBooks displays a message advising that it cannot record the change in an Accountant's Review copy.

If your computer's system date and time is earlier than the date and time that your client created the Accountant's Review copy, you will not be able to open the copy.

To correct the problem you'll need to determine which computer has the incorrect date and time, change the date and time, and try to reopen the copy. You may need to have your client cancel the first review copy and create another one for you.

To learn about...	Search the Help index for...
Creating a file to give to your client	accountant's review copy

Option 2: Have your accountant work onsite

If your accountant is local and amenable to working at your office, you can set him or her up as a user and he or she can work while another user inputs invoices and you pay bills.

Pros

- There is no need to make an Accountant's Review copy or a backup copy to give to your accountant.
- Your business can continue working as normal.
- Your accountant will make any necessary adjustments to the file.

Cons

- Only five users can simultaneously access QuickBooks Pro at a time.
- Your accountant may want to conduct some operations that are allowed in single-user mode only.
- Some reports your accountant generates may run slowly in multi-user mode.

To learn about...	Search the Help index for...
Setting up your accountant as a user	permissions

Option 3: Give your accountant a backup copy

If your accountant needs to conduct work for you not permitted by the Accountant's Review copy, you may want to give him or her a backup copy of your QuickBooks company file.

Consider this carefully.

The backup copy that your accountant reviews and changes will become your master company file! We recommend that you do not enter any transactions into QuickBooks while your accountant works on his or her copy.

Pros

- Your accountant will have complete access to all areas of your QuickBooks company.

- Your accountant can make any necessary adjustments to the file.

Cons

- **You cannot merge transactions between two regular files.**

    If you make any changes to your QuickBooks company file during the time your accountant is working on the other version, your changes will be lost when you accept your accountant's version as your new master company.

Creating a backup file for your accountant

Because you are giving your accountant a backup (compressed) version of your file, he or she will need to use the Restore command to access the data.

Note: If you have set up users and passwords, you must also set up your accountant as a user so he or she can access the file.

To learn about...	Search the Help index for...
Creating a backup copy of your QuickBooks company file	backups

Using your accountant's revised copy as your master copy

To learn about...	Search the Help index for...
Accessing your accountant's revised copy	restoring data

CHAPTER 25

Importing and exporting data

Importing and exporting to other software programs 456

Transferring QuickBooks lists between company files 457

How can I transfer information between QuickBooks and other software?

You can use the import and export commands to import from and export to word processors, spreadsheets, other bookkeeping software, and other QuickBooks companies. You can copy lists from one QuickBooks company to another, export list information to be opened in other software, and import transactions that are in a special format.

You cannot export transactions from QuickBooks.
However, you can create a report based on transactions and print the report to a file that can be read by a spreadsheet, database, or word processor.

Importing and exporting to other software programs

QuickBooks exports and imports data in a format called IIF (Intuit Interchange Format). This format is different from QIF (used by Quicken). QuickBooks imports only IIF data.

When you export information from QuickBooks, the program formats the data into IIF. You can then import the IIF file into spreadsheets, word processors, and database programs.

If you want to import data from other software applications, you need to create an IIF file from scratch or reformat data you already use to conform to IIF standards.

> **Note:** **Creating an IIF file from scratch or changing data from another accounting program into an IIF file is technically complex.** It is not recommended for those who do not have programming experience. However, you do not need to learn about the IIF format to export lists and import them back into QuickBooks.

Unless you have a very large customer database or more than 200 transactions, it may be easier and less time-consuming to enter the data directly into QuickBooks.

If you use Microsoft Word, Microsoft Excel, Microsoft Outlook, or Symantec ACT!

You can export QuickBooks Pro data to Microsoft Word or Excel. You can synchronize Microsoft Outlook and Symantec ACT! contact data with QuickBooks Pro.

- If you use Microsoft Word 97 as your word processing program and are using QuickBooks Pro, you can use the Write Letters feature. See "Writing letters" on page 441.

- If you use Microsoft Excel 97 and are using QuickBooks Pro, you can export your QuickBooks report data to Excel for further customization and filtering. See "Exporting the report to a Microsoft Excel spreadsheet" on page 410.

- If you use Microsoft Outlook or Symantec ACT!, you can synchronize contact information with QuickBooks Pro. See "Sharing QuickBooks Pro information with your contact manager" on page 438. (You should not import or export data from your contact manager to QuickBooks because of formatting problems that may occur.)

Importing customer names from a list

If you already have information about your customers in software such as a spreadsheet, you can prepare a file for import into your QuickBooks company file. The import file must be in Intuit Interchange Format (IIF), which is a type of ASCII text file with special headings to identify to QuickBooks the type of information it contains.

If you choose to import customer names from such a file, you will probably have to edit each customer to add additional information, such as payment terms or sales tax information.

Also, if you have unpaid balances for such customers, you will need to enter an invoice for each that, at the minimum, tells the total amount owed.

To learn about...	Search the Help index for...
Creating an IIF file for importing list information into QuickBooks	importing data
Creating invoices for customer balances that were unpaid as of the start date	invoices, creating

Transferring QuickBooks lists between company files

QuickBooks allows you to export most lists and their related information. You simply mark the lists that you would like to export and QuickBooks creates a file that can be easily imported into another QuickBooks company.

Importing list information with duplicate entries.

When you import lists into an existing QuickBooks company, QuickBooks considers the import file's entries more recent. It replaces any duplicate entries with ones from the import file.

This table compares the different methods of transferring data.

Method	What it does	Advantages	Disadvantages
Copying a file (through DOS or Windows)	Makes an exact copy (in QuickBooks .QBW format)	QuickBooks can open the copy without extra steps.	A large company file may not fit on one disk. Only QuickBooks can read the file.
Backing up a company file	Makes a compressed copy of everything in the original company file	More data fits on one 3.5-inch disk. Backup allows you to divide very large files among more than one 3.5-inch disk.	QuickBooks must restore the backed-up copy before it can open the file.
Printing to disk	Makes a copy in a format common to other software programs	You can use the file in a spreadsheet or word-processing program.	Only certain information can be printed to disk, such as lists and reports. QuickBooks cannot read files printed to disk.
Exporting	Puts lists into a file in IIF format, with one record per line and one column for each field	You can share lists with other company data files or use a list in a database, word processor, or spreadsheet program. You can add to the list and import it back into QuickBooks.	QuickBooks can export only lists, not transactions or reports.

To learn about...	Search the Help index for...
Importing data from other software programs	importing data
The import and export files that QuickBooks creates	■ importing data ■ IIF file format
Exporting lists to another QuickBooks company	exporting data
The process of backing up your company file	backups

APPENDIX A

Troubleshooting

How do I solve a QuickBooks problem?

Finding the information you need	460
Exploring problems on your own	462
Getting Technical Support	464

If you're having a problem using a particular form, or the program isn't acting as you expected, or you've received an error message, follow these steps until your problem is solved.

- Research all available documentation to see if you are performing the task correctly (see page 460).
- Follow the guidelines for solving typical problems (see page 462).
- Talk to an expert QuickBooks technical support representative who can walk you through the solution (Service charges may apply—see page 464).

Important: Terms, conditions, support plan pricing and offerings are subject to change without notice.

Finding the information you need

There are many ways to get information about using QuickBooks. The User's Guide provides general conceptual, setup, and usage information. The Information & Support window is a central location for information about using QuickBooks— see *Using the Information & Support window,* beginning on page 6. The onscreen Help provides detailed how-to instructions. Other tools, such as the Frequently Asked Questions section on the QuickBooks.com Web site and Fax on Demand, focus on providing answers to problems or common questions such as:

- What goes into box 14 of the W-2 Form?
- Why do some letters get cut off on QuickBooks forms?
- How do I resolve the error, "Insufficient memory"?

Using QuickBooks onscreen Help features

To get help about the window you're working in, press F1 or choose "Help on this window" from the Help menu. You can also use the How Do I menu if it's available.

To search for a particular subject, choose Help Index from the Help menu and enter your subject.

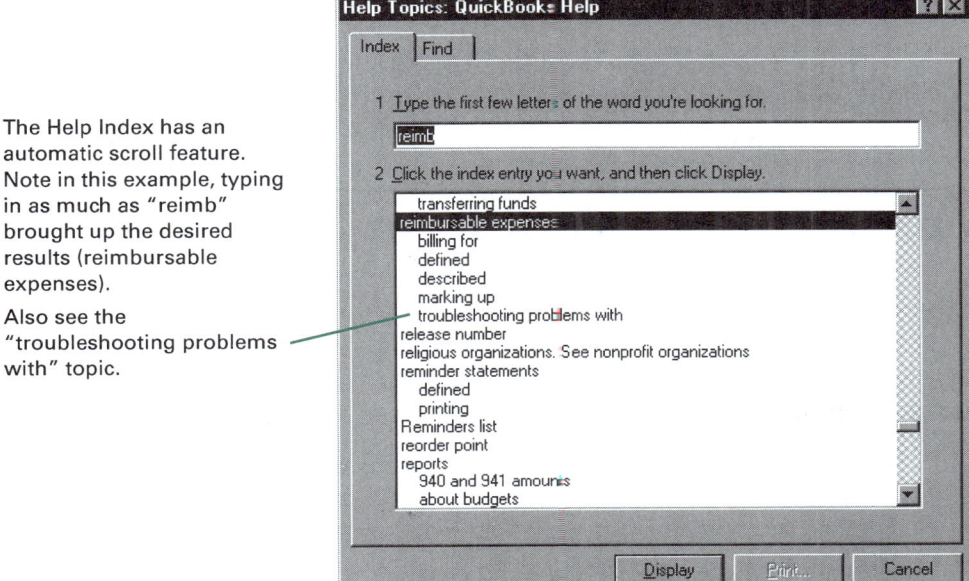

The Help Index has an automatic scroll feature. Note in this example, typing in as much as "reimb" brought up the desired results (reimbursable expenses).

Also see the "troubleshooting problems with" topic.

Frequently asked questions

Look to these resources to provide specific problem-solving procedures.

QuickBooks.com Web site

You can use this site (**www.quickbooks.com**) to search for answers to over 700 QuickBooks questions, including information about error messages. You may also want to access a QuickBooks User Group at the Web site to ask if any other users have had a similar experience or problem.

Fax on Demand (QuickFax) system

The Fax on Demand system offers 24-hour access to documents that answer hundreds of technical support questions. When you call the phone number, recorded prompts guide you through the process of ordering the documents.

After you enter the numbers of the documents you want, they are automatically faxed to you.

To find the Fax on Demand phone number, choose Phone Directory from the Help menu and click General Product Support.

Tip: The first time you call, order an updated index of all documents available for your version of QuickBooks.

Exploring problems on your own

Note: We recommend you back up your data on new, formatted disks before you start.

Guidelines for solving typical problems

Use the following examples as a guide to solving the problems you are having.

Try the procedure again

Start at the beginning. Examine windows where you filled in fields to be sure you are asking the program for what you want.

For example, if invoices you just entered are not showing on your profit and loss statement, you should ask questions such as:

- Does the date of the report include those invoices?
- Do the invoices appear if you change the report from Cash to Accrual basis?
- Does this problem occur with only invoices for one particular customer?
- Have you changed any filters on the report? (Try to create a new report from scratch to see if the problem is solved.)

Try a related procedure

For example, if you have a printing problem:

- Check that the printer is working by trying to print something else. If you have trouble printing checks, try printing a report. If you can't print a sales forms, try printing a similar form.

- If you can't print from QuickBooks, try printing from another program such as Windows Notepad. If nothing prints from Notepad, you know the problem is related to the printer, not the software. Check the printer connections, the printer driver, the print queue, and so forth.

Think about what has changed

If something used to work but no longer works, think about what's changed.

- Have you changed or added other programs on your computer recently?
- Have you added a new printer?
- Have you moved the QuickBooks company file to a new location?
- Have you changed a setting in the Preferences window?

If the program "hangs" or locks up on you

There are a number of reasons why your system could freeze while using QuickBooks. In that case, try restarting your computer to see if that solves the problem.

Note: **If you encounter a recurring problem with system freezes while using QuickBooks, you may want to call for technical support. Choose Phone Directory from the Help menu and click General Product Support.** But first see "Talking to a technical support representative: Be prepared when you call" on page 464.

If restarting doesn't help, go through the following list of questions and take any corresponding action:

- Does your computer system (and network) meet the minimum requirements necessary for QuickBooks? (See the *QuickBooks Installation and Conversion Guide*.)
- Are you making the best use of available system resources by shutting down other programs that may be running? (Check for programs that may be running in the background by pressing Alt+Tab.)

- Do you have enough hard disk space available? (This is particularly appropriate for those working in a multi-user, peer-to-peer network situation.)
- Do you have any conflicts with sound and video drivers?

For more information about these topics, go to the Support section of QuickBooks.com Web site (**www.quickbooks.com**) and use the Questions & Answers search feature.

Getting Technical Support

If you've followed the guidelines in "Exploring problems on your own" on page 462 and you're still unable to solve your problem, you can get expert assistance through the QuickBooks Support Network.

QuickBooks telephone support is flexibly priced to make it cost effective for any business.

Choose Phone Directory from the Help menu and click General Product Support for the number to call.

Important: Terms, conditions, support plan pricing, and offerings are subject to change without notice. (Calls about installation and conversion are currently provided for certain earlier versions of QuickBooks at no charge.)

Note: **Other support options are available, including automated telephone support and the Fax on Demand system.** For a description of these options, see "QuickBooks Support Network (QBSN)" on page 468.

Talking to a technical support representative: Be prepared when you call

When you call, you will get an answer more quickly if you:

- Make sure you have registered your copy of QuickBooks and have your registration number ready. To display your registration number, choose About QuickBooks from the Help menu.
- If your company file is set up with users (and permissions), you'll need to have enough permissions to areas of QuickBooks. You might want to switch to single-user mode.

- Be sure that you are at your computer with QuickBooks running. Try to remember the windows you opened and the tasks you did prior to encountering the problem.
- Important: know exactly what you did before the problem occurred, and the exact wording of any message appearing on the screen.
- In some cases, the following information is relevant to your problem. Have it ready when you call:
  - Computer type, model number, and amount of memory (RAM)
  - Windows version
  - Monitor type and printer manufacturer, type, and model
  - Network configuration and version
- Have a pencil and paper handy to take notes.

In case you need to restore a file

Restoring a backup copy of your company file

You may need to restore company data from your backup files in the following situations:

- You need to put the data on another computer.
- You want your data to revert to the state it was in at an earlier date.
- Your working data is damaged.
- Your hard disk has malfunctioned.

In the first two instances, you can restore your company data on your own. In the last two, you should use this approach only if a technical support representative has recommended it.

Because the Back Up command creates a compressed file, you must restore the backup data onto your hard disk by using the QuickBooks Restore command.

Note: **If QuickBooks finds a company file with the same name in the same directory on the hard disk, it asks you whether you want to replace the existing file on the hard disk.** If you answer "No," QuickBooks returns you to the Restore window. You must then designate a different name for the restored file. *We recommend entering a new name for the file when you restore so that you don't overwrite the current file. Once it has been overwritten, it cannot be retrieved.*

To learn about...	Search the Help index for...
Restoring your company data from a backup copy	restoring data

The Verify and Rebuild utilities

A technical support representative may have you run the QuickBooks Verify Data and Rebuild Data utilities to recover damaged transactions. The Verify utility detects any data errors; the Rebuild utility ensures that the errors are corrected.

Because Rebuild can cause additional problems to the data file that can increase the difficulty of recovering your data, we do not recommend running Rebuild on your own.

Note: **The Rebuild utility requires that you back up your company file first.** If a technical support representative asks you to run Rebuild, you will need to have formatted disks on hand for the backup.

APPENDIX B

Intuit services, supplies, and technical support

Intuit services and supplies 468

Want more help running your business?

Intuit has an extensive range of services, supplies, and support programs designed to meet the needs of your small business.

Check this appendix for information on:

- Intuit supplies, including checks, invoices, and many others.
- Services such as QuickBooks Payroll Services and Online Banking and Bill Payment.
- Support through the QuickBooks Support Network (QBSN), which includes QuickBooks Telephone Support, QuickStart Service, QuickBooks Automated Phone Support, QuickFax, and the QuickBooks.com Web site.
- Training provided through QuickBooks Training Seminars and the *QuickBooks Learning Guide*.
- Advice and consultation through the QuickBooks Professional Advisors Program.

Intuit services and supplies

Intuit supplies

Intuit offers a complete line of checks, invoices, envelopes, tax forms, forms leaders, printable deposit slips, and custom and standard logos that work with QuickBooks.

Your QuickBooks package includes an *Intuit Checks, Forms, & Supplies Catalog*. QuickBooks also includes a link to our checks and forms Web site, www.intuitmarket.com, where you can order and learn more about our supplies.

If you want to order by telephone, choose Phone Directory from the Help menu and click QuickBooks Supplies to find the phone number.

QuickBooks Support Network (QBSN)

The following technical support services are designed to help you get the most from your QuickBooks investment. You can find the phone numbers for the QuickBooks Support Network on the back cover of this book or in the phone directory. Choose Phone Directory from the Help menu and click General Product Support to find the phone number for the service you want.

Important: Terms, conditions, support plan pricing and offerings are subject to change without notice. Intuit reserves the right to limit any telephone call to one hour and to limit any call to one incident.

- **QuickBooks telephone support.**

    QuickBooks telephone support is flexibly priced to make it cost effective for any business.

    - **Premier Plan.** This 12-month membership plan provides telephone support, day and night**. Premier Plan membership includes a priority telephone number, a quarterly newsletter, and access to a members-only Web site—with electronic incident support.

    - **Basic Telephone Support.** If you choose not to purchase the Premier Plan, you can get telephone support that is billed to you by the minute.

*Excludes occasional downtime for server or system maintenance.
**Excludes U.S. holidays.

- **QuickStart Service.** Our QuickStart specialists can tailor QuickBooks for you and ensure that your QuickBooks company file is set up correctly for your business requirements and payroll needs. QuickStart has two modules—QuickStart Setup and QuickStart Consultation. With QuickStart Setup, a specialist will configure QuickBooks for you based on information you provide and will walk you through a brief tutorial of the QuickBooks software. QuickStart Consultation provides four, one-hour phone consultation sessions that address the QuickBooks features essential to your business. (QuickStart specialists do not provide technical support.)

- **QuickBooks automated telephone support.** Get recorded answers to frequently asked questions about QuickBooks by telephone, 24 hours a day, seven days a week*.

- **Fax-on-Demand.** Our automated QuickFax service provides answers by fax to the most frequently asked questions, 24 hours a day, seven days a week*.

- **Data recovery.** If your QuickBooks data file becomes damaged, data recovery is available for a fee. (There is no charge for unrecoverable files.)

- **Password removal.** If you forget your password, password removal is available for a fee.

QuickBooks Payroll Services

QuickBooks Payroll Services provides two levels of service—Basic and Deluxe—that are designed to meet a variety of payroll needs. Both are subscription-based and require that you have an Internet connection.

QuickBooks Basic Payroll

QuickBooks Basic Payroll lets you process your own payroll with the confidence that your federal and state tax tables will be updated with the latest payroll withholding regulations. For a monthly fee, the payroll service allows QuickBooks to automatically calculate federal and state payroll taxes and provide updates via the Internet whenever the tax information changes.

The service also provides the ability to prepare and print W-2, W-3, 940, 941, and Schedule B forms online, as well as tax forms for a

*Excludes occasional downtime for server or system maintenance.
**Excludes U.S. holidays.

selected number of states (available for the 2000 tax year). Also available, at an additional cost, is direct deposit, which deposits paychecks in up to two bank accounts per employee.

For contact information, choose Phone Directory from the Help menu and click QuickBooks Basic Payroll to find the phone number.

QuickBooks Deluxe Payroll

QuickBooks Deluxe Payroll is a more comprehensive solution that includes calculating your payroll to making your federal and state tax deposits for you. For a monthly fee, Deluxe Payroll customers get many of the features provided with Basic Payroll, plus the service:

- Makes federal and state payroll tax deposits from your company accounts.
- Prepares and files federal and state payroll tax forms required for your company.
- Prepares and delivers to you Forms W-2 for your employees.
- Files Form W-3 for your company at the end of the year.
- Provides a toll-free number for assistance with your payroll.

Direct deposit is also available to Deluxe Payroll customers at an additional cost.

For contact information, choose Phone Directory from the Help menu and click QuickBooks Deluxe Payroll to find the phone number.

QuickBooks Online Banking and Bill Payment

Through participating financial institutions, you can do banking and online bill payment through QuickBooks, day and night.

- Online account access lets you check account balances, make transfers, and see if a check has cleared, in addition to other banking tasks.
- Online payment gives you flexibility and control in paying your bills. You can schedule payments up to a year in advance.

*Excludes occasional downtime for server or system maintenance.
**Excludes U.S. holidays.

For contact information, choose Phone Directory from the Help menu and click "Online account access or online payment support" to find the phone number.

> Note: Service fees and offerings may vary by participating financial institution.

QuickBooks.com Web site

QuickBooks.com is the official site for QuickBooks users. You can get answers to small business and QuickBooks questions, important QuickBooks updates and e-mail notices, user-to-user forums, advice and articles from renowned small business experts, and industry-specific tools and advice.

If you have an Internet Service Provider, you can access this site (**www.quickbooks.com**) from the Help menu in QuickBooks.

QuickBooks Learning Guide

Intuit offers the *QuickBooks Learning Guide*, a self-study guide designed for self-motivated users who want to learn the basic QuickBooks and QuickBooks Pro features.

The learning guide is modular so you can learn at your own pace. Each lesson walks you through a key feature using true-to-life examples. You can skip lessons that don't apply to your business.

The guide comes with a 3.5-inch disk that contains sample data used in examples throughout the guide.

To order the guide, choose Phone Directory from the Help menu and click Intuit Direct Sales and Customer Service to find the phone number.

QuickBooks Certified Professional Advisors Program

Our Certified QuickBooks ProAdvisors are accounting professionals, competent in using QuickBooks and have completed a comprehensive curriculum and tests developed by Intuit. These professionals possess the resources and knowledge to help you optimize and master QuickBooks so you can manage your business better.

*Excludes occasional downtime for server or system maintenance.
**Excludes U.S. holidays.

Customers can find a QuickBooks Professional Advisor through the free referral service found at **www.quickbooks.com**. Your selected advisor will provide you with fee information.

If you are an accountant, bookkeeper, or computer consultant, consider becoming certified as a member of this community of professionals.

Whether you want to find a QuickBooks Professional Advisor or become one yourself, visit the **www.quickbooks.com** Web site.

QuickBooks Training Seminars

Intuit and an endorsed seminar provider, Real World Training, Inc., offer one- and two-day training seminars for users who want a comprehensive course on using QuickBooks or QuickBooks Pro.

Seminars are offered nationwide throughout the year. For full course descriptions and details on locations and pricing, visit the **www.quickbooks.com/training** Web site or call the phone number listed in the phone directory. Choose Phone Directory from the Help menu and click Intuit Direct Sales and Customer Service.

New services

New services that work with QuickBooks may become available at any time. For a listing of products and services that are available, choose QuickBooks Products & Services from the Company menu.

---

*Excludes occasional downtime for server or system maintenance.
**Excludes U.S. holidays.

Index

If you don't find the topic you are looking for here or in the *Installation and Conversion Guide*, try QuickBooks Help. From the QuickBooks Help menu, choose Help Index, enter the keyword, and press Enter.

Numbers

1096 forms
  ordering from Intuit, 468
  summary information for, 308
1099-MISC forms
  ordering from Intuit, 468
  printing and verifying, 308
  setting up for, 307
  vendors, specifying for, 216
401(k) plans, 360
403(b) plans, 360
408(k)(6)SEP plans, 360
457(b) plans, 360
501(c)(18)(D) plans, 360
5-User Value Pack, registering, 73
90% of job, invoicing for, 187
940 forms
  preparing and filing, 389
  up-to-date, 354
941 forms
  preparing and filing, 388
  tax tracking classification, effect on, 360
  up-to-date, 354

A

A/P, *see* accounts payable
A/R, *see* accounts receivable
access control, *see* passwords
account numbers
  bill payment checks, printing on, 213
  chart of accounts, 52
  online payees, 256
accountant's review feature, 450–452

accountants
  finding one, 9
  information, 6
  making adjustments, 449
  using a backup copy, 453
  working onsite, 453
  working with, 447
accounting
  method, defined, 11
  year-end entries, 423
accounting software, transferring data to QuickBooks from, 456
accounts (types)
  accounts payable, 14
  accounts receivable, 14
  asset, 14
  balance sheet, 13
  bank, 14
  cost of goods sold, 230
  credit card, 14
  depreciation, 305
  equity, 15
  expense, 16
  fixed asset, 14
  income, 16
  inventory asset, 230
  liability, 14
  long term liability, 15
  merchant credit card, 104
  non-posting, 13
  online, *see* online accounts
  other asset, 14
  other current asset, 14
  other current liability, 14
  sales tax payable, 287
  subaccounts, *see* subaccounts
accounts (working with)
  1099 categories, 307
  alphabetical order, 52
  applying for a merchant credit card account, 104
  automatically-created accounts, 13

balances, viewing, 15
business and personal, 97
chart of, *see* chart of accounts
editing, 30
fees and interest, entering, 107
hiding, 59
items, choosing for, 116
list of, 13
names, changing, 52
numerical, 30, 52
opening balances
   changing, 52
   entering, 99
payroll, 352
printing names on voucher checks, 255
reconciling, 108
registers, 16
removing from chart of accounts, 59
reorganizing order of, 52
subaccounts, *see* subaccounts
tax lines, assigning, 301
transferring money, 110

accounts payable, 256–264
   account for, 14, 255
   aging detail report, 220
   aging summary report, 263
   defined, 253
   historical transactions, 31
   register, 16
   reports, 263, 264
   unpaid bills detail report, 264
   vendor balance detail report, 264
   vendor balance summary report, 264
   see also bills from vendors

accounts receivable
   account for, 14
   aging summary report, 209
   collections report, 209
   customer registers, 158
   defined, 172
   graph, 208
   historical transactions, 31
   QuickReport of customer or job, 163
   reports about, 205
   see also customers; invoices

accrual basis
   adjustment during setup, 34
   defined, 35
   overview, 12

reporting, 398
sales tax, preference for, 286

ACT!, Symantec, synchronizing information with QuickBooks, 439

activities
   defined, 311
   detail, how much to track, 311
   editing or viewing Timer data about, 320
   exporting from Timer, 321
   importing into QuickBooks Pro, 322
   invoicing for, 197
   list of (time by job detail report), 333
   recording time for manually in QuickBooks, 324
   reports, 330–334
   single, recording, 325
   timing and recording in Timer, 318
   timing and recording with Stopwatch, 323

actuals, comparing to estimates, 207

adding, *look under what you want to add*

additions, payroll
   employee defaults, adding to, 362
   employees, individual, setting up for, 363
   payroll item for, 359

address
   company, 425
   synchronizing addresses from Symantec ACT! or Microsoft Outlook, 438

adjusting
   alignment when printing forms, 93
   income and expense accounts, 35
   inventory value, 241
   item prices or rates, 135
   liabilities for payroll items, 392
   paychecks, 381
   quantity on hand, 241
   sales tax owed, 291

adjusting entries, 449

Administrator, QuickBooks, 63

advance deposits from customers, 191

advances
   against salary, 360
   travel, payroll item for, 360

advertising firms, information, 6

aging
   defined, 398
   graph of A/R, 208

If you don't find the topic you are looking for here or in the *Installation and Conversion Guide*, try QuickBooks Help. From the QuickBooks Help menu, choose Help Index, enter the keyword, and press Enter.

reports
    A/P detail, 220, 263
    A/P summary, 263
    A/R summary, 209
    calculating, preference for, 210

alerts, 38

alignment adjustment when printing forms, 93

alphabetical order for accounts and lists, 52

annual salaries, *see* salaries

annual tasks, 422

architecture firms, information, 6

artists, information, 6

assets
    accounts for, 14
    balance sheet, viewing on, 17
    buying, 304
    buying with a loan, 111
    current, accounts for, 14
    defined, 17
    depreciation of, 305
    selling, 305
    theft or loss of, 306

ATM withdrawals, 103

attorneys, what they can do for you, 8

audit trail, 65–66

automatic recall of last transaction for a name, 255

automatic statement charge entry, 201

automatically entering transactions, *see* scheduling

average cost of inventory items
    how QuickBooks calculates, 242
    valuation summary report, 245

Avery labels, 443

B

back orders
    inventory sales, tracking, 238
    not filled automatically by QuickBooks, 225

backing up data, 66–67
    compared to other methods of transferring data, 458

bad checks from customers, 190

bad debt, 111

balance forward
    credit cards, 107
    statements to customers, 174

balance sheet accounts
    registers for, 16
    types of, 14
    viewing balances, 15

balance sheets, 17

balances
    current for customers and jobs, 155
    current for vendors, 217
    in letters, 441
    opening, *see* opening balances
    viewing for balance sheet accounts, 15

balancing accounts, *see* reconciling

bank accounts
    adding, 99
    description, 14
    fees and interest, entering, 107
    historical transactions, 99
    online, *see* online accounts
    opening balances for existing, 99
    reconciling, 108
    service charges, 107
    setting up, 99

banks, *see* financial institutions

Basic Payroll, 346

batch printing, 94

benefits for employees
   how QuickBooks tracks, 353
   payroll item for, 359
bids, *see* estimates
bill payments
   deleting, 262
   editing, 261
   history, 262
   making, 258
   online inquiry, 261
billing customers, *see* customers; invoices; statements
billing statements, 175–176
billing status
   deciding whether to make time billable, 310
   making billed time billable again, 329
   making expenses or item purchases billable, 57
   viewing on time activity detail report, 333
   viewing on unbilled costs by job report, 166
bills from vendors
   accounts payable, using to track and pay, 256–264
   deleting, 262
   discounts for early payment, 259
   editing, 261
   entering, 259
   expense accounts for, 248
   inventory, 234
   memorizing, 261
   paying after recording a bill, 258
   paying immediately (non-A/P), 264
   paying online, *see* online payment
   paying with cash, 269
   receiving items with, 263
   scheduling online payments, 256
   shipping charges, 257
   unpaid bills report, 221
   viewing history, 262
   see also vendors
bookkeeping software, transferring data to QuickBooks from, 456
books, closing, 64
borrowing money, *see* loans
bounced checks from customers, 111, 190

brokerages, real estate, information, 6
budgets
   checking periodically, 418
   creating, 418
   customizing, 418
   deleting, 418
   editing, 418
   graphs, 416
   planning and setting up, 417
   printing, 418
   reports, 415
   types of, 414
business and personal funds, 97
business assets, 304
business plans, creating, 8
business segments, tracking, 47
business situations, 3
buying, *see* bills from vendors; checks; credit cards; purchase orders

C

calculating
   sales forms, on, by using items, 121
   state withholding taxes, method used, 359
calendar year, 11, 300
capital investments, 54–55
cash
   paying for expenses with, 269
   petty, *see* petty cash
   sales, *see* cash sales
cash basis
   defined, 34
   overview, 12
   reporting, 398
   sales tax, preference for, 286
cash sales, 182–184
   cash drawer, 190
   daily summary, 184
   deleting, 200
   finding, 198
   memorizing and recalling, 201

If you don't find the topic you are looking for here or in the *Installation and Conversion Guide*, try QuickBooks Help. From the QuickBooks Help menu, choose Help Index, enter the keyword, and press Enter.

receipts
    customizing, 84–91
        printing, 184
    recording, 183
    voiding, 200

cash vs. accrual
    reporting, 304
    sales tax liability, 286

centers
    Company Center, 38
    Customer Center, 153
    Customer Detail Center, 154
    Vendor Detail Center, 212

changing, *look under what you want to change*

charges
    bank, 107
    credit card, *see* credit cards
    finance, *see* finance charges
    statement, *see* statement charges

chart of accounts
    adding accounts, 30
    automatically-created accounts, 13
    explained, 13
    how to keep simple while tracking detail, 40
    numerical, 52
    reorganizing, 52

charts, *see* graphs

checking accounts
    checkbook management, 101
    historical transactions, 32
    reconciling, 108
    register, 101
    see also bank accounts

checklist for setting up payroll, 356–357

checks
    bounced from customers, 111, 190
    cancel online payment, 103
    duplicate numbers, warning about, 255
    editing information, 103
    expenses on, 265
    finding, 103
    fonts, 102
    handwritten, 252
    items on, 265
    logos on, 102
    memorizing, 267
    online payment, 265
    paying bills with, 265
    payroll
        printing, 385
        reviewing and correcting, 384
        writing, 381–383
    paystubs, printing, 385
    preferences, 255
    printing, 102
        payroll, 385
        paystubs, 385
    stubs, *see* paystubs; voucher checks
    voiding or deleting, 103, 266
    writing, 266

classes
    adding, 49
    compared to jobs, customer types, and job types, 49
    employees, grouping by, 363
    income and expenses, tracking for, 57
    payroll expenses, tracking by, 351
    profit and loss by class report, 43
    turning on preference for, 49
    uses for, in QuickBooks, 47

clients, *see* customers

closing books or period, 64

COGS, *see* cost of goods sold

collection letters, 441

collections report, 209

columns
    changing for reports, 400
    changing on forms, 88

combining, *see* merging

commissions
    employee defaults, adding to, 362
    paychecks, entering on, 381
    payroll item for, 359

companies
　address, 425
　backing up, 66–67
　changing information, 425
　creating, 23–37
　federal ID, 26, 425
　passwords, 62–65
　restoring data, 465
　sample, 5

company at a glance, 38

Company Center, 38

company contributions
　employee defaults, adding to, 362
　employees, individual, setting up for, 363
　payroll item for, 359

company file, *see* companies; files

company lists, *see* lists

company logo, *see* logos

company name and address, 425

compensation
　see also salaries; wages

computer consultants, information, 6

condensing data, 426
　compared to hiding, deleting, and merging names on lists, 59

consignment sales, 225

construction industry
　information, 6
　standard categories, tracking, 48

consulting companies, information, 6

contact management, 437–445
　contact lists, 441
　customer contact list, 162
　notes about customers and jobs, 157
　synchronizing with other software, 440

continuous-feed printers, 94

copying
　compared to other methods of transferring data, 458
　see also memorizing

corporations
　defined, 55
　equity accounts for, 55
　officer salaries, 358

correcting, *look under what you want to change or edit*

correspondence, with QuickBooks data, 441

cost of goods sold
　account for, 230
　how QuickBooks calculates, 243
　location on profit and loss statement, 18

costs
　average for inventory items, 242
　invoicing for, 193
　items, *see* prices
　passing through, *see* reimbursable expenses
　revenues, comparing to, 165

CPA firms, information, 6

craftspersons, information, 6

creating, *look under what you want to create*

credit
　customer, applying to refund or outstanding charge, 189
　debits and, 449
　sales tax agency, from, 293
　vendor, entering, 263
　vendor, for return of items, 240
　see also credit cards

credit card payments from customers
　recording for cash sales, 182
　recording for invoices or statements, 190
　recording for merchant credit cards, 104
　refunds for, 192

credit cards
　accepting payments through a merchant account, 104
　accounts, 14, 99
　annual fee, 107
　applying for a merchant account, 104
　choosing the right card, 98
　credit for returned merchandise, 268
　customer charges, *see* credit card payments from customers
　deleting charges recorded, 268
　expenses on, 267
　finance charges, 107
　inventory purchases, 237
　items purchased by, 267
　online banking, 98
　reconciling, 108
　recording charges, 267

If you don't find the topic you are looking for here or in the *Installation and Conversion Guide*, try QuickBooks Help. From the QuickBooks Help menu, choose Help Index, enter the keyword, and press Enter.

transactions, 103
voiding charges recorded, 268
see also merchant accounts

credit limit from vendors, 216

credit memos
 applying refund checks to, 191
 creating, 191
 customizing, 84–91
 finding, 198
 logos on, 88
 ordering from Intuit, 468
 outstanding charges, applying to, 192
 refund check, applying to, 192

current assets, accounts for, 14

current balances, *see* balances

custom fields
 adding to forms, 58
 filtering reports for, 403
 for customers, 58
 for employees, 376
 for items, 125
 for vendors, 215
 setting up, 58

Customer Center, 153

Customer Detail Center, 154

customer registers
 browsing, 158
 entering statement charges, 187

customer reports
 described, 162–167
 list of customers, 162
 open balance report, 164
 phone list, 162
 QuickReport, 163

customer support, *see* technical support

customer types, 145, 160

customers, 141–167
 adding new, 148
 centers, 153
 costs, recording, 57
 current balances, 155

custom fields for, 58
Customer:Job list, 155
defined, 142
deleting, 157
editing information for, 157
hiding, 156
importing list information, 457
inactive, 156
job tracking, turning on or off, 148
letters to, 441
list report, 162
notes about, 157
opening balances
 changing, 159
 creating invoices for, 457
out-of-state, nontaxable sales, 284
payments from, 189
payroll expenses, tracking by, 350
products and materials purchased for, 127
register, 158
removing from list, 156
reports about, 162–167
Rolodex cards for, 443
showing all, 156
types, 145, 160

customizing
 budgets, 418
 checks, 102
 forms, 58, 84–91
 graphs, 408
 reports, 400

D

daily cash sales summary, 184

data
 audit trail of, 65–66
 backing up, 66–67
 condensing, 426
 exporting from QuickBooks, 456–458
 exporting from Timer, 321
 importing from other software, 456–458
 importing Timer data into QuickBooks Pro, 322

organizing effectively, 39–59
passwords, 62–65
protecting, 61–66
refreshing, 75
reports out of sync, 399
restoring, 465
safeguarding last year's, 423
synchronizing with Symantec ACT! or Microsoft Outlook, 438
see also files

databases, transferring data to and from QuickBooks, 456

dates
report ranges, 404
scheduling for online payment, 256
start date, 25–26

debit card payments, 182

debits and credits, 449

decision tools
calculating depreciation for more accurate financial statements, 305
getting paid faster, 201

deductions, payroll
employee defaults, adding to, 362
employees, individual, setting up for, 363
payroll item for, 359

defaults
accounts created, 13
employee, for payroll, 361–362

deleting, *look under what you want to delete*

delivery charges, item for on invoice, 120

Deluxe Payroll
description, 347
subscribing to, 354

departments, tracking, 47

dependant care, 360

deposit slips, printing, 106

deposits
cash back, 106
direct via QuickBooks Payroll Services, 378
down payments on sales, 191
finding, 105
making, 105
of nonpayment income (donations, etc.), 106

payments from customers, 190
printing slips and summaries, 106

depreciation, 305
decision tool, 305
if tracking for tax purposes, consult your tax advisor, 305
tracking in QuickBooks only to get more accurate financial statements, 305

detail
how to track in QuickBooks, 51–59
where to track in QuickBooks, 40–51

direct deposit, 378

disability insurance, 360

discount items
creating, 124
description, 120
using on sales forms, 131

discounts
customer, for early payment, 190
sales tax agency, from, 293
vendor
entering on checks, 270
entering when paying bills, 259

disks
installing Timer from, 336
saving disk space, 426

displaying, *look under what you want to display*

distributors, information, 6

dividends for stockholders, 56

donations to charity, deducting from paycheck, 360

down payments from customers, 191

downloading
transactions, 110
update to QuickBooks, 432
see also online banking

dues, payroll item for, 360

duplicate names on lists, *see* merging

E

early payment discount
for customers, 190

If you don't find the topic you are looking for here or in the *Installation and Conversion Guide*, try QuickBooks Help. From the QuickBooks Help menu, choose Help Index, enter the keyword, and press Enter.

from vendors on checks, 270
from vendors when paying bills, 259
EasyStep Interview, 23
editing, *look under what you want to edit*
electronic funds transfer (EFT) to online payees, 254
e-mail messages to financial institutions, 112
employee defaults, 361–362
employees
    adding, 375
    benefits, *see* benefits for employees
    categorizing, 363
    custom fields, 58, 376
    defaults for payroll, 361–362
    deleting, 376
    duplicate names, 376
    editing information about, 376
    hiding, 376
    letters to, 441
    list of, 374
    loan repayment, 360
    merging names, 376
    notes about, 376
    passwords, *see* passwords
    paying, 381–383
    payroll information
        changing, 376
        setting up, 361–362
        year-to-date summaries, 365
    permissions, *see* permissions
    preferences for, 355
    raises, 376
    releasing, 375
    removing from list, 376
    reports about, 396
    sharing QuickBooks on a network, 69–75
    time tracking, 309–334
employer identification number (EIN), 301
Employer's Quarterly Tax Return, 422
employment taxes, *see* payroll taxes
encryption, 98
ending balances for balance sheet accounts, 16

envelopes
    ordering from Intuit, 468
    windowed for sender and return address, 91
equity
    accounts, 15
        created by QuickBooks, 53
        setting up, 53–56
    balance sheet, viewing on, 17
    corporations, in, 55
    defined, 53
    partnerships, in, 54
    redistributing during setup, 35
    retained earnings from, 36
    sole proprietorships, in, 53
    stockholders', 55
    transferring from Opening Bal Equity, 36
erasing, *look under what you want to delete or edit*
error messages, 461
estimates, 184
    actuals, comparing to, 207
    adding fields to, 58
    alternative proposals for the same job, 185
    amounts, viewing for all jobs, 155
    copy, starting from, 201
    creating, 185
    customizing, 84–91
    finding, 185
    list of, 185
    logos on, 88
    markup on, 185
    memorizing and recalling, 201
    preferences, 179
    printing, 91, 185
    reports comparing to actuals, 207
    turning on, 179
Excel, *see* Microsoft Excel
expense accounts
    assigning on bills, 257
    assigning on checks, 265
    assigning on credit card charges, 267
    at year-end, 422
    defined, 16
    level of detail, 248

opening balances, 35
tax implications, 249
Uncategorized, 34

expenses, 247–272
accounts payable, using to track and pay, 256–264
billable to customers, 57
budgeting for, 413
invoicing for, 187
monitoring with a budget, 413
paying for (situation table), 251
paying immediately (non-A/P), 264
paying with cash, 269
paying with personal funds, 271
payroll, 349
setting up to track and pay, 255
tracking by class, 58
tracking by customer and job, 249
tracking by job, 57
tracking, defined, 247

exporting
compared to other methods of transferring data, 458
data, 456–458
lists for use in Timer, 317
QuickBooks data into Microsoft Word letters, 441
reports to Microsoft Excel, 410
Timer data for use by QuickBooks, 321

F

F1 key for help, 460

farming, information, 6

Fax on Demand, 461

faxing forms from QuickBooks, 94

federal identification number, 301, 425

federal payroll taxes
employee defaults, adding to, 362
employees, individual, setting up for, 363
paying, 386–387
payroll item for, 360
tax forms, filing, 388–390

federal taxes, *see* federal payroll taxes; income tax

fees
ATM, 96
bank accounts, entering, 107
see also finance charges

FICA taxes, *see* social security; Medicare

fields
adding to forms, 87
changing on forms, 88
customizing, *see* custom fields
filtering reports with, 403
finding information about, 5

FIFO (first in, first out), 225

files
backing up, 66–67
condensing, 426
network location, 71, 72
opening, 29
protecting, 61–66
restoring, 465

filing system for your paper documents, 20

filing tax forms, *see* tax forms

filtering reports, 402

finance charges
assessing for overdue payments, 190
credit cards, 107
setting up, 179

financial institutions
choosing the right one, 96
online banking, 98
sending messages, 112

finding, *look under what you want to find*

fiscal year, 11, 67
adjust for mid-year QuickBooks start date, 35
budgets for, 417
changing, 425
year-end tasks, 422

fixed assets
buying, 304
depreciation, 305
selling, 305
tracking loans used to purchase, 304, 305

fixing, *look under what you want to change or edit*

flexible spending plans, 360

floppy disks, *see* disks

fonts
checks, 102
forms, 88
reports, 400

footers in reports, 402

formatting, *see* customizing

If you don't find the topic you are looking for here or in the *Installation and Conversion Guide*, try QuickBooks Help. From the QuickBooks Help menu, choose Help Index, enter the keyword, and press Enter.

forms
 customizing, 84–91
 printer setup, 91
 sales, *see* sales forms
 tax, *see* tax forms

franchises, information, 6

freight charges
 inventory purchases, 234
 inventory sales, 238
 item for on invoice, 120

fund accounting
 income and expenses, tracking, 57
 overview, 42

funds
 business and personal, 97
 loans, looking for, 99
 transferring between accounts, 110

FUTA (federal unemployment tax)
 credit, 389
 liability, adjusting, 392

G

garnished wages, payroll item for, 360

general journal entries, 449

general ledger, 449

goals, setting for your business, 8

government resources, 9

graphic design profession, information, 6

graphs, 407
 accounts receivable, 208
 budget vs. actual, 416
 budgets, 418
 creating, 408
 interpreting, 408
 preferences, 398, 408
 printing, 410
 sales, 139, 205
 setting up, 398

group items
 compared to subitems, 122
 creating, 124
 description, 120
 inventory, 231
 sales tax, 281
 uses of, 130
 using to hide details, 130

group-term life insurance, 360

growth financing programs, 99

H

hardware requirements
 QuickBooks *see Installation and Conversion Guide*
 Timer, 335

headers in reports, 402

health insurance for employees, 360

help
 How do I menus, 4
 index, 4, 460
 onscreen, 460
 see also technical support, 506

hiding and showing
 accounts on chart of accounts, 59
 customers, 156
 details on sales forms, using group items, 130
 employees, 376
 items, 135
 jobs, 156
 list entries, 59
 navigation bar, 37
 payroll items, 373
 vendors, 218

historical transactions, 31

hourly wages, *see* wages

hours worked
 entering on paychecks, 382
 invoicing for, 193
 recording manually in QuickBooks, 324

Index | 483

recording with Stopwatch, 324
recording with Timer, 318
viewing on timesheets, 325
see also time reports

How do I menus, 4

I

identification numbers
    employer, 26
    employer (EIN), 26
    federal, 26, 425
    state employer, 356

IIF file format, 456, 458

importing
    activities from Timer, 322
    customer list information, 457
    data from other software programs, 458
    lists from other QuickBooks companies, 458
    QuickBooks Pro lists into Timer, 317

income accounts
    at year-end, 422
    choosing for items, 116
    defined, 16
    opening balances, 35
    Uncategorized, 34

income statements, *see* profit and loss statements

income tax, 297–303
    changes, 298
    expert advice, 298
    form for your company, 27, 300, 425
    reporting, 302
    setting up, 300
    tracking, 300
    TurboTax, 304
    up-to-date information, 302
    year, 425

income, tracking, 169–210
    by class, 57

industry information, 5

installing
    maintenance releases, 435
    QuickBooks again *see Installation and Conversion Guide*
    Timer, 335–337

insurance for employees, 360

insurance industry, information, 6

interest on bank accounts, 107

Internal Revenue Service (IRS), assistance for small businesses, 9

interview for company setup, 23

Intuit
    new services available in maintenance releases, 432
    ordering checks and supplies from, 468
    phone numbers, choose Phone Directory from the Help menu (see the back of the User's Guide for main phone numbers)
    QuickBooks.com Web site, 10, 461
    technical support, 464

Intuit Online Payment service, 98

inventory, 223–246
    accounts
        effect on, 242
        needed for tracking, 230
    adjusting quantity on hand and value, 241
    back orders
        not filled automatically, 225
        tracking, 238
    cost, how QuickBooks calculates, 242
    items, *see* inventory part items
    layaways, 238
    LIFO or FIFO not used by QuickBooks, 225
    manufacturing businesses, 224
    ordering, 233, 234
    purchasing by check or cash, 236
    quantities, *see* quantity on hand; quantity on order
    receipt for, 234
    renting or leasing, 225
    reordering, 244
    reports, 244–246
    returning to vendors, 240
    returns from customers, 240
    turning on, 228
    value, *see* value of inventory

inventory part items
    accounts to associate with, 230
    average cost, 242, 245
    description, 120
    grouped for unit sales or purchase, 231
    setting up, 230
    subitems, 231
    tips for setting up, 231

If you don't find the topic you are looking for here or in the *Installation and Conversion Guide*, try QuickBooks Help. From the QuickBooks Help menu, choose Help Index, enter the keyword, and press Enter.

invoice items, *see* items

invoices
   basing on estimates, 187
   copy, starting from, 201
   creating, 185–187
   customizing, 84–91
   deleting, 200
   finding, 198
   logos on, 88
   memorizing and recalling, 201
   payment items on, 132
   payments for, 189
   pending, 238
   printed, illustration, 173
   printing, 91, 187
   sales tax on, 134
   time and costs, charging for, 193
   voiding, 200
   when to use, 172
   see also bills from vendors; sales forms

IRS, assistance for small businesses, 9

item reports
   item listing report, 138
   item price list report, 138
   item profitability, 245
   price list, 244
   QuickReport for inventory item, 245
   stock status by item, 244
   time by item, 333
   valuation summary, 245

items, 113–140
   accounts, how affected by, 116
   benefits of setting up, 114
   billable to customers, 57
   changing prices, 135
   custom fields for, 58, 125
   defined, 171
   deleting, 136
   discount, *see* discount items
   editing, 136
   group, *see* group items
   hiding, 135
   inventory part, *see* inventory part items
   list of, 118
   non-inventory part, 120, 124
   nontaxable, 288
   ordering, 233
   other charge, 120, 124
   payment, *see* payment items
   payroll, *see* payroll items
   price list of, 244
   prices, changing, 135
   QuickReports for, 137
   reimbursable costs, for, 125
   reports about, 137–140
   returning to vendors, 240
   sales tax group, *see* sales tax group items
   sales tax, *see* sales tax items
   service, 119, 124
   subitems, 122, 125
   subtotal, *see* subtotal items
   taxability
      changing on sales form, 288
      specifying, 281
   types
      included in reports by item, 139
      restrictions on changing, 135
      table of, 119

J

job costing, *see* job reports; jobs

job estimates or proposals, *see* estimates

job reports, 162–167
   estimates vs. actuals reports, 207
   job profitability detail report, 165
   job profitability summary report, 165
   QuickReport, 163
   time by job, 332
   unbilled costs by job, 166

job types, 145, 160

jobs, 141–167
   adding new, 150
   compared to classes, customer types, and job types, 49

comparing actuals to estimates, 207
costs, recording, 57
current balances, 155
Customer:Job list, 155
defined, 143
deleting, 157
hiding, 156
inactive, 156
notes about, 157
opening balances, changing, 159
payment for multiple, 189
payments for, 189
payroll expenses, tracking by, 350
products and materials purchased for, 127
QuickReport, 163
removing from list, 156
reports, *see* job reports
showing all, 156
status
    editing names for, 151
    viewing for all jobs, 155
types, 145

journal entries, 449

justifying, *see* reconciling

K

keyboard shortcuts, *see last page of manual*

L

L & I tax, 359

label printing, 443

labor and industries tax, 359

late-payment charges
    from vendors, 259
    to customers, 190

law firms, information, 6

layaways of inventory, 238

Layout Designer, 89

lead time for online payments, 254

leasing of inventory, 225

legal company name, 425

lending institutions, 111

letterhead printing issues, 92

letters, using Microsoft Word with your QuickBooks data, 441

liabilities
    accounts for, 14
    adjusting for payroll item, 392
    balance sheet, viewing on, 17
    defined, 17
    loans, *see* loans
    payroll, *see* payroll liabilities
    sales tax, *see* sales tax: liabilities

life insurance for employees, 360

LIFO (last in, first out), 225

line items
    defined, 129
    see also items

lists
    activating inactive entries, 136
    alphabetizing, 52
    customer reports, 162
    customer type, 160
    Customer:Job, 155
    deleting, hiding, or merging entries, 59
    employees, 374
    exporting for use in Timer, 317
    exporting to other QuickBooks companies, 457
    importing from other QuickBooks companies, 457
    item, 118
    job type, 160
    Payroll Item, 371
    reorganizing, 52
    Sales Rep, 210
    sorting, 119
    To Do notes, 444
    updating for Timer, 321
    Vendor, 217

loans
    accounts for, 111
    employee, deducting repayments, 360
    looking for, 99
    paying for assets, 111
    setting up and tracking, 111

local payroll taxes, *see* payroll taxes, local/other

locations, tracking, 47

login, 64

If you don't find the topic you are looking for here or in the *Installation and Conversion Guide*, try QuickBooks Help. From the QuickBooks Help menu, choose Help Index, enter the keyword, and press Enter.

logos
adding to checks, 102
printing on forms, 88
long term liability accounts, 15
loss of a fixed asset, 306

M

mailing labels, printing, 443
maintenance releases
definition, 432
installing, 435
installing for multiple users, 436
making active, *look under what you want to make active*
making inactive, *look under what you want to make inactive*
managing your business
Company Center, 38
Customer Center, 153
Customer Detail Center, 154
Vendor Detail Center, 212
manufacturer's representatives, information, 6
manufacturing inventory, 224
markup
estimates, on, 185
item prices, 135
maximum number of users, 73
medical practices, information, 6
medical saving accounts (MSAs), 360
Medicare tax, *see* federal payroll taxes
memorizing
bills from vendors, 261
checks, 267
estimates, invoices, and cash sales receipts, 200
reports, 405
statement charges, 201
see also scheduling
Merchant Account Service, 104, 190

merchant accounts
accepting credit card payments, 190
applying for online in QuickBooks, 104
processing fees, 104
merchant credit cards, *see* merchant accounts
merging
compared to deleting, hiding or condensing data, 59
customer or job records, 59
employee records, 376
item records, 59
vendor records, 218
messages
error, 461
financial institutions, sending to, 112
Microsoft Excel, exporting reports to, 410
Microsoft Outlook, synchronizing information with QuickBooks, 439
Microsoft Word letters, using with QuickBooks data, 441
midyear setup, 35
miscellaneous charges
items for, 124
reimbursable charges, 127
modes, multi-user and single-user
defined, 70
switching between, 74
modifying, *look under what you want to customize or edit*
monthly tasks, 421
moving data, *see* transferring
moving expenses, 360
multipurpose forms, 92
multi-user mode, 69–75
defined, 70
file location, 71, 72
maximum number of users, 73
performance, 75
setting up for, 73
switching to, 74

N

names
  company, 425
  Rolodex cards for, 443
  see also merging

navigation bar, 37

navigator, 37

net worth, 15

networks
  how QuickBooks works on, 70
  installing QuickBooks maintenance releases, 436
  maximum number of users, 73
  performance of QuickBooks, 75
  setting up QuickBooks on, 73
  sharing QuickBooks on, 69–75

new company, creating, 23–37

non-inventory part items
  creating, 124
  description, 120

non-posting accounts on chart of accounts, 13

nonprofit organizations
  information, 6
  see also fund accounting

nontaxable items, 288

nontaxable sales, 288
  out-of-state sales, 283
  resale customers, 284

notes
  about customer or job, 157
  about vendor, 219
  Timer activities, adding to, 319
  To Do notes, 444

number format in reports, 400

numerical accounts on chart of accounts, 52

O

office supplies, ordering from Intuit, 468

Office, *see* Microsoft Excel; Microsoft Word

officer salaries, 358

online accounts
  downloading transactions, 110
  editing information about, 112
  e-mail messages, 112
  PIN/password, 100
  reconciling, 109
  transferring funds, 110

online banking
  accounts, *see* online accounts
  advantages, 97
  credit cards, 98
  going online, 100
  Intuit Online Payment service, 98
  setting up, 99
  see also online payment

online payment
  account numbers, 256
  accounts, *see* online accounts
  advantages, 97
  anyone can use, 98
  canceling a payment, 266
  delivery date information, 254
  electronic funds transfer (EFT), 254
  features, 253
  going online, 100
  Intuit Online Payment service, 98
  lead time, 254
  remittance information, adding on checks, 265
  report about payments, 264
  scheduling, 97, 256
  setting up, 99, 256
  see also online banking

online payroll, *see* QuickBooks Payroll Services

onscreen help, 460

open balance report
  customer, 164
  vendor, 221

Opening Bal Equity account, 36
  adjusting balance during setup, 35
  described, 53
  transferring equity out of, 56

opening balances
  balance sheet accounts, changing, 52
  customer or job, changing, 159
  customers, invoices for, 457
  entering in EasyStep Interview, 28

options, *see* preferences

488 | Index

If you don't find the topic you are looking for here or in the *Installation and Conversion Guide*, try QuickBooks Help. From the QuickBooks Help menu, choose Help Index, enter the keyword, and press Enter.

ordering
    checks and supplies from Intuit, 468
    logos, 468
    see also inventory; purchase orders

other asset accounts, 14

other charge items
    creating, 124
    description, 120
    using for taxable shipping and handling, 290

other current asset accounts, 14

other current liability accounts, 14

other payroll taxes, *see* payroll taxes, local/other

Other, on reports, 44

Outlook, Microsoft, synchronizing information with QuickBooks, 439

out-of-state sales
    nontaxable, 283
    tax on, 289
    taxable, 282

overages, tracking for daily sales, 184

overdue bills, invoices, and statements, *see* aging

overpayments, 190
    payroll liability, refund check for, 387
    refund check, applying to, 192

owner's draws, 54

owner's equity, 53–54

owners/partners
    paying for business expenses with personal funds, 271
    paying for personal expenses with business funds, 272
    paying for time worked, 326

P

packing slips, 238

paid-in capital, 55

paper options for printing, 92

partial payment on invoice, 132

partnerships
    defined, 54
    equity accounts for, 54
    income and expenses, tracking by partner, 48
    time worked, paying partners for, 326

passwords, 62–65
    changing, 64
    deleting, 64

patching QuickBooks, *see* maintenance releases

payables, *see* accounts payable

paychecks
    deleting, 384
    editing, 384
    historical, entering, 365
    printing, 385
    printing paystubs, 385
    voiding, 384
    writing, 381–383

payees, online, setting up, 256

paying
    bills, 258
    employees, 381–383
    payroll liabilities, 386–387
    sales tax, 292

payment items
    creating, 124
    description, 121
    using on sales forms, 132

payment terms
    customer, 149
    vendor, setting up, 216

payments
    applying, preferences for, 179
    cash, *see* cash sales
    correcting application to invoices or statement charges, 199
    credit card, *see* credit card payments from customers
    depositing, 190
    discounts for early, 190
    finding, 158

payroll (*continued*)
   getting paid faster, decision tool, 201
   loans, 111
   multiple jobs, one payment for, 189
   online, *see* online payment
   partial on invoice, 132
   receiving, 105, 189

payroll
   accounts, 349
   basic service, 346
   checklist for setting up, 356–357
   customizing accounts for, 352
   expenses, 349
   features, description of, 343–345
   historical transactions, entering, 364–368
   items, *see* payroll items
   liabilities, *see* payroll liabilities
   online, *see* QuickBooks Online Payroll
   preferences for, 355
   reports, 393, 394
   setting up, 355
   subaccounts, 352
   taxes, *see* payroll taxes
   tracking expenses, 351
   turning on or off, 379

payroll expenses
   class, tracking by, 351
   customer, tracking by, 350
   job, tracking by, 350
   reports, 349
   service item, tracking by (Pro only), 351

payroll items, 371–373
   additions, 359
   changes, effects of, 372
   commissions, 359
   company contributions, 359
   created by QuickBooks, 358
   deductions, 359
   deleting, 373
   editing, 371–372
   examples of common items, 360
   federal taxes, for, 360
   hiding, 373
   hourly wages, 358
   liabilities, adjusting, 392
   list, 371
   local/other taxes, for, 359
   merging, 373
   officer salaries, 358
   order of, effect on amounts and gross pay, 363
   removing from Payroll Item list, 373
   reports, 395
   salaries, 358
   showing, 373
   state taxes, for, 358
   taxes, for, 360

payroll liabilities
   adjusting, 392
   discounts for, 387
   how QuickBooks tracks, 352
   paying, 386–387
   penalties, 387
   report, 393
   year-to-date summaries for setup, 368

payroll reports, 393–396

payroll taxes
   company-paid, how QuickBooks tracks, 353
   depositing, 112
   employee defaults, adding to, 362
   employees, individual, setting up for, 363
   federal, *see* federal payroll taxes
   historical, 364
   how QuickBooks calculates, 387
   liabilities, *see* payroll: liabilities
   local/other
      employee defaults, adding to, 362
      employees, individual, setting up, 363
      list of QuickBooks supported, 359
      payroll items for, 359
   miscellaneous, 360
   paying, 112, 386–387
   payments, entering year-to-date summaries, 368
   questions about amount due, 387
   refunds for overpayments, 387
   state, *see* state payroll taxes
   tax forms, filing, 388–390
   withholding amounts, up-to-date, 354
   see also payroll; payroll expenses; tax tables

paystubs, printing, 385

pending invoices, 238

performance in multi-user mode, 75

periodic billing, information, 6

periodic tasks, 419–429

permissions, 64 *see also* passwords

personal finances, 97

personal funds, using for business expenses, 271

If you don't find the topic you are looking for here or in the *Installation and Conversion Guide*, try QuickBooks Help. From the QuickBooks Help menu, choose Help Index, enter the keyword, and press Enter.

petty cash
  ATM withdrawals, 103
  back from your deposit, 106
  items purchased with, 236
  paying for expenses with, 269

phone list report
  for customers, 162
  for vendors, 221

phone numbers, Intuit, choose Phone Directory from the Help menu (see the back of the User's Guide for main phone numbers)

photographers, information, 6

pie charts, *see* graphs

PIN/password for online accounts, 100

point-of-sale scanning systems, 225

preferences
  checking, 255
  employee, 355
  estimates, 179
  graphs, 408
  job tracking, turning on or off, 148
  payroll, 355
  reminders, 255
  reports, 398
  sales and customers, 179
  sales tax, 280
  users, 74
  using classes, turning on, 49

preprinted forms
  printing issues, 92
  using with customized forms, 92

previewing reports, 410

price list, 138, 244

prices of items, changing, 135

printer setup, 91

printing
  alignment issues, 93
  budgets, 418
  checks, 102
  customized invoices on multipurpose forms, 92
  estimates, 185

  files to disk, compared to other methods of transferring data, 458
  fonts, *see* fonts
  graphs, 410
  invoices, 187
  logos, 88
  mailing labels, 443
  paychecks, 385
  paystub reports, 385
  receipts for cash sales, 184
  reports, 410
  Rolodex cards, 443
  statements, 189
  "T's" for taxable items on sales, 281
  timesheets, 325

printing industry, information, 6

prior liability payments, 368

procedures, finding, 3, 4

product lines, tracking by, 48

product support, *see* technical support

professional associations and societies, 10

profit and loss statement
  by class, 43
  by job, 165
  example, 18

profitability
  report by item, 245
  report by job, 165

progress invoices
  creating, 186
  definition, 177
  turning on, 179

projects, *see* jobs

proposals, *see* estimates

protecting your data, 61–66

public relations firms, information, 6

purchase orders
  adding fields to, 58
  customizing, 84–91
  finding, 234

list of, 234
logos on, 88
ordering items or services, 251
printing, 91
turning on, 255
writing, 233

purchasing, *see* bills from vendors; checks; credit cards; purchase orders

Q

quantity on hand
    adjusting, 241
    initial, 231
    transactions affecting, 245
    viewing, 239

quantity on order
    initial, 229
    list of purchase orders for an item, 245
    viewing, 239

quarterly payroll tax forms
    federal, 388
    state, 391

quarterly tasks, 422

Quick Reference Sheet for Timer, 338

QuickBooks
    company, setting up, 23–37
    documentation, how to use, 1
    navigation bar, 37
    navigator, 37
    network, sharing on, 69–75
    performance in multi-user mode, 75
    sample company, 5
    setting up a company, 23–37
    training seminars, 472
    transferring data, 456–458
    updating current version, 432

QuickBooks Administrator, 63

QuickBooks and Your Industry, 5

QuickBooks Learning Guide, 471

QuickBooks Payroll Services, 346, 347
    direct deposit, 378

QuickBooks Professional Advisors Program, 9

QuickBooks Support Network, 464

QuickBooks Tax Table Update Service, *see* QuickBooks Payroll Services

QuickBooks Update Service, 432

QuickBooks user communities, 10

QuickBooks.com Web site, 10, 461

QuickReports, 406
    customer or job, 163
    inventory item, 245
    item, 137

QuickStatement for online accounts, 109

QuickZoom, 408

quotes, *see* estimates

R

ranching, information, 6

rates
    items, changing, 135
    sales tax
        changing, 293
        most common, 281
        setting up, 281

real estate brokerages, information, 6

rearranging elements on forms, *see* customizing

rearranging order of entries on lists, *see* reorganizing

receipts for cash sales, *see* cash sales

receivables, *see* accounts receivable

receiving payments, 105

reconciling
    accounts, 108
    canceling before completing, 108
    online accounts, 109
    skipped months, 108
    transactions added earlier, 108

recordkeeping of old documents, 424

reducing file size, *see* condensing data

refreshing data, 75, 399

refund checks
    creating, 192
    credit memos and overpayment, 191
    payroll liability, 387

If you don't find the topic you are looking for here or in the *Installation and Conversion Guide*, try QuickBooks Help. From the QuickBooks Help menu, choose Help Index, enter the keyword, and press Enter.

registers
    checking, 101
    customer, 158
    description, 16
    entering transactions in, 32
    fees and interest, entering in, 107
    sales tax payable, 291
    sorting by different criteria, 103

reimbursable expenses
    items for, 125
    miscellaneous charges, items for, 127
    paychecks, entering on, 381
    QuickBooks, 194–195
    QuickBooks Pro, 195–196
    unbilled costs by job report, 166

reimbursed expenses
    definition, 180
    tracking as income, 180

release date for an employee, 375

reminder statements, 174

reminders
    deposits, to make, 105
    preferences, 255
    to customers, 174

removing, *look under what you want to delete or hide*

rental of inventory, 225

reordering
    inventory, 244
    see also reorganizing

reorganizing
    accounts on chart of accounts, 52
    columns on forms, 88
    fields on forms, 88
    lists, 52
    transactions in registers, 103
    transactions in reports, 401

repeating, *see* automatic recall; memorizing; scheduling

Report Finder, 399

reports
    aging preferences, 398
    cash vs. accrual based, 398
    changing the scope of the information, 402
    customizing the look, 400
    date ranges, 404
    descriptions of
        A/P aging detail, 220, 263
        A/P aging summary, 263
        A/R aging summary, 209
        accounts receivable, 205
        audit trail, 65
        budget actual, 415
        budget by job budget overview, 415
        budget by job comparison, 415
        budget overview, 415
        budget, balance sheet comparison, 416
        budget, balance sheet overview, 415
        collections, 209
        customer, 162–167
        customer contact, 162
        customer open balance, 164
        customer phone list, 162
        estimates vs. actuals, 207
        inventory, 244
        item listing, 138
        item price list, 138, 244
        item profitability, 245
        job, 162–167
        job estimates vs. actuals, 207
        job profitability detail, 165
        job profitability summary, 165
        open balance for vendors, 221
        payroll, 393–396
        payroll item detail, 395
        payroll liabilities, 393
        payroll summary, 394
        profit and loss by class, 43
        profit and loss by job, 165
        sales, 205
        sales tax liability, 294
        stock status by item, 244
        time by item, 333
        time by job, 332
        time by job detail, 333
        time by name, 330

    unbilled costs by job, 166
    unpaid bills detail, 264
    valuation summary, 245
    vendor balance detail, 264
    vendor balance summary, 264
    vendor phone list, 221
  exporting to Microsoft Excel, 410
  file, saving to, 410
  filtering, 402
  finding the report you want, 399
  generating, 399
  investigating values on reports and graphs, 408
  memorizing, 405
  multi-user environment, in, 399
  "Other" on, 44
  printing, 410
  QuickReports, *see* QuickReports
  QuickZoom, 408
  saving the customization and filtering, 405
  setting up, 398
representative (sales rep), tracking sales by, 210
representatives, sales, information, 6
requisitions, *see* purchase orders
resale customers, nontaxable sales to, 284
restaurants, information, 6
restoring company data, 465
retail businesses
  information, 6
  inventory tracking, 224
retainage, 187
retained earnings
  account, 53
  description, 15
  transferring equity from Opening Bal Equity, 56
  year-end adjustment by QuickBooks, 423
retainers received, 191
retirement plans, 360
returns
  customer, recording, 191
  inventory, from customers, 240
  inventory, to vendors, 240
revenues, comparing to costs, 165
Rolodex cards, printing on, 443
routing number formats, 378

S

salaries
  employee, changing, 376
  employee, entering, 363
  officer, payroll item for, 358
  payroll item for, 358
  removing from bonus check, 360
  year-to-date, entering for setup, 365
sales, 169–210
  cash, *see* cash sales
  credit card, *see* credit card payments from customers
  graphs, 205
  nontaxable, 288
  overages and shortages, tracking, 184
  preferences, 179
  reports about, 205
  tax, *see* sales tax
  taxable, 287–288
  time and costs, charging for, 193
  tracking by sales rep, 210
  see also invoices; statement charges
sales forms
  customizing, 58, 84–91
  logos on, 88
  printing, 91
sales items, *see* items
sales representatives
  information about, 6
  tracking sales by, 210
sales tax, 275–296
  account for, 287, 291
  agencies, 277
  amount owed at start date, 34
  applying to a sale, 287–289
  applying to shipping and handling, 290
  cash basis vs. accrual basis, preference for, 286
  changing rates, 293
  credits or discounts from tax agency, 293
  customers exempt from, 284
  historical data, 34
  items for sales tax, *see* sales tax items
  liabilities, *see* sales tax liabilities
  multiple taxes, 281
  nontaxable items, 288
  nontaxable sales, 288

If you don't find the topic you are looking for here or in the *Installation and Conversion Guide*, try QuickBooks Help. From the QuickBooks Help menu, choose Help Index, enter the keyword, and press Enter.

out-of-state sales, 289
   nontaxable, 283
   taxable, 282
paying, 292
preferences, 280
rates
   changing, 293
   most common, 281
   setting up, 281
reimbursable expenses, 194, 196
reports about, 294
resale customers, nontaxable sales to, 284
sales forms, how QuickBooks applies to, 287
sales tax group items, *see* sales tax group items
sales tax items, *see* sales tax items
"T's," printing on sales forms, 281
turning on, 280
unusual situations, 289

sales tax group items
   changing, 293
   creating, 281
   description, 121
   where to use, 134

sales tax items
   changing, 293
   creating, 281
   description, 121
   taxability
      changing on sales form, 288
      specifying, 281
   where to use, 134

sales tax liabilities
   adjusting, 291
   paying, 292
   period covered, 286
   register for, 291
   report, 294

sample company, 5

saving, *see* backing up

Schedule B (Form 941), *see* 941 forms

scheduling
   online payments, 97, 256
   repeated charges, 200

SDI tax, *see* state payroll taxes

Section 125 plans, 360

security, 62–65
   online banking and online payment, 98
   see also passwords

service businesses
   benefits of setting up items, 114
   information for, 6

service items
   creating, 124
   description, 119
   tracking payroll expenses by (Pro only), 351

services, new in maintenance releases, 432

session report, *see* audit trail

setting up
   employee payroll information, 361–362
   employee year-to-date payroll summaries, 365
   merchant account, 104
   payroll, 355
   QuickBooks company, 23–37
   Web site for your business, 78
   also look under what you want to set up

setup, *see* installing; setting up

sharing QuickBooks on a network, 69–75

shipping charges
   adding to a bill, 257
   adding to a check, 265
   adding to a credit card charge, 267
   inventory purchases, 234
   inventory sales, 238
   item for on invoice, 120
   making taxable, 290

shortages, tracking for daily sales, 184

shrinking data, *see* condensing data

sick pay plans, 360

sick time
   accrual period and hours, entering on employee defaults, 362
   employees, setting up for, 363

entering, 363
year-to-date, entering, 366

SIMPLE retirement plans, 360

single activities
   entering details about in QuickBooks, 325
   list of, 333
   timing, 323

single-user mode
   defined, 70
   switching to, 74

social security number, 301

social security tax, *see* federal payroll taxes

sole proprietorships, 53

sorting
   by zip code, 443
   lists, 119

sorting, *see also* reorganizing

spreadsheets
   exporting reports to, 410
   transferring data to and from QuickBooks, 456

start date, 25–26

start-up financing programs, 99

state employer ID number, 356

state payroll taxes
   additional, 359
   disability insurance (SDI), 359
   employee defaults, adding to, 362
   employees, individual, setting up, 363
   income, method of calculation for, 359
   list of QuickBooks supported, 359
   miscellaneous taxes, 360
   paying, 386–387
   payroll items for, 358
   tax forms, 391
   unemployment insurance (SUI), 359
   withholding, 358

statement charges
   automatic entry, 201
   businesses appropriate for, 177
   entering, 187
   finding, 198
   payments for, 189
   when to use, 175

statements, 188–189
   billing, 175–176
   cash flow, 19
   customizing, 84–91
   logos on, 88
   ordering from Intuit, 468
   payments for, 189
   printing, 91, 189
   reconciling, 108
   reminder, illustration and description, 174

statements of financial condition, *see* balance sheets

STEP (Small Business Tax Education Program), 9

step-by-step instructions, finding, 3, 4

stock status by item report, 244

stockholders' equity, 55

Stopwatch
   setting up QuickBooks to use, 314
   timing activities with, 323
   when to use, 313

storage boxes, ordering, 468

stubs, *see* paystubs; voucher checks

subaccounts
   adding to chart of accounts, 52
   advantages of using, 43
   entering on transactions, 56
   payroll, 352

subclasses, 49

subcontractors
   deciding whether to track time for, 311
   services performed by, 126
   time worked, paying for, 326

subitems
   compared to group items, 122
   creating, 125
   inventory, 231

subtotal items
   creating, 124
   description, 120
   using on sales forms, 130

subtotals on reports, 401

SUI tax, *see* state payroll taxes

summary of daily cash sales, 184

summary transactions, 428

If you don't find the topic you are looking for here or in the *Installation and Conversion Guide*, try QuickBooks Help. From the QuickBooks Help menu, choose Help Index, enter the keyword, and press Enter.

supplies, ordering from Intuit, 468

Symantec ACT!, synchronizing information with QuickBooks, 439

T

"T," printing next to taxable items, 281

tax forms
  1099-MISC, 307
  changing which one you file, 425
  Form 940, 389
  Form 941, 388
  Form W-2 and Form W-3, 390
  payroll, 388–390
    up-to-date, 354

tax lines, assigning, 301

tax preparation
  software, 298
  see also income tax

tax preparer, finding one, 9

tax tables, payroll, up-to-date, required, 354

tax tracking classification, effect on tax forms, 360

tax year, 11

taxable items, "T's," printing or hiding, 281

taxable, non-cash fringe benefits, 360

taxes
  income, *see* income tax
  labor and industries, 359
  payroll, *see* payroll taxes
  sales, *see* sales tax
  TurboTax, 304

technical support
  answers by fax, 461
  before you call, 464
  frequently asked questions, 461
  phone numbers, choose Phone Directory from the Help menu or see the back cover of the User's Guide for main numbers
  talk to a representative, 464
  Web site, 10, 461

telephone numbers, *see* phone numbers

templates
  business forms, 86
  default, 86
  list of form templates, 86

Templates list, 86

terms, *see* payment terms

theft of a fixed asset, 306

time
  invoicing for, 193
  paying nonemployees for, 326
  see also time reports; time tracking; Timer

time reports, 330–334

time tracking, 309–328
  deciding whether to make time billable, 310
  options for tracking, 313
  recording time in Timer, 318
  recording time manually in QuickBooks, 324
  recording time with Stopwatch in QuickBooks, 323
  reports, 330–334
  setting up QuickBooks for, 314
  see also Timer

Timer
  creating disks for, 336
  data
    backing up, restoring, or condensing, 321
    exporting to QuickBooks Pro, 321
    files, creating, 317
    importing into QuickBooks Pro, 322
  hardware requirements, 335
  install disks, creating, 336
  installing, 335–337
  lists
    exporting from QuickBooks Pro, 317
    importing from QuickBooks Pro, 317
    updating to match changes in QuickBooks Pro, 321
  Quick Reference Sheet, 338
  recording activities in, 318

setting up, 315
when to use, 313

timesheets
filling out, 325
reports, 330–334
viewing, 325

tips employees receive, 360

titles, changing
forms, 88
reports, 404

To Do notes
creating, 444
for vendors, 219
list of, 444
viewing, 420

tracking
income, 169–210
inventory, *see* inventory
payroll expenses, 351
retainers, 191
sales tax, 275–296
sales, *see* sales
time, *see* time tracking

training seminars for QuickBooks, 472

transaction history, accounts payable, 262

transactions
audit trail, 65
automatic recall of last transaction for a name, 255
deleted during condensing, 426
deleting, 200
downloading, 110
exporting, 455
historical, 31
memorizing, *see* memorizing
online *see* online banking; online payment
retained, 427
sorting
in registers, 103
in reports, 401
summary, created during condensing process, 428

transferring
data between other software and QuickBooks, 456
data to a new QuickBooks company, 457
money between online accounts, 110

troubleshooting, *see* problems

TurboTax, 302, 304

TurboTax for Business, 298

turning on
audit trail, 66
class tracking, 49
estimates, 179
inventory, 228
numerical accounts on chart of accounts, 52
payroll, 379
progress invoicing, 179
purchase orders, 255
sales tax, 280

type face, *see* fonts

types
account, *see* accounts (types)
customer, 145
changing, 160
compared to classes, jobs, and job types, 49
item
included in reports by, 139
restrictions on changing, 135
table of, 119
job, 145
changing, 160
compared to classes, jobs, and customer types, 49
vendor, 214

U

U.S. Small Business Administration (SBA)
loan programs, 99

unbilled costs by job report, 166

Uncategorized Expenses, 34, 35

Uncategorized Income, 34, 35

uncollectable charges, 111

undeposited funds
account for, 104
cash sales, recording proceeds with, 182
customer payments, recording with, 190
depositing, 190

unemployment insurance, *see* payroll taxes

union dues, payroll item, 360

unpaid bills detail report, 221, 264

updating, QuickBooks, current version, 432

If you don't find the topic you are looking for here or in the *Installation and Conversion Guide*, try QuickBooks Help. From the QuickBooks Help menu, choose Help Index, enter the keyword, and press Enter.

user groups
    QuickBooks users, 461
    using QuickBooks to manage, 6

users
    auditing, 65
    login, 64
    maximum number, 73
    setting up, 63

V

vacation time
    accrual period and hours, entering on employee defaults, 362
    employees, setting up for, 363
    entering, 363
    year-to-date, entering, 366

value of inventory, 230
    how QuickBooks calculates, 242
    initial, 231
    report of, 245

Vendor Detail Center, 212

vendor reports, 220–221, 264

vendors, 211–221
    1099-MISC, 216
    adding, 212–215, 216
    balance report, 264
    balances, current, 217
    credit from, 263
    custom fields for, 58, 215
    deleting, 219
    detail center, 212
    discounts
        entering on checks, 270
        entering when paying bills, 259
    editing, 218
    hiding and showing, 218
    letters to, 441
    making inactive and active, 218
    merging records, 219
    notes about, 219
    phone list, 221
    reports about, 220–221
    returning inventory to, 240
    Rolodex cards for, 443
    time worked, paying for, 326
    types, 214
    Vendor list, 217
    see also bills from vendors; bill payments

version, updating QuickBooks, 432

viewing, *look under what you want to view*

voiding
    checks, 103, 266
    paychecks, 384
    sales transactions, 200

voucher checks
    ordering from Intuit, 468
    printing account names on, 255
    printing paychecks on, 385

W

W-2 forms
    ordering from Intuit, 468
    preparing and filing, 390
    tax tracking classification, effect on, 360
    up-to-date, 354

W-2 tracking, *see* tax tracking

W-3 forms
    ordering from Intuit, 468
    preparing and filing, 390
    up-to-date, 354

wage bases
    defined, 367
    employee year-to-date setup, viewing, 367
    viewing on reports, 395

wages
    employee
        changing hourly rates or salary, 376
        entering hourly rates, 363
        entering salary, 363
    garnished, payroll item for, 360
    hourly, payroll item for, 358

officer salary, payroll item for, 358
salary, payroll item for, 358
year-to-date, entering for setup, 365

Web sites
creating for your business, 78
QuickBooks.com, 10, 461
technical support, 10, 461
TurboTax, 298

weekly tasks, 420

weekly timesheets, *see* timesheets

wholesalers
information, 6
inventory tracking, 224

window envelopes
designing forms to fit, 91
ordering from Intuit, 468

Windows, versions required to install Timer, 335

withholding, *see* payroll taxes

word processors, transferring data to and from QuickBooks, 456

Word, *see* Microsoft Word

World Wide Web, *see* Web sites

write-offs, 111

writers, information, 6

writing
checks, 266
paychecks, 381–383

Y

year 2000 compliance, *see* www.intuit.com/y2k

year-end tasks, 422

year-to-date amounts
general, *see* reports: descriptions of
payroll, entering, 364–368

Z

zip code sorting, 443

QuickBooks Keyboard Shortcuts

General	Key
To start QuickBooks without a company file	Ctrl + double-click
To suppress the desktop windows (at Open Company window)	Alt (while opening)
Display information about QuickBooks	Ctrl + 1 (one)
Cancel	Esc
Record (when black border is around OK, Next, or Previous button)	↵
Record (always)	Ctrl + ↵

Dates	Key
Next day	+ (plus key)
Previous day	– (minus key)
Today	T
First day of the **W**eek	W
Last day of the wee**K**	K
First day of the **M**onth	M
Last day of the mont**H**	H
First day of the **Y**ear	Y
Last day of the yea**R**	R
Date calendar	Alt + down arrow

Editing	Key
Edit transaction selected in register	Ctrl + E
Delete character to right of insertion point	Del
Delete character to left of insertion point	Backspace
Delete line from detail area	Ctrl + Del
Insert line in detail area	Ctrl + Ins
Cut selected characters	Ctrl + X
Copy selected characters	Ctrl + C
Paste cut or copied characters	Ctrl + V
Increase check or other form number by one	+ (plus key)
Decrease check or other form number by one	– (minus key)
Undo changes made in field	Ctrl + Z

Help window	Key
Display Help in context	F1
Select next option or topic	Tab
Select previous option or topic	Shift + Tab
Display selected topic	↵
Close popup box	Esc
Close Help window	Esc

Activity	Key
Account list, display	Ctrl + A
Check, write	Ctrl + W
Copy transaction in register	Ctrl + O
Customer:Job list, display	Ctrl + J
Delete check, invoice, transaction, or item from list	Ctrl + D
Edit lists or registers	Ctrl + E
QuickFill and Recall (type first few letters of name and press Tab, name fills in)	*abc* Tab
Find transaction	Ctrl + F
Go to register of transfer account	Ctrl + G
Help in context, display	F1
History of A/R or A/P transaction	Ctrl + H
Invoice, create	Ctrl + I
List (for current field), display	Ctrl + L
Memorize transaction or report	Ctrl + M
Memorized transaction list, display	Ctrl + T
New invoice, bill, check or list item	Ctrl + N
Paste copied transaction in register	Ctrl + V
Print	Ctrl + P
QuickZoom on report	↵
QuickReport on transaction or list item	Ctrl + Q
Register, display	Ctrl + R
Show list	Ctrl + S
Use list item	Ctrl + U
Transaction journal, display	Ctrl + Y

Moving around a window	Key
Next field	Tab
Previous field	Shift + Tab
Toggle between form and navigation bar	Ctrl + 0 (zero)
Report column to the right	Right arrow
Report column to the left	Left arrow
Beginning of current field	Home
End of current field	End
Line below in detail area or on report	Down arrow
Line above in detail area or on report	Up arrow
Down one screen	Page Down
Up one screen	Page Up
Next word in field	Ctrl + →
Previous word in field	Ctrl + ←
First item on list or previous month in register	Ctrl + Page Up
Last item on list or next month in register	Ctrl + Page Down
Close active window	Esc or Ctrl + F4